VIZ GRAPHIC NOVEL

Ceres™
Celestial Legend

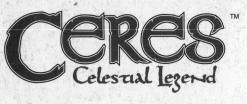

VOL. 1: AYA

CERES™
Celestial Legend
VOL. 1: Aya
Shôjo Edition

This volume contains the CERES: CELESTIAL LEGEND installments from
Part 1, Issue 1, through Part 1, Issue 6, in their entirety.

STORY & ART BY YÛ WATASE

English Adaptation/Gary Leach

Translaton/Lillian Olsen
Touch-Up Art & Lettering/Bill Schuch
Cover Design/Hidemi Sahara
Graphic Design/Carolina Ugalde
Editor/Frances E. Wall
Shôjo Edition Editors/Elizabeth Kawasaki & Andy Nakatani

Managing Editor/Annette Roman
Editor-in-Chief/Alvin Lu
Sr. Director of Licensing and Acquisitions/Rika Inouye
Production Manager/Noboru Watanabe
Vice President of Marketing/Liza Coppola
V.P. of Sales/Joe Morici
Sr. Vice President of Editorial/Hyoe Narita
Publisher/Seiji Horibuchi

Printed in Canada

Published by VIZ, LLC
P.O. Box 77010 • San Francisco, CA 94107

Shôjo Edition
10 9 8 7 6 5 4 3 2
First printing, October 2003
Second printing, August 2004

store.viz.com

www.viz.com

VIZ GRAPHIC NOVEL

CERES
Celestial Legend
VOL. 1: AYA

Story and Art by
YÛ WATASE

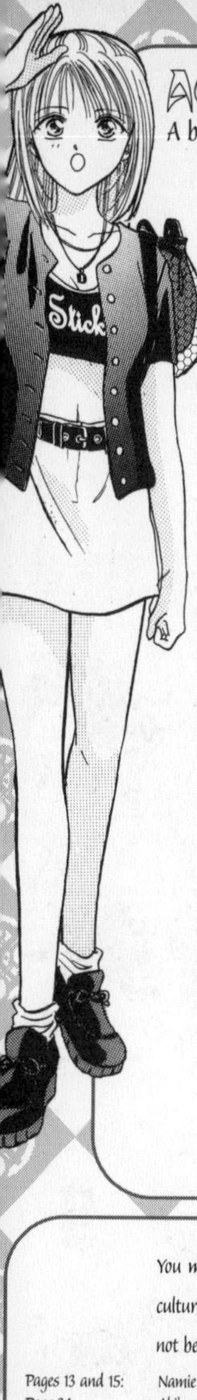

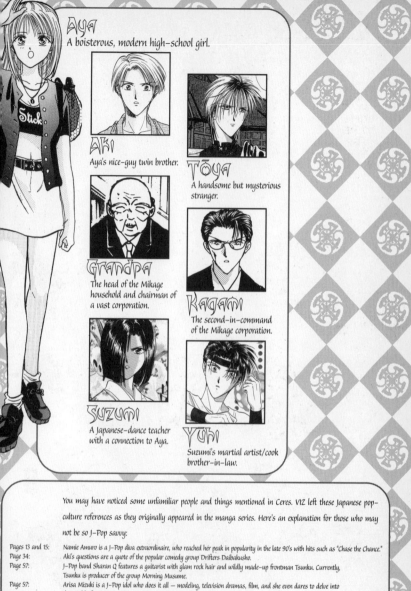

Aya
A boisterous, modern high-school girl.

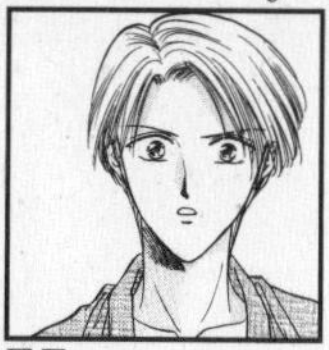

Aki
Aya's nice-guy twin brother.

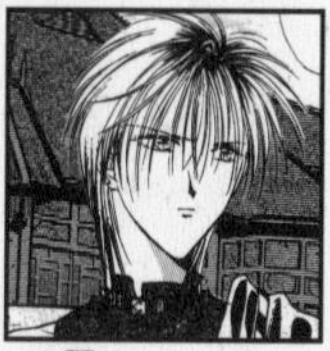

Tōya
A handsome but mysterious stranger.

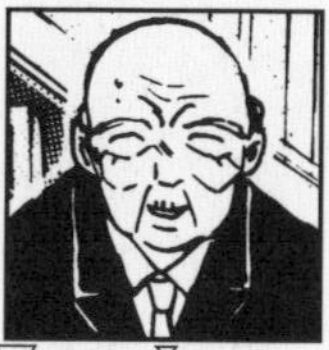

Grandpa
The head of the Mikage household and chairman of a vast corporation.

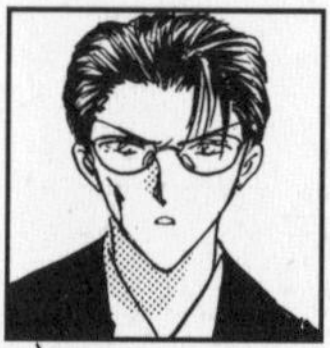

Kagami
The second-in-command of the Mikage corporation.

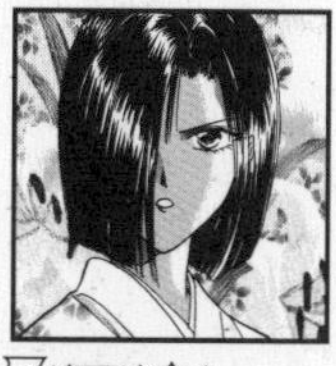

Suzumi
A Japanese-dance teacher with a connection to Aya.

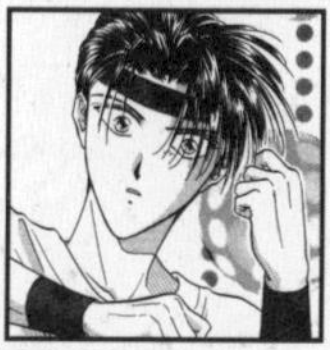

Yūhi
Suzumi's martial artist/cook brother-in-law.

You may have noticed some unfamiliar people and things mentioned in Ceres. VIZ left these Japanese pop-culture references as they originally appeared in the manga series. Here's an explanation for those who may not be so J-Pop savvy:

Pages 13 and 15: Namie Amuro is a J-Pop diva extraordinaire, who reached her peak in popularity in the late 90's with hits such as "Chase the Chance."

Page 34: Aki's questions are a quote of the popular comedy group Drifters Daibakusho.

Page 57: J-Pop band Sharan Q features a guitarist with glam rock hair and wildly made-up frontman Tsunku. Currently, Tsunku is producer of the group Morning Musume.

Page 57: Arisa Mizuki is a J-Pop idol who does it all — modeling, television dramas, film, and she even dares to delve into the world of J-Pop music.

Page 66: Nanase Aikawa is the purveyor of power pop hits combining J-Pop idol appeal with a Joan Jett edge.

Page 116: Mrs. Q's name (Oda Kyû) and appearance both pay comical homage to the classical anime series, Obake no Kyu-Taro ("Kyu-Taro the Ghost")

Page 118: In Japan, Formula-1 champion Ayrton Senna is much idolized for his incredible driving prowess.

Page 151: A reference to the famous cook Rokusaburo Michiba from the infamously melodramatic cooking show Iron Chef, which pits culinary geniuses against one another.

Page 184: Totsuzen Tonari No Gohan Gomen ("Intruding Suddenly: Next Door's Dinner") is a show in which an ordinary housewife is filmed making dinner.

Ceres
Celestial Legend

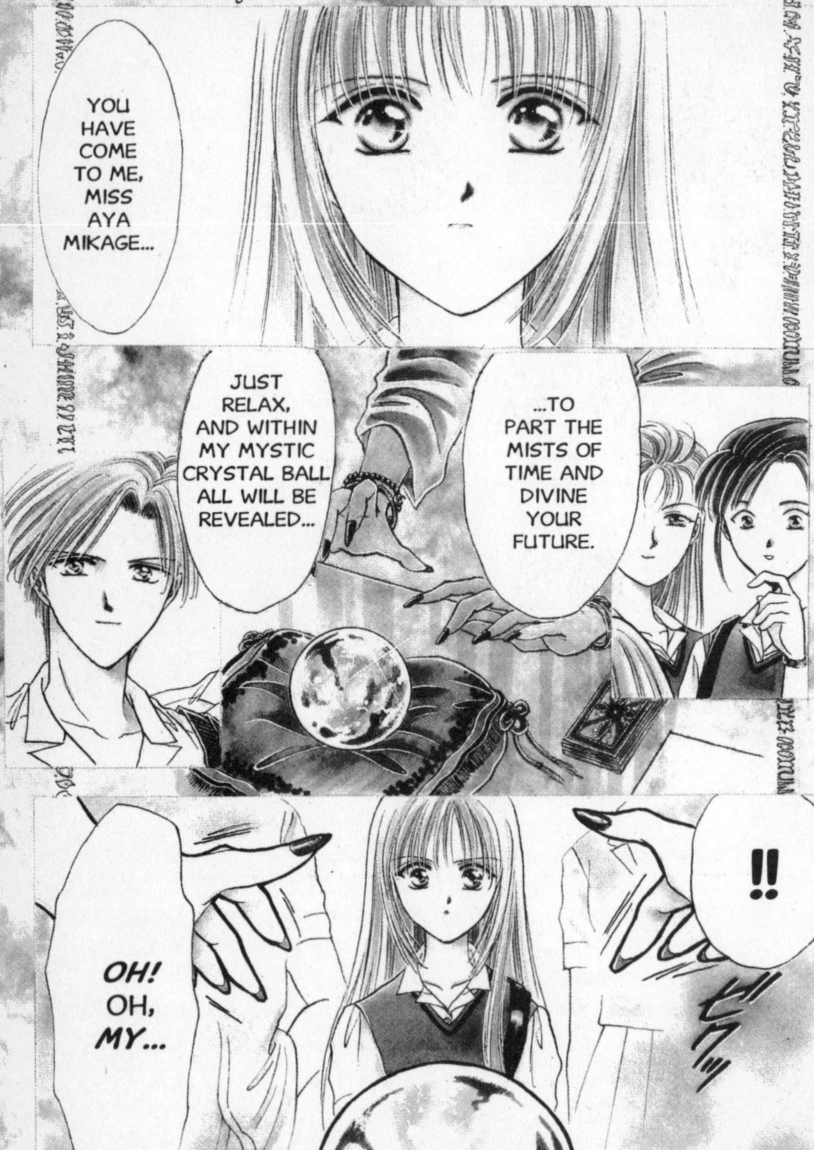

YOU HAVE COME TO ME, MISS AYA MIKAGE...
...TO PART THE MISTS OF TIME AND DIVINE YOUR FUTURE.
JUST RELAX, AND WITHIN MY MYSTIC CRYSTAL BALL ALL WILL BE REVEALED...
!!
OH! OH, MY...

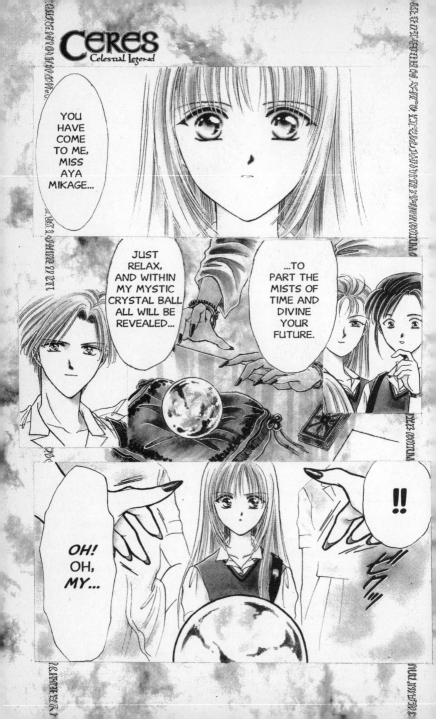

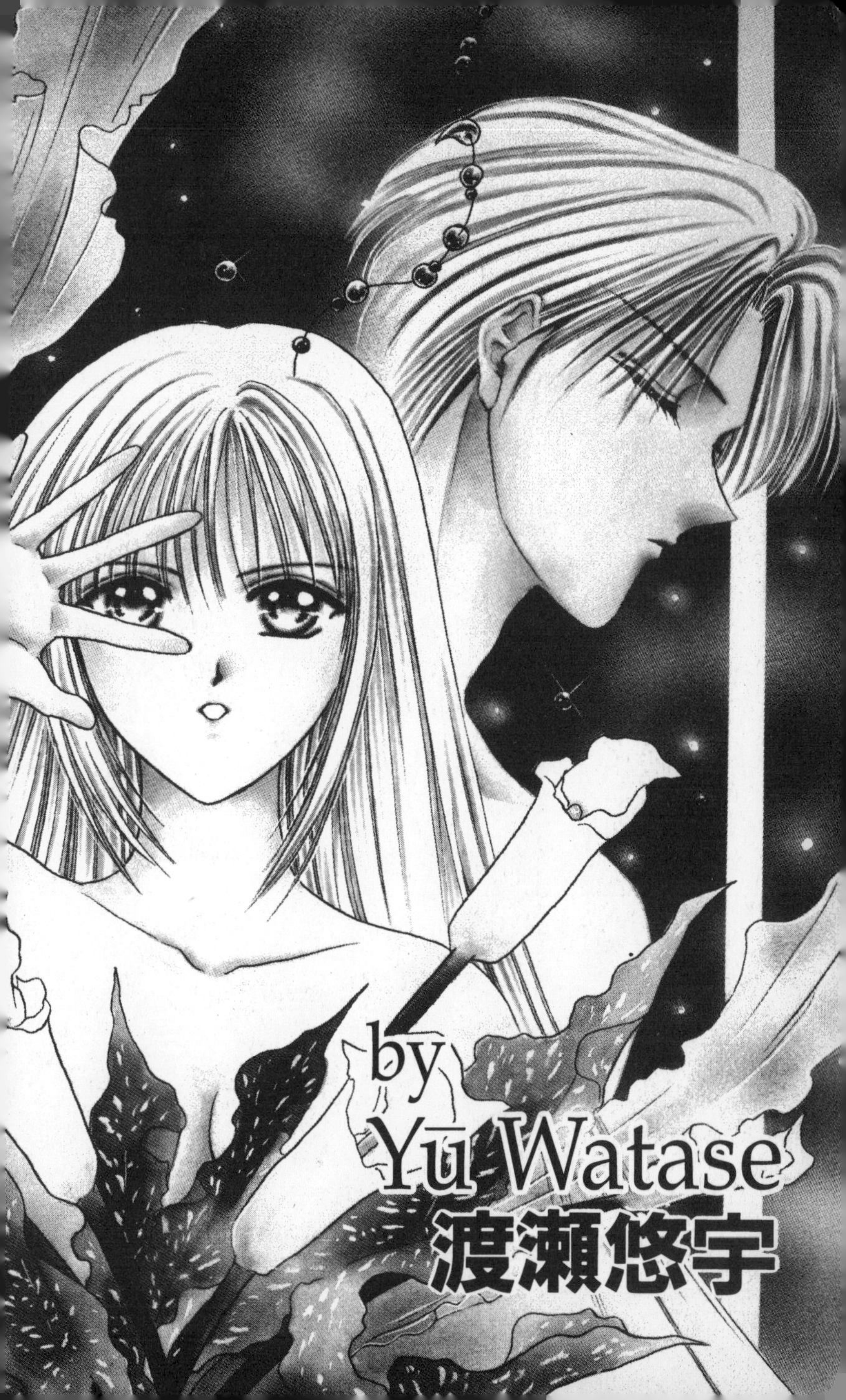
by
Yū Watase
渡瀬悠宇

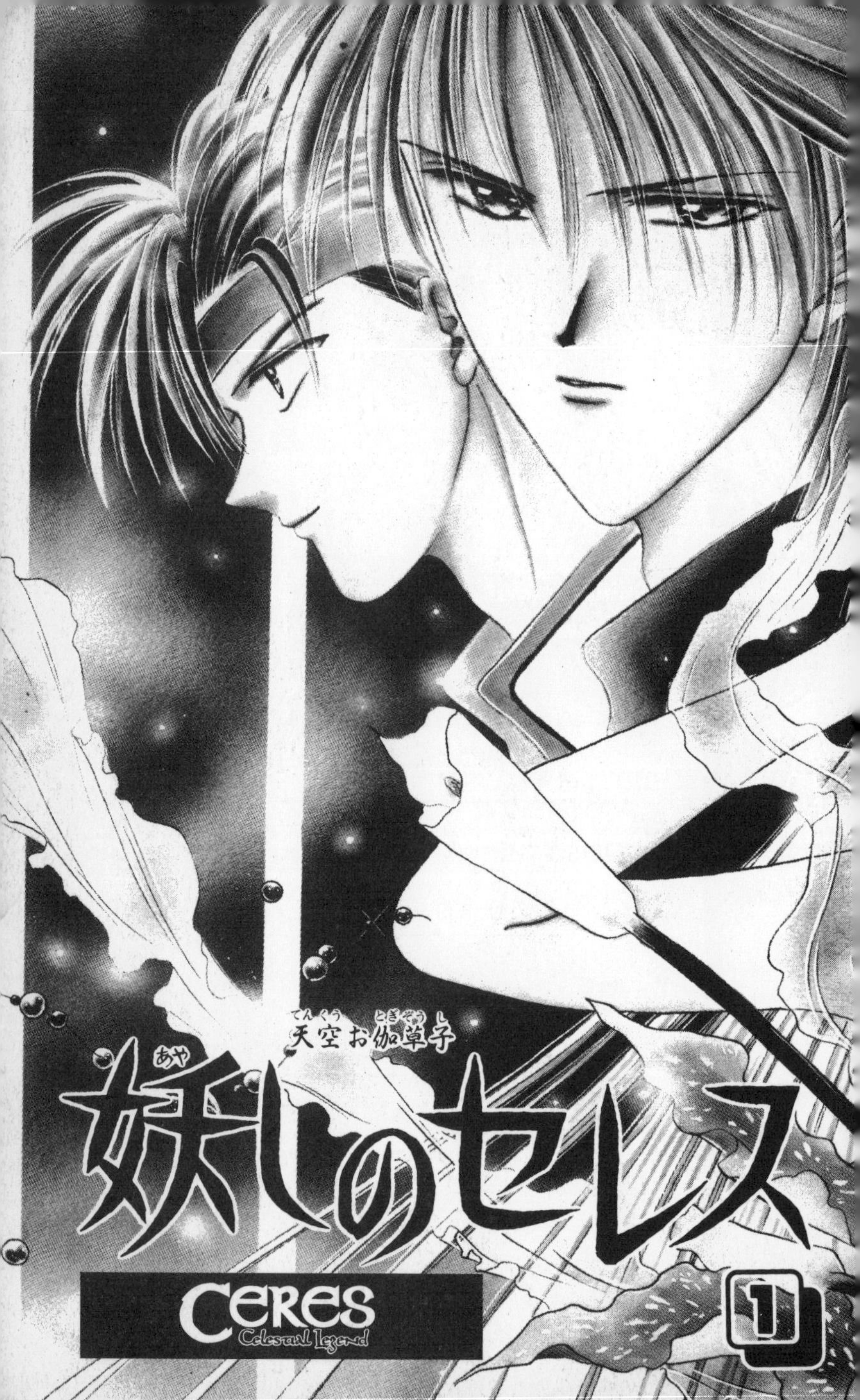
天空お伽草子
妖しのセレス
CERES
Celestial Legend
1

BIRTHDAY: September 24, a Libra!

BLOODTYPE: O

HEIGHT: 5'5" BUST: 33" WAIST: 22 1/2" HIPS: 34"

HOBBY: Karaoke, gabbing on the phone, collecting cool jewelry

SPECIAL TALENT: Bouncing back, mimicking pop stars

AYA MIKAGE

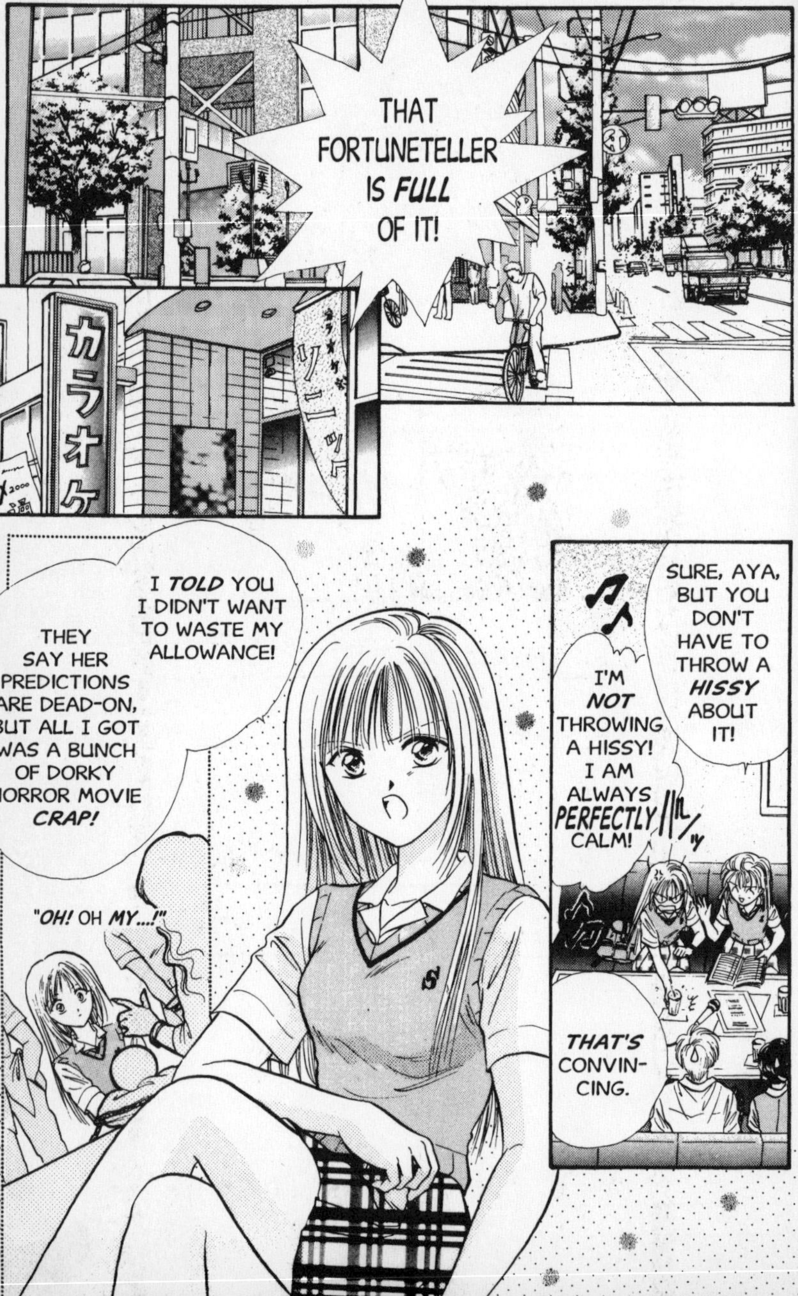
THAT FORTUNETELLER IS FULL OF IT!
カラオケ
I TOLD YOU I DIDN'T WANT TO WASTE MY ALLOWANCE!
THEY SAY HER PREDICTIONS ARE DEAD-ON, BUT ALL I GOT WAS A BUNCH OF DORKY HORROR MOVIE CRAP!
"OH! OH MY...!"
SURE, AYA, BUT YOU DON'T HAVE TO THROW A HISSY ABOUT IT!
I'M NOT THROWING A HISSY! I AM ALWAYS PERFECTLY CALM!
THAT'S CONVIN-CING.

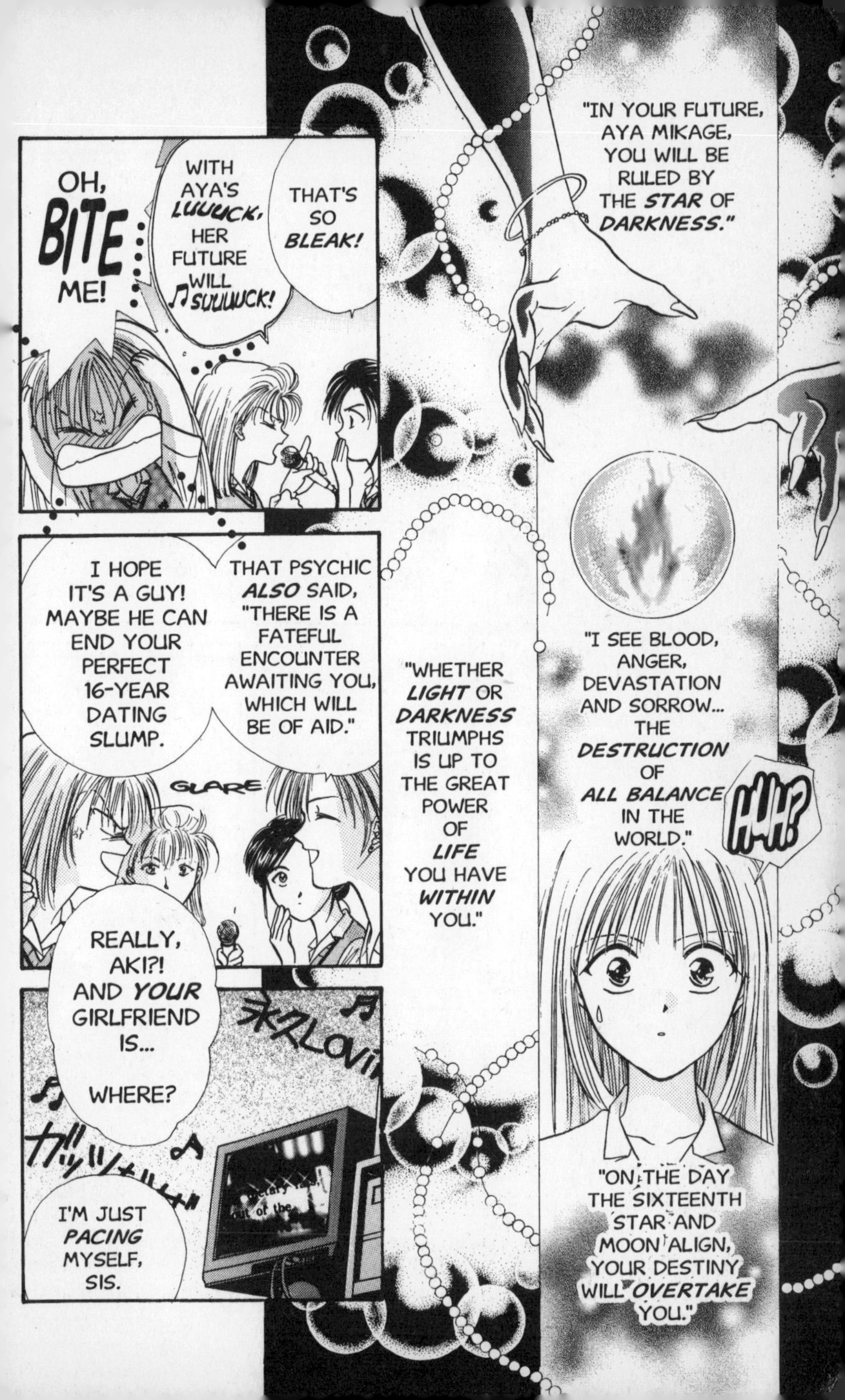
"IN YOUR FUTURE, AYA MIKAGE, YOU WILL BE RULED BY THE *STAR* OF *DARKNESS.*"
"I SEE BLOOD, ANGER, DEVASTATION AND SORROW... THE *DESTRUCTION* OF *ALL BALANCE* IN THE WORLD."
HUH?
"ON THE DAY THE SIXTEENTH STAR AND MOON ALIGN, YOUR DESTINY WILL *OVERTAKE* YOU."
"WHETHER *LIGHT* OR *DARKNESS* TRIUMPHS IS UP TO THE GREAT POWER OF *LIFE* YOU HAVE *WITHIN* YOU."
THAT'S SO *BLEAK!*
WITH AYA'S *LUUUCK,* HER FUTURE WILL ♫ *SUUUCK!*
OH, BITE ME!
THAT PSYCHIC *ALSO* SAID, "THERE IS A FATEFUL ENCOUNTER AWAITING YOU, WHICH WILL BE OF AID."
I HOPE IT'S A GUY! MAYBE HE CAN END YOUR PERFECT 16-YEAR DATING SLUMP.
GLARE
REALLY, AKI?! AND *YOUR* GIRLFRIEND IS... WHERE?
I'M JUST *PACING* MYSELF, SIS.

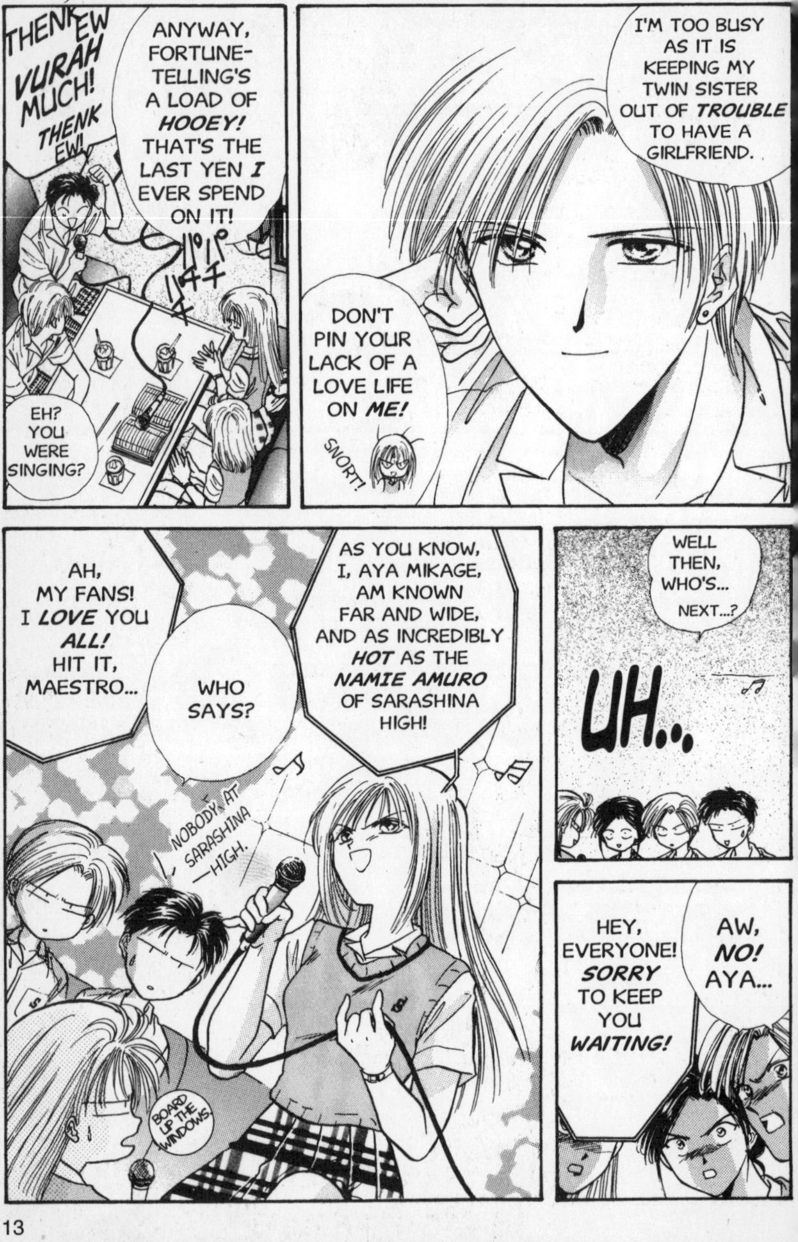
I'M TOO BUSY AS IT IS KEEPING MY TWIN SISTER OUT OF *TROUBLE* TO HAVE A GIRLFRIEND.
DON'T PIN YOUR LACK OF A LOVE LIFE ON *ME!*
SNORT!
ANYWAY, FORTUNE-TELLING'S A LOAD OF *HOOEY!* THAT'S THE LAST YEN *I* EVER SPEND ON IT!
THENK EW VURAH MUCH! THENK EW!
EH? YOU WERE SINGING?
WELL THEN, WHO'S... NEXT...?
UH...
AW, *NO!* AYA...
HEY, EVERYONE! *SORRY* TO KEEP YOU *WAITING!*
AS YOU KNOW, I, AYA MIKAGE, AM KNOWN FAR AND WIDE, AND AS INCREDIBLY *HOT* AS THE *NAMIE AMURO* OF SARASHINA HIGH!
WHO SAYS?
AH, MY FANS! I *LOVE* YOU *ALL!* HIT IT, MAESTRO...
NOBODY AT SARASHINA—HIGH.
BOARD UP THE WINDOWS.

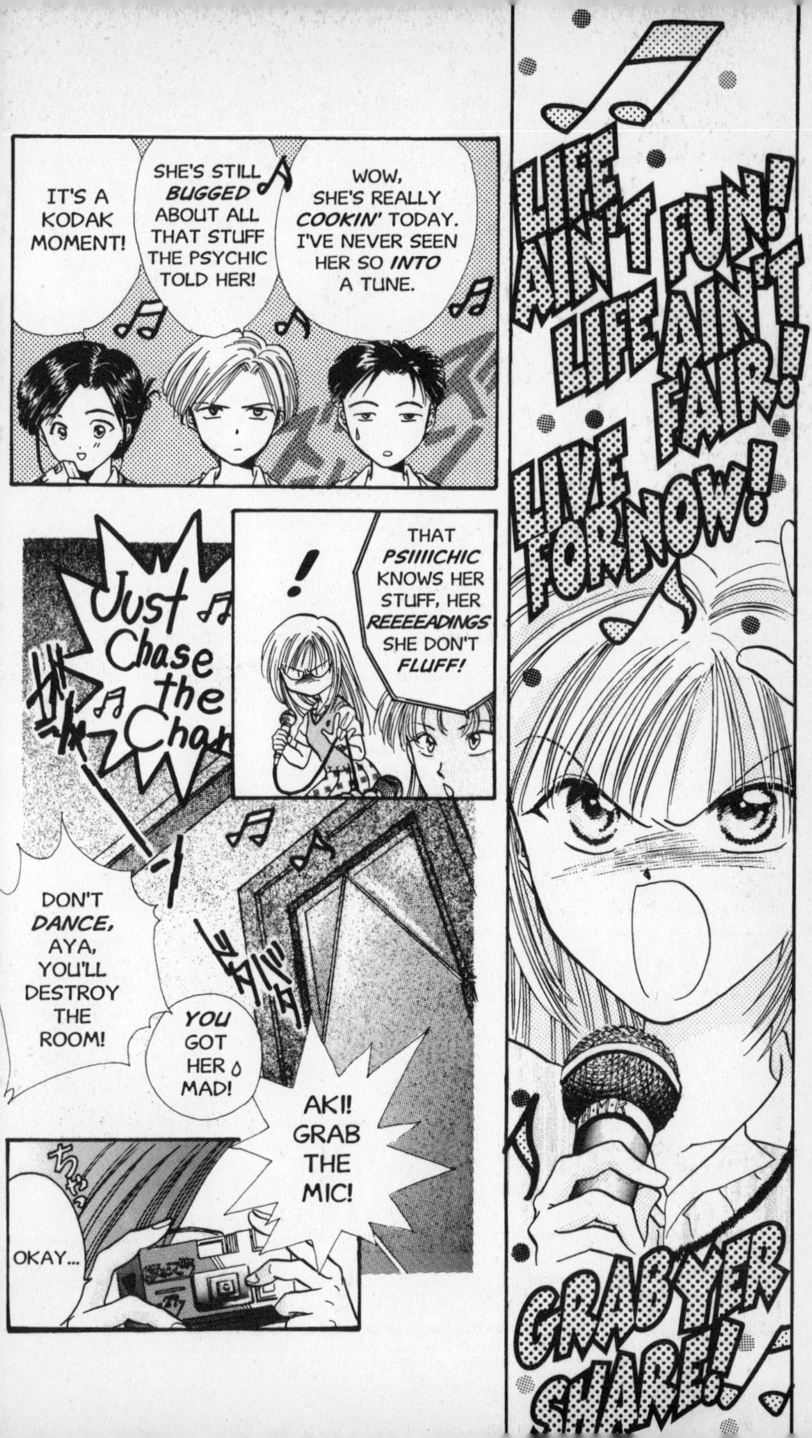
LIFE AIN'T FUN! LIFE AIN'T FAIR! LIVE FOR NOW!
GRAB YER SHARE!!
WOW, SHE'S REALLY *COOKIN'* TODAY. I'VE NEVER SEEN HER SO *INTO* A TUNE.
SHE'S STILL *BUGGED* ABOUT ALL THAT STUFF THE PSYCHIC TOLD HER!
IT'S A KODAK MOMENT!
!
THAT *PSIIIICHIC* KNOWS HER STUFF, HER *REEEEADINGS* SHE DON'T *FLUFF!*
Just Chase the Chan
DON'T *DANCE,* AYA, YOU'LL DESTROY THE ROOM!
YOU GOT HER MAD!
AKI! GRAB THE MIC!
OKAY...

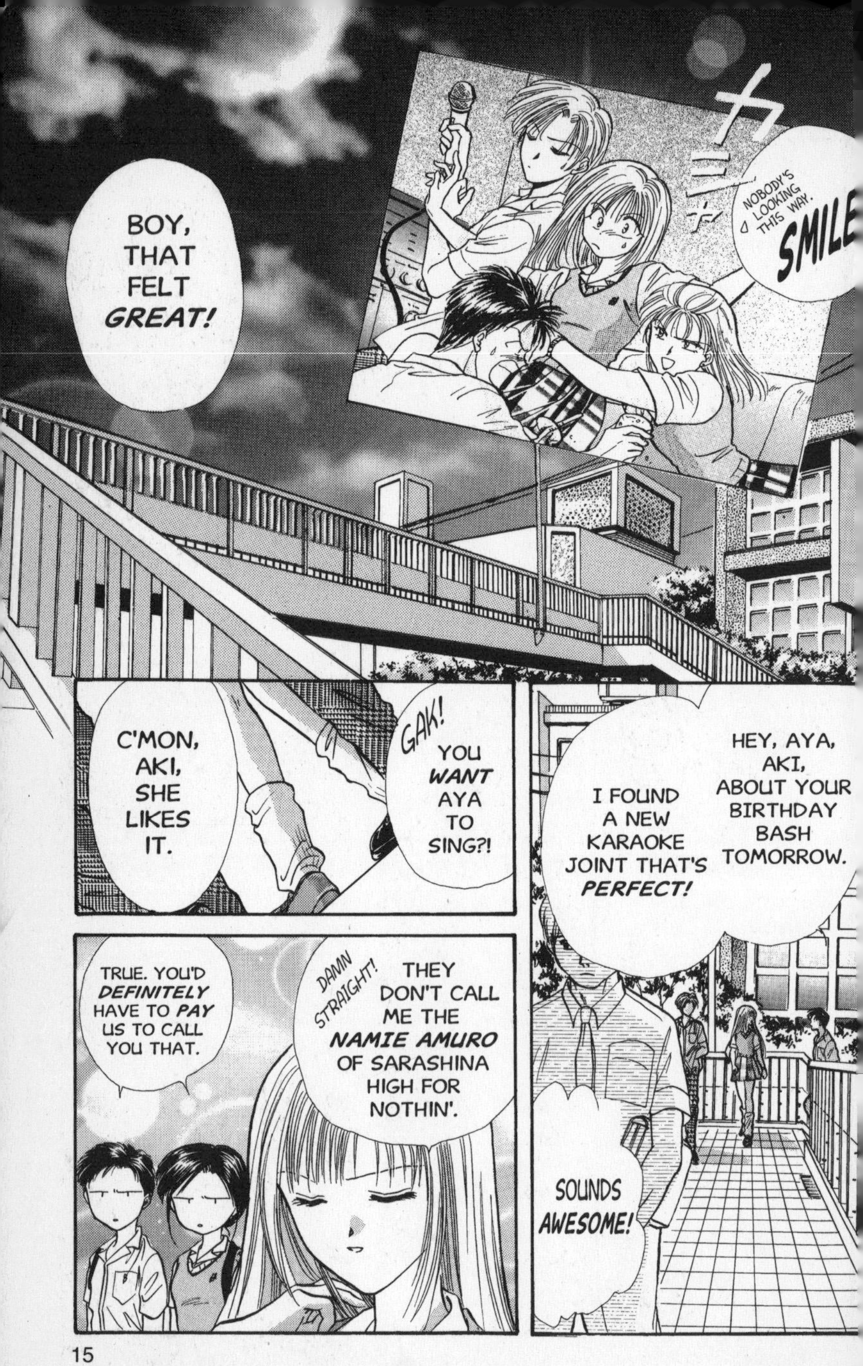
NOBODY'S LOOKING THIS WAY.
SMILE
BOY, THAT FELT GREAT!
HEY, AYA, AKI, ABOUT YOUR BIRTHDAY BASH TOMORROW.
I FOUND A NEW KARAOKE JOINT THAT'S PERFECT!
SOUNDS AWESOME!
GAK!
YOU WANT AYA TO SING?!
C'MON, AKI, SHE LIKES IT.
DAMN STRAIGHT!
THEY DON'T CALL ME THE NAMIE AMURO OF SARASHINA HIGH FOR NOTHIN'.
TRUE. YOU'D DEFINITELY HAVE TO PAY US TO CALL YOU THAT.

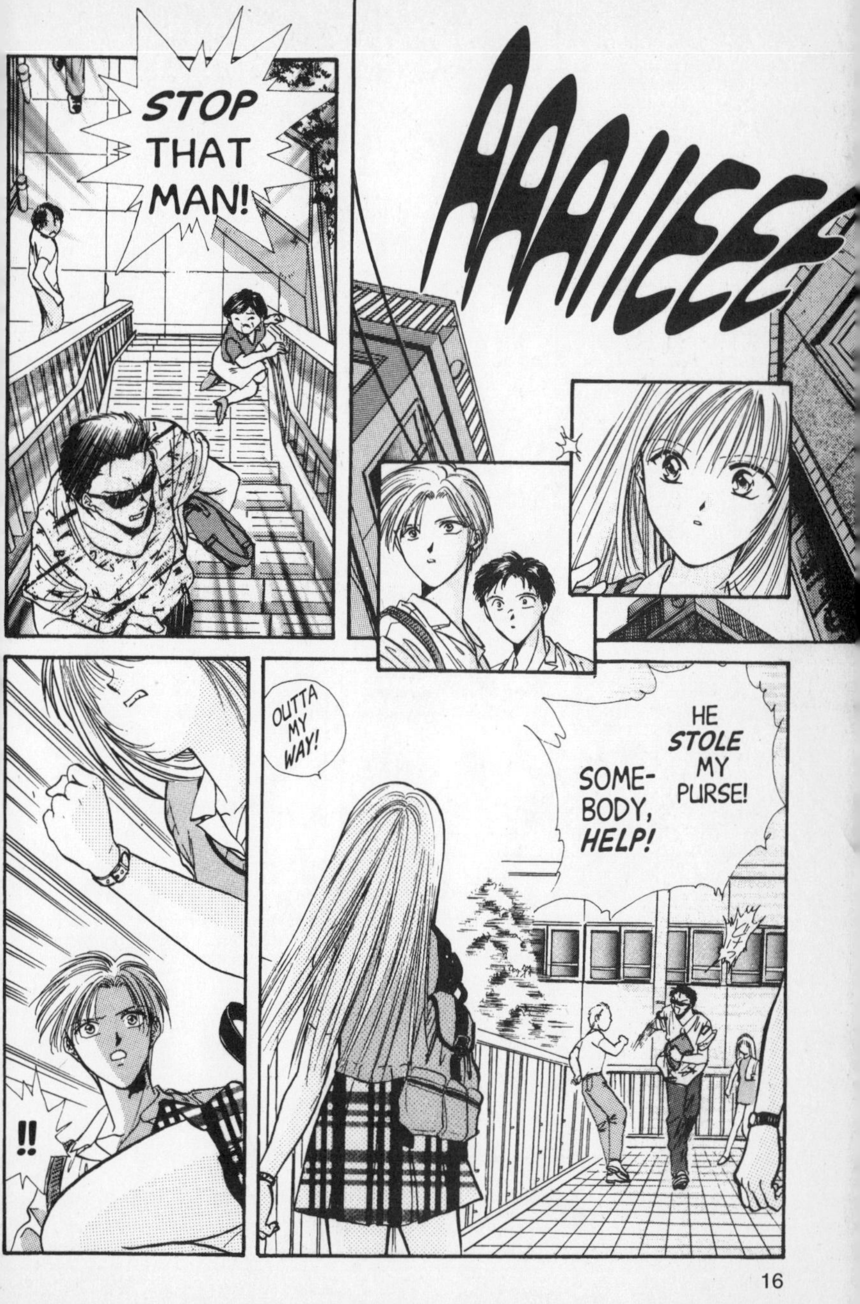

AAAIIEEE
STOP THAT MAN!
HE STOLE MY PURSE!
SOME-BODY, HELP!
OUTTA MY WAY!
!!

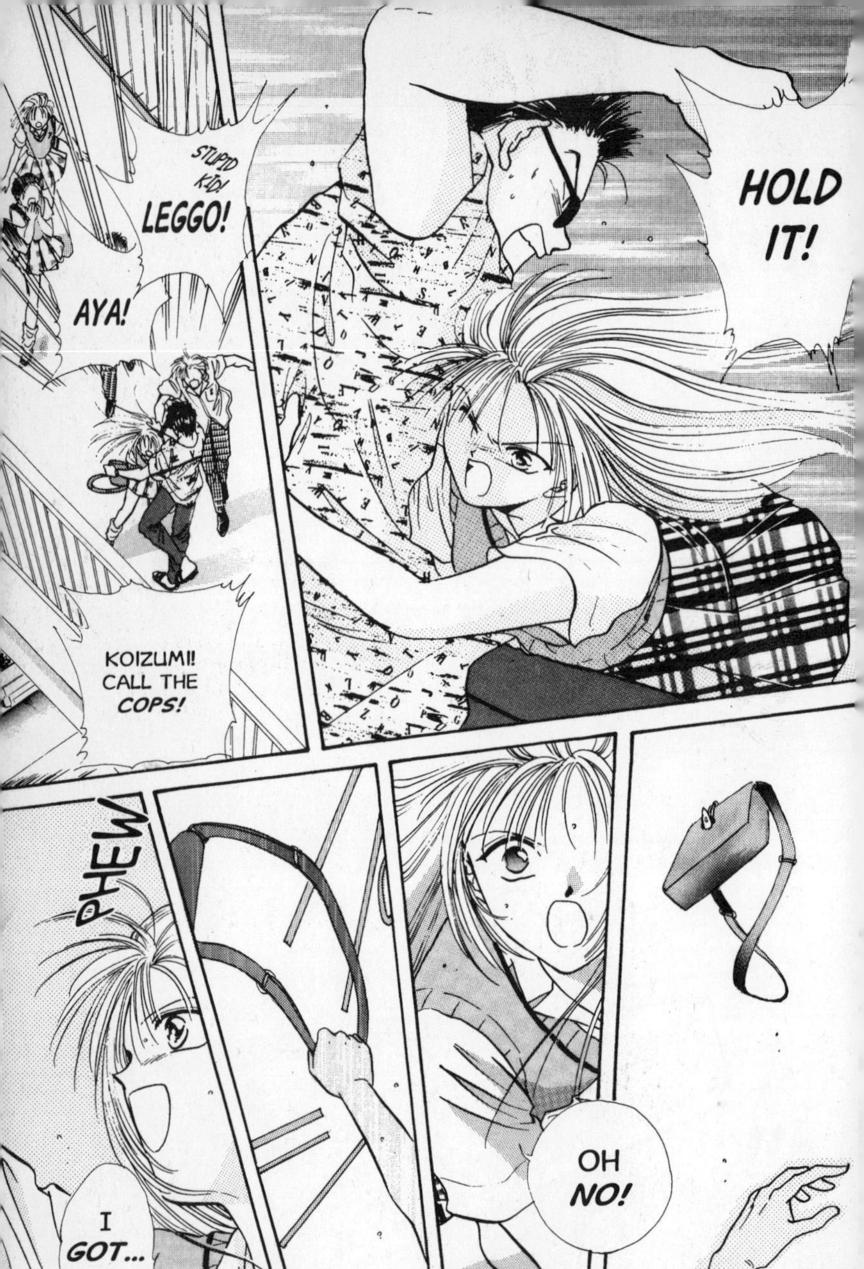
HOLD IT!
STUPID KID! LEGGO!
AYA!
KOIZUMI!! CALL THE COPS!
OH NO!
PHEW
I GOT...

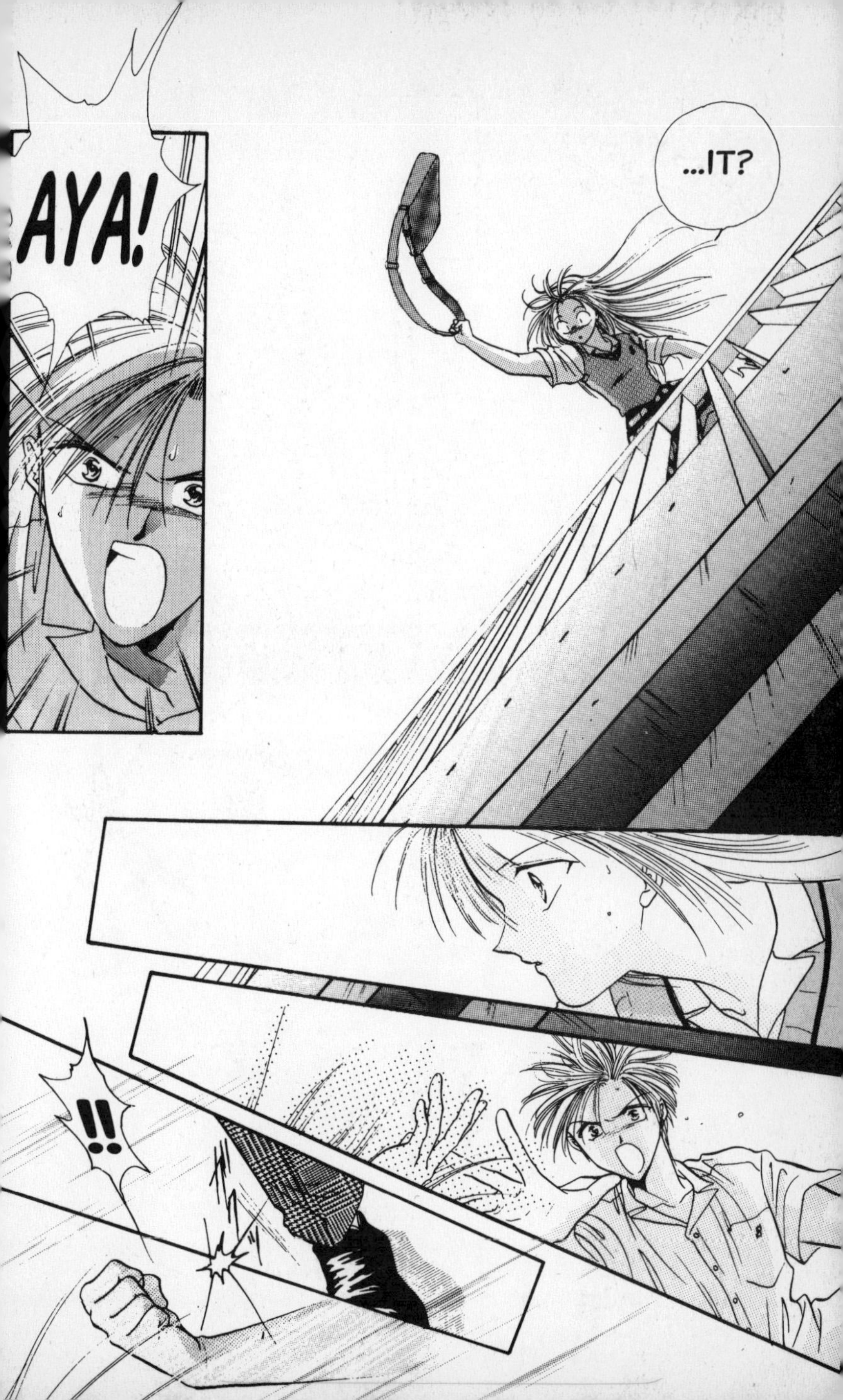
...IT?
AYA!
!!

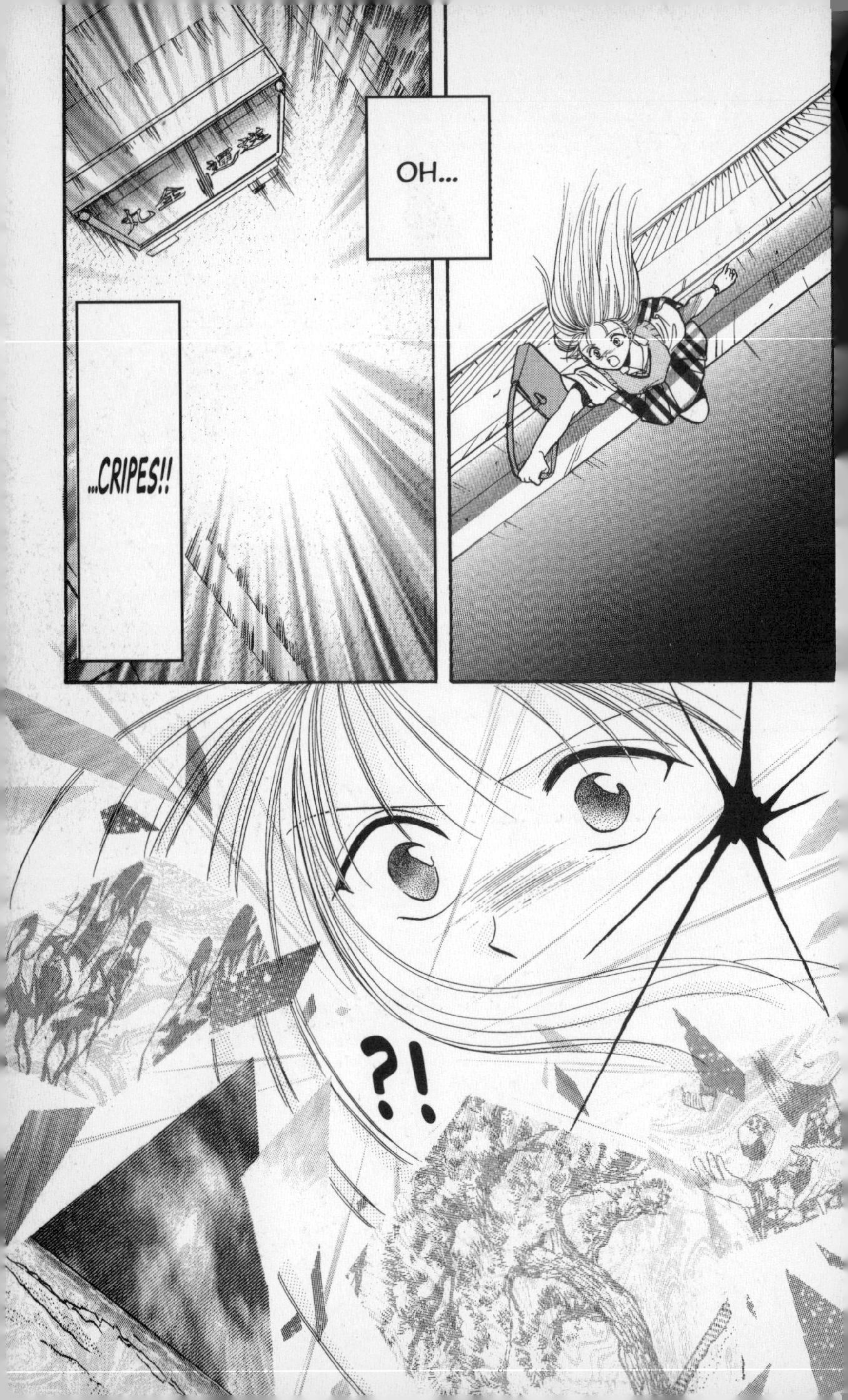
OH...
...CRIPES!!
?!

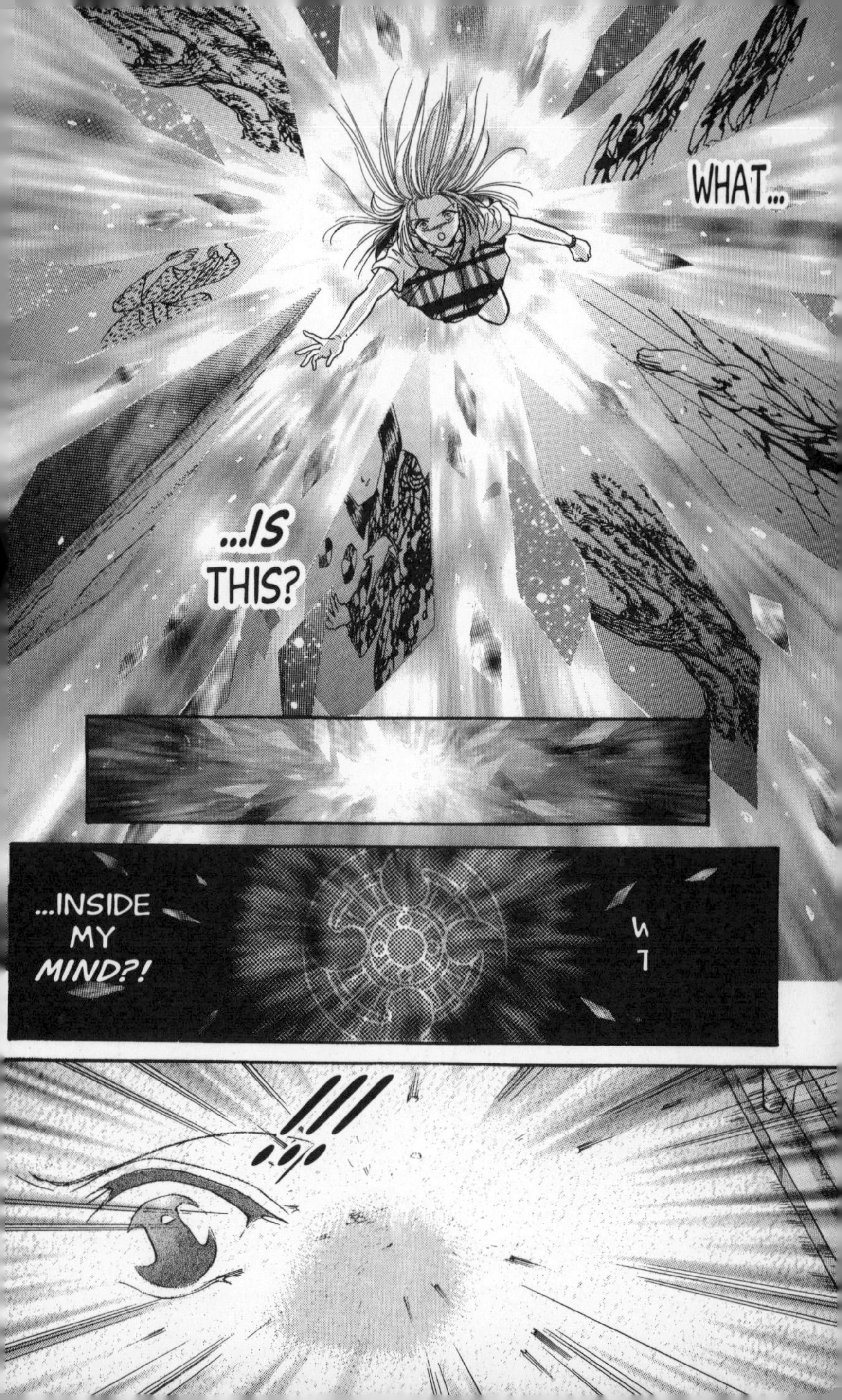
WHAT...
...IS THIS?
...INSIDE MY MIND?!

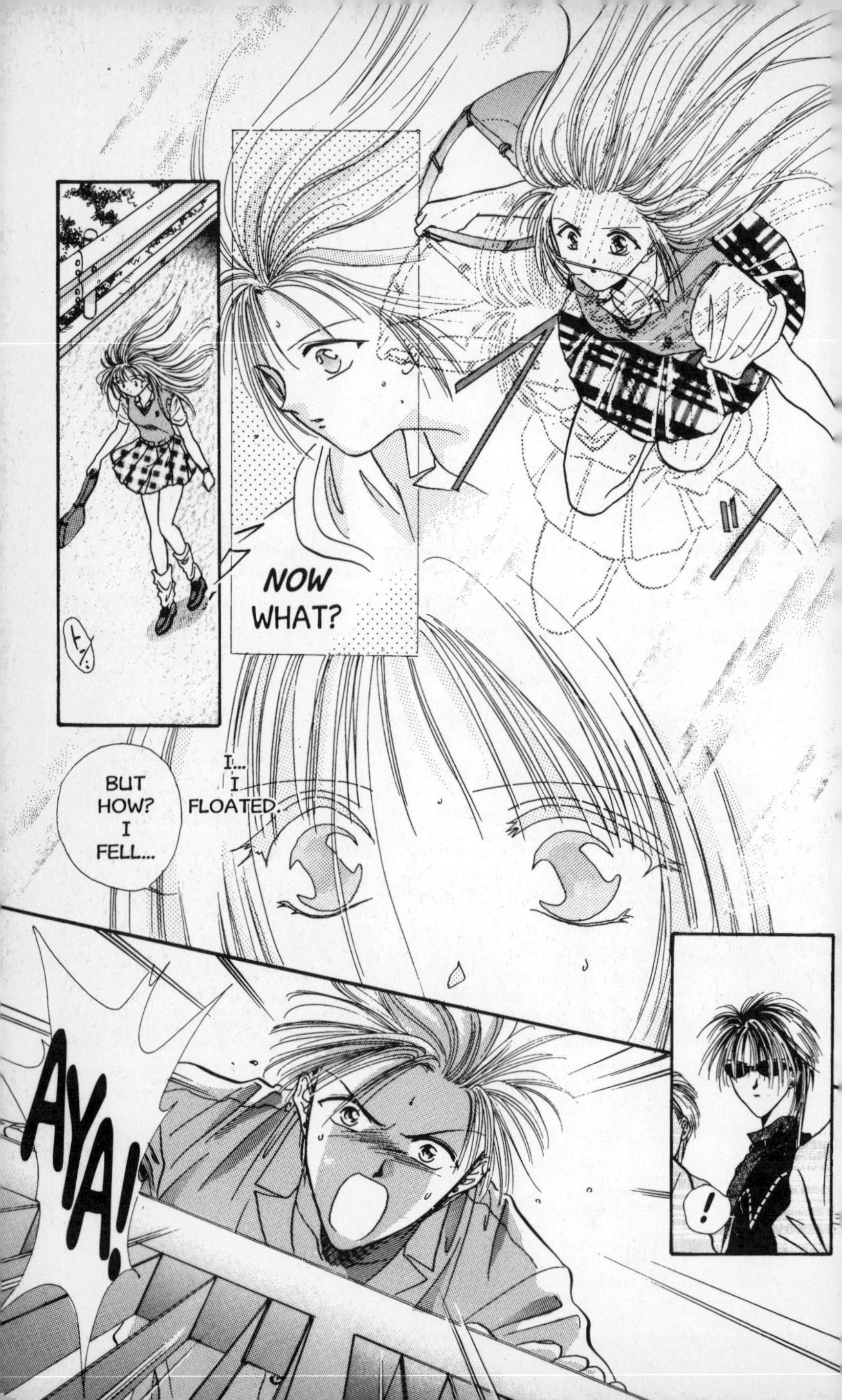
NOW WHAT?
I... I FLOATED.
BUT HOW? I FELL...
!
AYA!

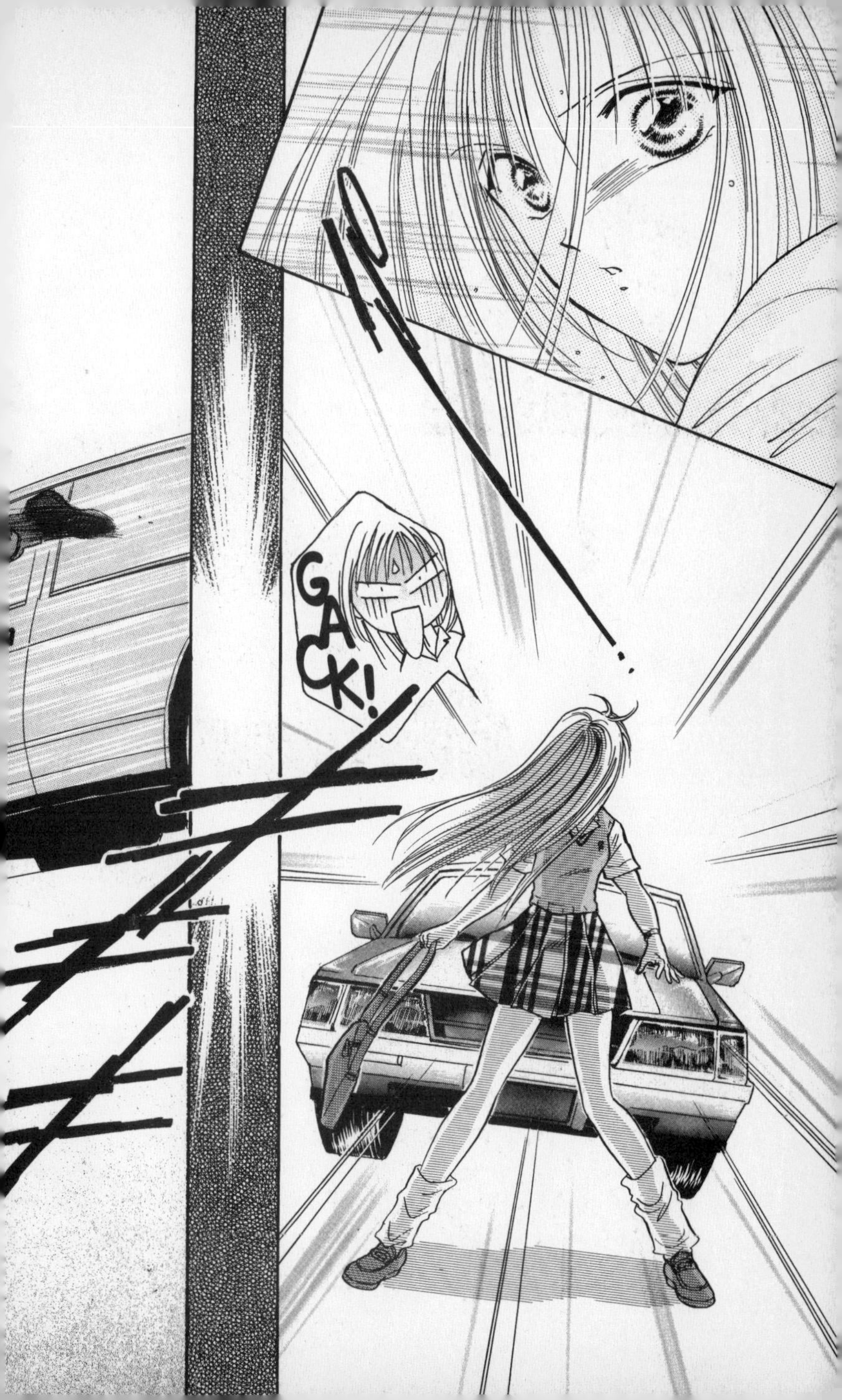
GACK!

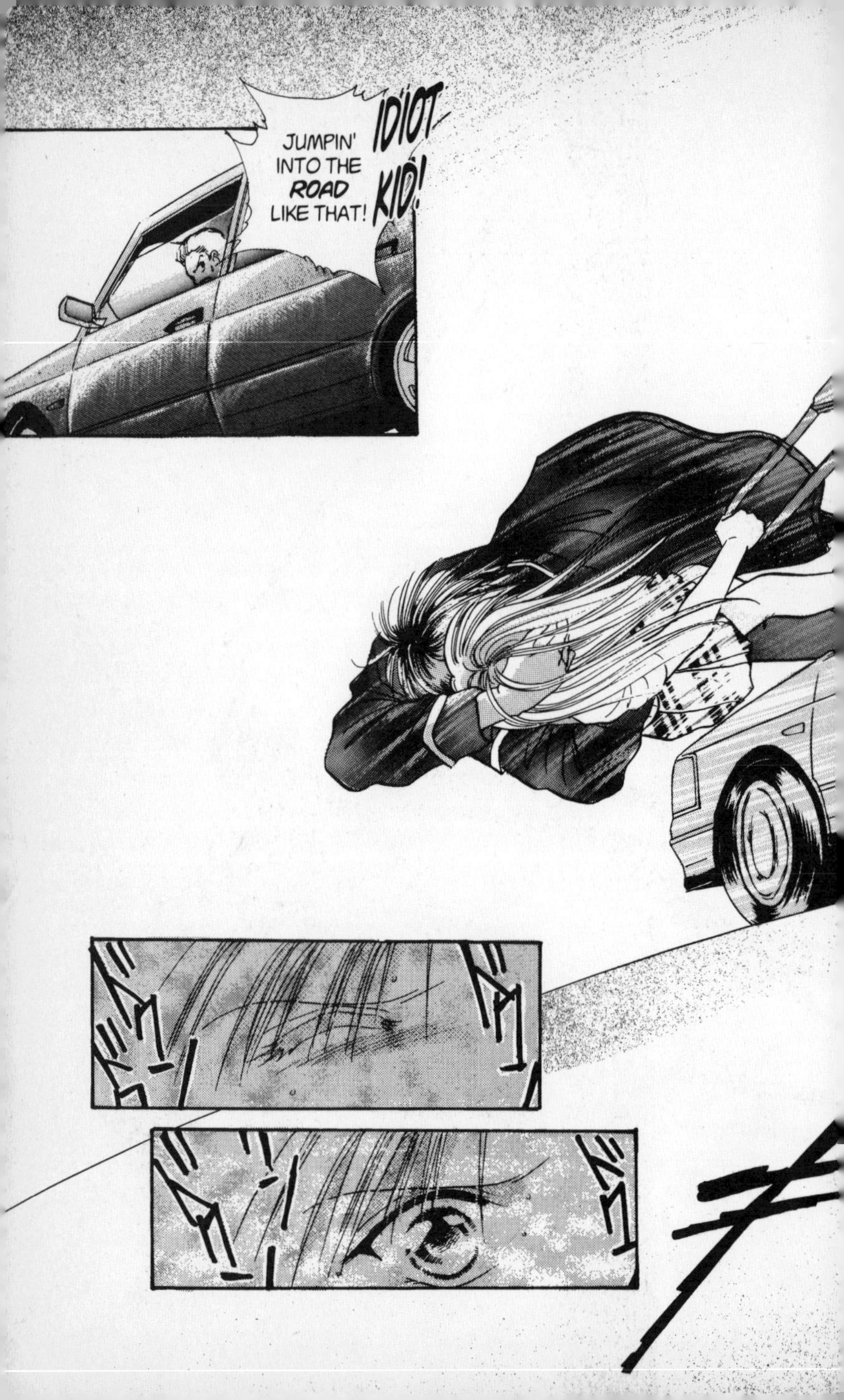

JUMPIN' INTO THE ROAD LIKE THAT!
IDIOT KID!

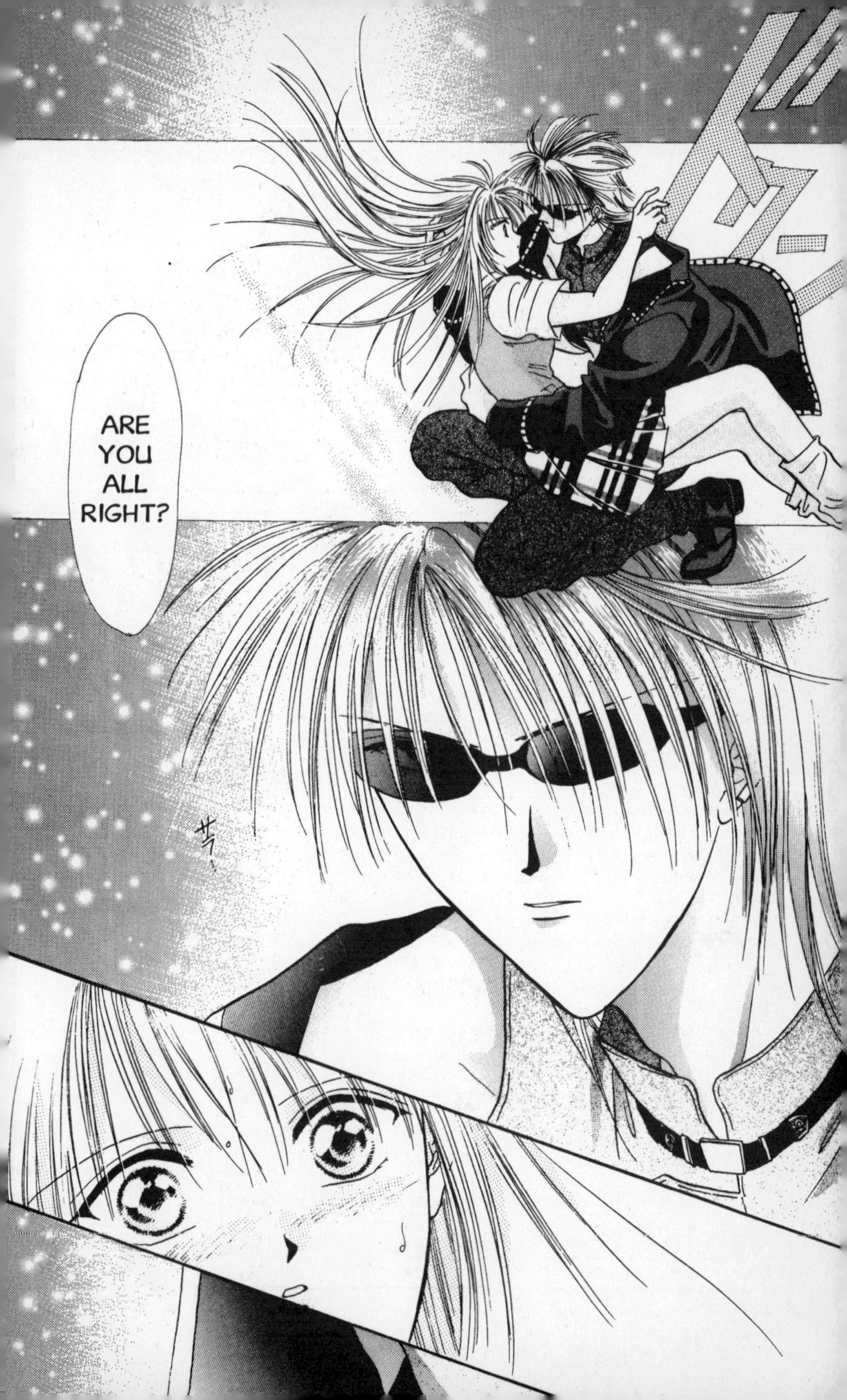
ARE YOU ALL RIGHT?

Yes! This is my new series! For people reading for the first time, and those continuing from Fushigi Yûgi, hello.
I thought up this story when I was a senior in high school (here we go again) — even before the idea for FY. "Aya" was born then, and had a more occult story, but I've changed things around here and there, so I hope there'll be a different kind of "horror."
The meaning of the subtitle, "Celestial Legend," will eventually become clear.
Of course, the rhythm and the atmosphere are different from my previous work, but I'd like to try my best to depict Aya's strength, unusual characters, a different form of love, etc., while I tell the story. There might be something here that will contradict what I've tried to communicate in my other works, but I guess that's because the characters' ways of life, or their ways of thinking, are different. What's especially new to me are the standard minor characters which are essential to shôjo manga. I've never used these types of characters in my previous work, so it should be interesting.
And then there's Aya. She has one feature that is clearly different from my previous heroines -- she has slanting eyes. (Since they're twins, Aki has the same eyes.) They're a distinctive feature for the character... or rather...well...it's intentional. She's the new Watase heroine who bleaches her hair, is a little vulgar and headstrong, and does what she wants and lives how she wants.

Please treat her kindly!

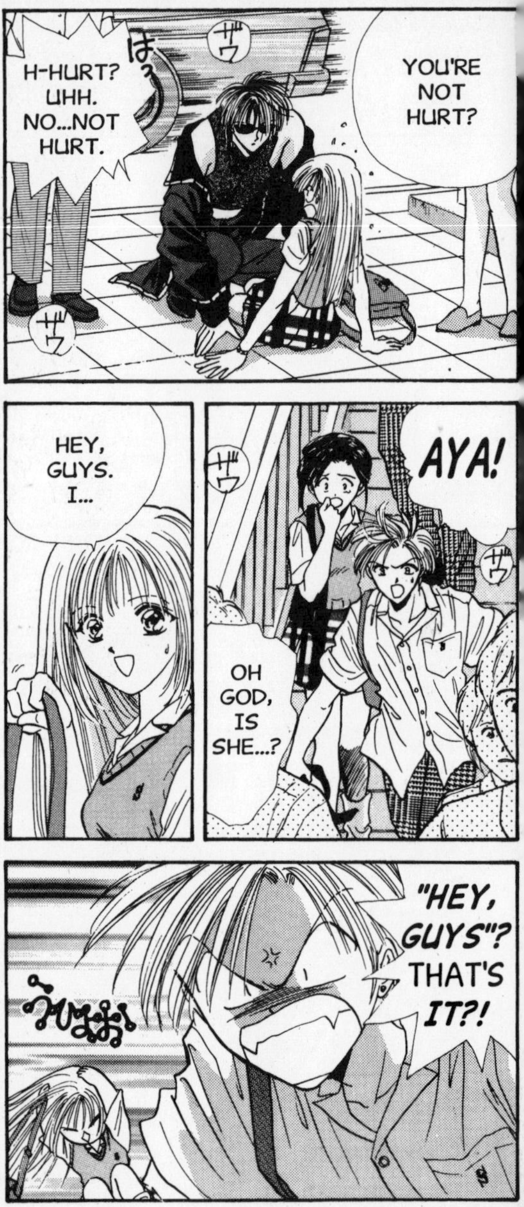
YOU'RE NOT HURT?
H-HURT? UHH. NO...NOT HURT.
AYA!
OH GOD, IS SHE...?
HEY, GUYS. I...
"HEY, GUYS"? THAT'S IT?!

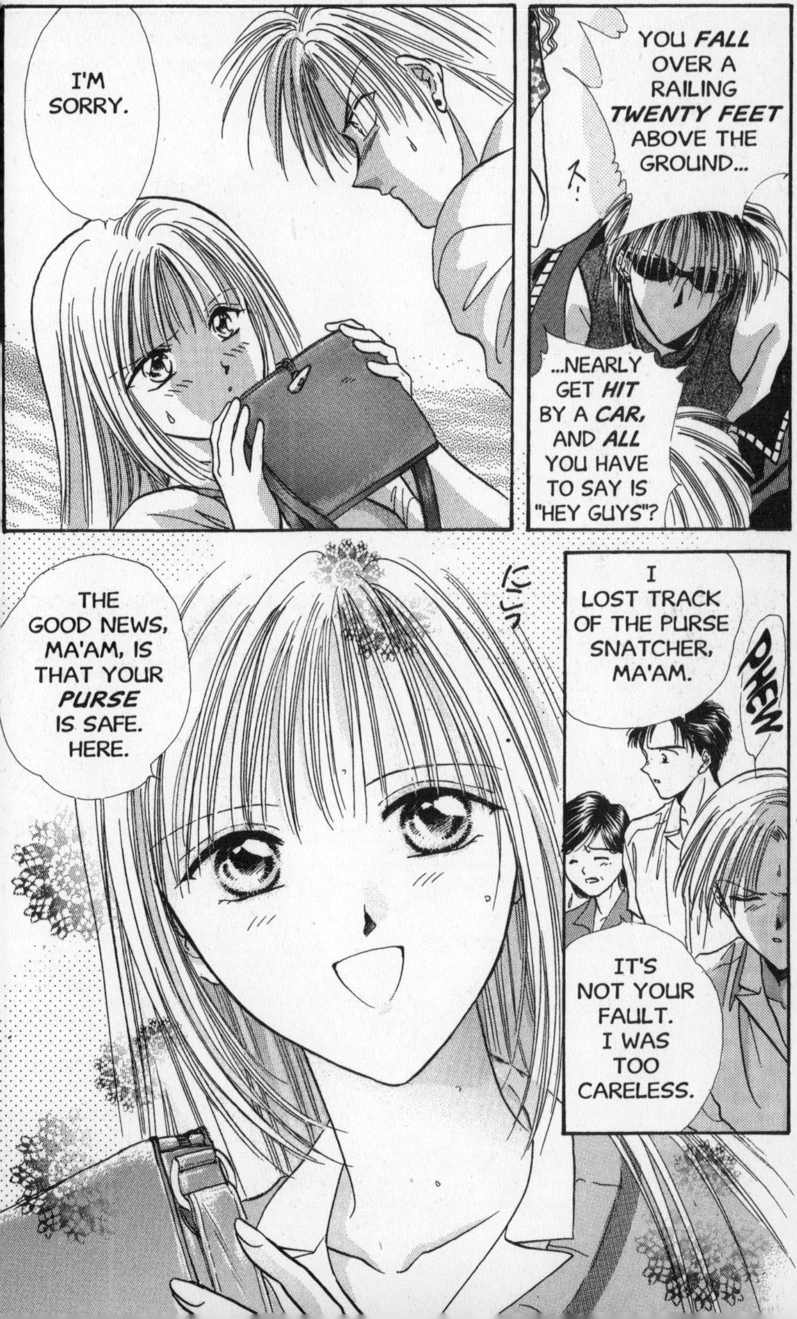
YOU FALL OVER A RAILING TWENTY FEET ABOVE THE GROUND...
...NEARLY GET HIT BY A CAR, AND ALL YOU HAVE TO SAY IS "HEY GUYS"?
I'M SORRY.
I LOST TRACK OF THE PURSE SNATCHER, MA'AM.
PHEW
IT'S NOT YOUR FAULT. I WAS TOO CARELESS.
THE GOOD NEWS, MA'AM, IS THAT YOUR PURSE IS SAFE. HERE.

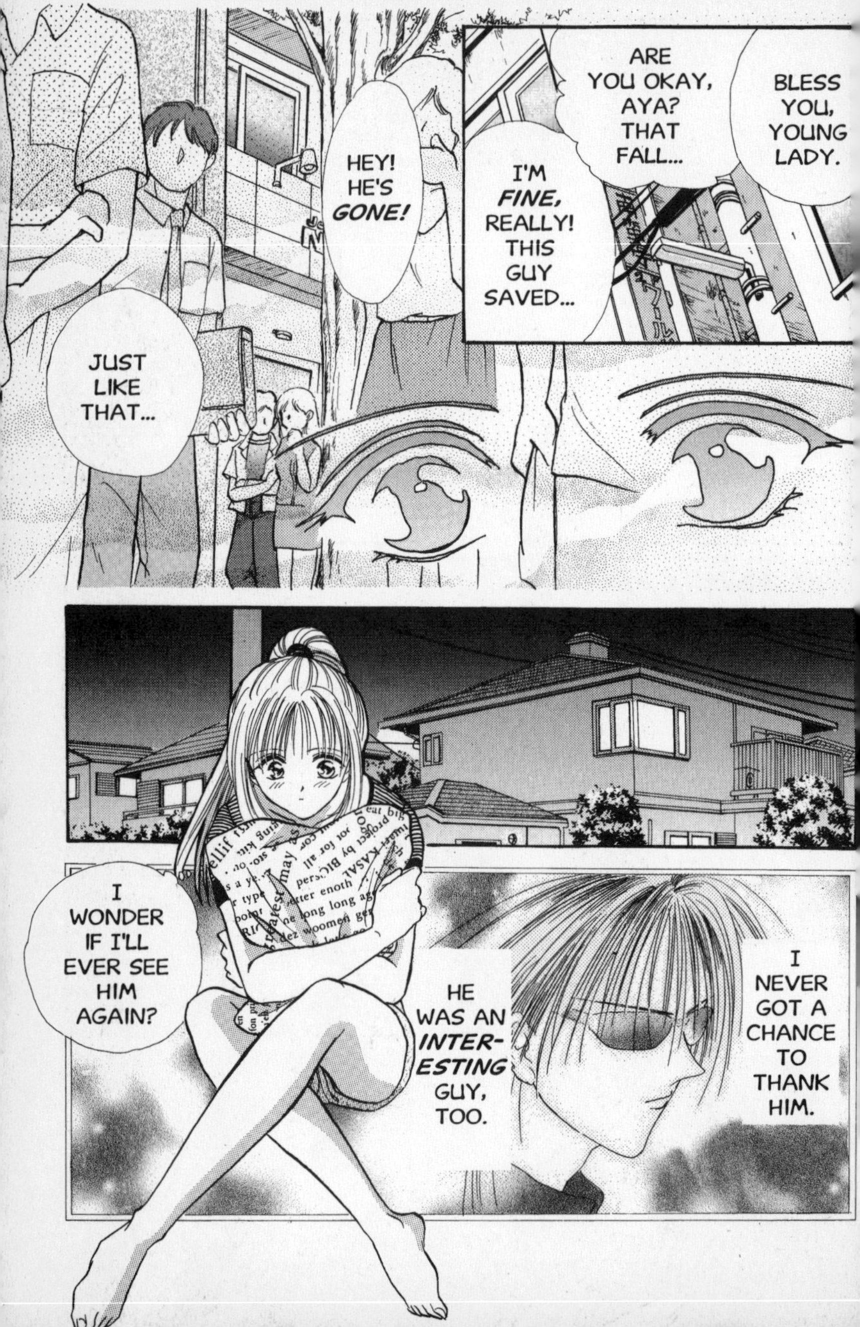
BLESS YOU, YOUNG LADY.
ARE YOU OKAY, AYA? THAT FALL...
I'M *FINE,* REALLY! THIS GUY SAVED...
HEY! HE'S *GONE!*
JUST LIKE THAT...
I NEVER GOT A CHANCE TO THANK HIM.
HE WAS AN *INTER-ESTING* GUY, TOO.
I WONDER IF I'LL EVER SEE HIM AGAIN?

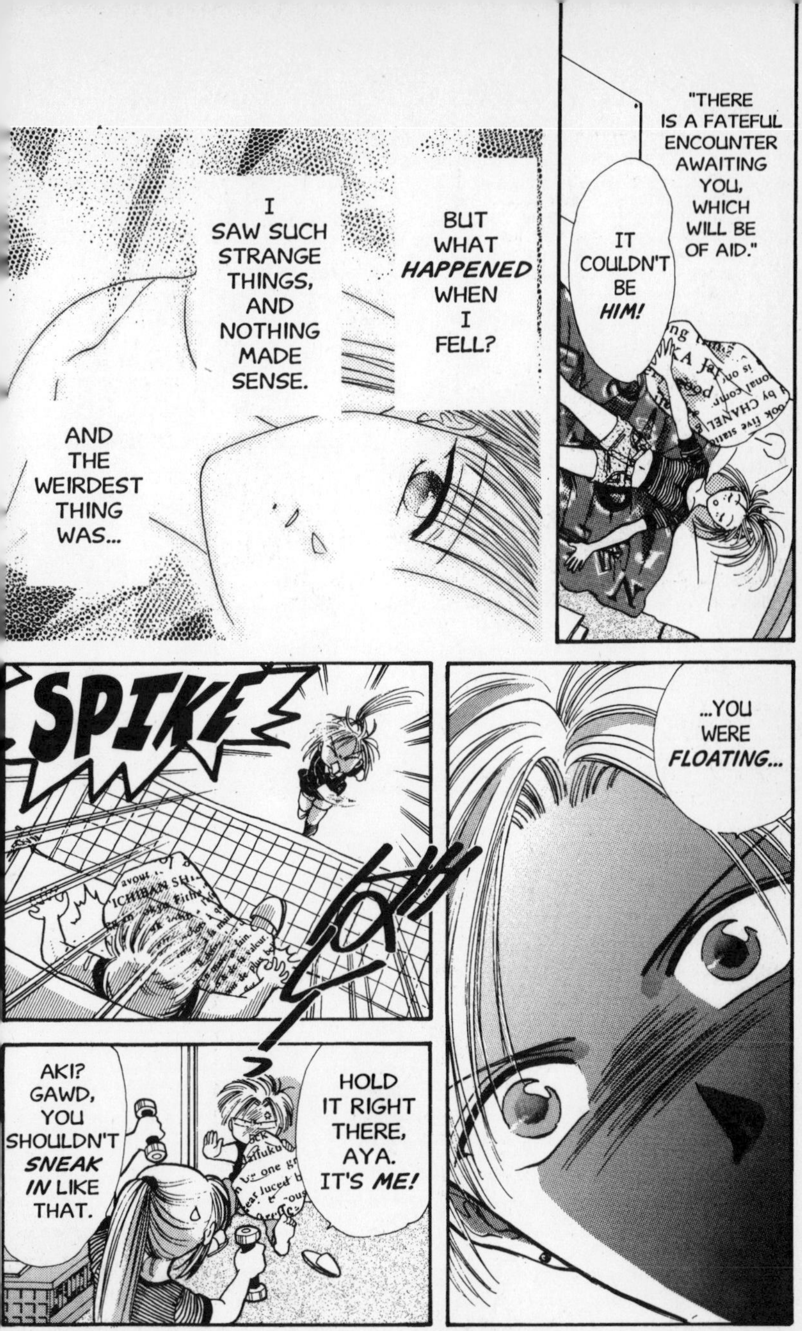
"THERE IS A FATEFUL ENCOUNTER AWAITING YOU, WHICH WILL BE OF AID."
IT COULDN'T BE HIM!
BUT WHAT HAPPENED WHEN I FELL?
I SAW SUCH STRANGE THINGS, AND NOTHING MADE SENSE.
AND THE WEIRDEST THING WAS...
...YOU WERE FLOATING...
SPIKE
HOLD IT RIGHT THERE, AYA. IT'S ME!
AKI? GAWD, YOU SHOULDN'T SNEAK IN LIKE THAT.

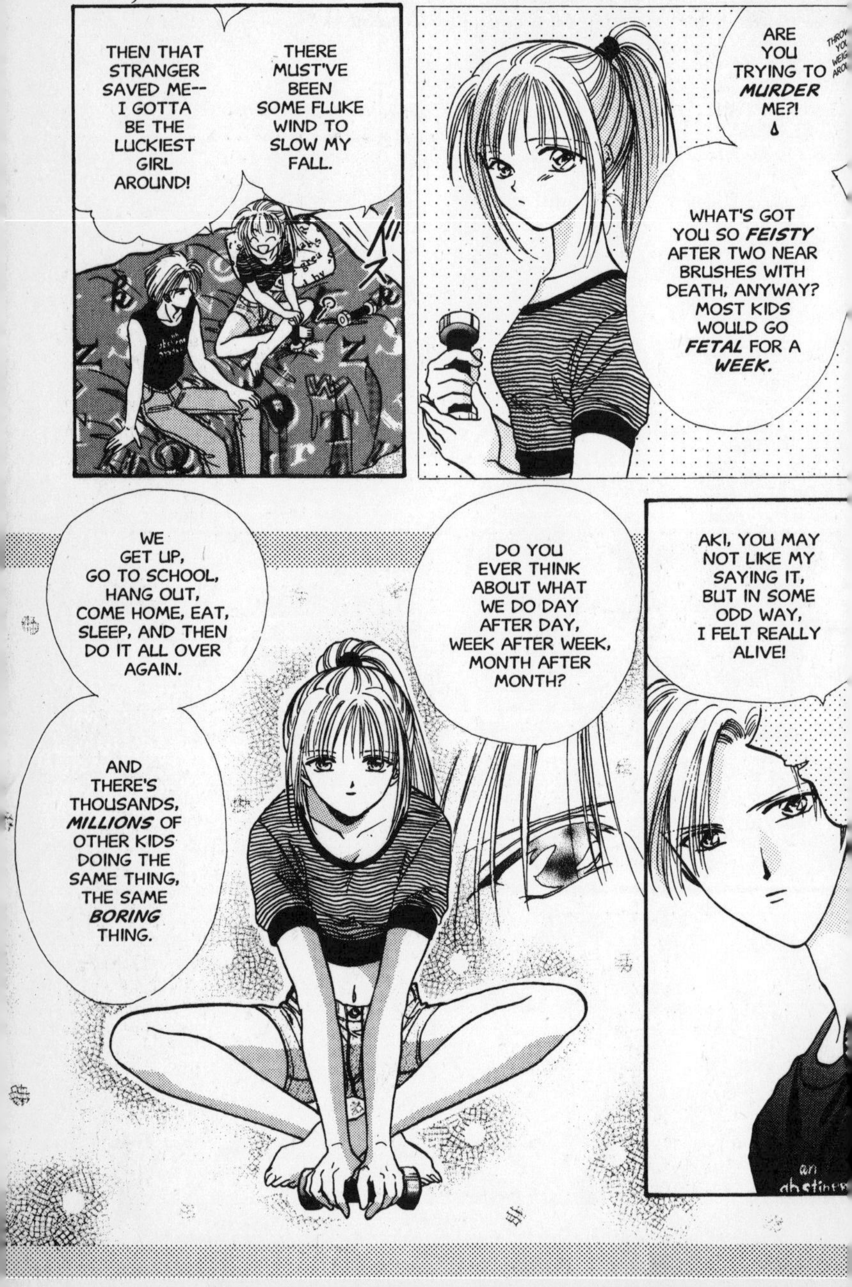
ARE YOU TRYING TO MURDER ME?!
WHAT'S GOT YOU SO FEISTY AFTER TWO NEAR BRUSHES WITH DEATH, ANYWAY? MOST KIDS WOULD GO FETAL FOR A WEEK.
THERE MUST'VE BEEN SOME FLUKE WIND TO SLOW MY FALL.
THEN THAT STRANGER SAVED ME-- I GOTTA BE THE LUCKIEST GIRL AROUND!
AKI, YOU MAY NOT LIKE MY SAYING IT, BUT IN SOME ODD WAY, I FELT REALLY ALIVE!
DO YOU EVER THINK ABOUT WHAT WE DO DAY AFTER DAY, WEEK AFTER WEEK, MONTH AFTER MONTH?
WE GET UP, GO TO SCHOOL, HANG OUT, COME HOME, EAT, SLEEP, AND THEN DO IT ALL OVER AGAIN.
AND THERE'S THOUSANDS, MILLIONS OF OTHER KIDS DOING THE SAME THING, THE SAME BORING THING.

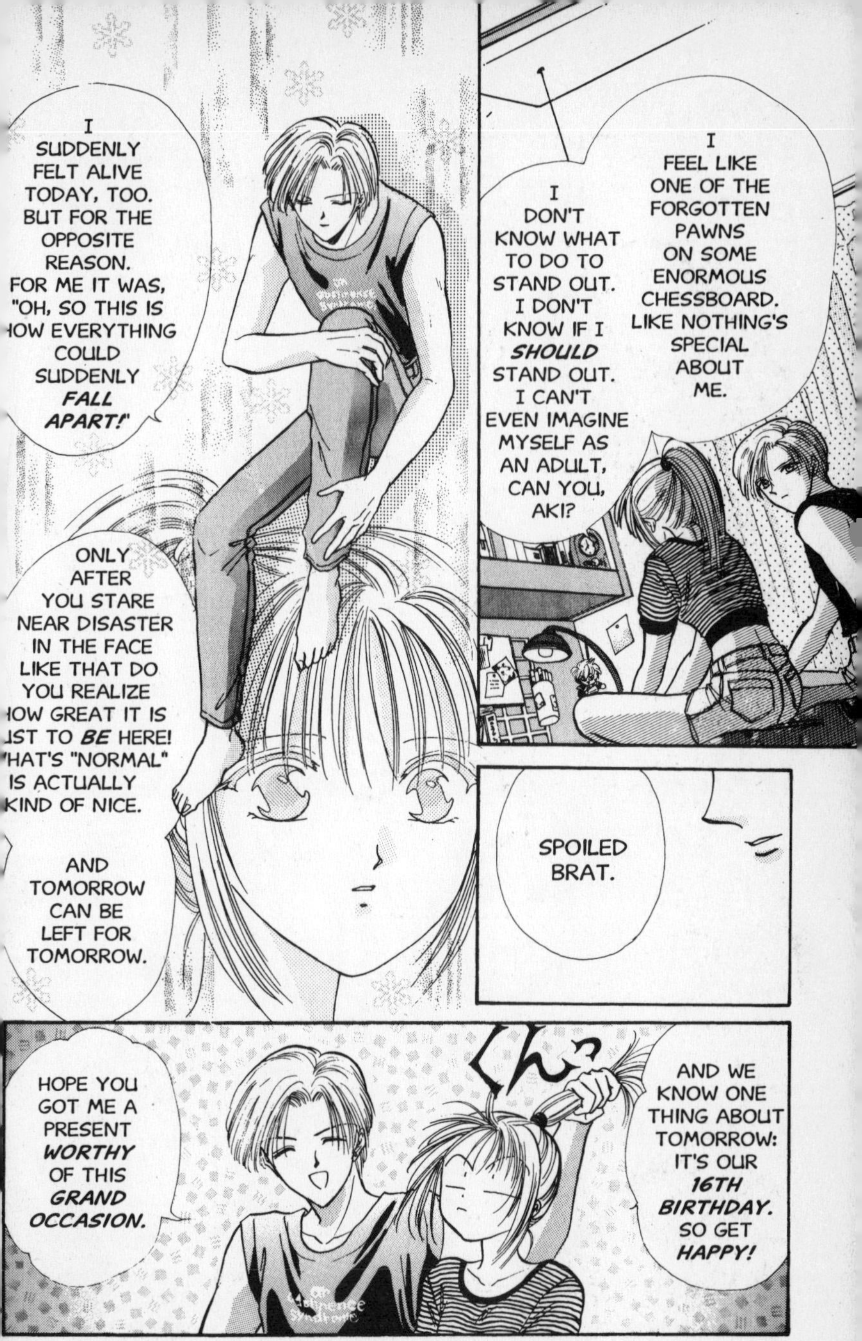
I FEEL LIKE ONE OF THE FORGOTTEN PAWNS ON SOME ENORMOUS CHESSBOARD. LIKE NOTHING'S SPECIAL ABOUT ME.
I DON'T KNOW WHAT TO DO TO STAND OUT. I DON'T KNOW IF I *SHOULD* STAND OUT. I CAN'T EVEN IMAGINE MYSELF AS AN ADULT, CAN YOU, AKI?
SPOILED BRAT.
I SUDDENLY FELT ALIVE TODAY, TOO. BUT FOR THE OPPOSITE REASON. FOR ME IT WAS, "OH, SO THIS IS IOW EVERYTHING COULD SUDDENLY *FALL APART!*"
ONLY AFTER YOU STARE NEAR DISASTER IN THE FACE LIKE THAT DO YOU REALIZE IOW GREAT IT IS IST TO *BE* HERE! 'HAT'S "NORMAL" IS ACTUALLY KIND OF NICE.
AND TOMORROW CAN BE LEFT FOR TOMORROW.
AND WE KNOW ONE THING ABOUT TOMORROW: IT'S OUR *16TH BIRTHDAY.* SO GET *HAPPY!*
くんっ
HOPE YOU GOT ME A PRESENT *WORTHY* OF THIS *GRAND OCCASION.*

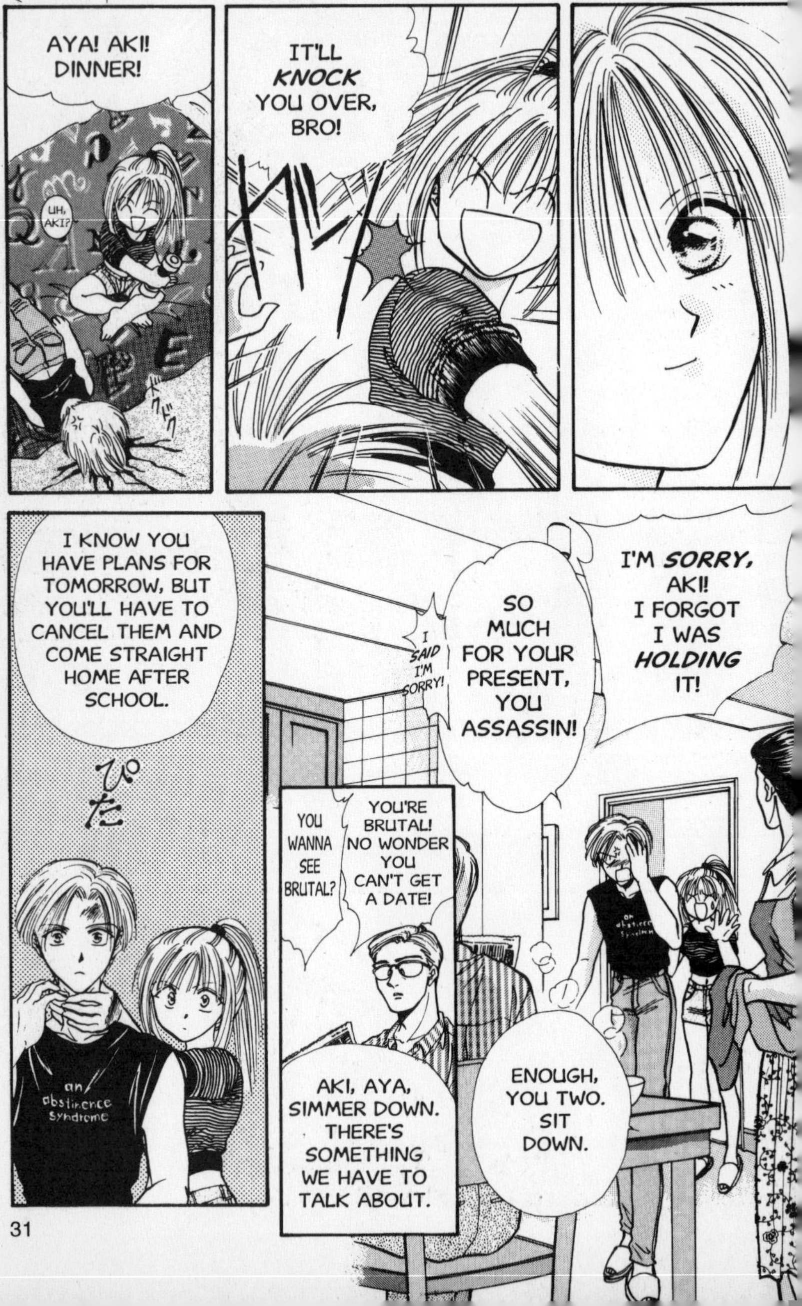
IT'LL *KNOCK* YOU OVER, BRO!
AYA! AKI! DINNER!
UH, AKI?
I'M *SORRY,* AKI! I FORGOT I WAS *HOLDING* IT!
SO MUCH FOR YOUR PRESENT, YOU ASSASSIN!
I *SAID* I'M SORRY!
YOU'RE BRUTAL! NO WONDER YOU CAN'T GET A DATE!
YOU WANNA SEE BRUTAL?
ENOUGH, YOU TWO. SIT DOWN.
AKI, AYA, SIMMER DOWN. THERE'S SOMETHING WE HAVE TO TALK ABOUT.
I KNOW YOU HAVE PLANS FOR TOMORROW, BUT YOU'LL HAVE TO CANCEL THEM AND COME STRAIGHT HOME AFTER SCHOOL.
ぴた
an abstinence syndrome

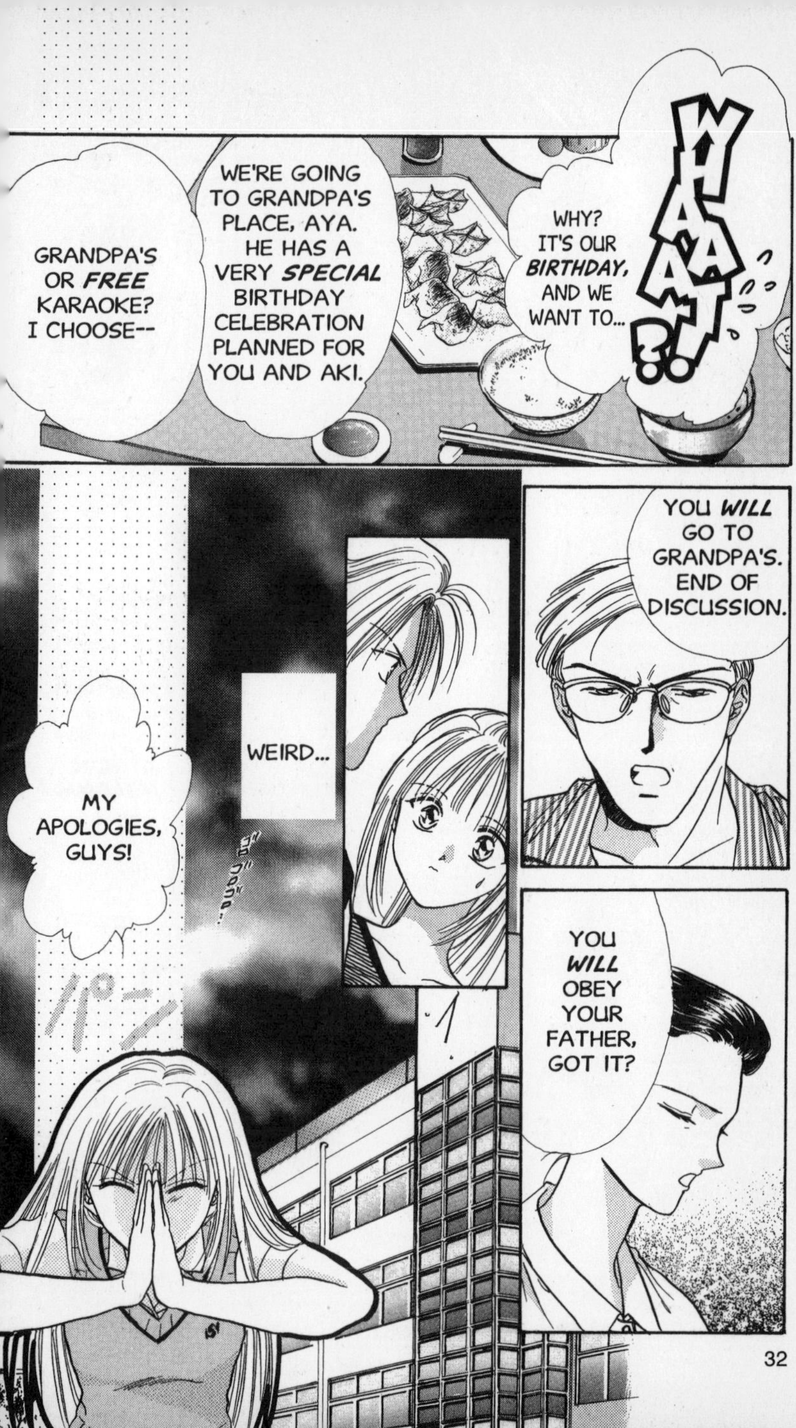
WHAAA!?
WHY? IT'S OUR *BIRTHDAY,* AND WE WANT TO...
WE'RE GOING TO GRANDPA'S PLACE, AYA. HE HAS A VERY *SPECIAL* BIRTHDAY CELEBRATION PLANNED FOR YOU AND AKI.
GRANDPA'S OR *FREE* KARAOKE? I CHOOSE--
YOU *WILL* GO TO GRANDPA'S. END OF DISCUSSION.
YOU *WILL* OBEY YOUR FATHER, GOT IT?
WEIRD...
MY APOLOGIES, GUYS!

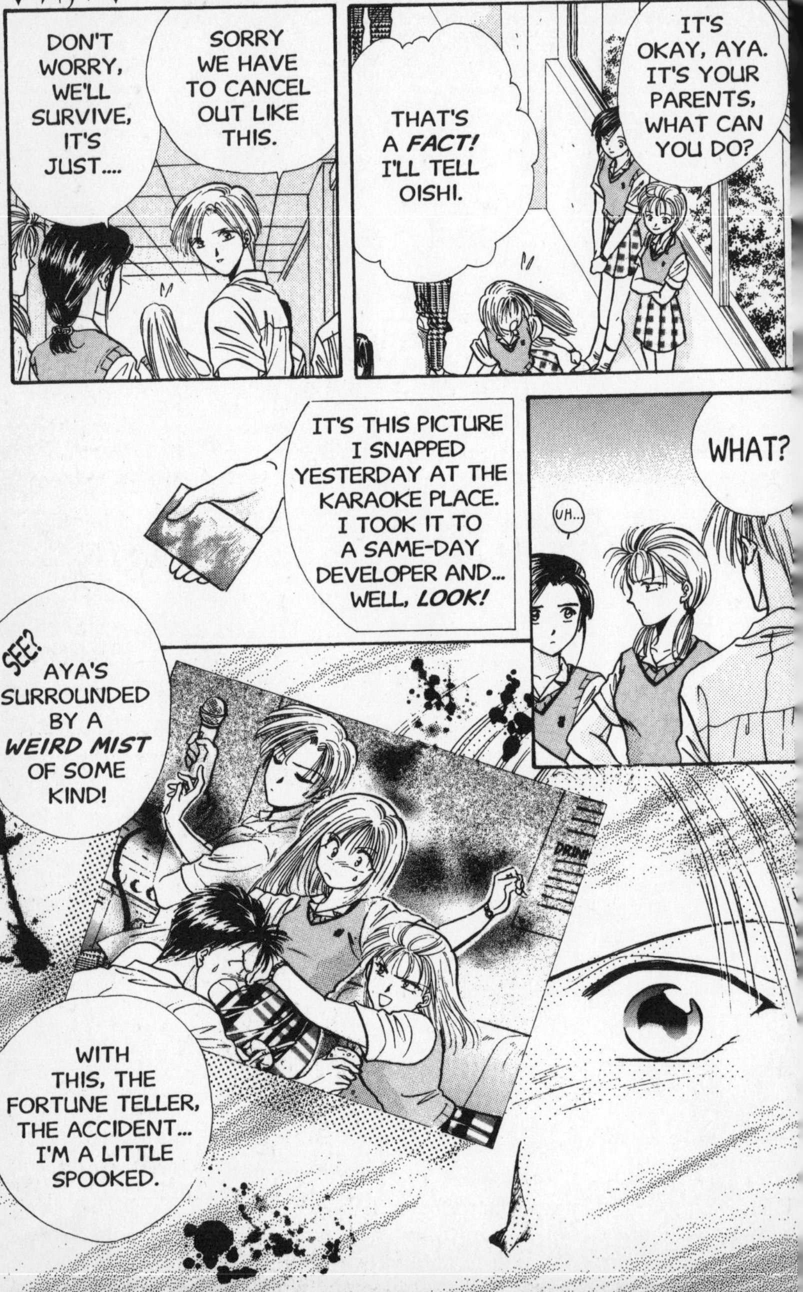
IT'S OKAY, AYA. IT'S YOUR PARENTS, WHAT CAN YOU DO?
THAT'S A FACT! I'LL TELL OISHI.
SORRY WE HAVE TO CANCEL OUT LIKE THIS.
DON'T WORRY, WE'LL SURVIVE, IT'S JUST....
WHAT?
UH...
IT'S THIS PICTURE I SNAPPED YESTERDAY AT THE KARAOKE PLACE. I TOOK IT TO A SAME-DAY DEVELOPER AND... WELL, LOOK!
SEE? AYA'S SURROUNDED BY A WEIRD MIST OF SOME KIND!
WITH THIS, THE FORTUNE TELLER, THE ACCIDENT... I'M A LITTLE SPOOKED.

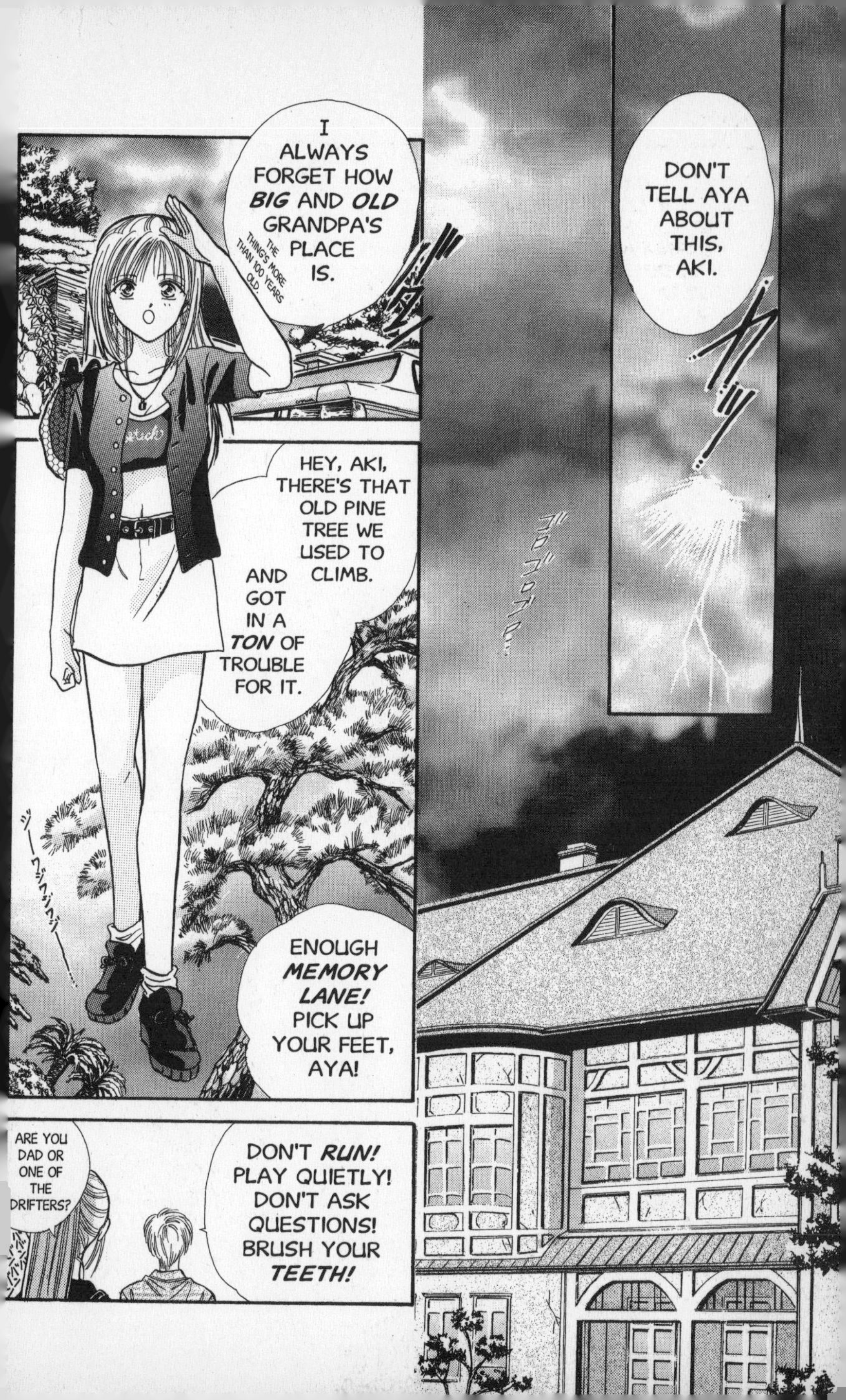
DON'T TELL AYA ABOUT THIS, AKI.
I ALWAYS FORGET HOW BIG AND OLD GRANDPA'S PLACE IS.
THE THING'S MORE THAN 100 YEARS OLD.
HEY, AKI, THERE'S THAT OLD PINE TREE WE USED TO CLIMB.
AND GOT IN A TON OF TROUBLE FOR IT.
ENOUGH MEMORY LANE! PICK UP YOUR FEET, AYA!
DON'T RUN! PLAY QUIETLY! DON'T ASK QUESTIONS! BRUSH YOUR TEETH!
ARE YOU DAD OR ONE OF THE DRIFTERS?

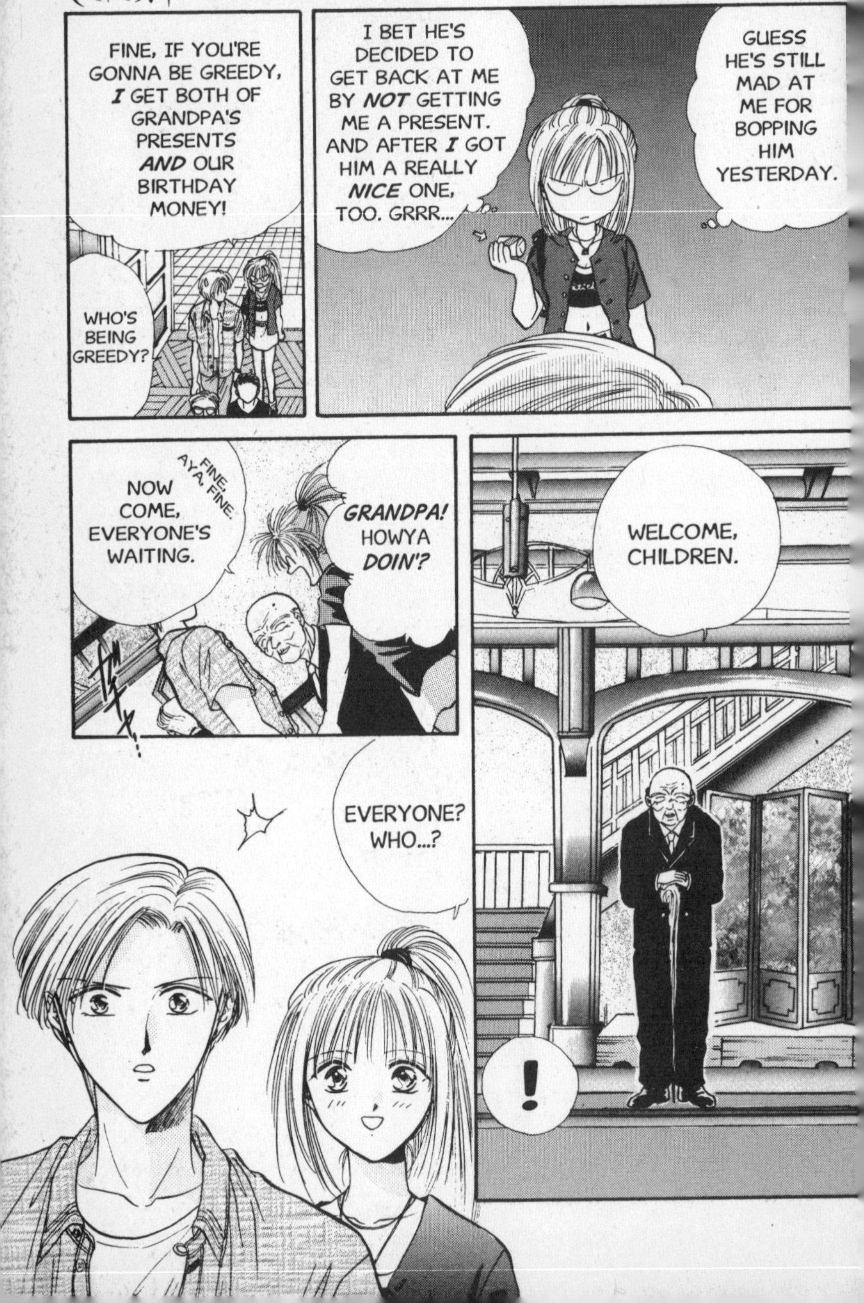
GUESS HE'S STILL MAD AT ME FOR BOPPING HIM YESTERDAY.
I BET HE'S DECIDED TO GET BACK AT ME BY *NOT* GETTING ME A PRESENT. AND AFTER *I* GOT HIM A REALLY *NICE* ONE, TOO. GRRR...
FINE, IF YOU'RE GONNA BE GREEDY, *I* GET BOTH OF GRANDPA'S PRESENTS *AND* OUR BIRTHDAY MONEY!
WHO'S BEING GREEDY?
WELCOME, CHILDREN.
!
GRANDPA! HOWYA *DOIN'?*
FINE, AYA, FINE.
NOW COME, EVERYONE'S WAITING.
EVERYONE? WHO...?

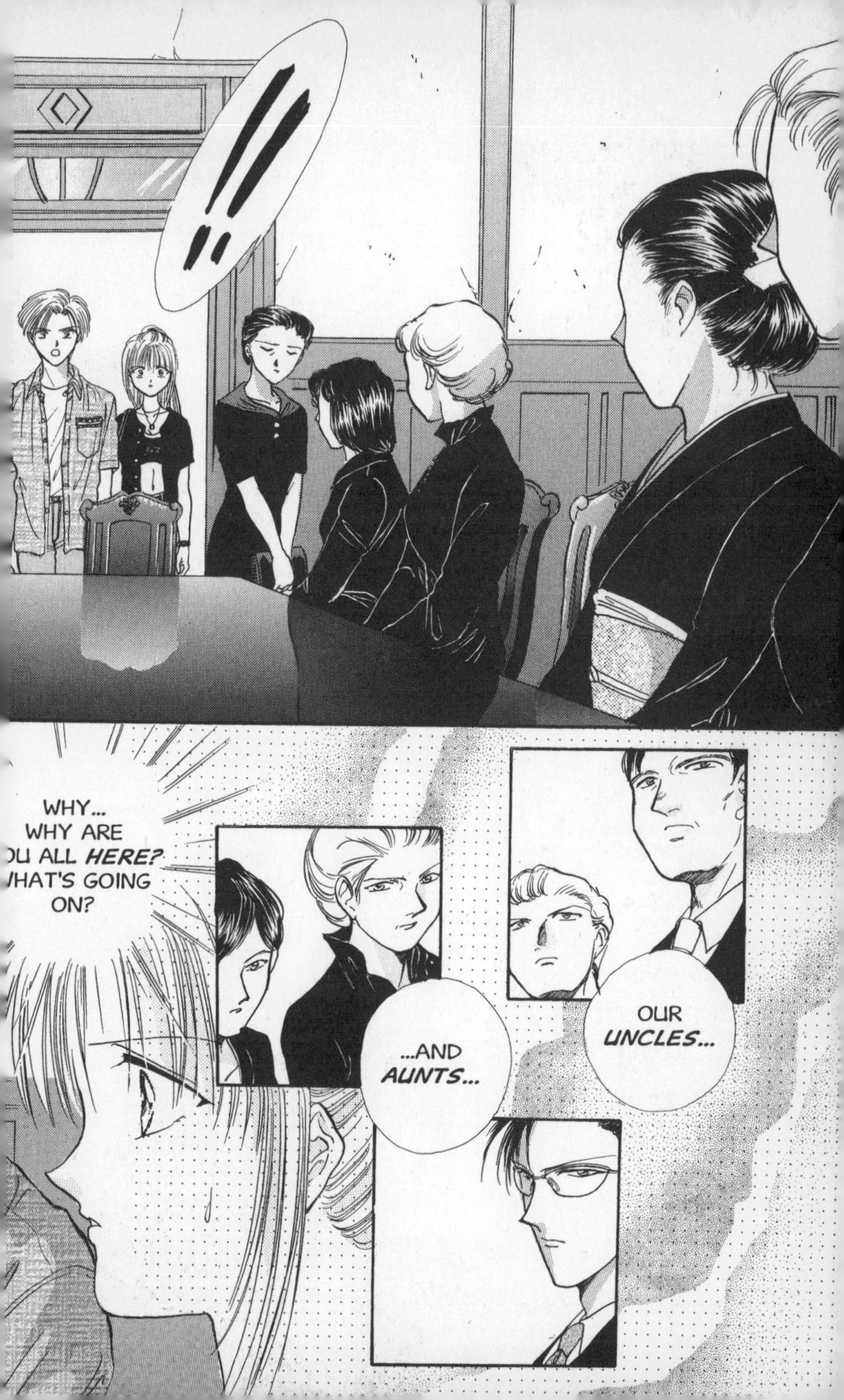
!!
OUR UNCLES...
...AND AUNTS...
WHY... WHY ARE OU ALL HERE? HAT'S GOING ON?

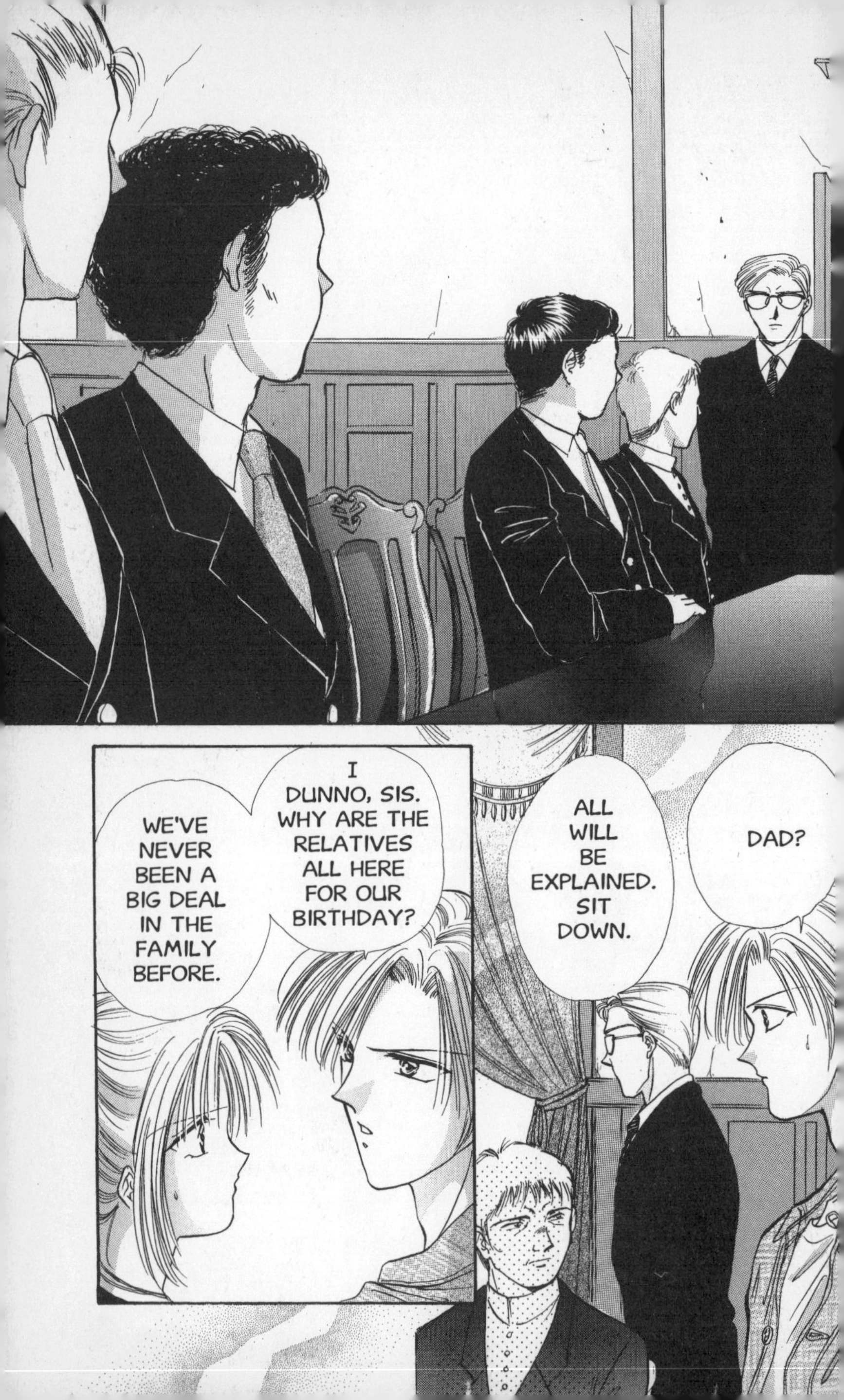
DAD?
ALL WILL BE EXPLAINED. SIT DOWN.
I DUNNO, SIS. WHY ARE THE RELATIVES ALL HERE FOR OUR BIRTHDAY?
WE'VE NEVER BEEN A BIG DEAL IN THE FAMILY BEFORE.

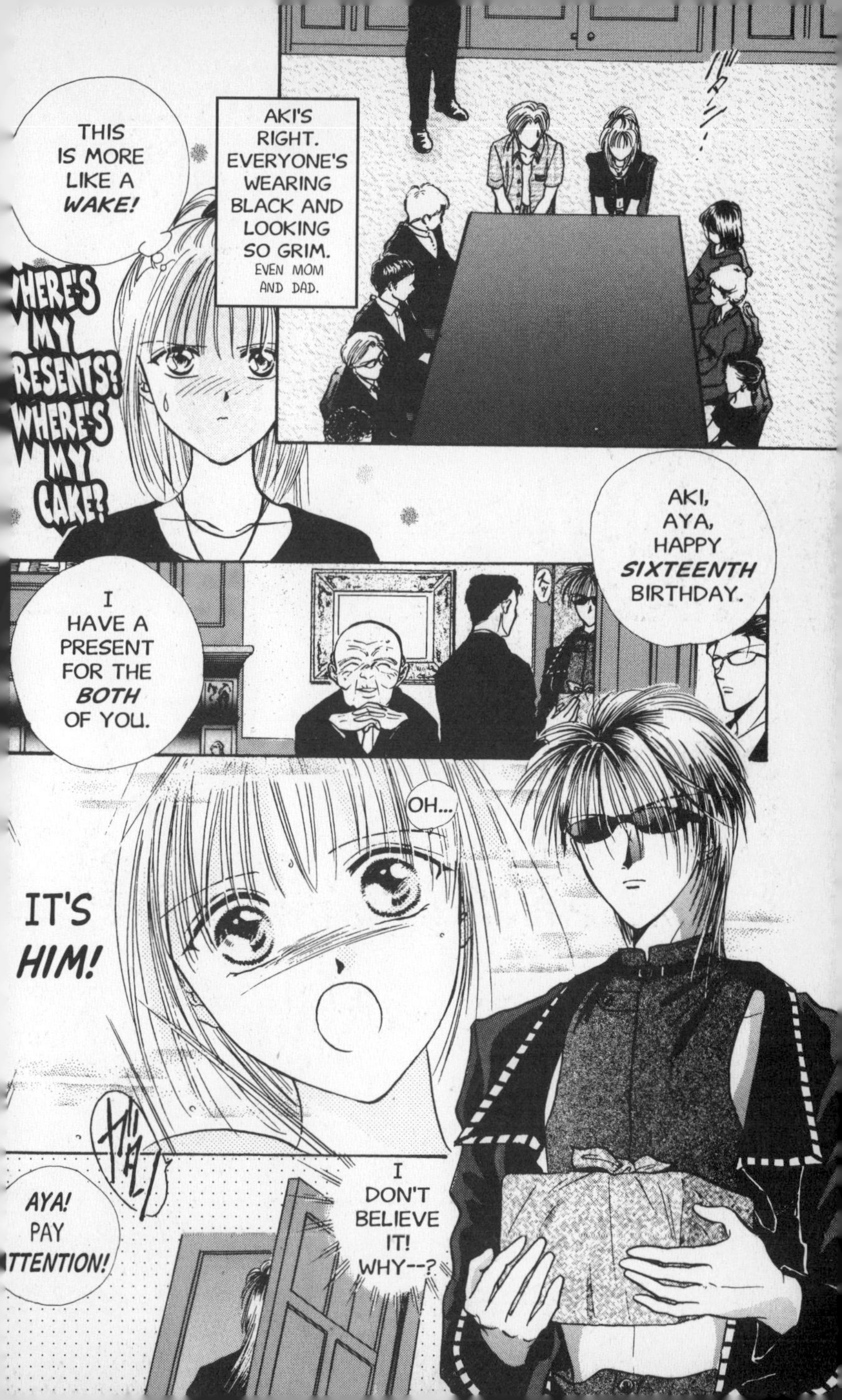

AKI'S RIGHT. EVERYONE'S WEARING BLACK AND LOOKING SO GRIM. EVEN MOM AND DAD.
THIS IS MORE LIKE A *WAKE!*
WHERE'S MY PRESENTS? WHERE'S MY CAKE?
AKI, AYA, HAPPY *SIXTEENTH* BIRTHDAY.
I HAVE A PRESENT FOR THE *BOTH* OF YOU.
OH...
IT'S *HIM!*
I DON'T BELIEVE IT! WHY--?
AYA! PAY *TTENTION!*

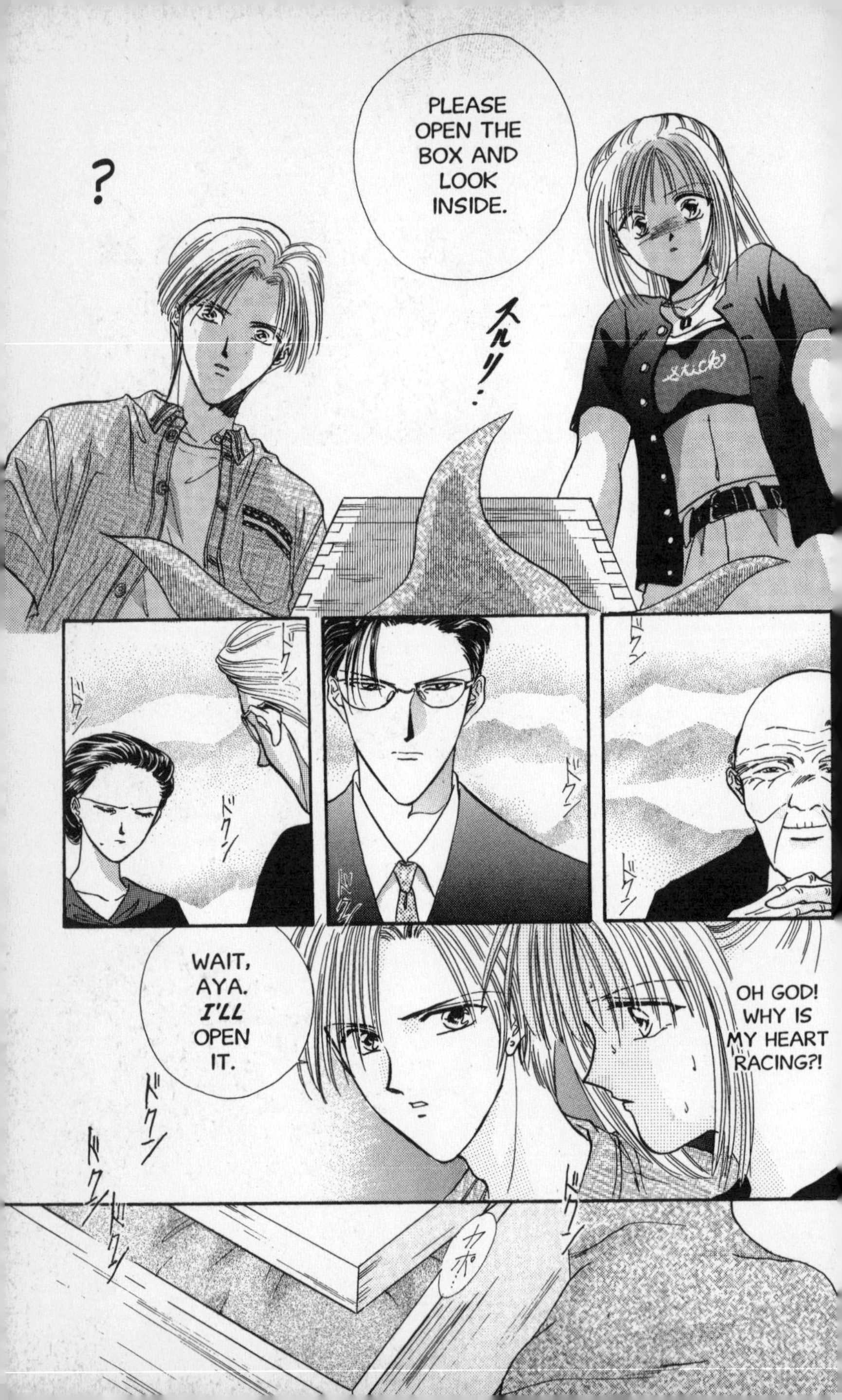
PLEASE OPEN THE BOX AND LOOK INSIDE.
スルリ…
?
ドクン
ドクン
ドクン
ドクン
ドクン
ドクン
ドクン
OH GOD! WHY IS MY HEART RACING?!
WAIT, AYA. *I'LL* OPEN IT.
ドクン
ドクン
ドクン
ドクン
カポ…

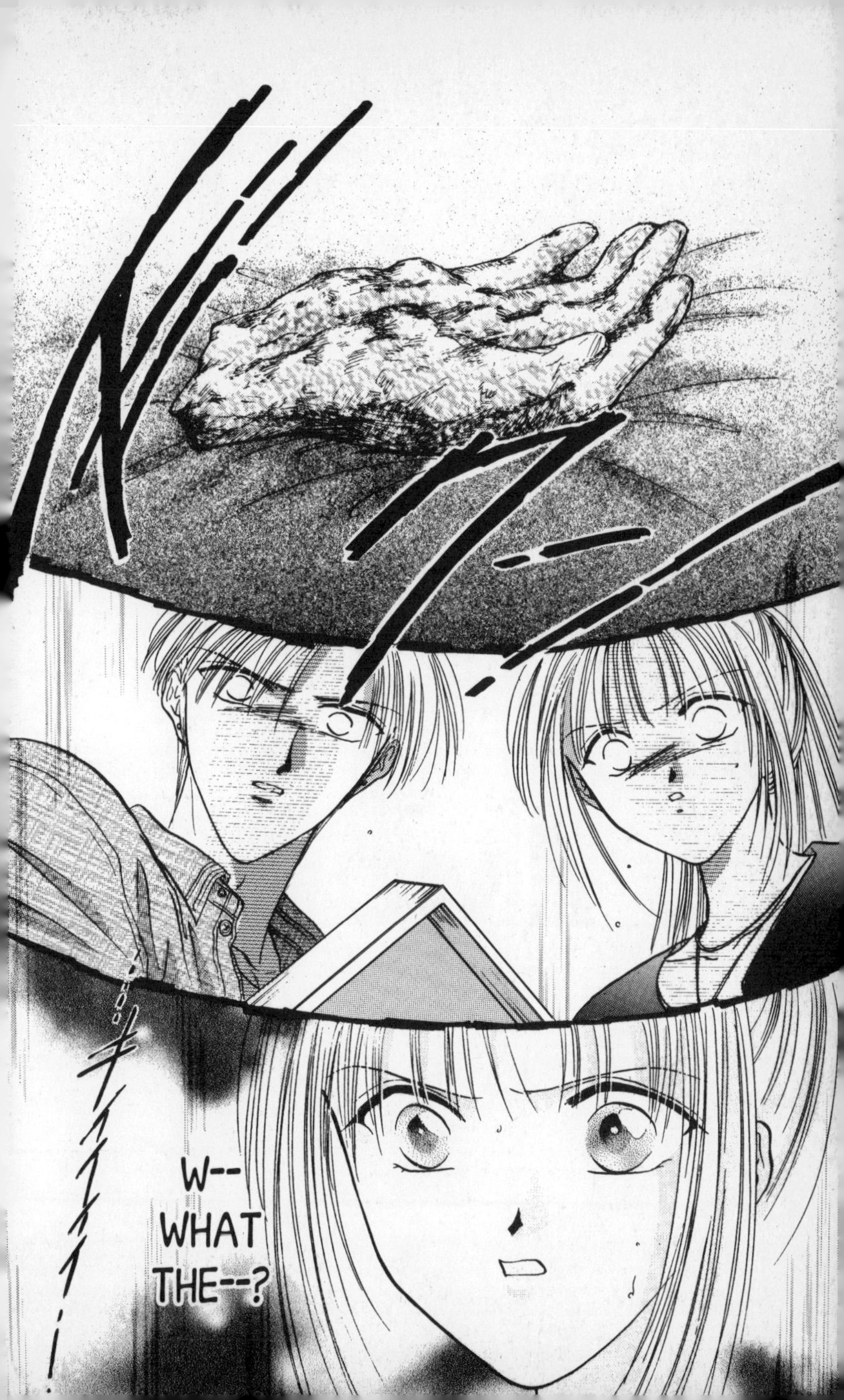
W-- WHAT THE--?

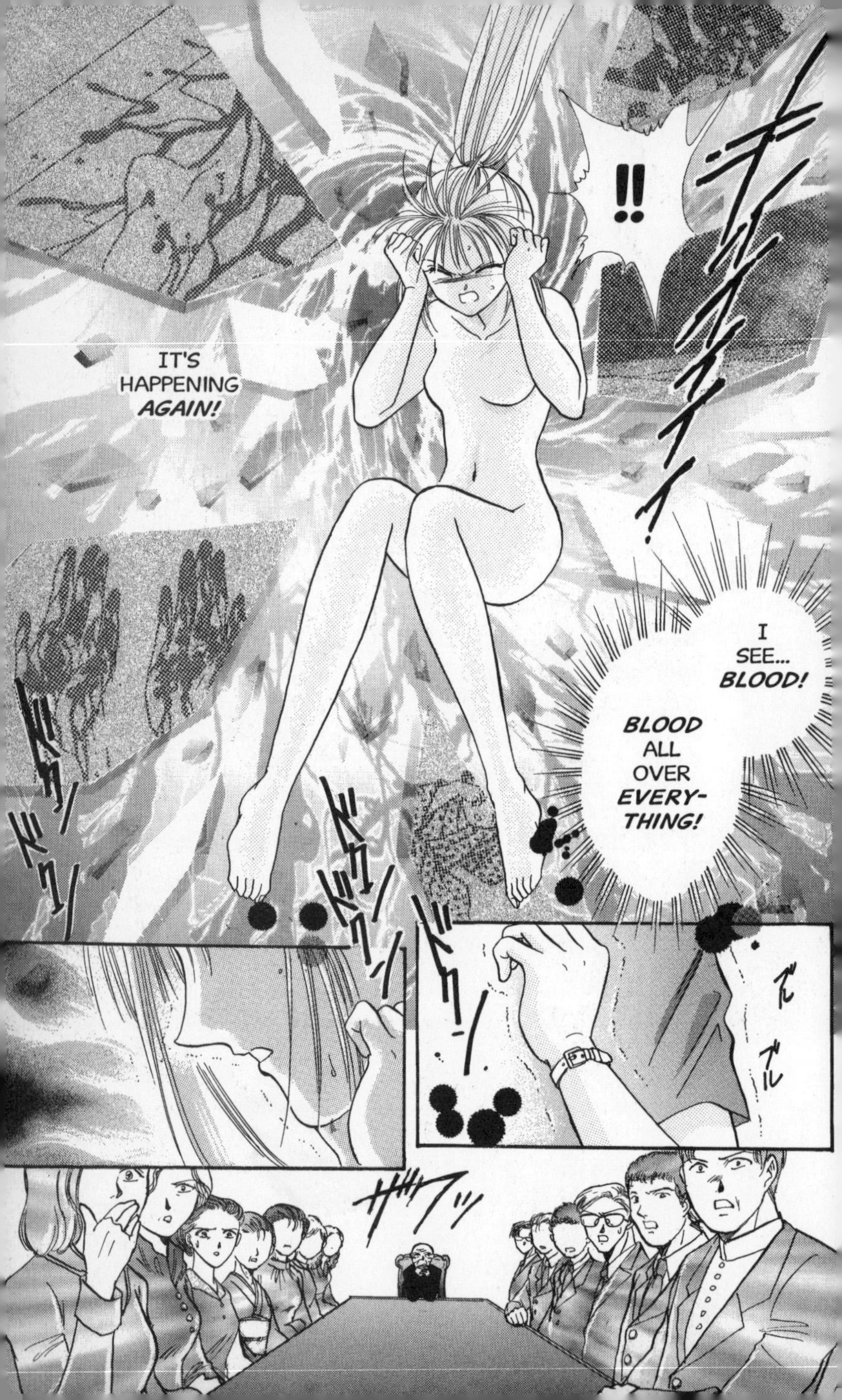
!!
IT'S HAPPENING AGAIN!
I SEE... BLOOD!
BLOOD ALL OVER EVERYTHING!

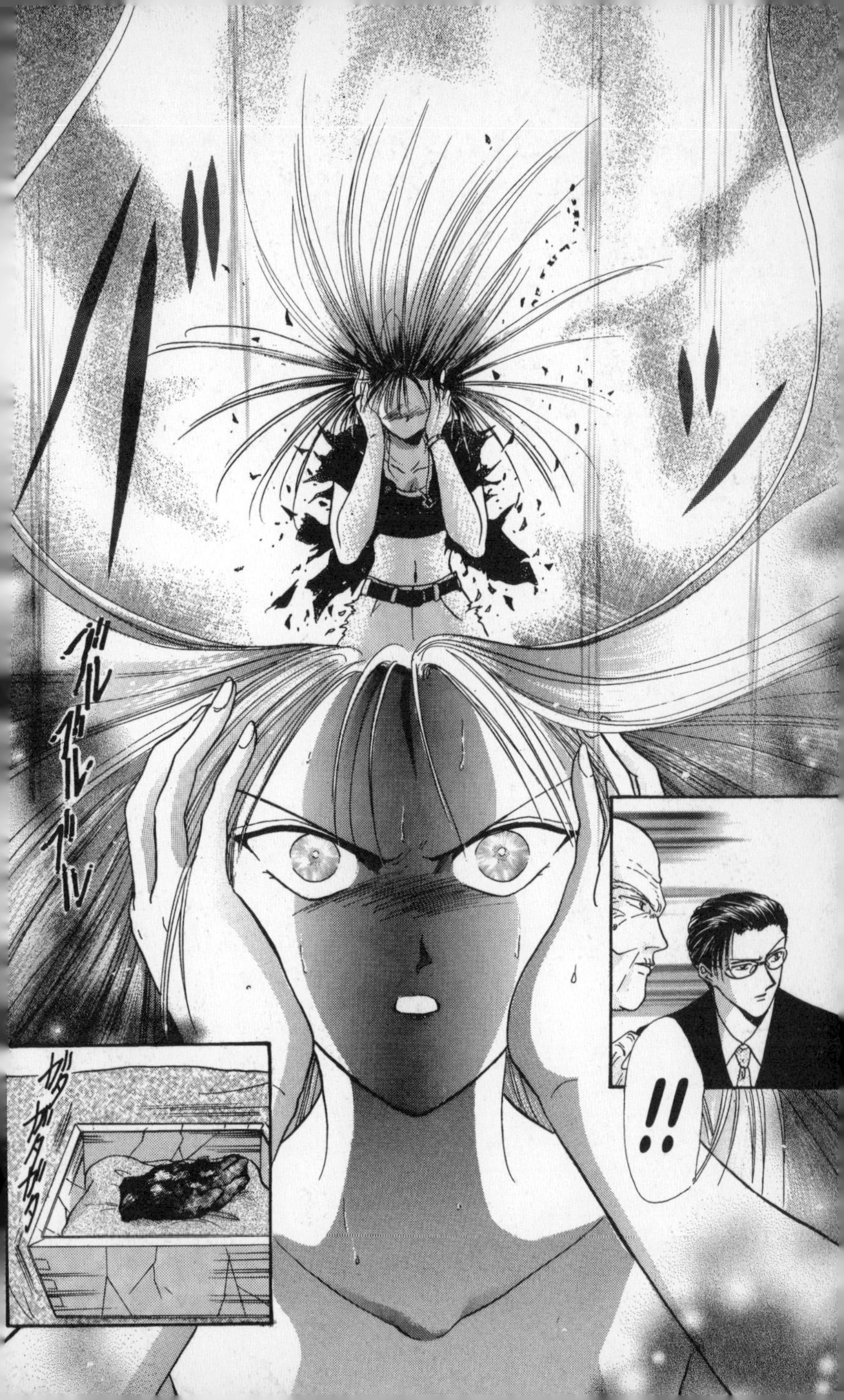

ブルブルブル
!!
ガタガタ

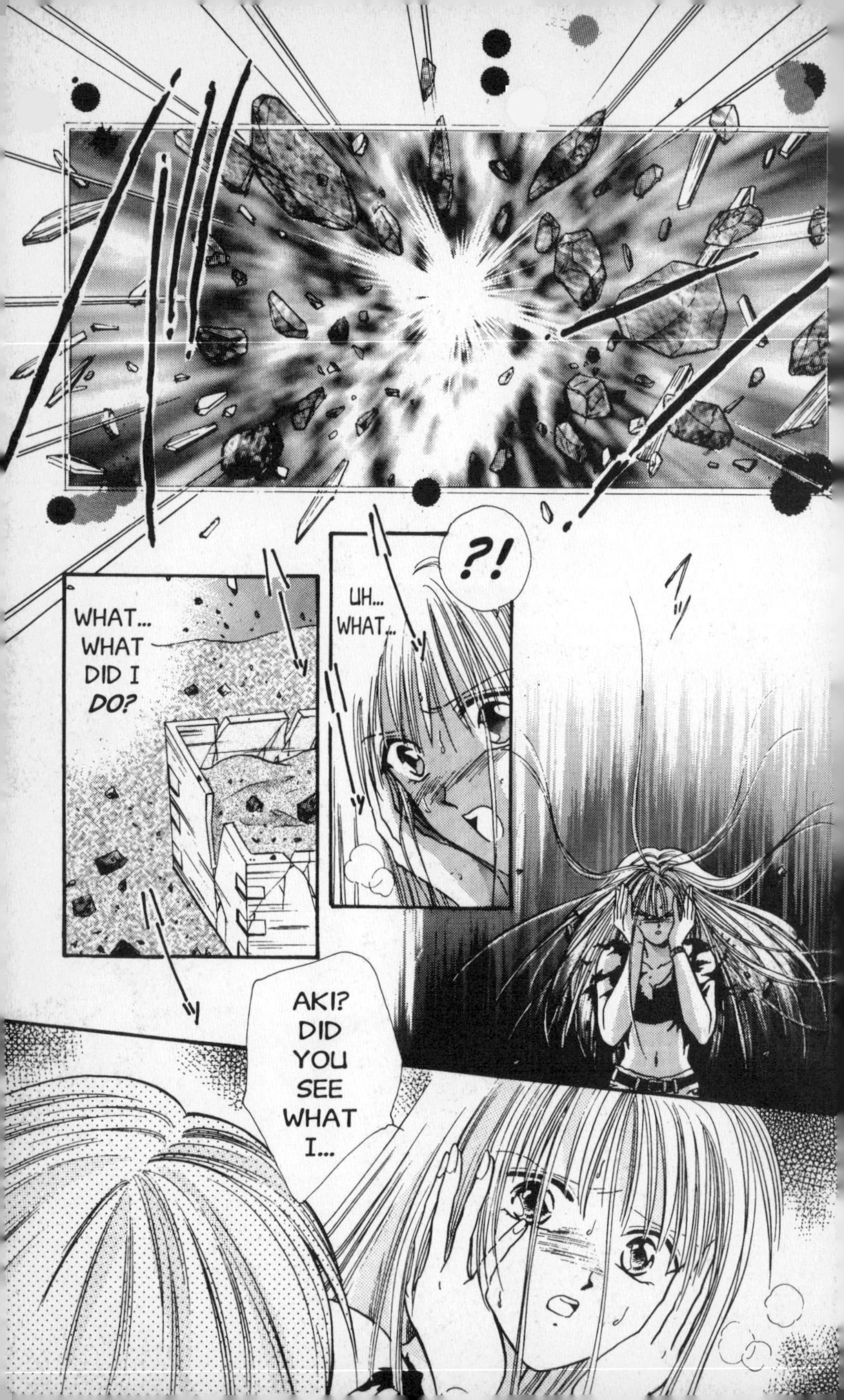

?!
UH... WHAT...
WHAT... WHAT DID I *DO?*
AKI? DID YOU SEE WHAT I...

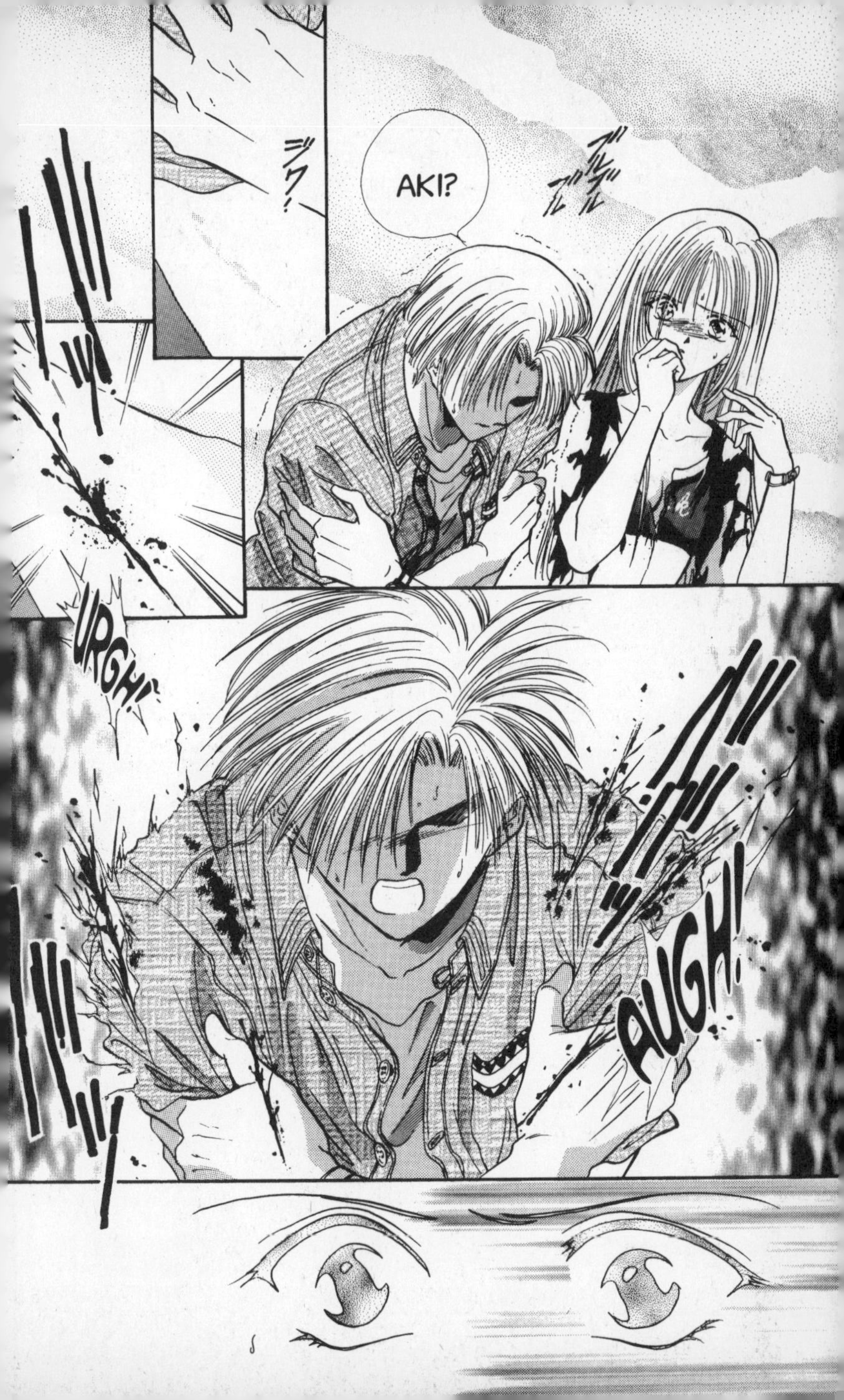

ブルブル
AKI?
ジク!
AUGH!
URGH!

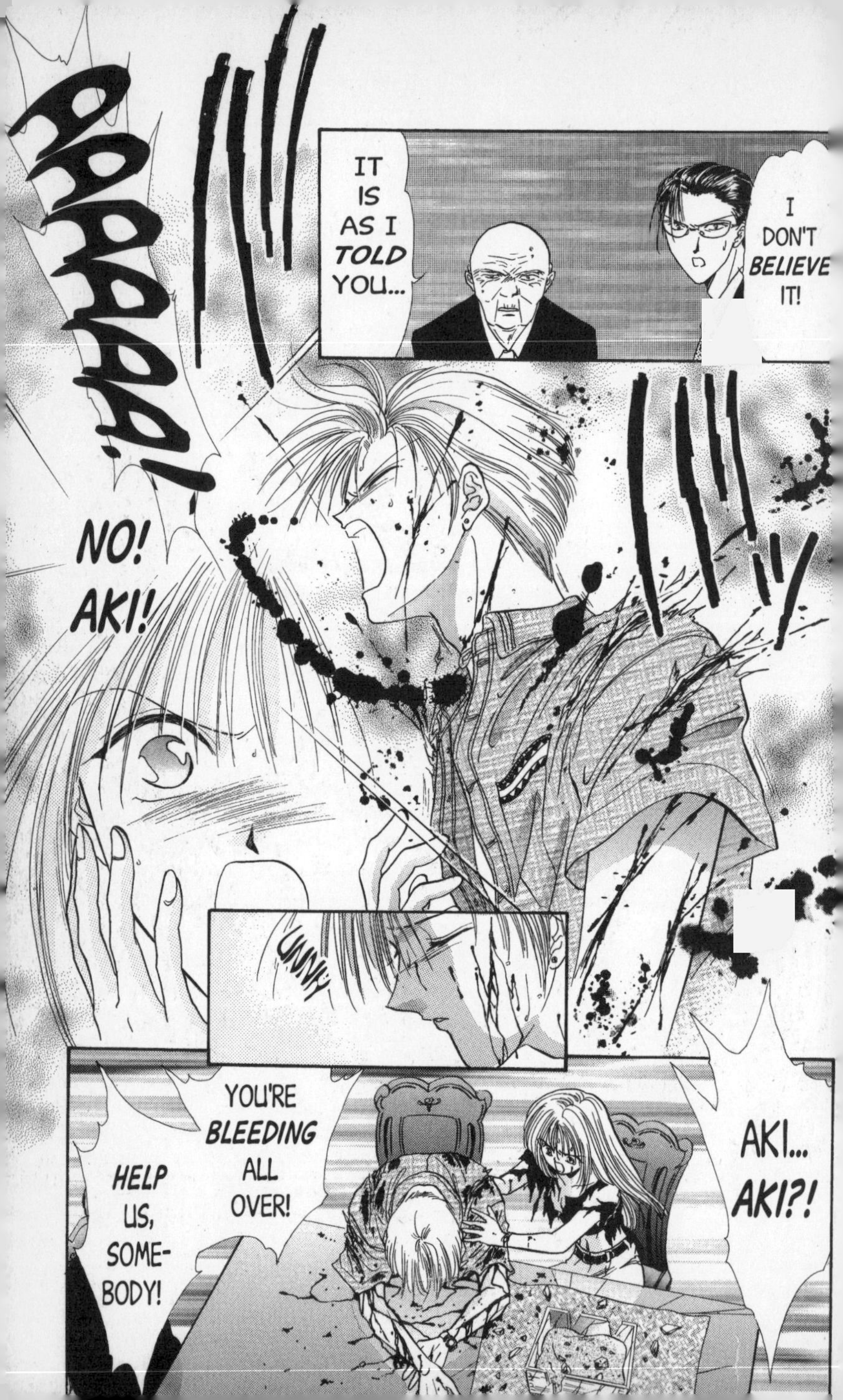

I DON'T *BELIEVE* IT!
IT IS AS I *TOLD* YOU...
AAAAAAA!
NO! AKI!
UNNH
AKI... AKI?!
YOU'RE *BLEEDING* ALL OVER!
HELP US, SOME-BODY!

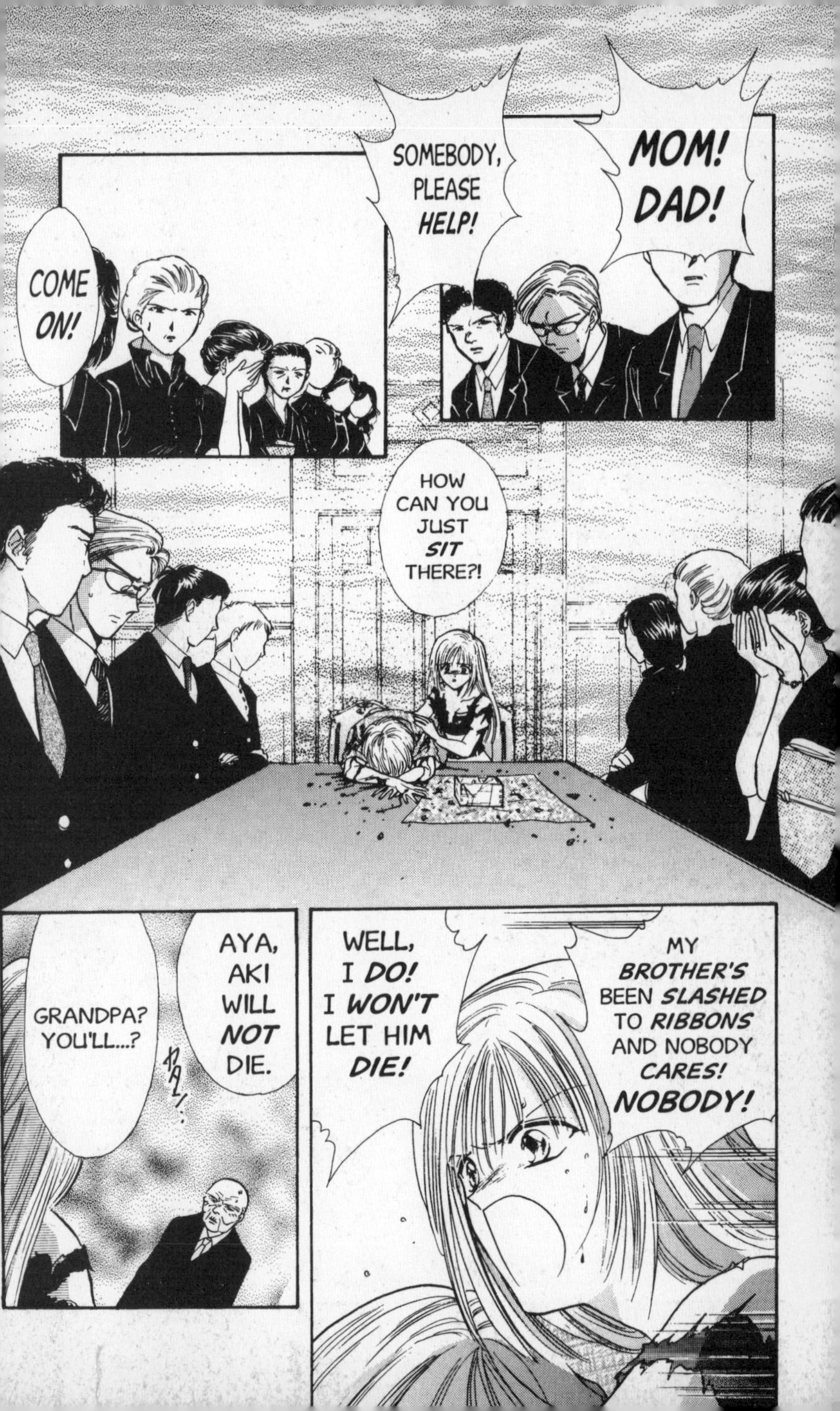

MOM! DAD!
SOMEBODY, PLEASE HELP!
COME ON!
HOW CAN YOU JUST SIT THERE?!
MY BROTHER'S BEEN SLASHED TO RIBBONS AND NOBODY CARES! NOBODY!
WELL, I DO! I WON'T LET HIM DIE!
AYA, AKI WILL NOT DIE.
GRANDPA? YOU'LL...?

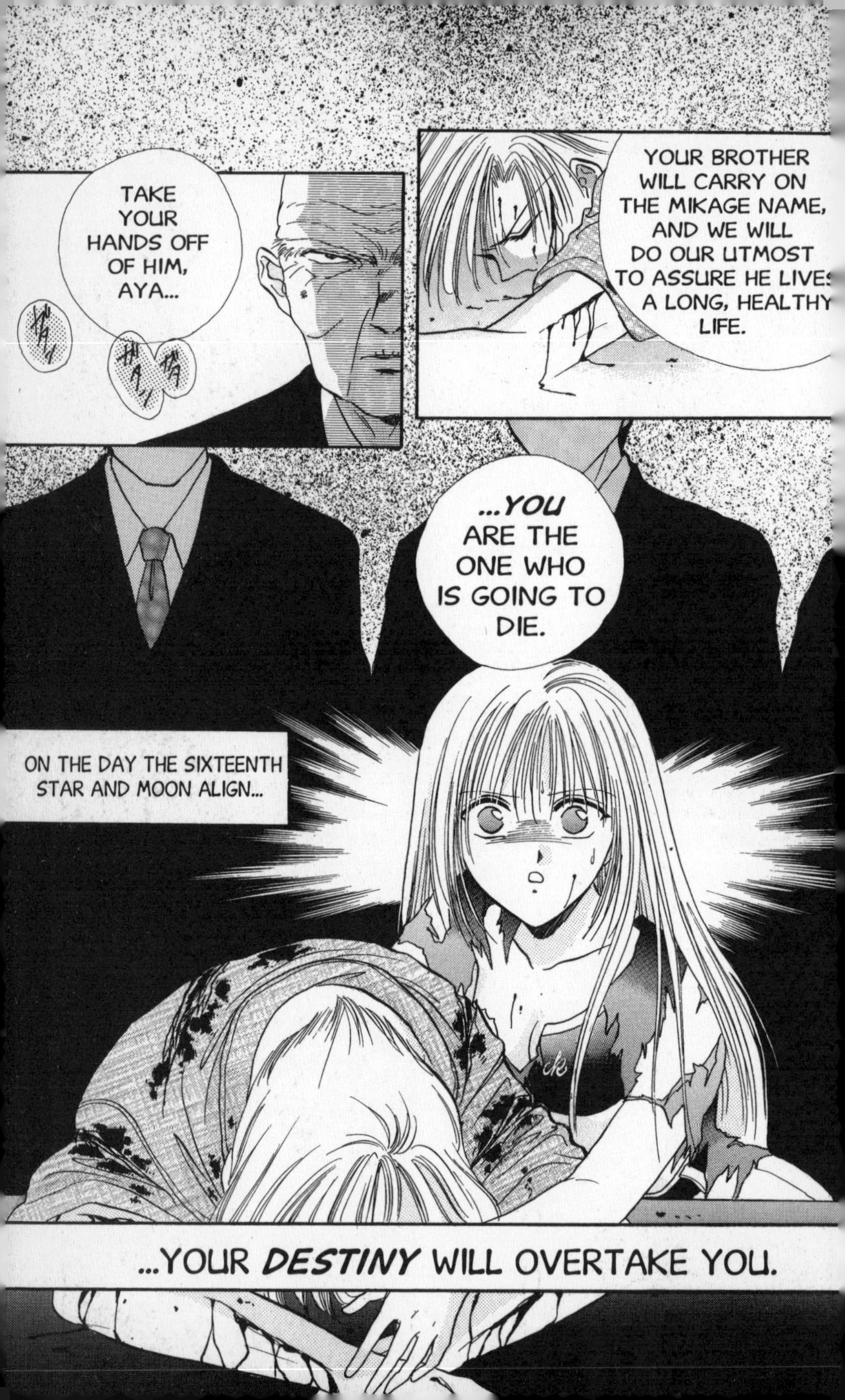
YOUR BROTHER WILL CARRY ON THE MIKAGE NAME, AND WE WILL DO OUR UTMOST TO ASSURE HE LIVES A LONG, HEALTHY LIFE.
TAKE YOUR HANDS OFF OF HIM, AYA...
...YOU ARE THE ONE WHO IS GOING TO DIE.
ON THE DAY THE SIXTEENTH STAR AND MOON ALIGN...
...YOUR DESTINY WILL OVERTAKE YOU.

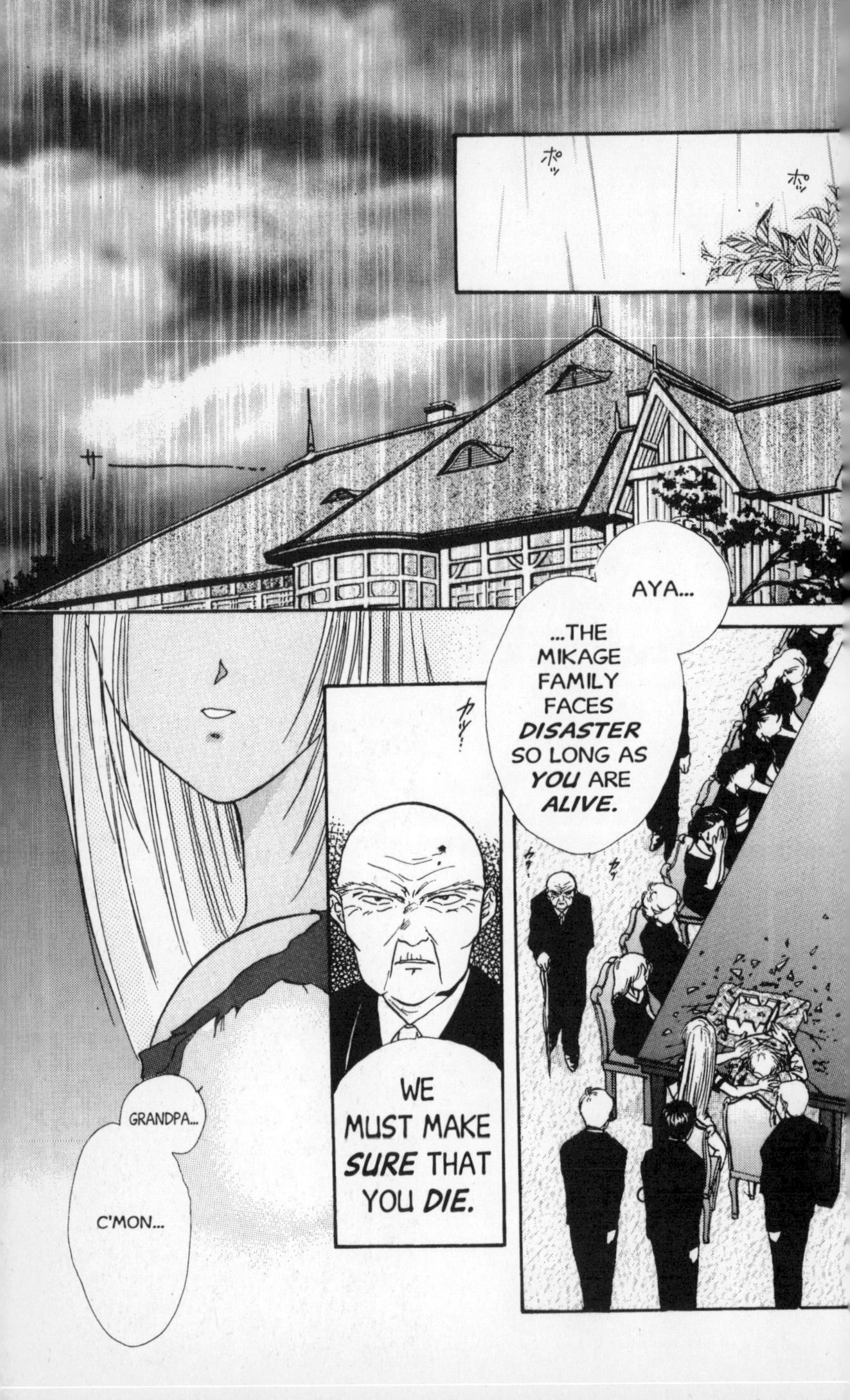
ポッ
ポッ
サー
AYA...
...THE MIKAGE FAMILY FACES **DISASTER** SO LONG AS **YOU** ARE **ALIVE.**
WE MUST MAKE **SURE** THAT YOU **DIE.**
GRANDPA...
C'MON...

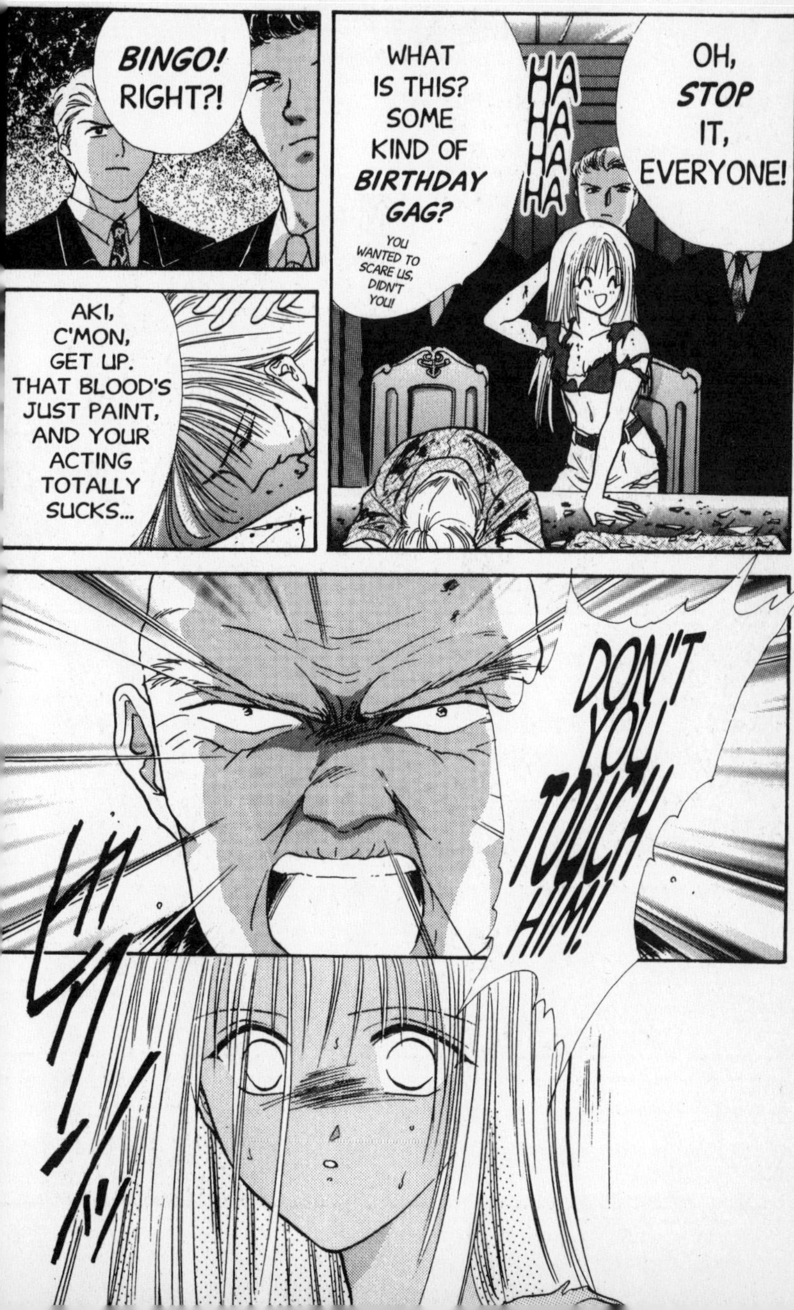
OH, STOP IT, EVERYONE!
HAHAHAHA
WHAT IS THIS? SOME KIND OF BIRTHDAY GAG?
YOU WANTED TO SCARE US, DIDN'T YOU!
BINGO! RIGHT?!
AKI, C'MON, GET UP. THAT BLOOD'S JUST PAINT, AND YOUR ACTING TOTALLY SUCKS...
DON'T YOU TOUCH HIM!!

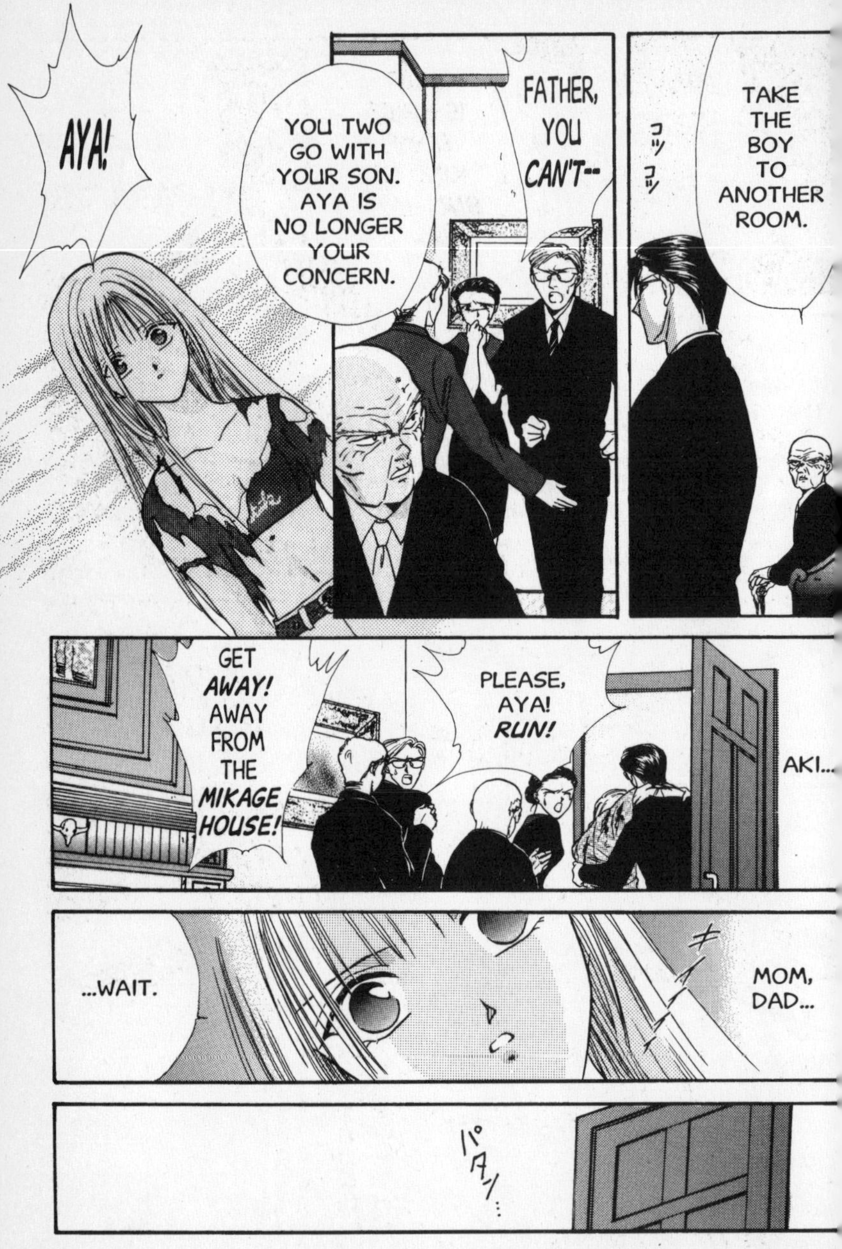

TAKE THE BOY TO ANOTHER ROOM.
コツ コツ
FATHER, YOU CAN'T--
YOU TWO GO WITH YOUR SON. AYA IS NO LONGER YOUR CONCERN.
AYA!
AKI...
PLEASE, AYA! RUN!
GET AWAY! AWAY FROM THE MIKAGE HOUSE!
MOM, DAD...
...WAIT.
パタン…

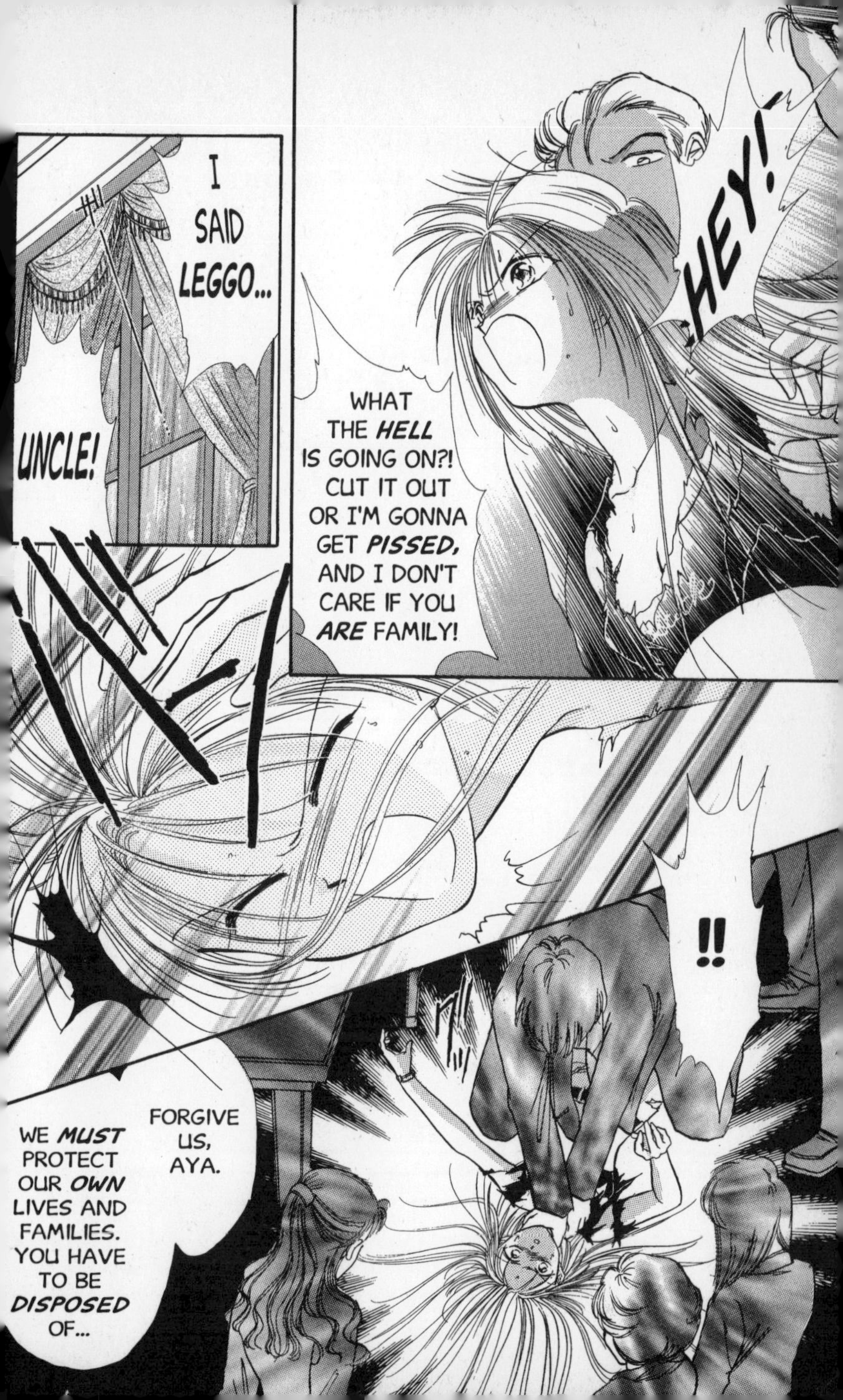

HEY!
WHAT THE HELL IS GOING ON?! CUT IT OUT OR I'M GONNA GET PISSED, AND I DON'T CARE IF YOU ARE FAMILY!
I SAID LEGGO...
UNCLE!
!!
FORGIVE US, AYA.
WE MUST PROTECT OUR OWN LIVES AND FAMILIES. YOU HAVE TO BE DISPOSED OF...

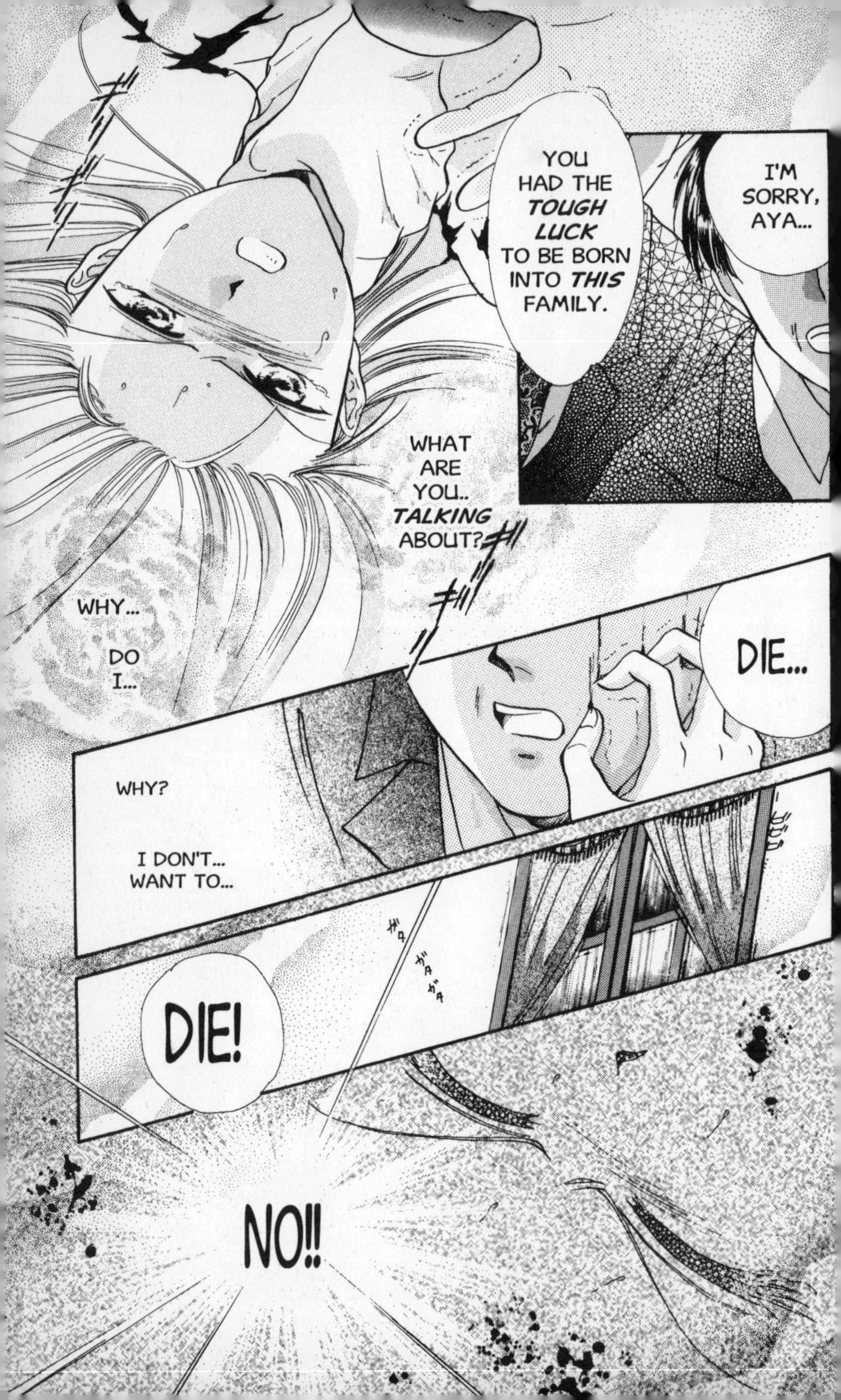
I'M SORRY, AYA...
YOU HAD THE TOUGH LUCK TO BE BORN INTO THIS FAMILY.
WHAT ARE YOU.. TALKING ABOUT?
WHY... DO I...
DIE...
WHY?
I DON'T... WANT TO...
DIE!
NO!!

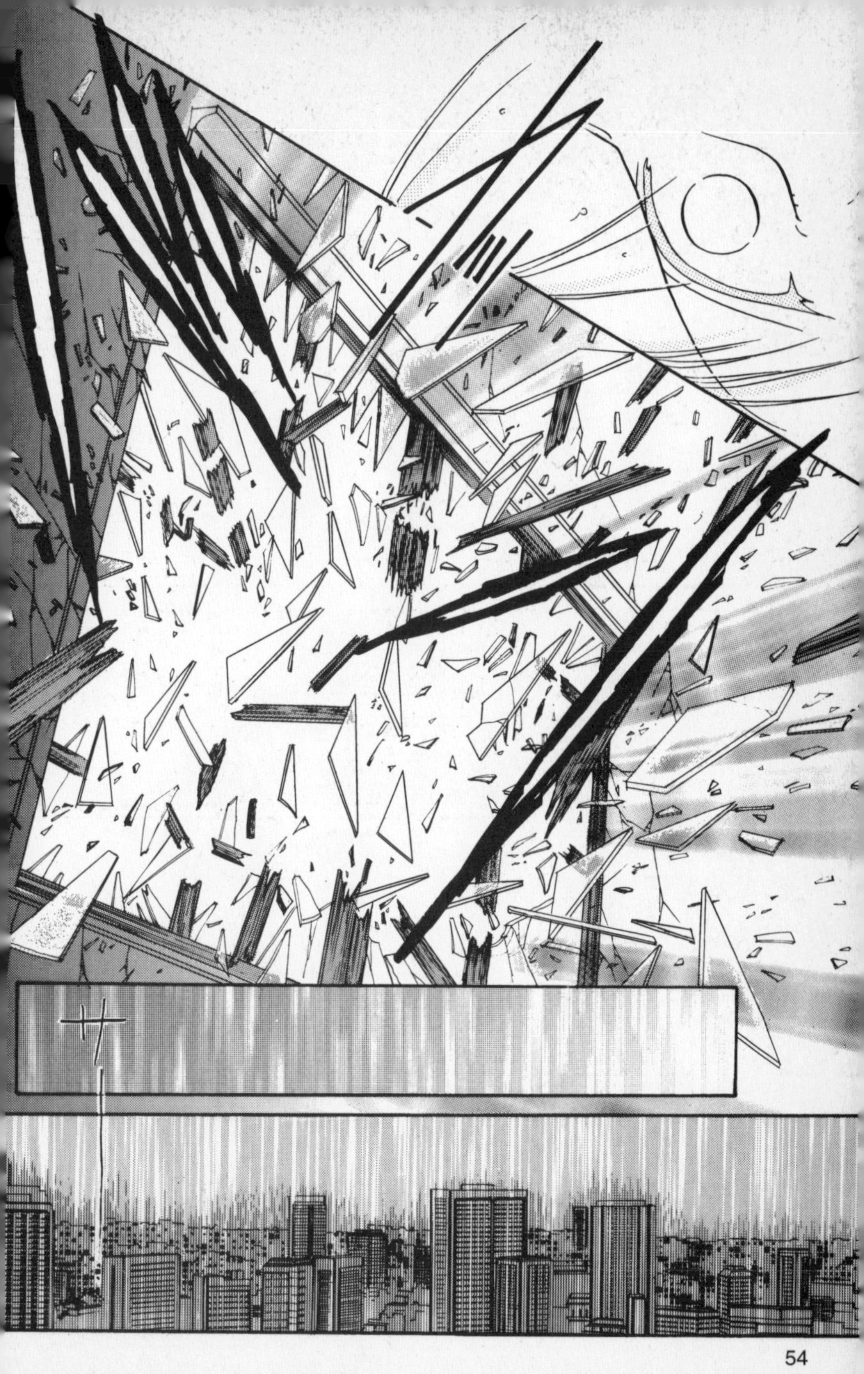

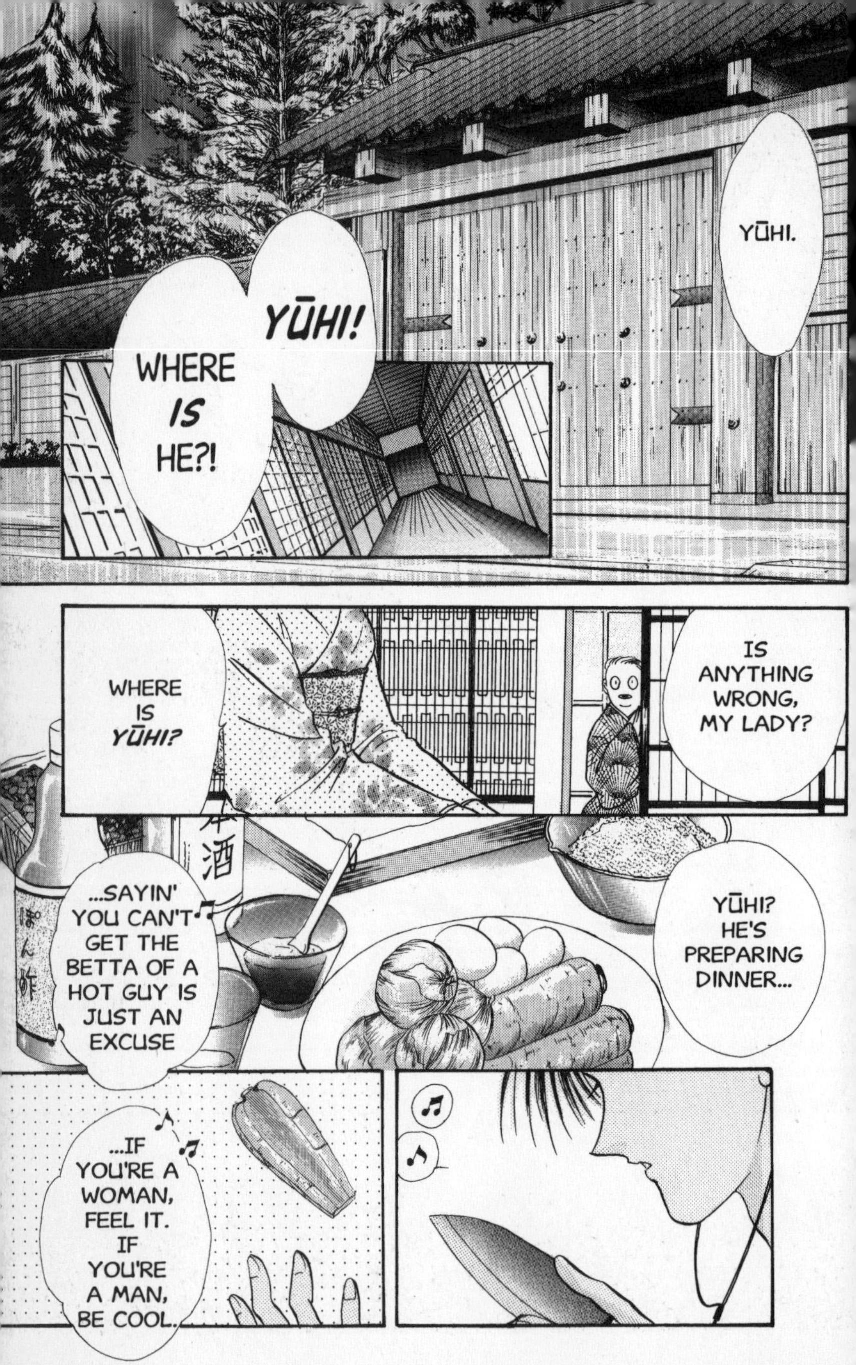
YŪHI.
YŪHI! WHERE IS HE?!
IS ANYTHING WRONG, MY LADY?
WHERE IS YŪHI?
YŪHI? HE'S PREPARING DINNER...
...SAYIN' YOU CAN'T GET THE BETTA OF A HOT GUY IS JUST AN EXCUSE
...IF YOU'RE A WOMAN, FEEL IT. IF YOU'RE A MAN, BE COOL.

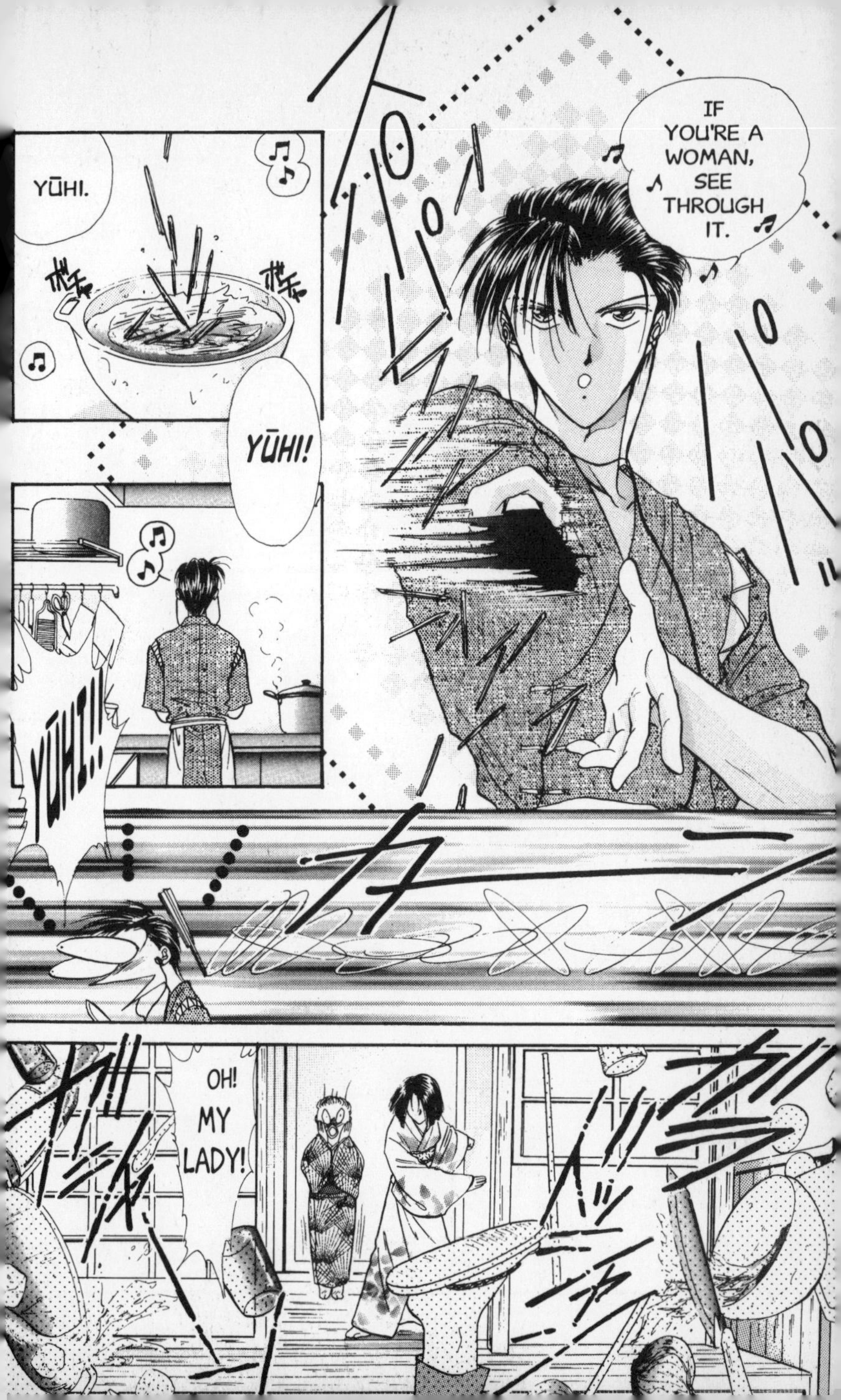
IF YOU'RE A WOMAN, SEE THROUGH IT.
YŪHI.
YŪHI!
YŪHI!!!
OH! MY LADY!

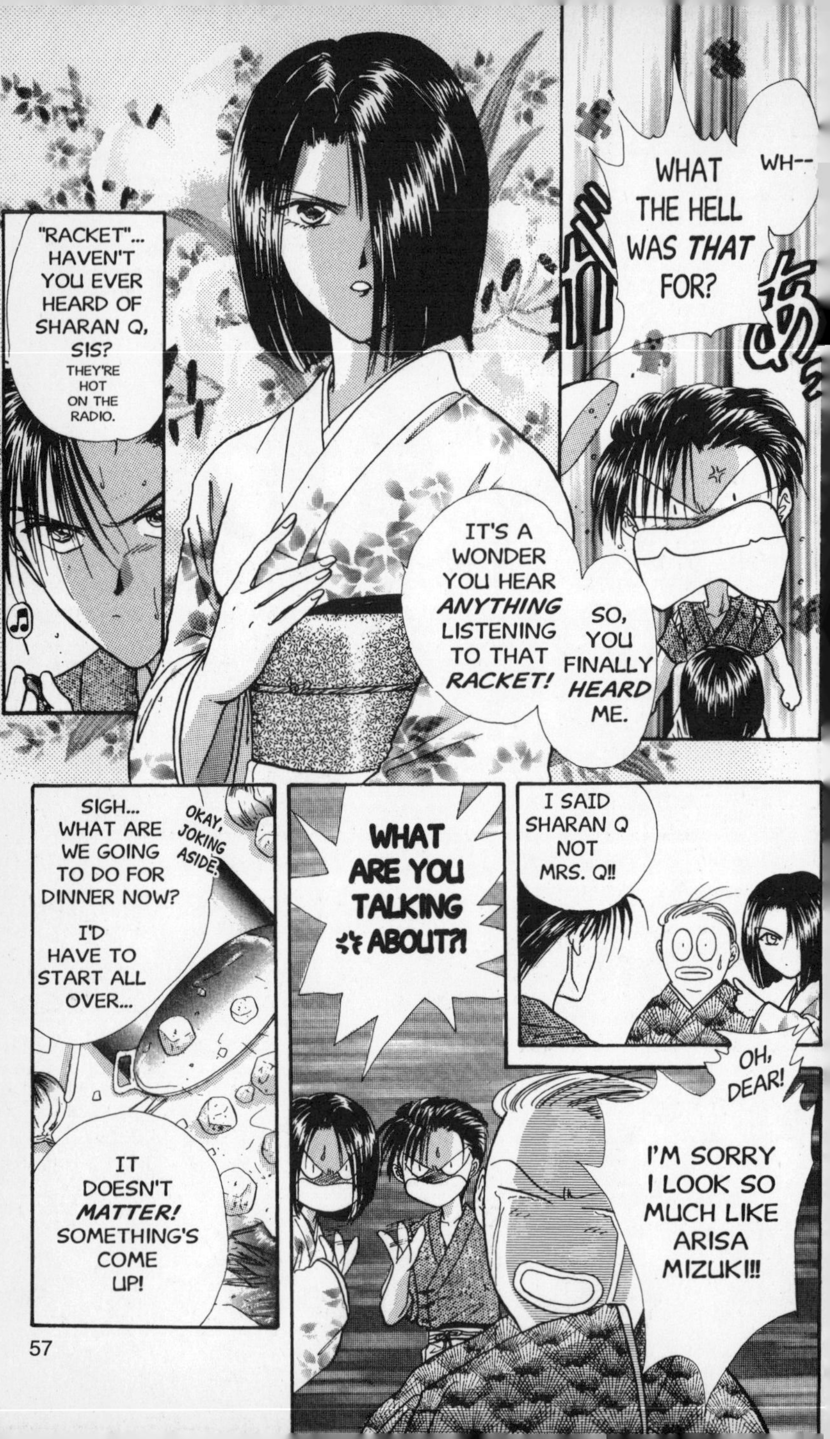
WH--
WHAT THE HELL WAS THAT FOR?
SO, YOU FINALLY HEARD ME.
IT'S A WONDER YOU HEAR ANYTHING LISTENING TO THAT RACKET!
"RACKET"... HAVEN'T YOU EVER HEARD OF SHARAN Q, SIS?
THEY'RE HOT ON THE RADIO.
I SAID SHARAN Q NOT MRS. Q!!
OH, DEAR!
I'M SORRY I LOOK SO MUCH LIKE ARISA MIZUKI!!
WHAT ARE YOU TALKING ABOUT?!
OKAY, JOKING ASIDE.
SIGH... WHAT ARE WE GOING TO DO FOR DINNER NOW?
I'D HAVE TO START ALL OVER...
IT DOESN'T MATTER! SOMETHING'S COME UP!

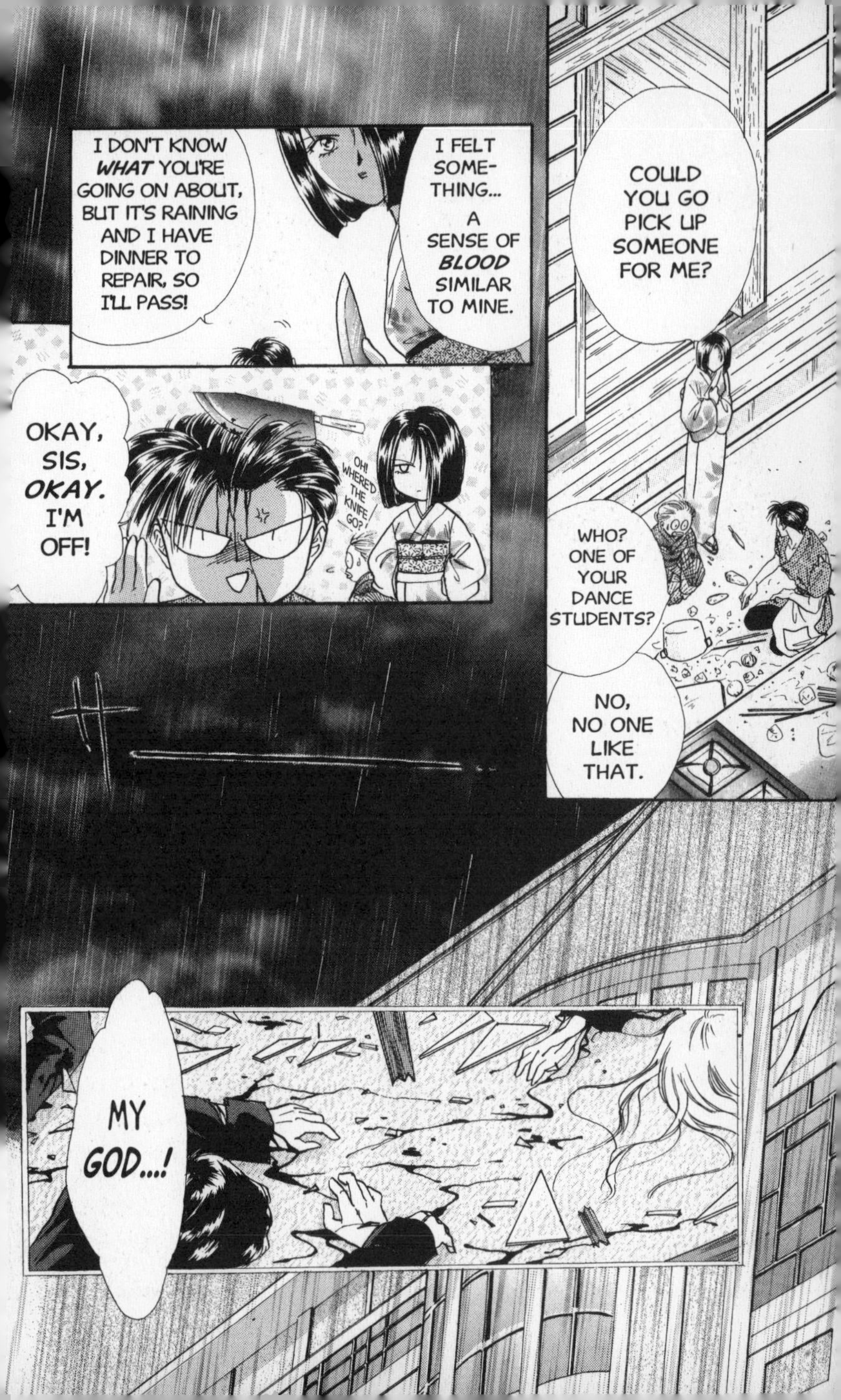
COULD YOU GO PICK UP SOMEONE FOR ME?
WHO? ONE OF YOUR DANCE STUDENTS?
NO, NO ONE LIKE THAT.
I FELT SOME-THING... A SENSE OF BLOOD SIMILAR TO MINE.
I DON'T KNOW WHAT YOU'RE GOING ON ABOUT, BUT IT'S RAINING AND I HAVE DINNER TO REPAIR, SO I'LL PASS!
OH! WHERE'D THE KNIFE GO?
OKAY, SIS, OKAY. I'M OFF!
MY GOD...!

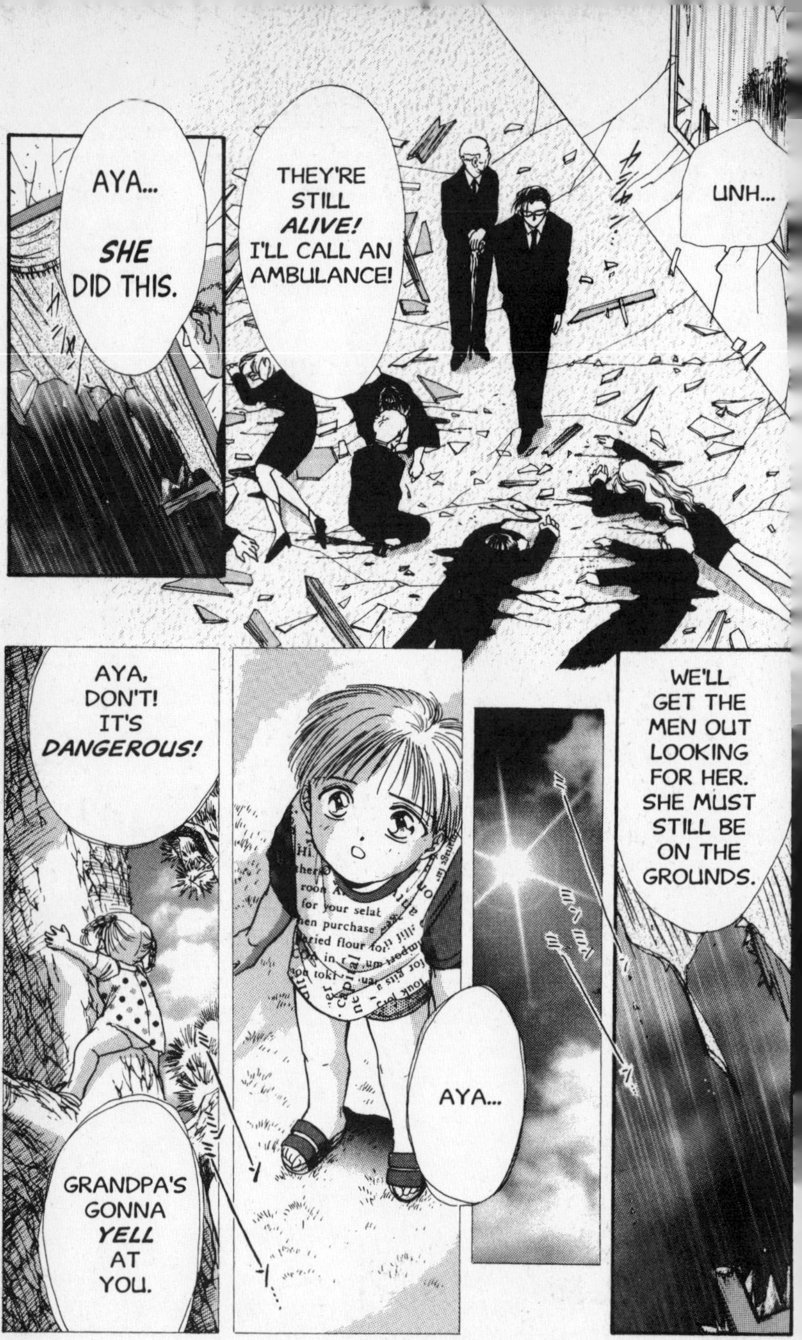
UNH...
THEY'RE STILL *ALIVE!* I'LL CALL AN AMBULANCE!
AYA... *SHE* DID THIS.
WE'LL GET THE MEN OUT LOOKING FOR HER. SHE MUST STILL BE ON THE GROUNDS.
AYA...
AYA, DON'T! IT'S *DANGEROUS!*
GRANDPA'S GONNA *YELL* AT YOU.

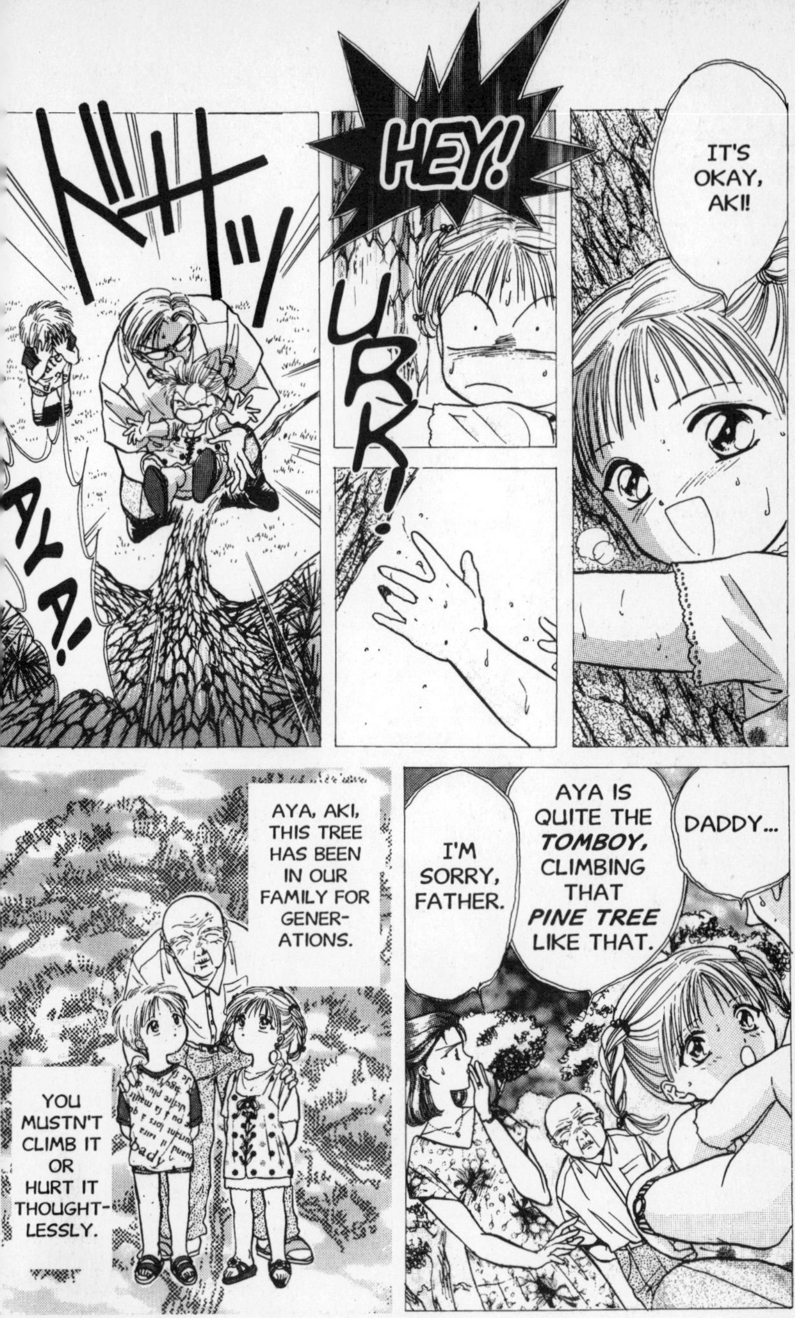

IT'S OKAY, AKI!
HEY!
URK!
ドサッ
AYA!
DADDY...
AYA IS QUITE THE *TOMBOY,* CLIMBING THAT *PINE TREE* LIKE THAT.
I'M SORRY, FATHER.
AYA, AKI, THIS TREE HAS BEEN IN OUR FAMILY FOR GENER-ATIONS.
YOU MUSTN'T CLIMB IT OR HURT IT THOUGHT-LESSLY.

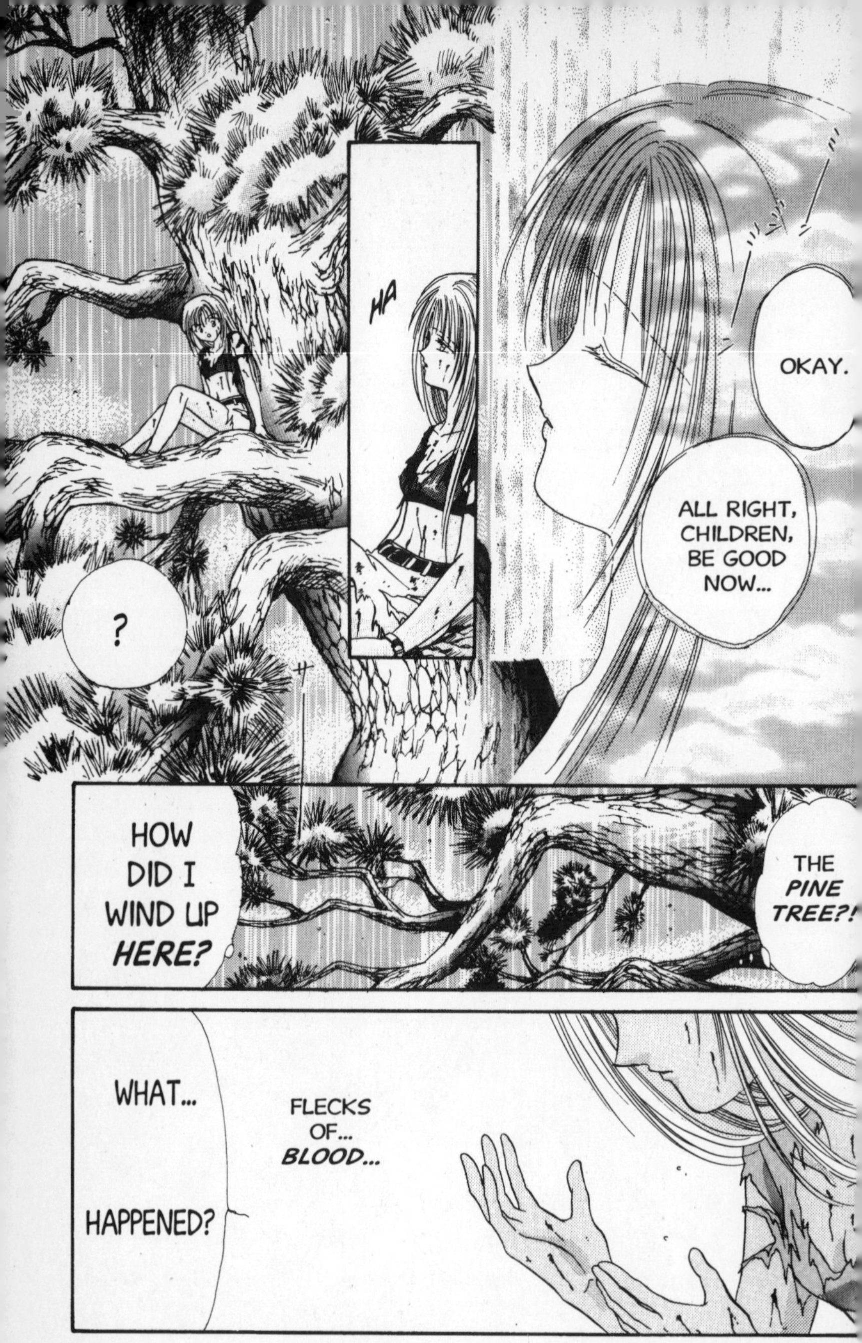
OKAY.
ALL RIGHT, CHILDREN, BE GOOD NOW...
HA
?
THE *PINE TREE?!*
HOW DID I WIND UP *HERE?*
FLECKS OF... *BLOOD...*
WHAT... HAPPENED?

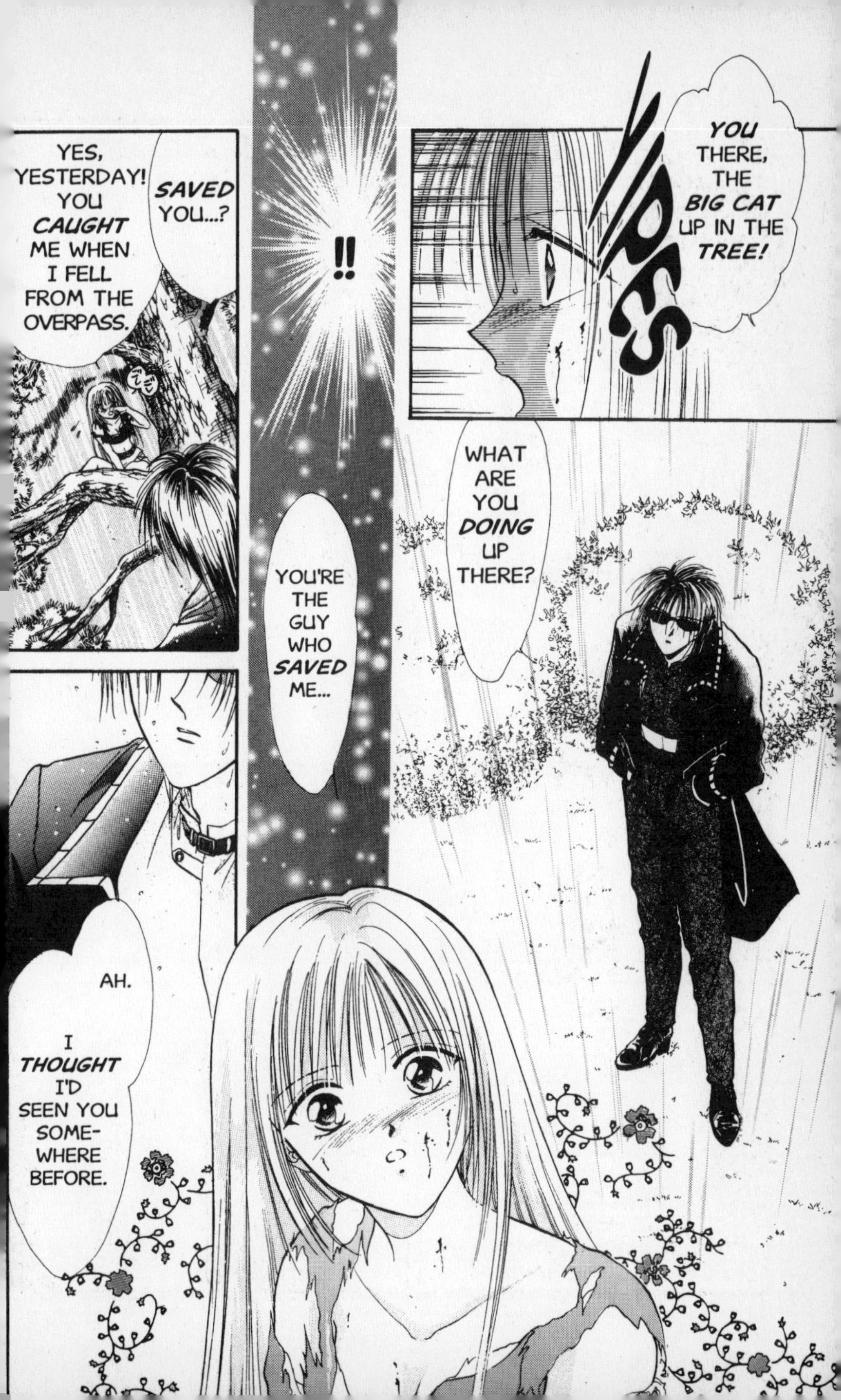
VIPS
YOU THERE, THE BIG CAT UP IN THE TREE!
WHAT ARE YOU DOING UP THERE?
!!
YOU'RE THE GUY WHO SAVED ME...
SAVED YOU...?
YES, YESTERDAY! YOU CAUGHT ME WHEN I FELL FROM THE OVERPASS.
AH.
I THOUGHT I'D SEEN YOU SOME-WHERE BEFORE.

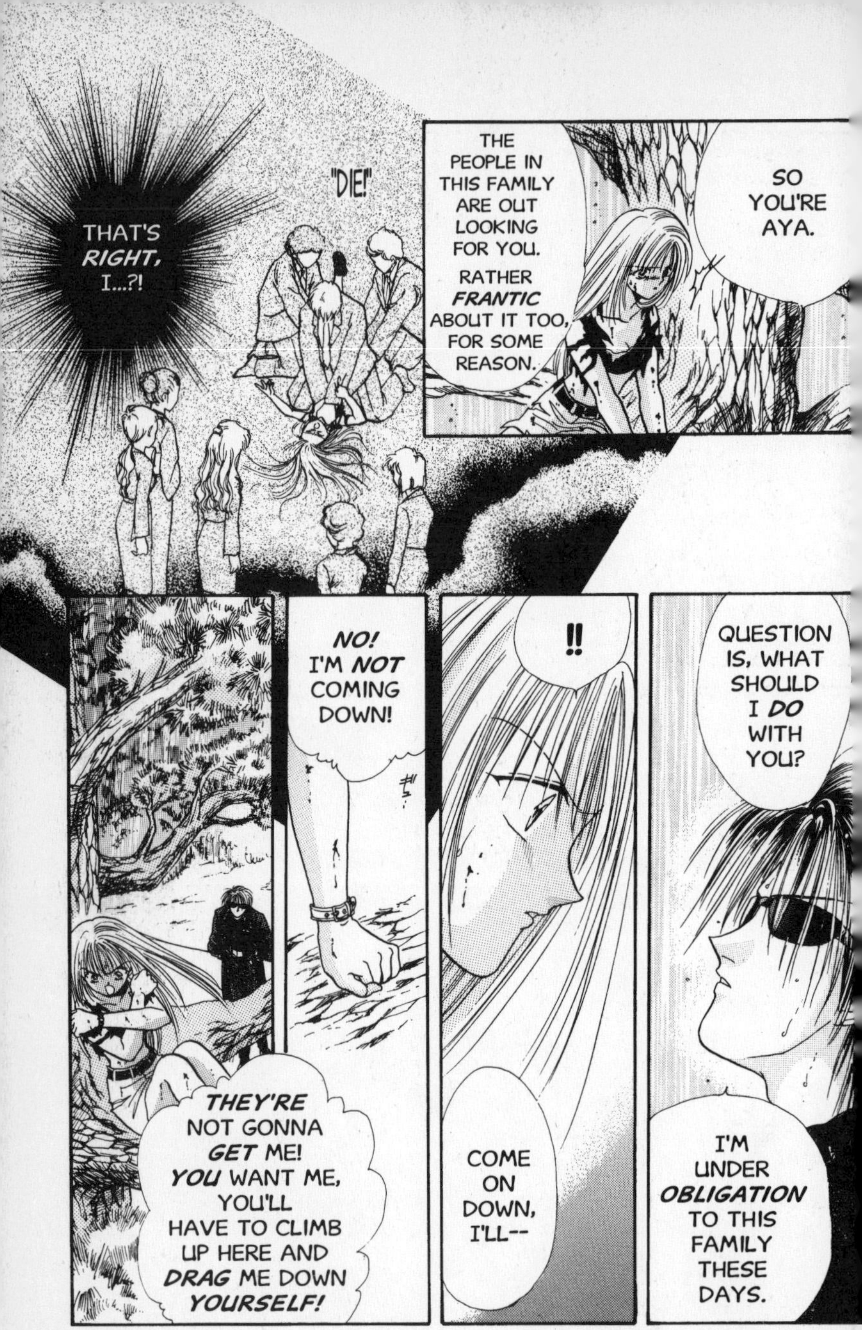
SO YOU'RE AYA.
THE PEOPLE IN THIS FAMILY ARE OUT LOOKING FOR YOU.
RATHER FRANTIC ABOUT IT TOO, FOR SOME REASON.
"DIE!"
THAT'S RIGHT, I...?!
QUESTION IS, WHAT SHOULD I DO WITH YOU?
I'M UNDER OBLIGATION TO THIS FAMILY THESE DAYS.
!!
COME ON DOWN, I'LL--
NO! I'M NOT COMING DOWN!
THEY'RE NOT GONNA GET ME! YOU WANT ME, YOU'LL HAVE TO CLIMB UP HERE AND DRAG ME DOWN YOURSELF!

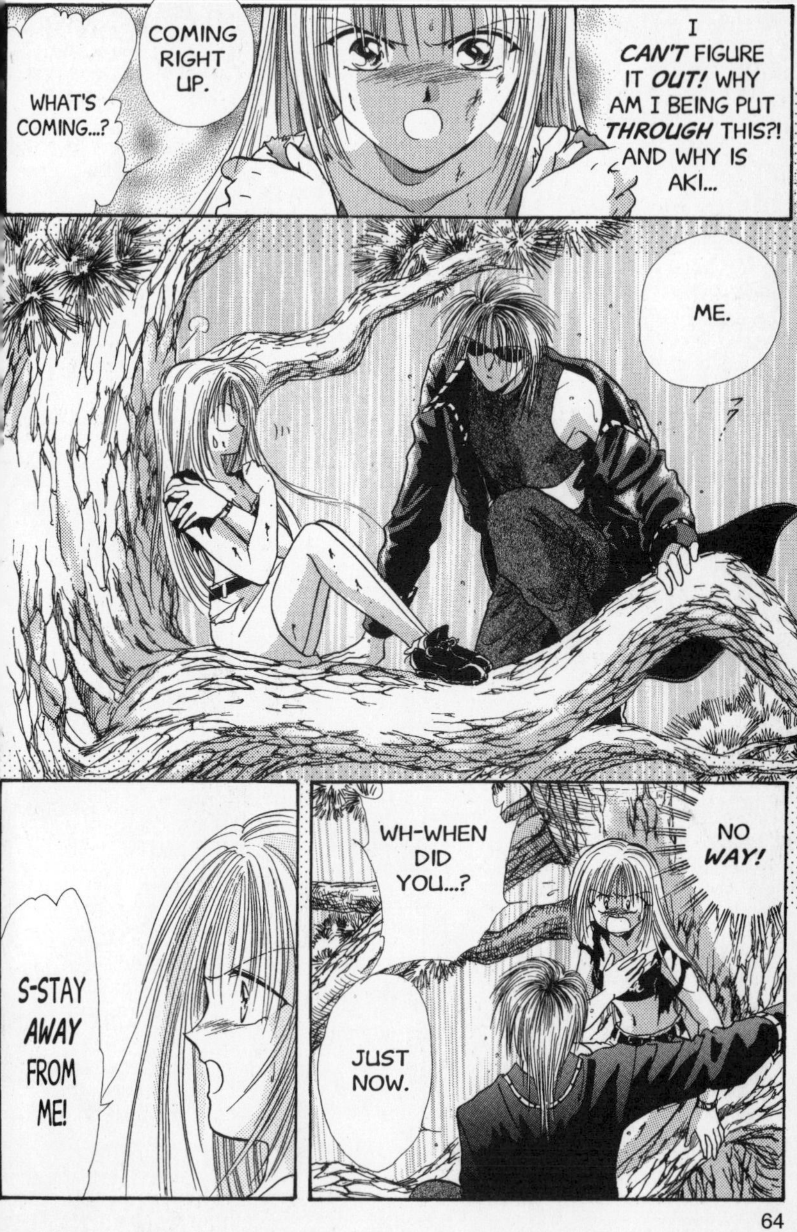

I CAN'T FIGURE IT OUT! WHY AM I BEING PUT THROUGH THIS?! AND WHY IS AKI...
COMING RIGHT UP.
WHAT'S COMING...?
ME.
NO WAY!
WH-WHEN DID YOU...?
JUST NOW.
S-STAY AWAY FROM ME!

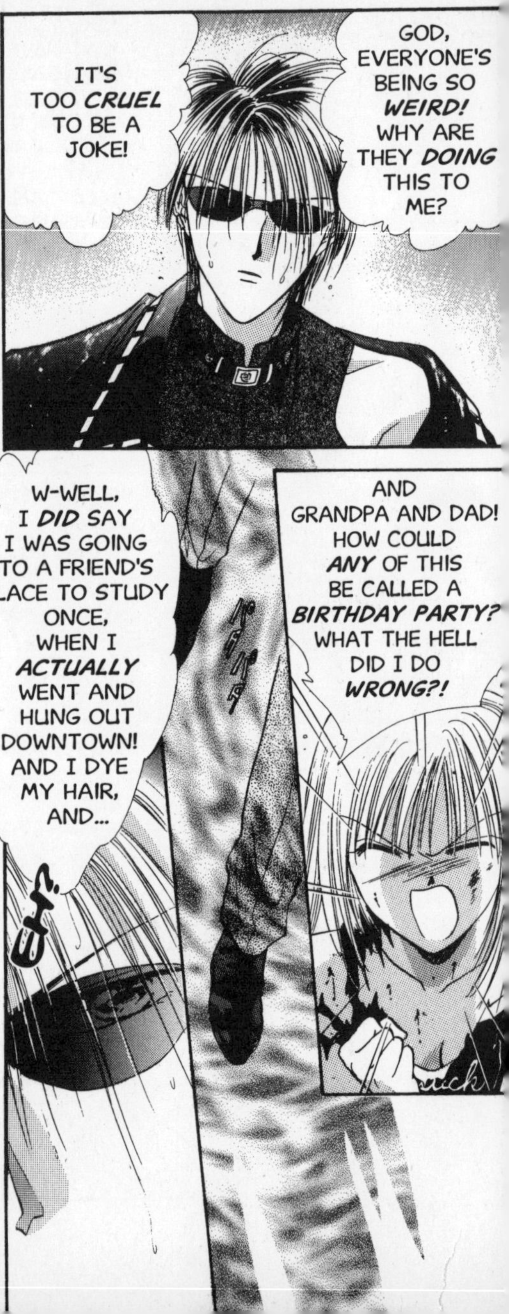
GOD, EVERYONE'S BEING SO *WEIRD!* WHY ARE THEY *DOING* THIS TO ME?
IT'S TOO *CRUEL* TO BE A JOKE!
AND GRANDPA AND DAD! HOW COULD *ANY* OF THIS BE CALLED A *BIRTHDAY PARTY?* WHAT THE HELL DID I DO *WRONG?!*
W-WELL, I *DID* SAY I WAS GOING TO A FRIEND'S PLACE TO STUDY ONCE, WHEN I *ACTUALLY* WENT AND HUNG OUT DOWNTOWN! AND I DYE MY HAIR, AND...

♦ Aya ♦

Now then, I'd like to talk a bit about the Fushigi Yûgi OAV wrap-up celebration event, held on 8/30 and 31. On the 30th in Osaka, the participants were me, Mr. Hajime Kamegaki the director, Mr. Hideyuki Motohashi the character designer and art director, the voice actors Ms. Kae Araki, Mr. Hikaru Midorikawa, and Mr. Takehito Koyasu, and the singers Ms. Akemi Sato and Ms. Saori Ishizuka. I stayed at the same hotel as the director the night before, and we all had fried octopus, and I got drunk on Oolong High and chatted with Mr. Motohashi. He is a really friendly guy. But I was nervous around Mr. Director. Like a student faced with her teacher.

The day started with the opening (of the anime) without credits, and the best lines of the characters, (the voice actors came in dresses and tuxedos. It was like the Oscars!) plus songs, a Q&A session, and a giveaway of telephone cards, autographs, and the script, etc., for a total of two hours. And there was something called "a letter to Miaka from Tamahome," and Mr. Midorikawa came forward on stage and read it as Tama- home. I thought the audience reaction was funny. "They're all closing their eyes and swooning!" I had made Tamahome say lots and lots of cheesy lines in the manga (partly to be funny), but... it was still pretty embarrassing.

And on the 31st in Tokyo, Mr. Koyasu missed out, but we were joined by Ms. Chika Sakamoto and Mr. Tomokazu Seki.

To be continued

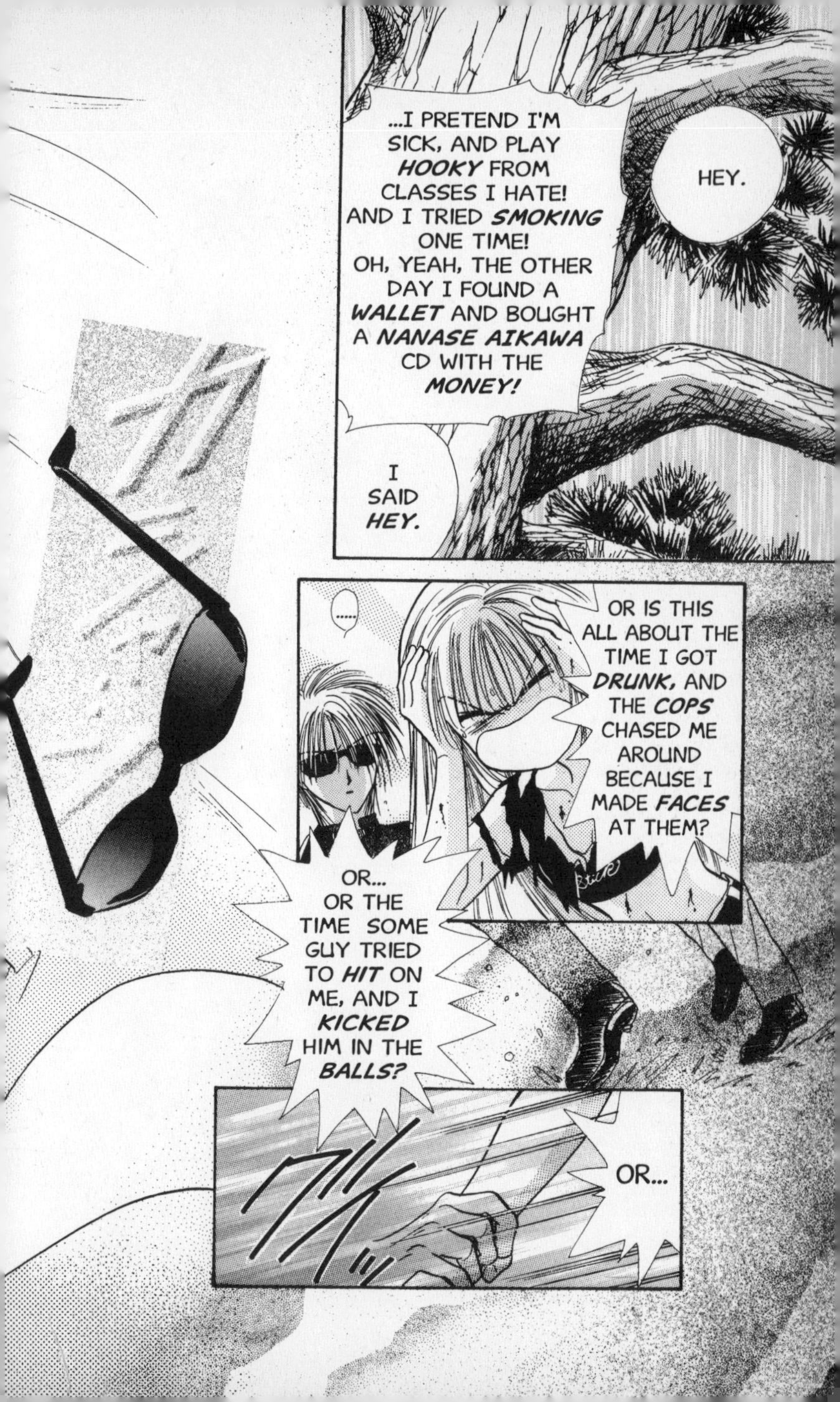

HEY.
...I PRETEND I'M SICK, AND PLAY HOOKY FROM CLASSES I HATE! AND I TRIED SMOKING ONE TIME! OH, YEAH, THE OTHER DAY I FOUND A WALLET AND BOUGHT A NANASE AIKAWA CD WITH THE MONEY!
I SAID HEY.
OR IS THIS ALL ABOUT THE TIME I GOT DRUNK, AND THE COPS CHASED ME AROUND BECAUSE I MADE FACES AT THEM?
.....
OR... OR THE TIME SOME GUY TRIED TO HIT ON ME, AND I KICKED HIM IN THE BALLS?
OR...

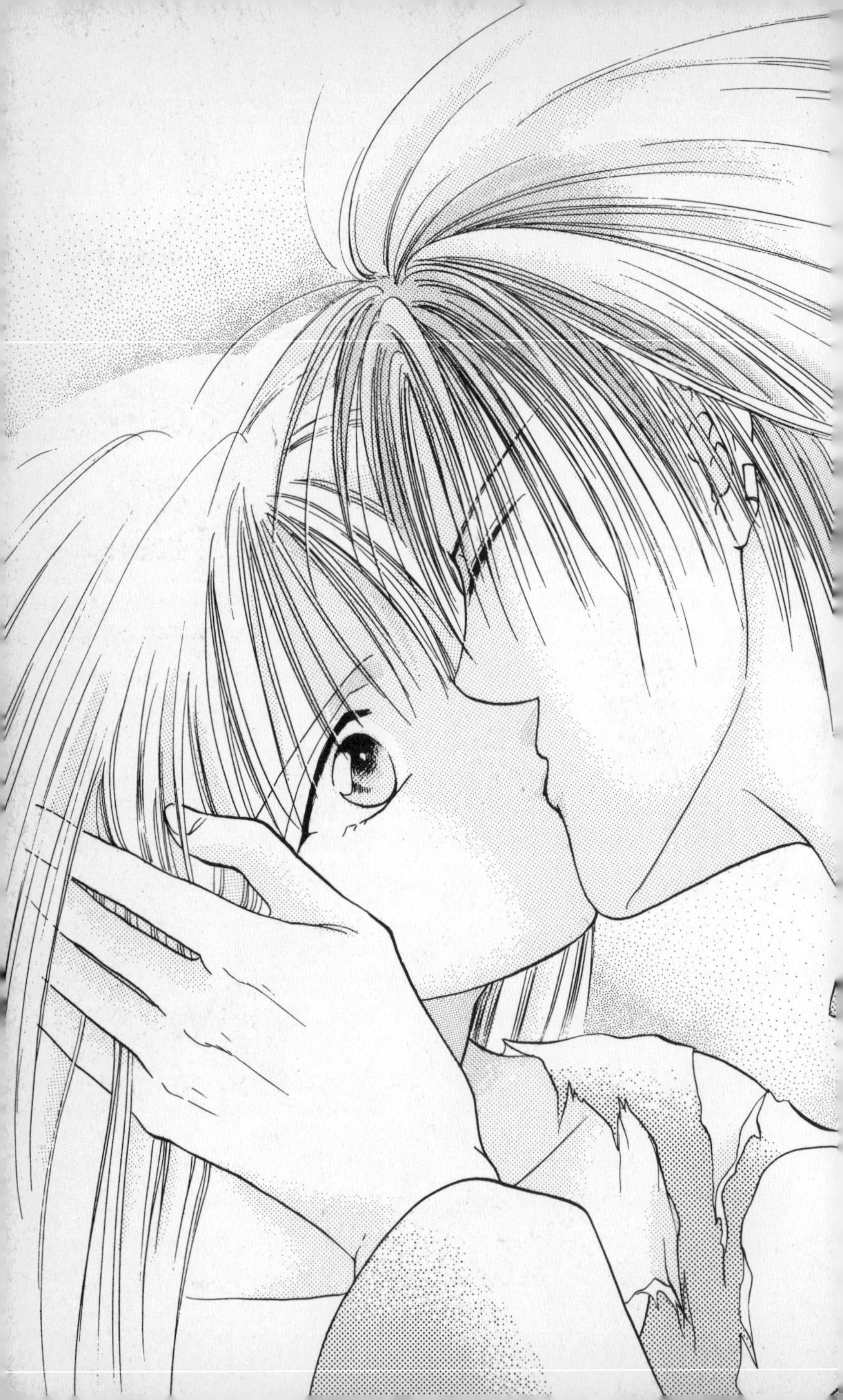

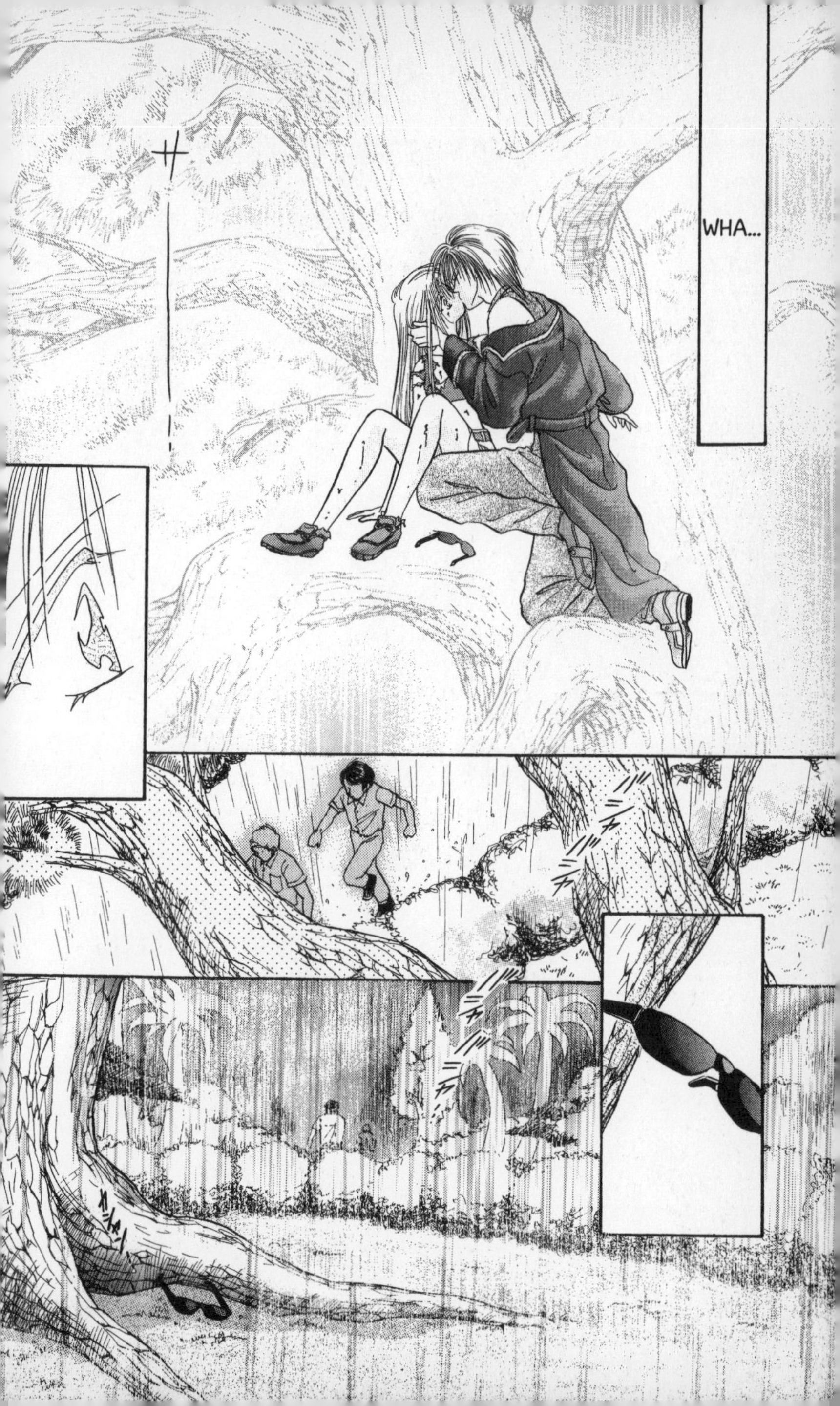
WHA...

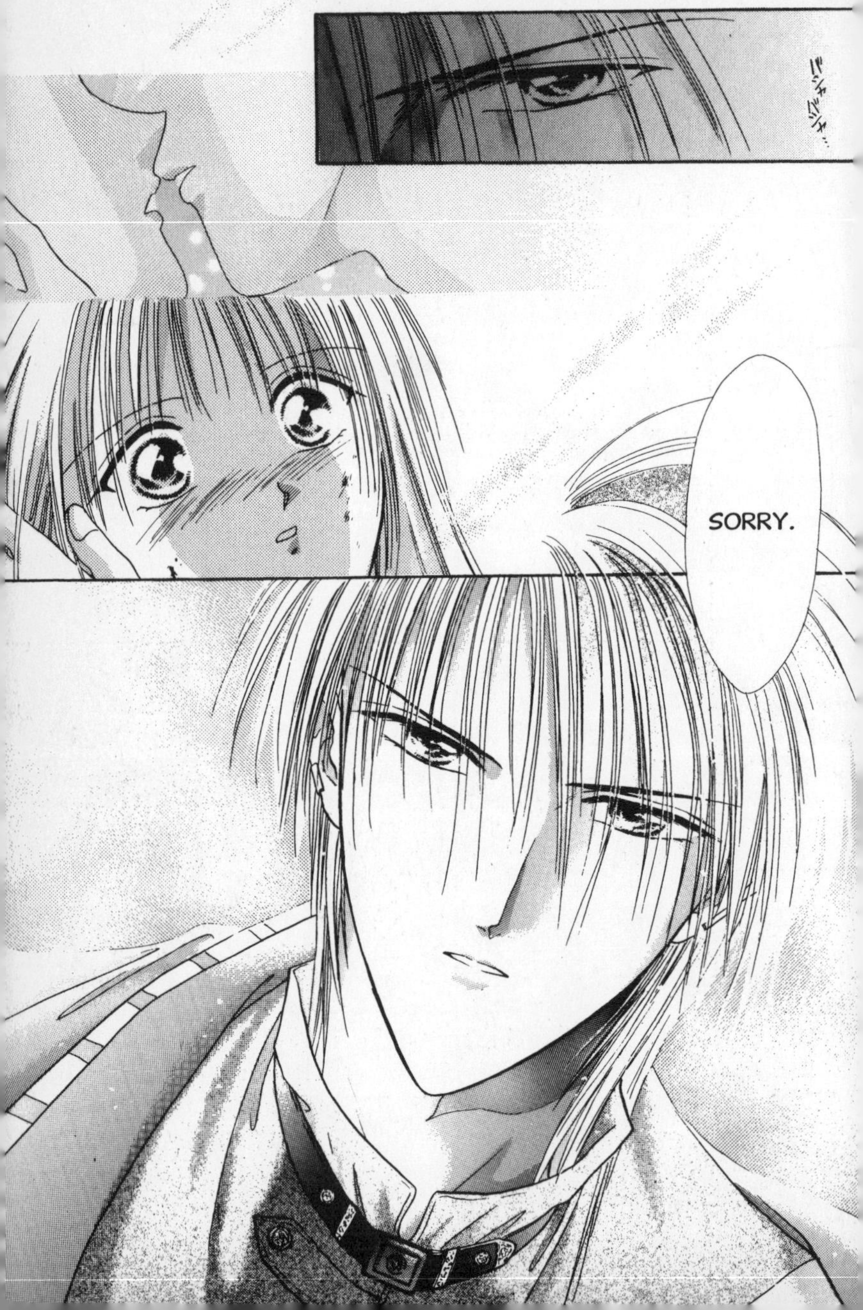
バシャバシャ‥
SORRY.

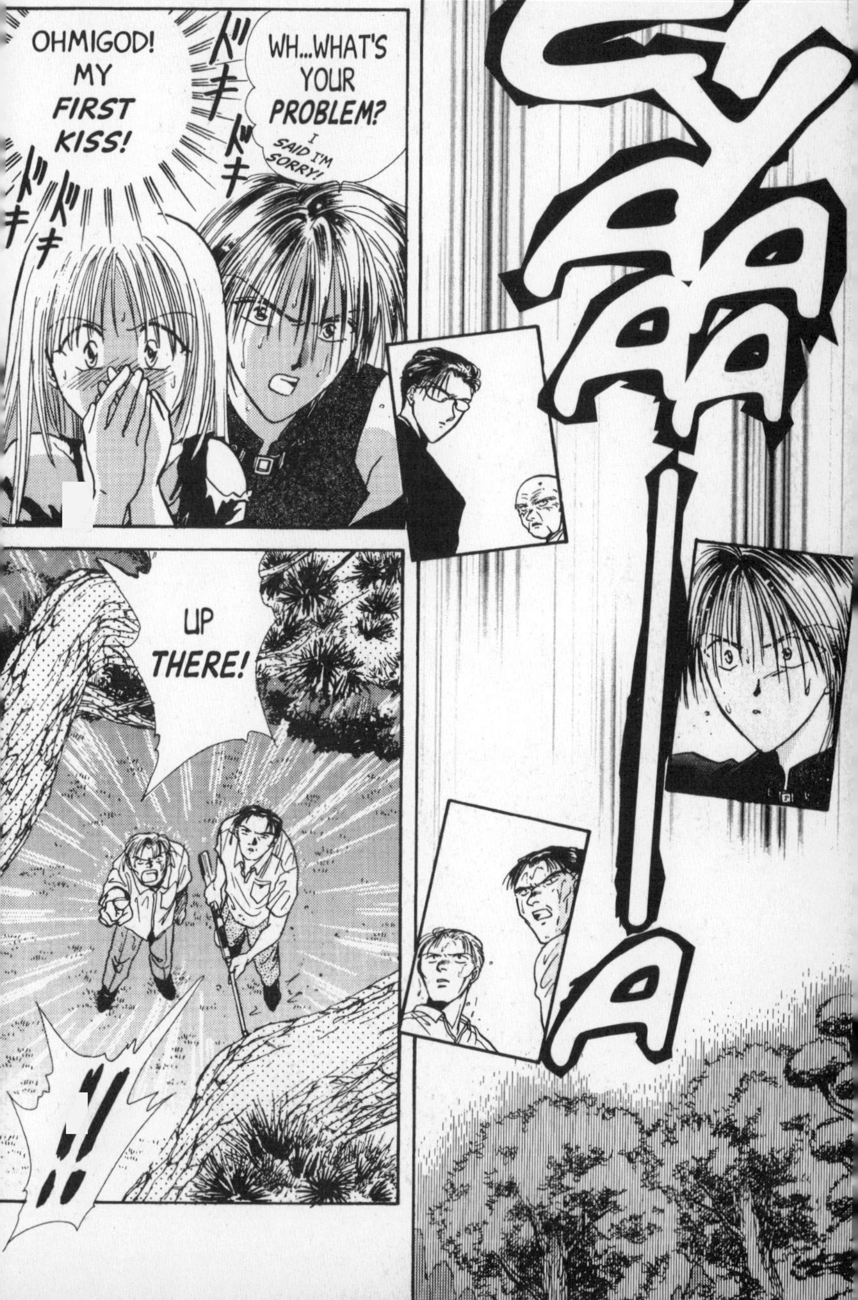
GYAAAAA
WH...WHAT'S YOUR PROBLEM?
I SAID I'M SORRY!
ドキ ドキ
OHMIGOD! MY FIRST KISS!
ドキ ドキ
UP THERE!
!!

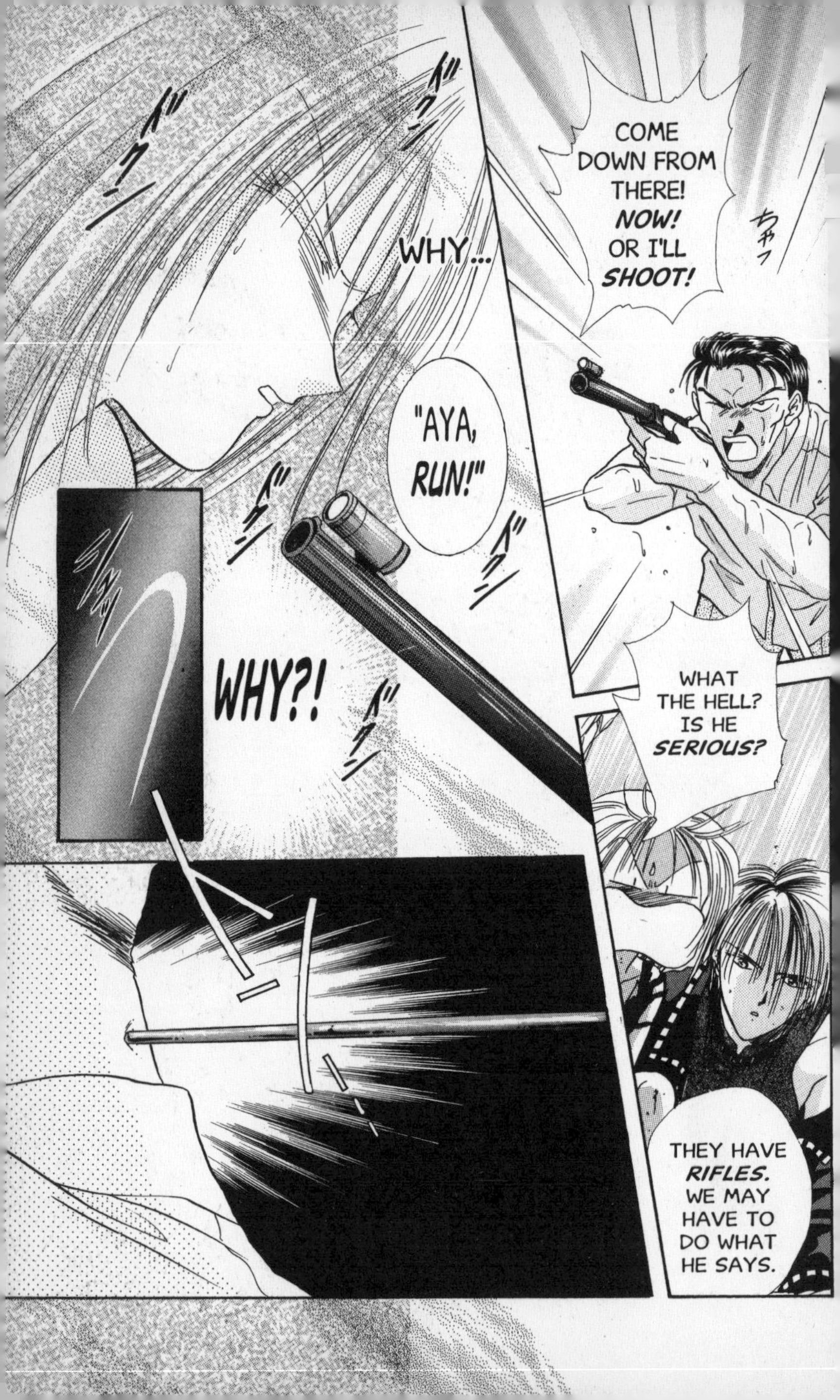
COME DOWN FROM THERE! NOW! OR I'LL SHOOT!
WHAT THE HELL? IS HE SERIOUS?
THEY HAVE RIFLES. WE MAY HAVE TO DO WHAT HE SAYS.
WHY...
"AYA, RUN!"
WHY?!

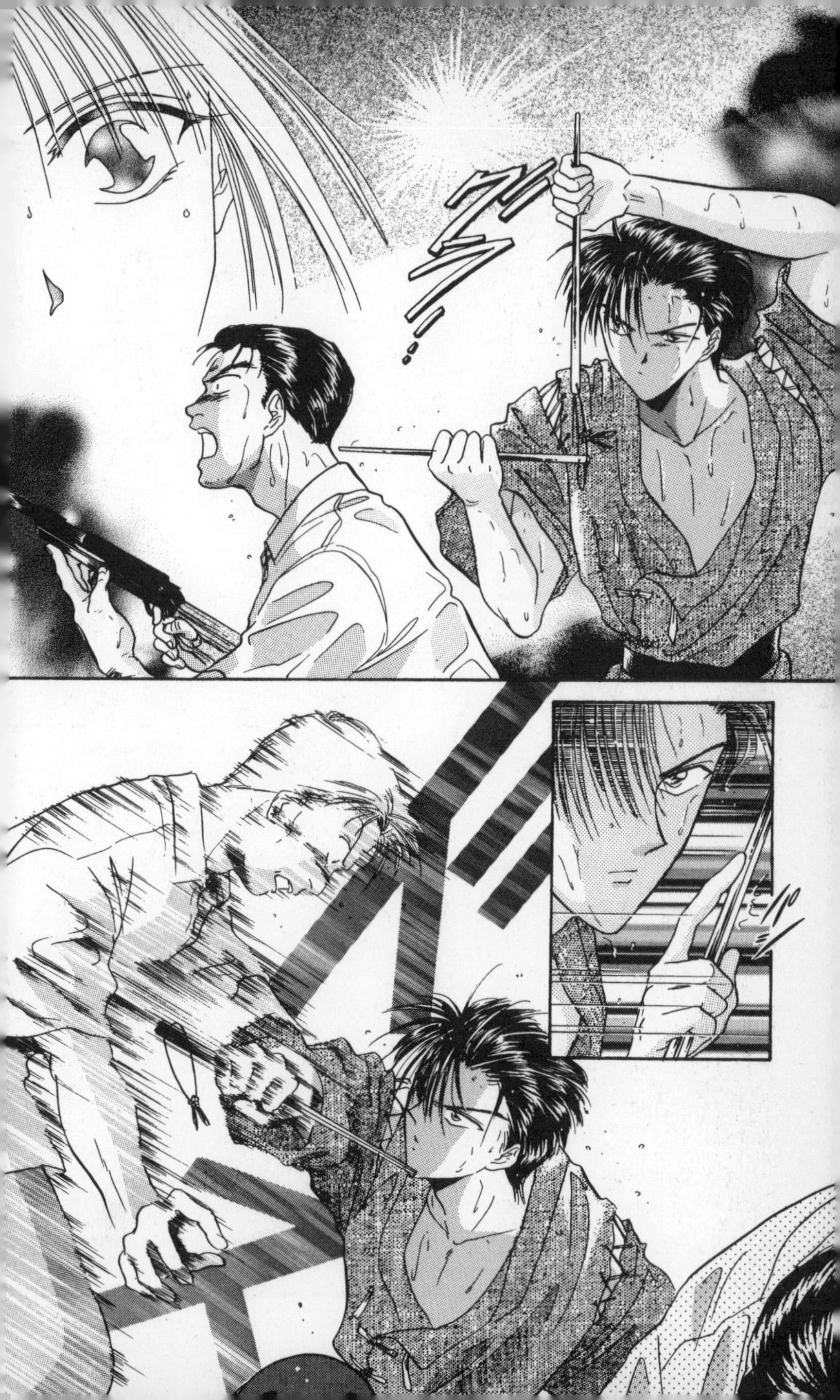
ブツ

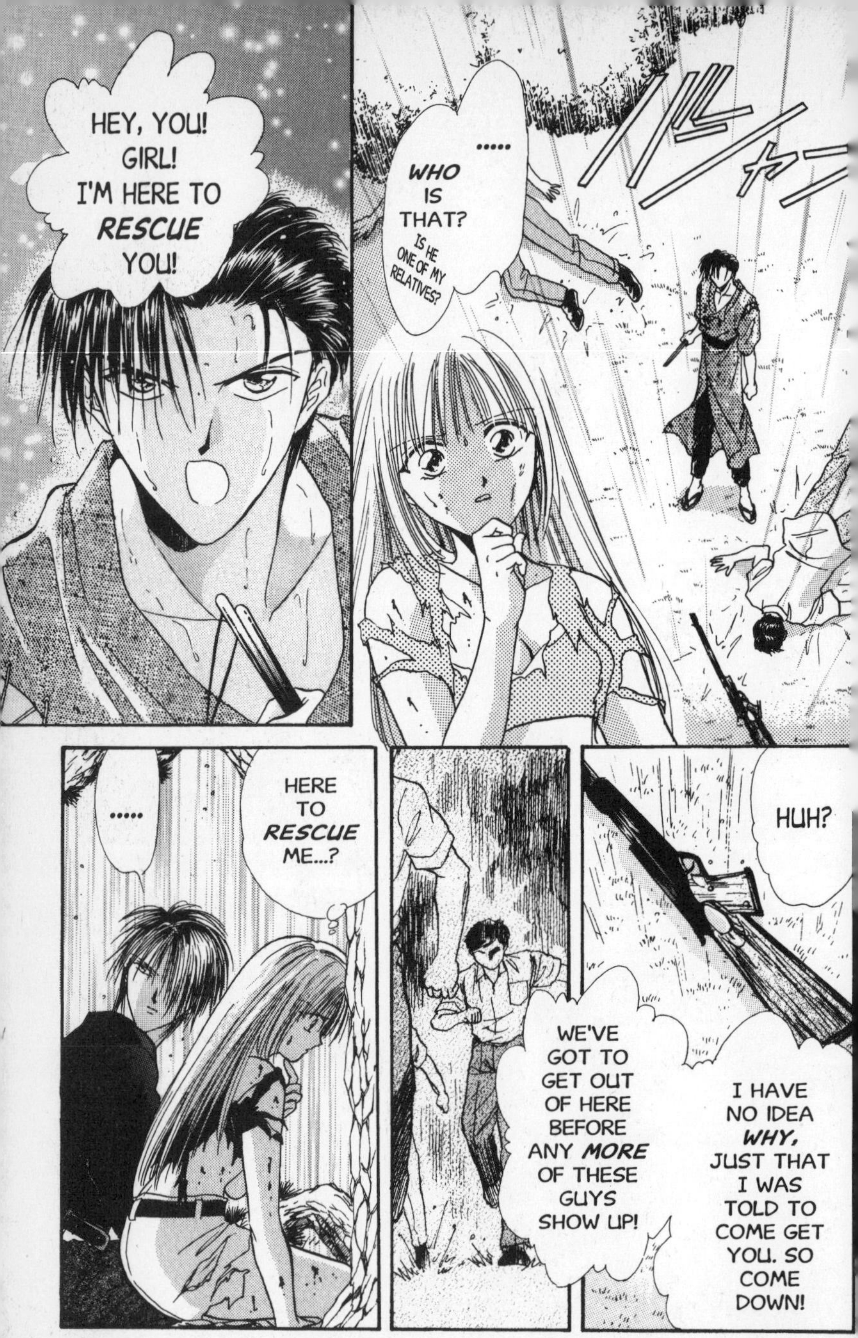
.....
WHO IS THAT?
IS HE ONE OF MY RELATIVES?
HEY, YOU! GIRL! I'M HERE TO RESCUE YOU!
HUH?
I HAVE NO IDEA WHY, JUST THAT I WAS TOLD TO COME GET YOU. SO COME DOWN!
WE'VE GOT TO GET OUT OF HERE BEFORE ANY MORE OF THESE GUYS SHOW UP!
.....
HERE TO RESCUE ME...?

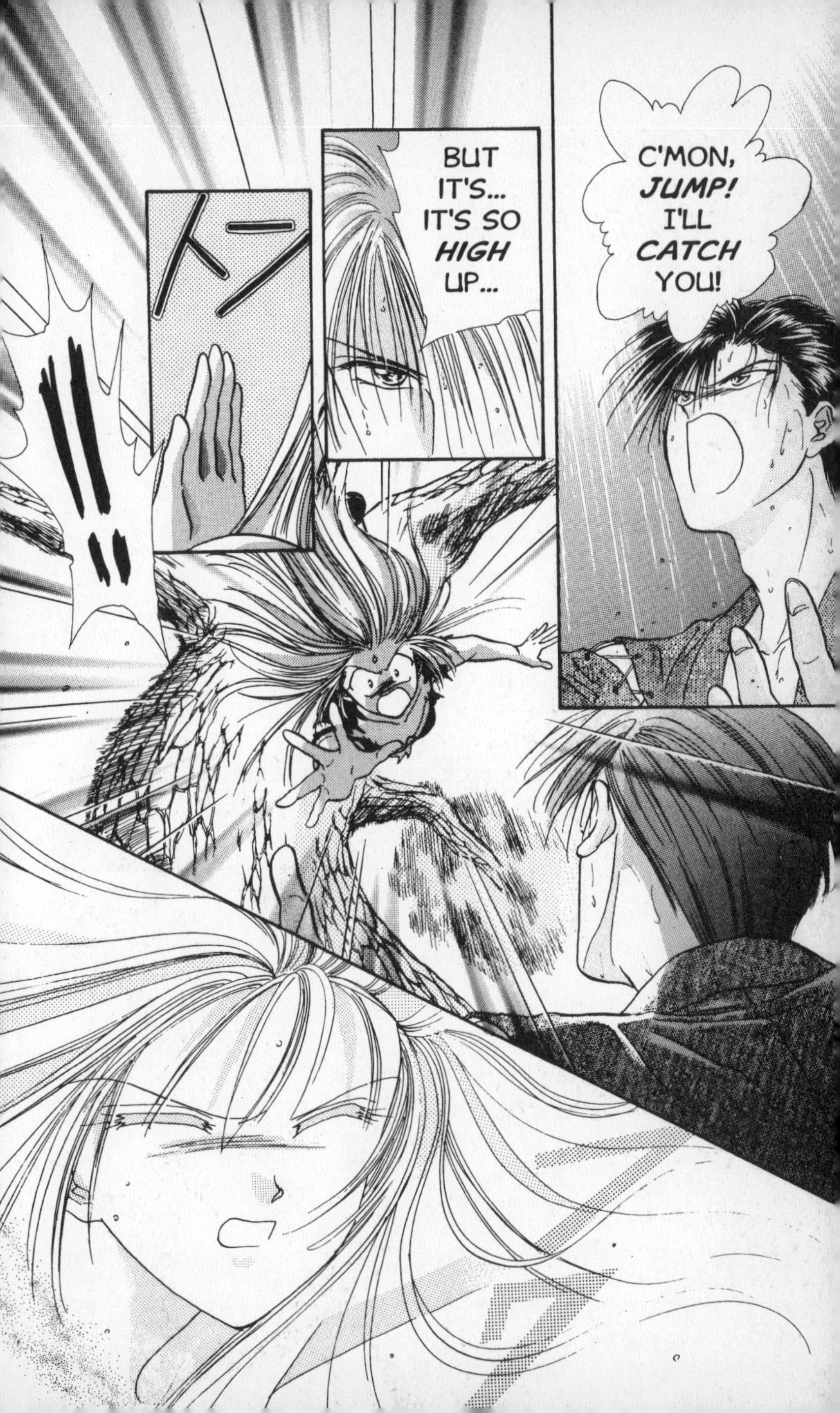
C'MON, *JUMP!* I'LL *CATCH* YOU!
BUT IT'S... IT'S SO *HIGH* UP...
トーン

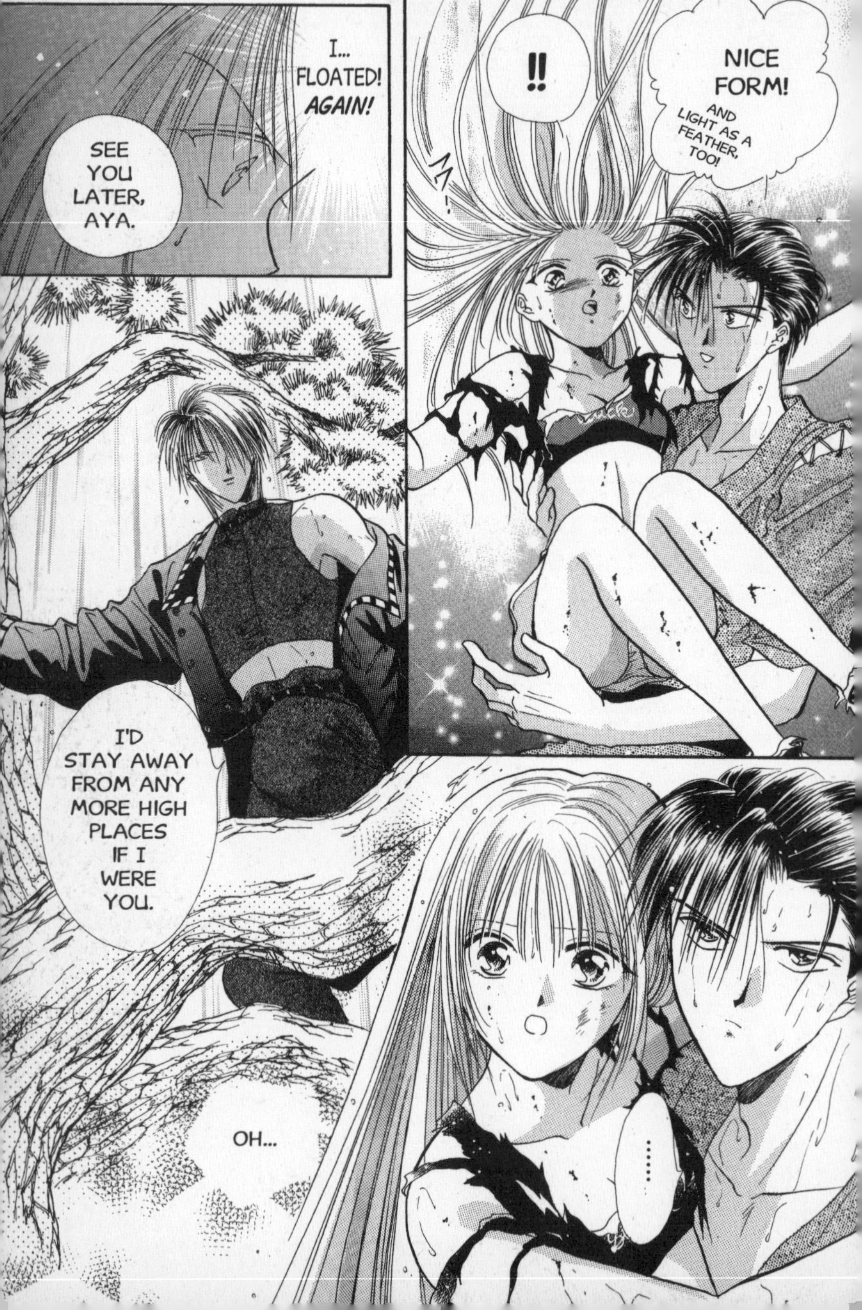
!!
NICE FORM!
AND LIGHT AS A FEATHER, TOO!
I... FLOATED! AGAIN!
SEE YOU LATER, AYA.
I'D STAY AWAY FROM ANY MORE HIGH PLACES IF I WERE YOU.
......
OH...

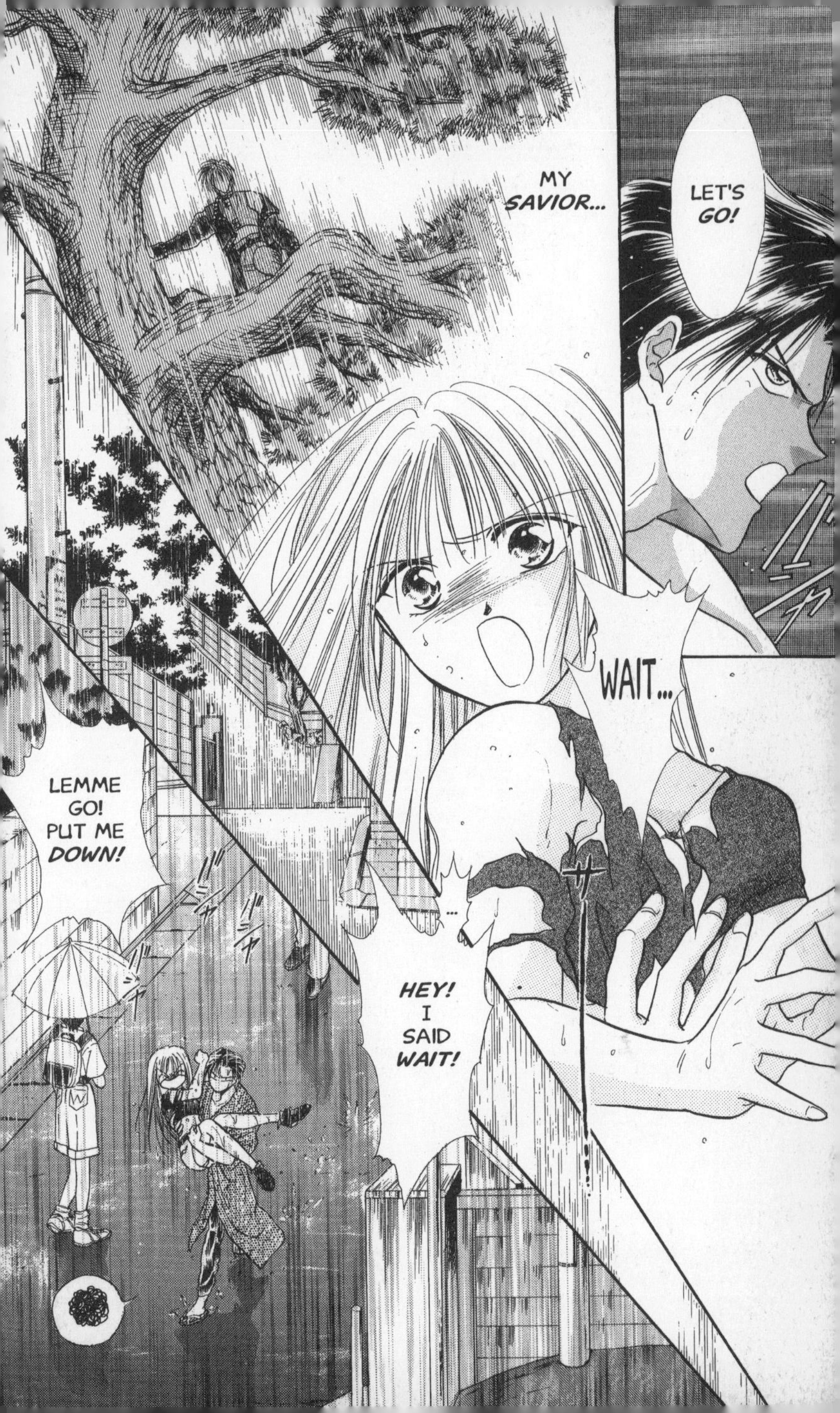
LET'S GO!
MY SAVIOR...
WAIT...
...
HEY! I SAID WAIT!
LEMME GO! PUT ME DOWN!

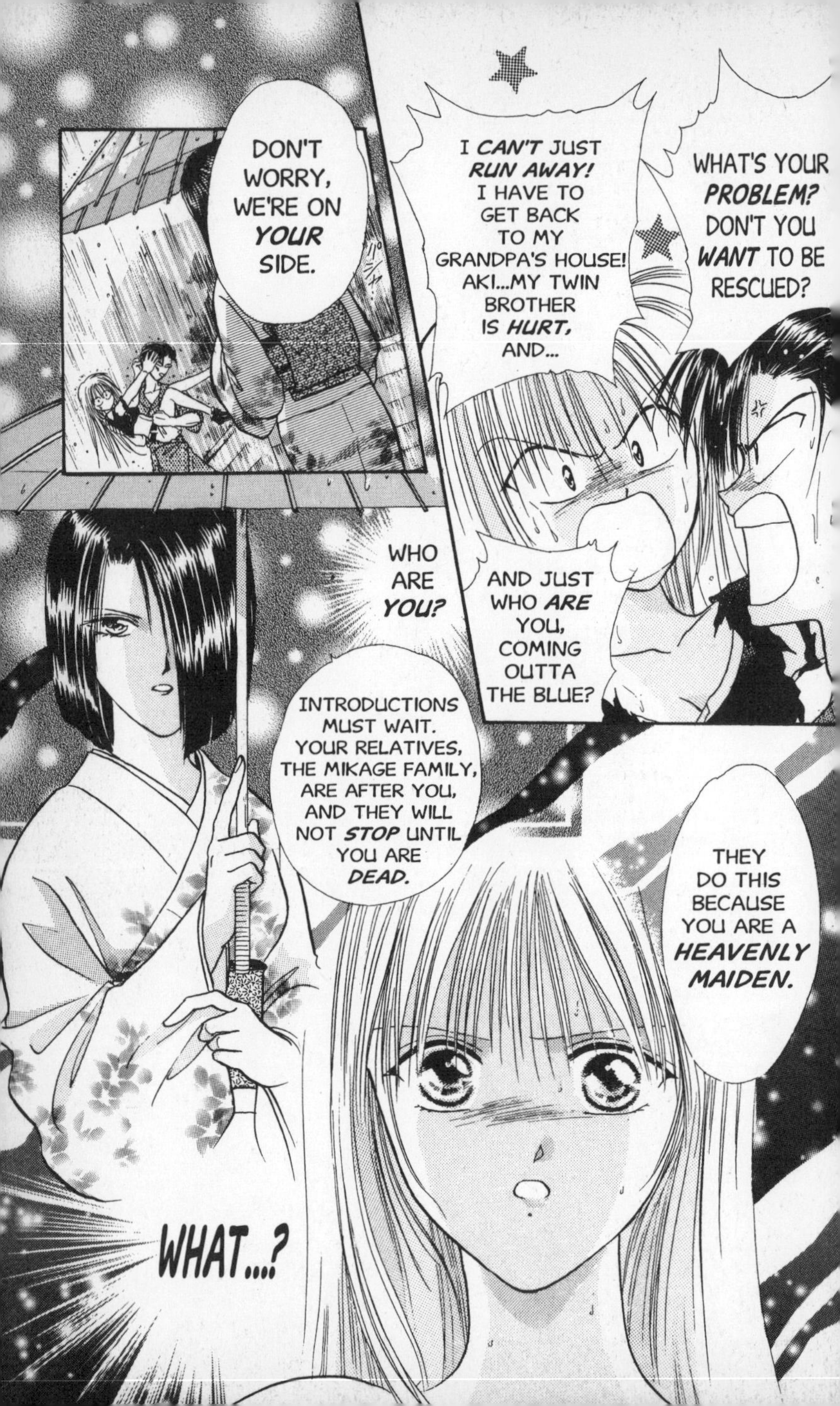
WHAT'S YOUR PROBLEM? DON'T YOU WANT TO BE RESCUED?
I CAN'T JUST RUN AWAY! I HAVE TO GET BACK TO MY GRANDPA'S HOUSE! AKI...MY TWIN BROTHER IS HURT, AND...
AND JUST WHO ARE YOU, COMING OUTTA THE BLUE?
DON'T WORRY, WE'RE ON YOUR SIDE.
WHO ARE YOU?
INTRODUCTIONS MUST WAIT. YOUR RELATIVES, THE MIKAGE FAMILY, ARE AFTER YOU, AND THEY WILL NOT STOP UNTIL YOU ARE DEAD.
THEY DO THIS BECAUSE YOU ARE A HEAVENLY MAIDEN.
WHAT...?

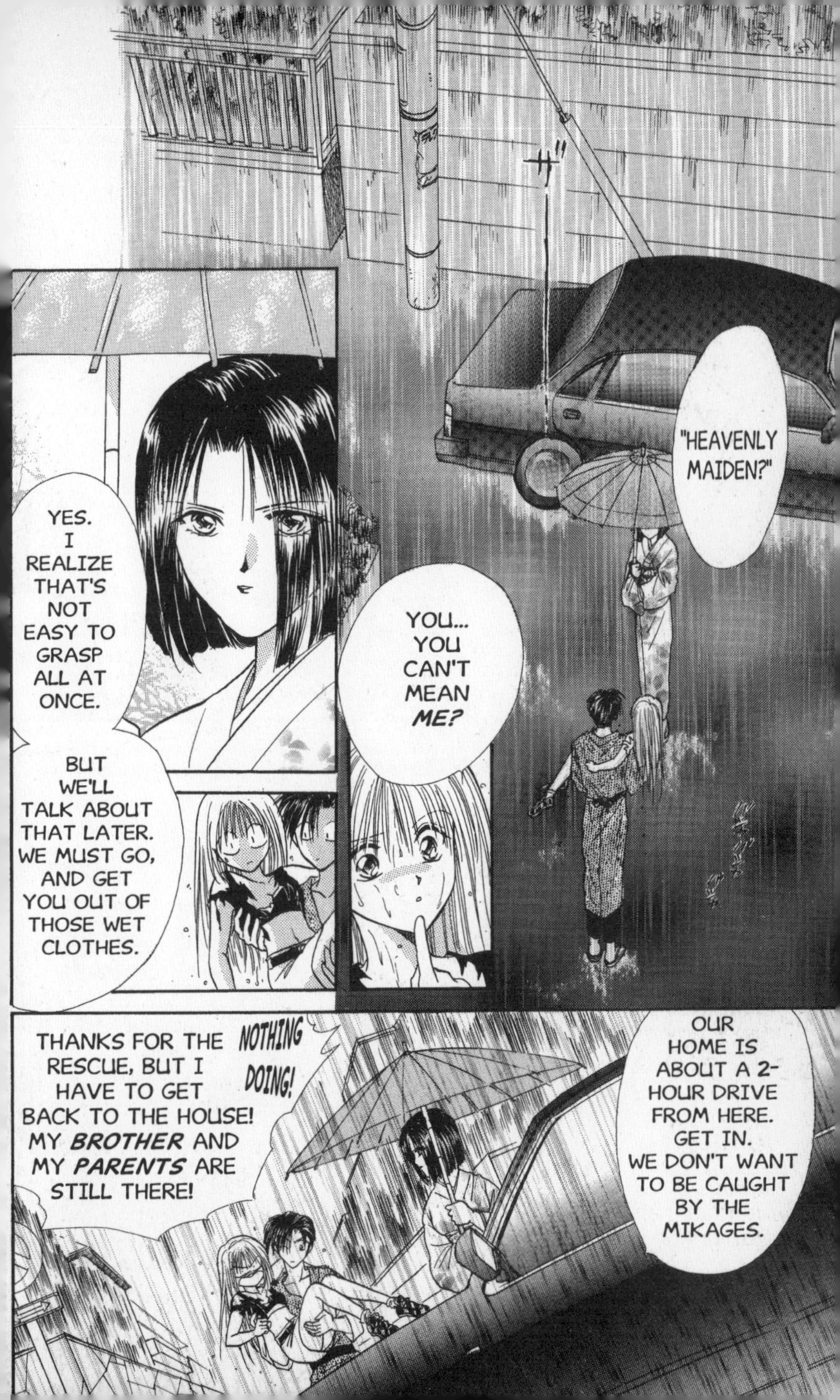
"HEAVENLY MAIDEN?"
YOU... YOU CAN'T MEAN *ME?*
YES. I REALIZE THAT'S NOT EASY TO GRASP ALL AT ONCE.
BUT WE'LL TALK ABOUT THAT LATER. WE MUST GO, AND GET YOU OUT OF THOSE WET CLOTHES.
OUR HOME IS ABOUT A 2-HOUR DRIVE FROM HERE. GET IN. WE DON'T WANT TO BE CAUGHT BY THE MIKAGES.
NOTHING DOING!
THANKS FOR THE RESCUE, BUT I HAVE TO GET BACK TO THE HOUSE! MY *BROTHER* AND MY *PARENTS* ARE STILL THERE!

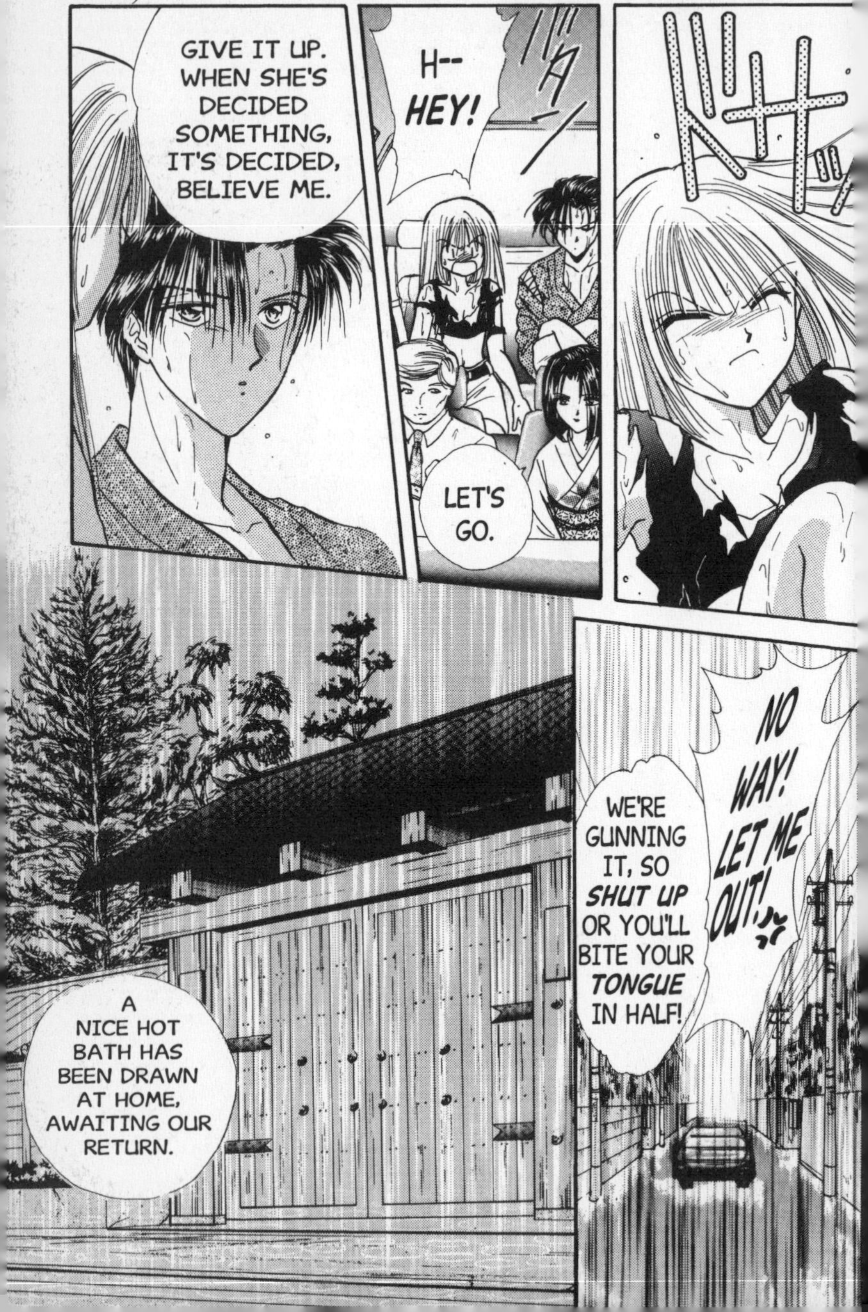
H-- HEY!
LET'S GO.
GIVE IT UP. WHEN SHE'S DECIDED SOMETHING, IT'S DECIDED, BELIEVE ME.
NO WAY! LET ME OUT!
WE'RE GUNNING IT, SO SHUT UP OR YOU'LL BITE YOUR TONGUE IN HALF!
A NICE HOT BATH HAS BEEN DRAWN AT HOME, AWAITING OUR RETURN.

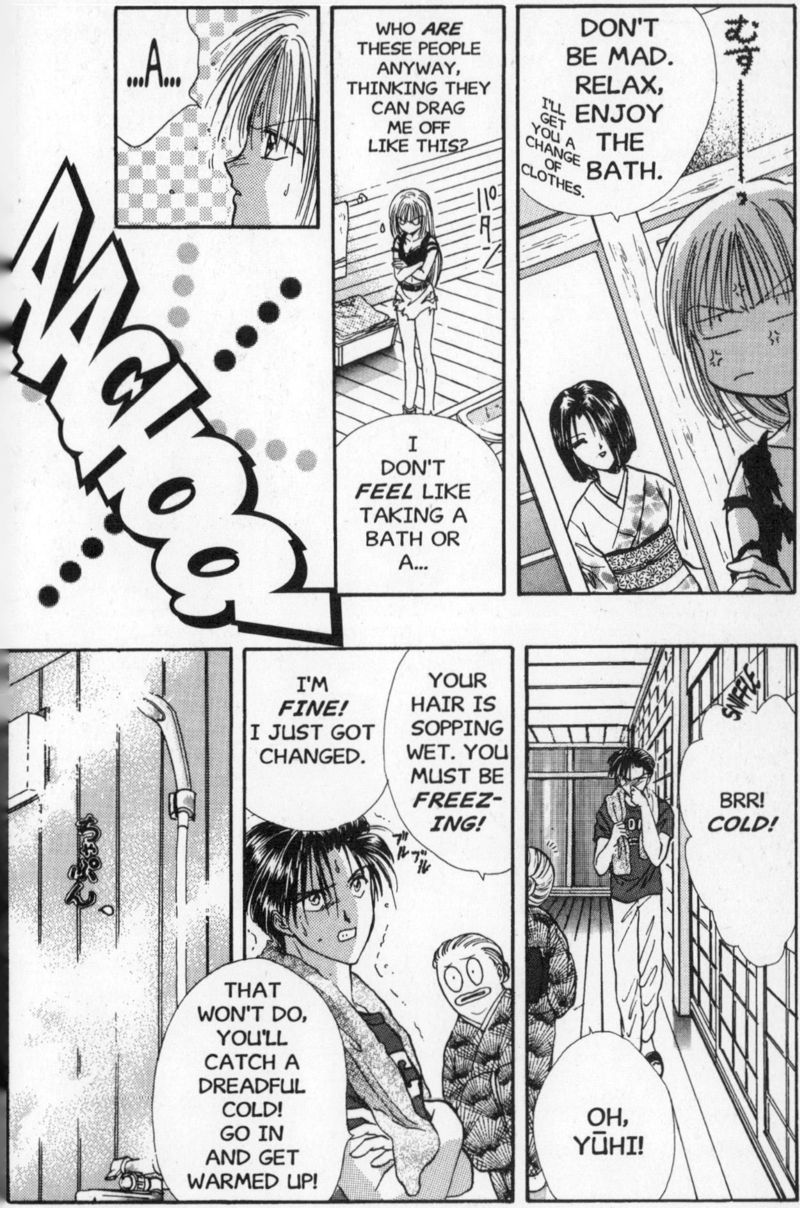
むす
DON'T BE MAD. RELAX, ENJOY THE BATH.
I'LL GET YOU A CHANGE OF CLOTHES.
WHO *ARE* THESE PEOPLE ANYWAY, THINKING THEY CAN DRAG ME OFF LIKE THIS?
I DON'T *FEEL* LIKE TAKING A BATH OR A...
...A...
SNIFFLE
BRR! *COLD!*
OH, YŪHI!
YOUR HAIR IS SOPPING WET. YOU MUST BE *FREEZ-ING!*
I'M *FINE!* I JUST GOT CHANGED.
THAT WON'T DO, YOU'LL CATCH A DREADFUL COLD! GO IN AND GET WARMED UP!
ちゃぷん

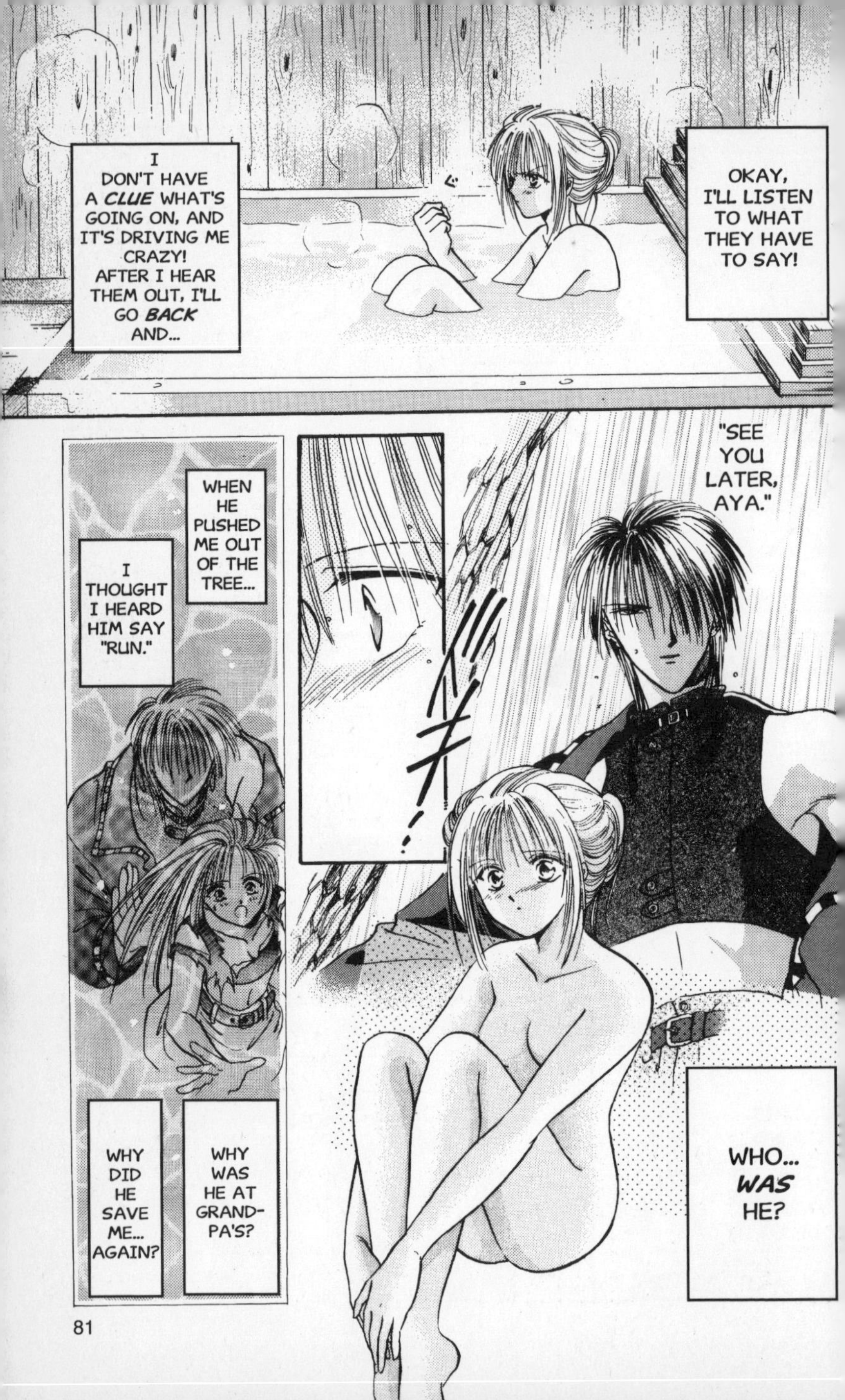
OKAY, I'LL LISTEN TO WHAT THEY HAVE TO SAY!
I DON'T HAVE A *CLUE* WHAT'S GOING ON, AND IT'S DRIVING ME CRAZY! AFTER I HEAR THEM OUT, I'LL GO *BACK* AND...
"SEE YOU LATER, AYA."
WHO... *WAS* HE?
WHEN HE PUSHED ME OUT OF THE TREE...
I THOUGHT I HEARD HIM SAY "RUN."
WHY WAS HE AT GRAND-PA'S?
WHY DID HE SAVE ME... AGAIN?

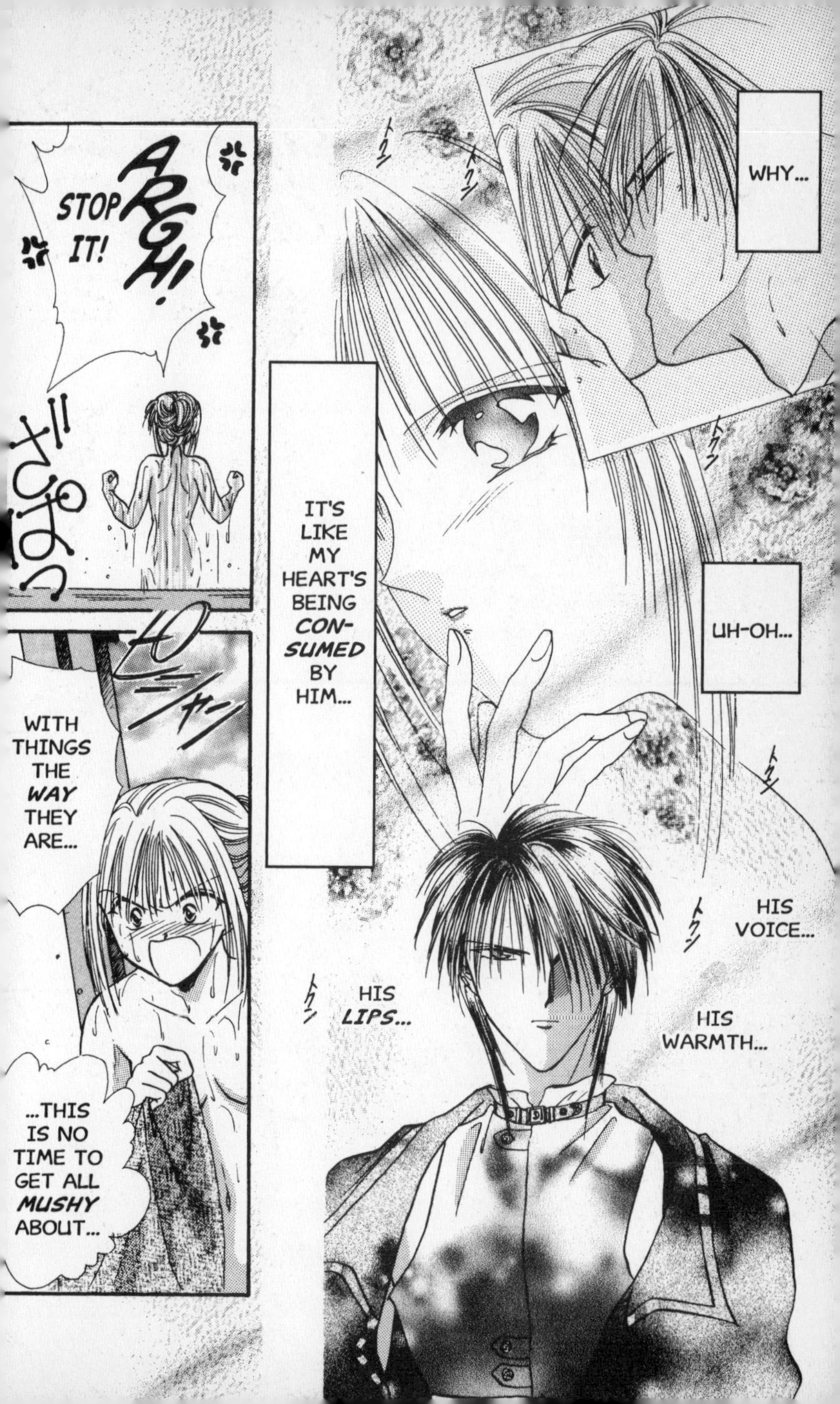

WHY...
UH-OH...
IT'S LIKE MY HEART'S BEING *CON-SUMED* BY HIM...
HIS VOICE...
HIS WARMTH...
HIS *LIPS*...
ARGH!
STOP IT!
WITH THINGS THE *WAY* THEY ARE...
...THIS IS NO TIME TO GET ALL *MUSHY* ABOUT...

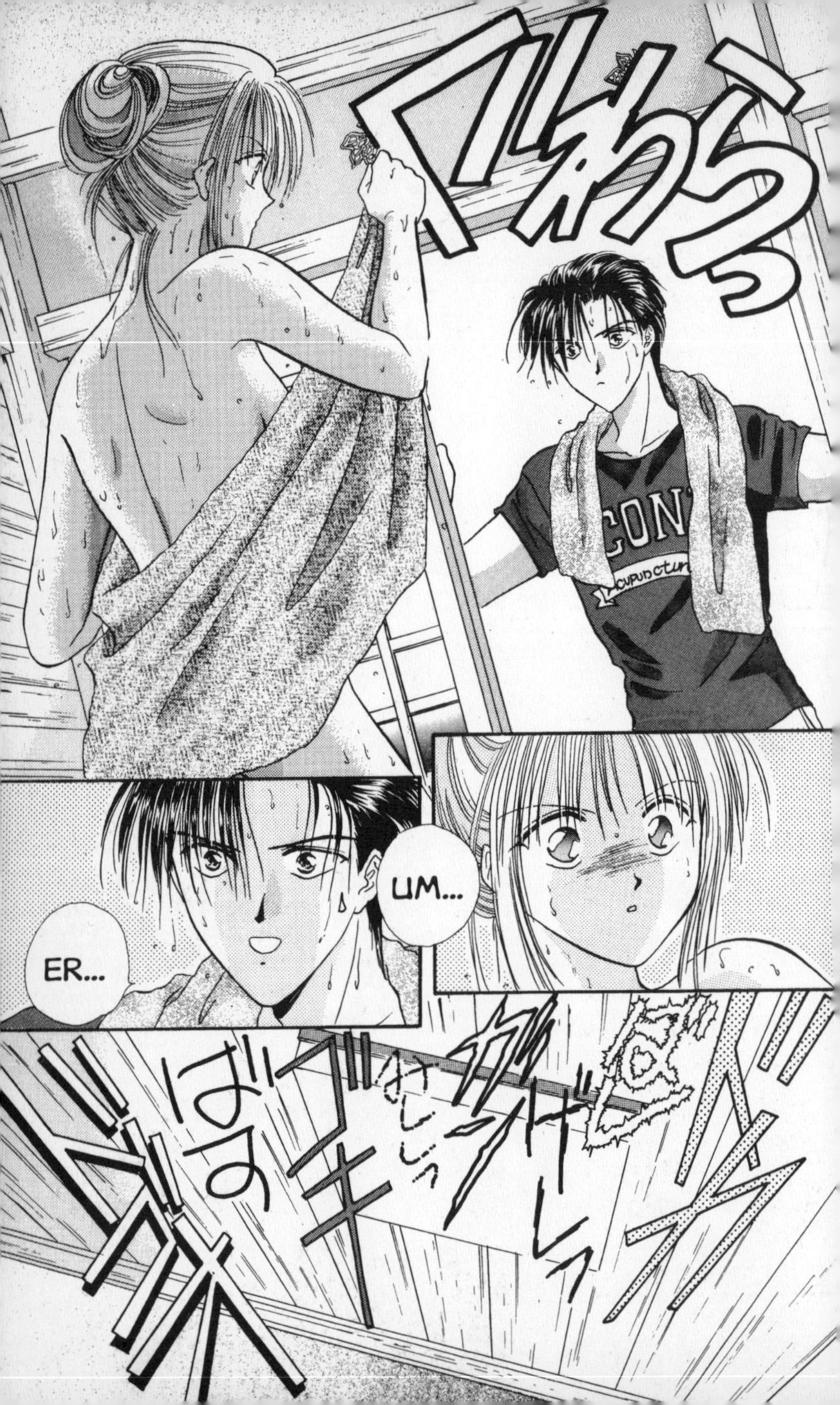
UM...
ER...

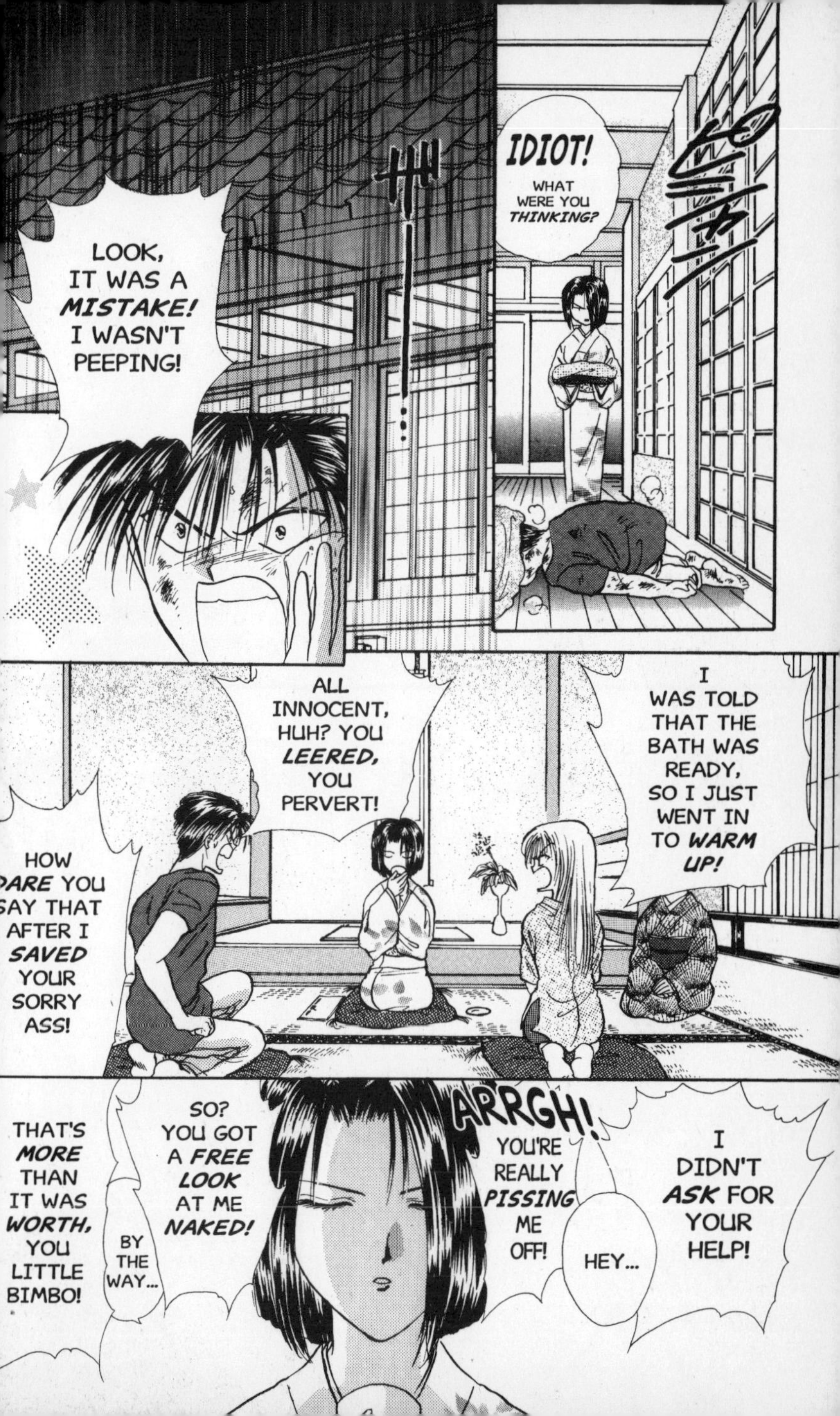
IDIOT! WHAT WERE YOU THINKING?
LOOK, IT WAS A MISTAKE! I WASN'T PEEPING!
I WAS TOLD THAT THE BATH WAS READY, SO I JUST WENT IN TO WARM UP!
ALL INNOCENT, HUH? YOU LEERED, YOU PERVERT!
HOW DARE YOU SAY THAT AFTER I SAVED YOUR SORRY ASS!
I DIDN'T ASK FOR YOUR HELP!
ARRGH!
YOU'RE REALLY PISSING ME OFF!
HEY...
BY THE WAY...
SO? YOU GOT A FREE LOOK AT ME NAKED!
THAT'S MORE THAN IT WAS WORTH, YOU LITTLE BIMBO!

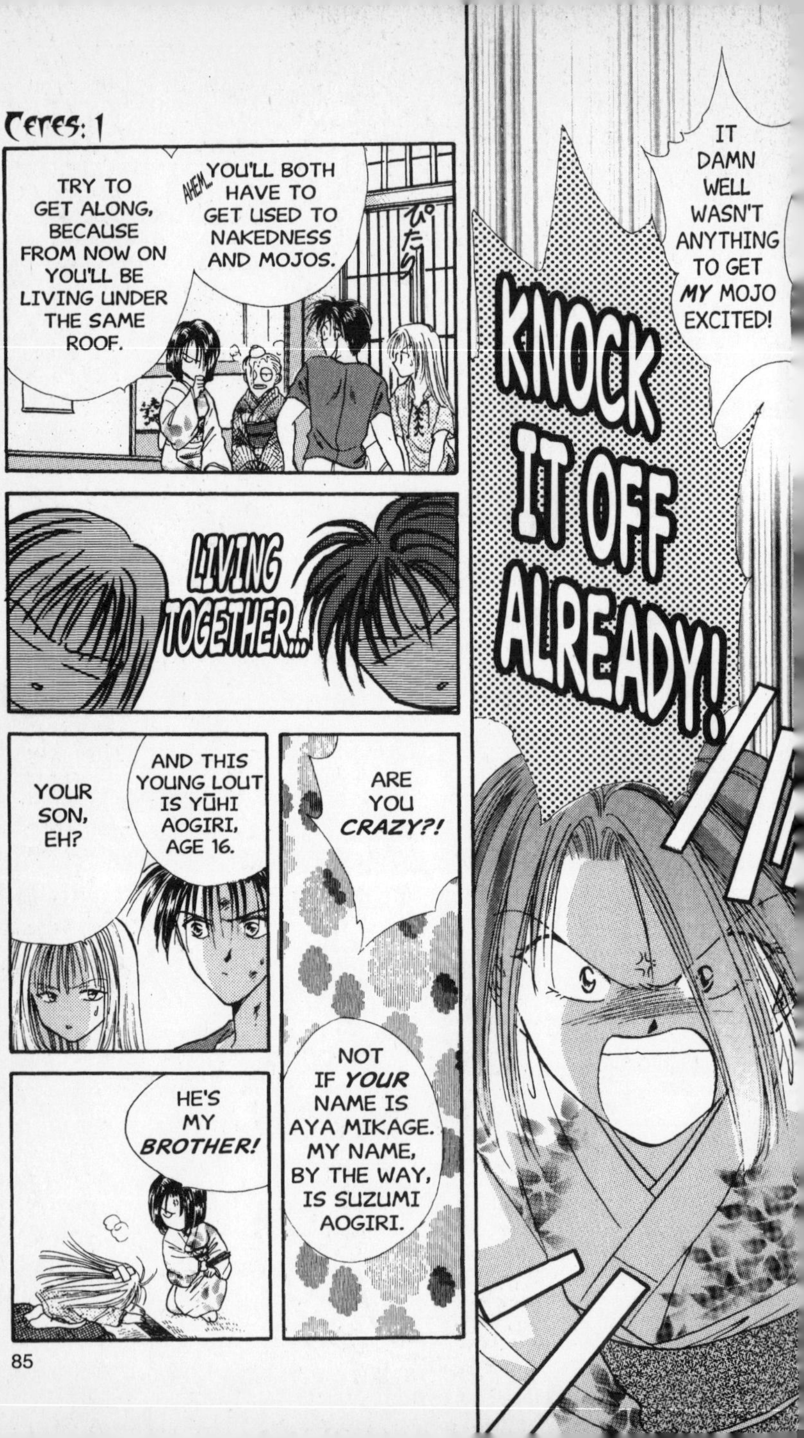
IT DAMN WELL WASN'T ANYTHING TO GET *MY* MOJO EXCITED!
KNOCK IT OFF ALREADY!
AHEM...
YOU'LL BOTH HAVE TO GET USED TO NAKEDNESS AND MOJOS.
ぴたり
TRY TO GET ALONG, BECAUSE FROM NOW ON YOU'LL BE LIVING UNDER THE SAME ROOF.
LIVING TOGETHER...
ARE YOU *CRAZY?!*
NOT IF *YOUR* NAME IS AYA MIKAGE. MY NAME, BY THE WAY, IS SUZUMI AOGIRI.
AND THIS YOUNG LOUT IS YŪHI AOGIRI, AGE 16.
YOUR SON, EH?
HE'S MY *BROTHER!*

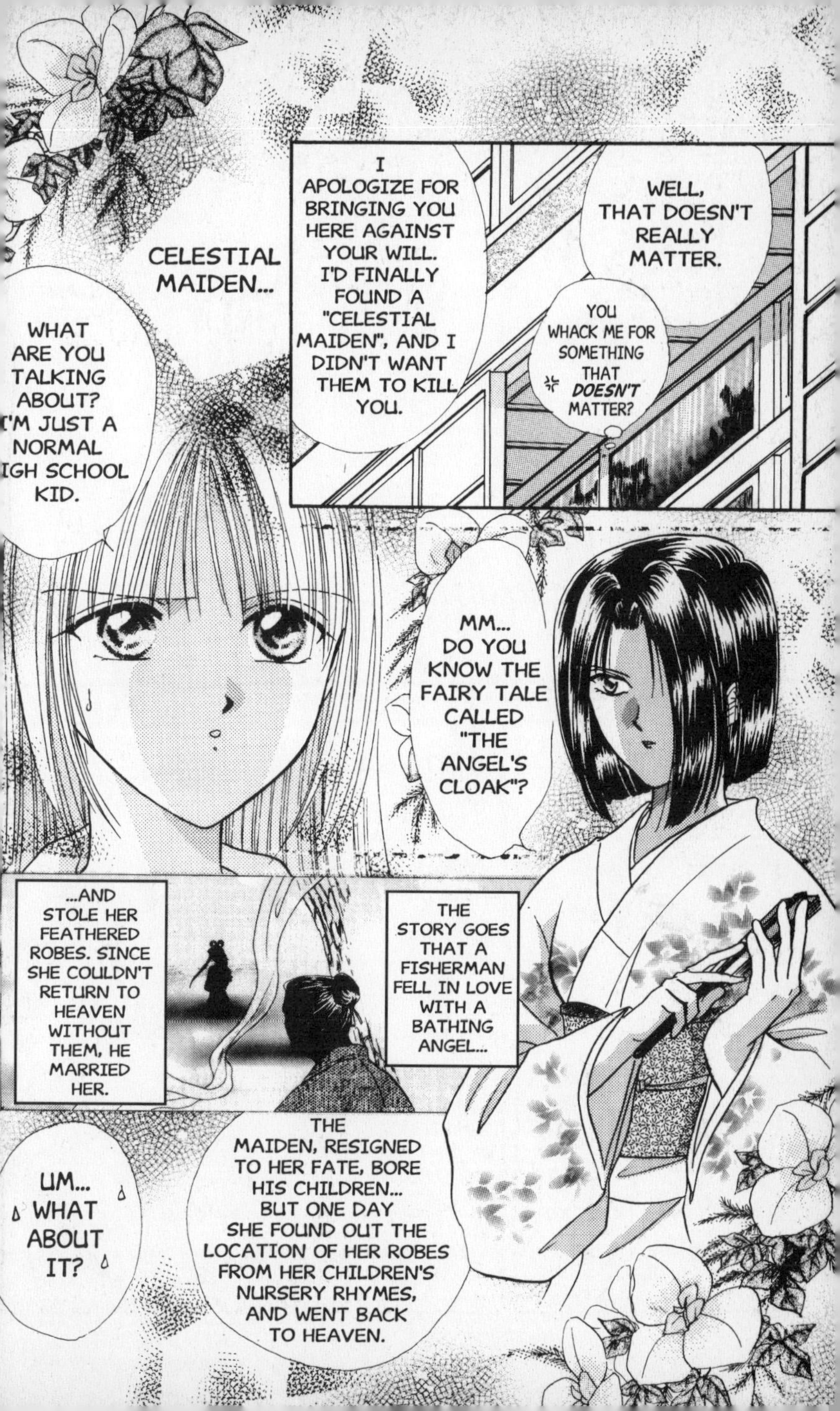
WELL, THAT DOESN'T REALLY MATTER.
YOU WHACK ME FOR SOMETHING THAT DOESN'T MATTER?
I APOLOGIZE FOR BRINGING YOU HERE AGAINST YOUR WILL. I'D FINALLY FOUND A "CELESTIAL MAIDEN", AND I DIDN'T WANT THEM TO KILL YOU.
CELESTIAL MAIDEN...
WHAT ARE YOU TALKING ABOUT? I'M JUST A NORMAL IGH SCHOOL KID.
MM... DO YOU KNOW THE FAIRY TALE CALLED "THE ANGEL'S CLOAK"?
THE STORY GOES THAT A FISHERMAN FELL IN LOVE WITH A BATHING ANGEL...
...AND STOLE HER FEATHERED ROBES. SINCE SHE COULDN'T RETURN TO HEAVEN WITHOUT THEM, HE MARRIED HER.
THE MAIDEN, RESIGNED TO HER FATE, BORE HIS CHILDREN... BUT ONE DAY SHE FOUND OUT THE LOCATION OF HER ROBES FROM HER CHILDREN'S NURSERY RHYMES, AND WENT BACK TO HEAVEN.
UM... WHAT ABOUT IT?

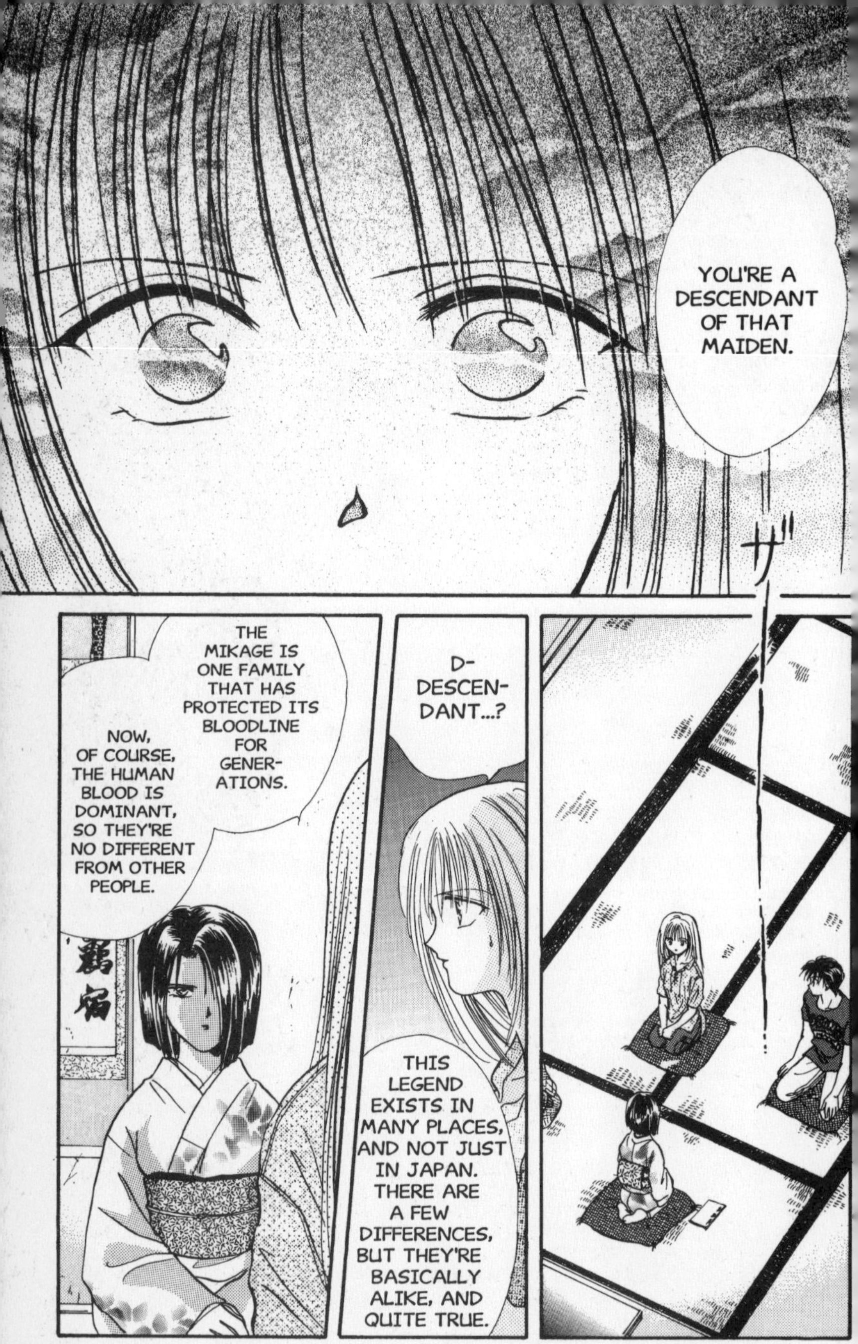
YOU'RE A DESCENDANT OF THAT MAIDEN.
ザ
D-DESCENDANT...?
THIS LEGEND EXISTS IN MANY PLACES, AND NOT JUST IN JAPAN. THERE ARE A FEW DIFFERENCES, BUT THEY'RE BASICALLY ALIKE, AND QUITE TRUE.
THE MIKAGE IS ONE FAMILY THAT HAS PROTECTED ITS BLOODLINE FOR GENERATIONS.
NOW, OF COURSE, THE HUMAN BLOOD IS DOMINANT, SO THEY'RE NO DIFFERENT FROM OTHER PEOPLE.

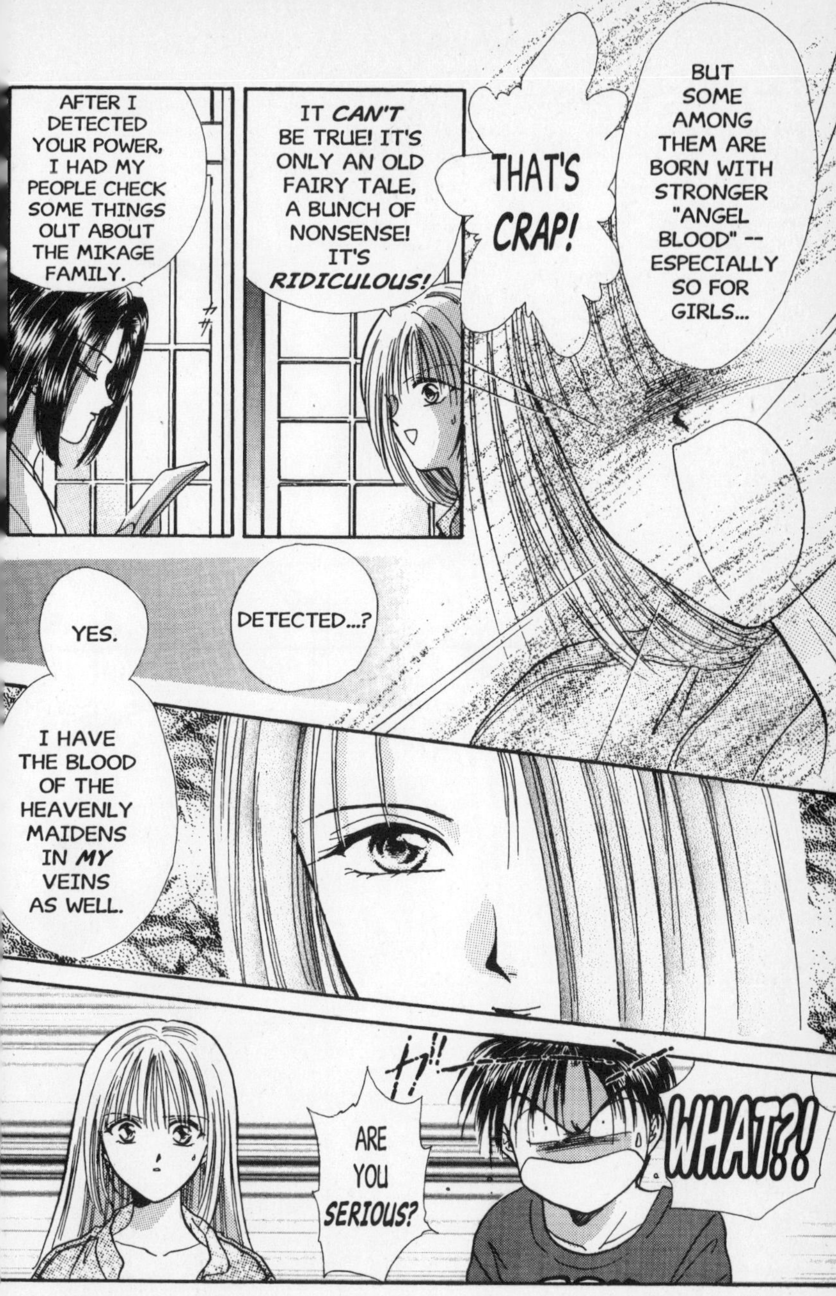

BUT SOME AMONG THEM ARE BORN WITH STRONGER "ANGEL BLOOD" -- ESPECIALLY SO FOR GIRLS...
THAT'S CRAP!
IT *CAN'T* BE TRUE! IT'S ONLY AN OLD FAIRY TALE, A BUNCH OF NONSENSE! IT'S *RIDICULOUS!*
AFTER I DETECTED YOUR POWER, I HAD MY PEOPLE CHECK SOME THINGS OUT ABOUT THE MIKAGE FAMILY.
DETECTED...?
YES.
I HAVE THE BLOOD OF THE HEAVENLY MAIDENS IN *MY* VEINS AS WELL.
WHAT?!
ARE YOU *SERIOUS?*

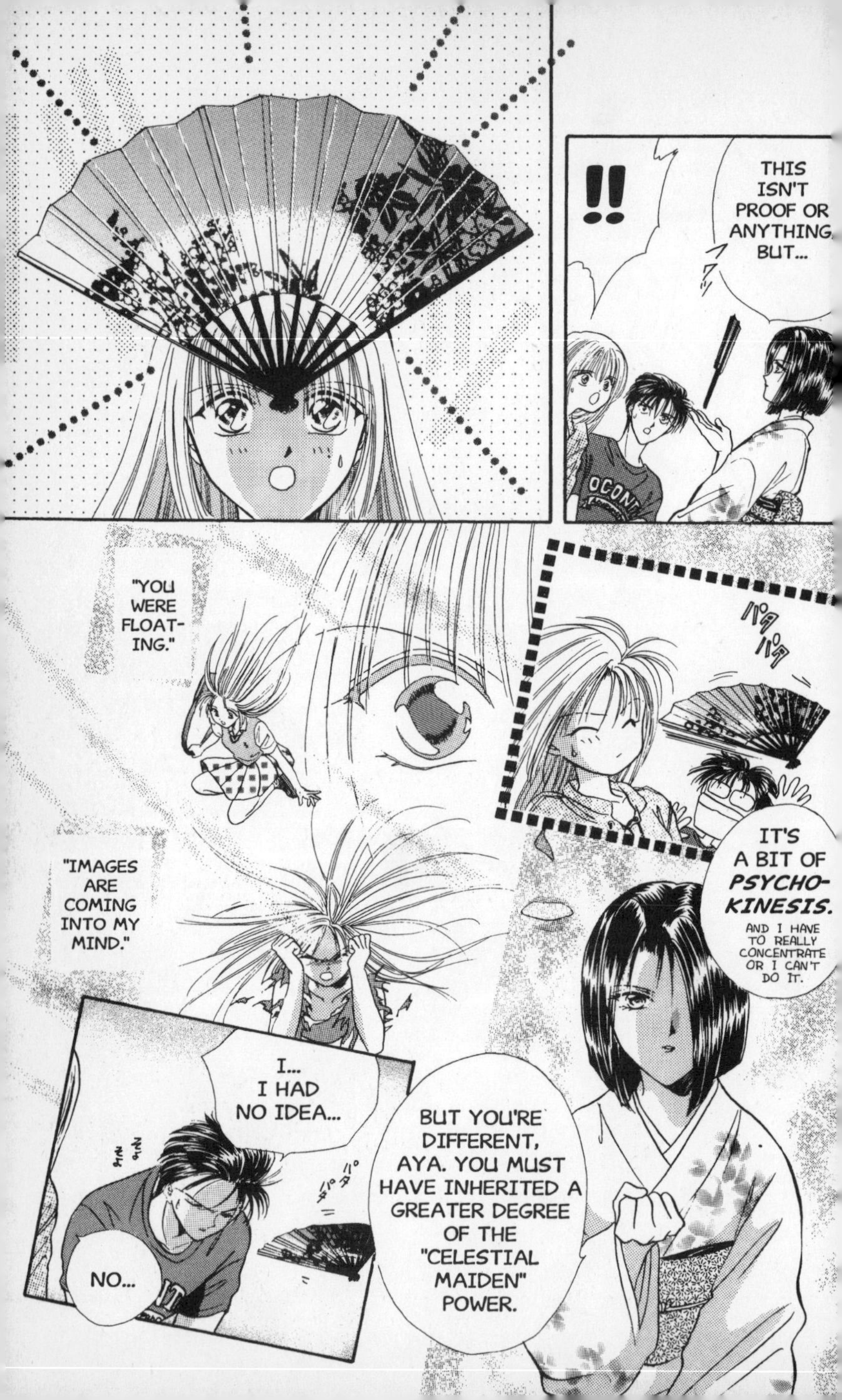
!!
THIS ISN'T PROOF OR ANYTHING, BUT...
パタ パタ
IT'S A BIT OF *PSYCHOKINESIS.*
AND I HAVE TO REALLY CONCENTRATE OR I CAN'T DO IT.
"YOU WERE FLOATING."
"IMAGES ARE COMING INTO MY MIND."
BUT YOU'RE DIFFERENT, AYA. YOU MUST HAVE INHERITED A GREATER DEGREE OF THE "CELESTIAL MAIDEN" POWER.
I... I HAD NO IDEA...
NO...

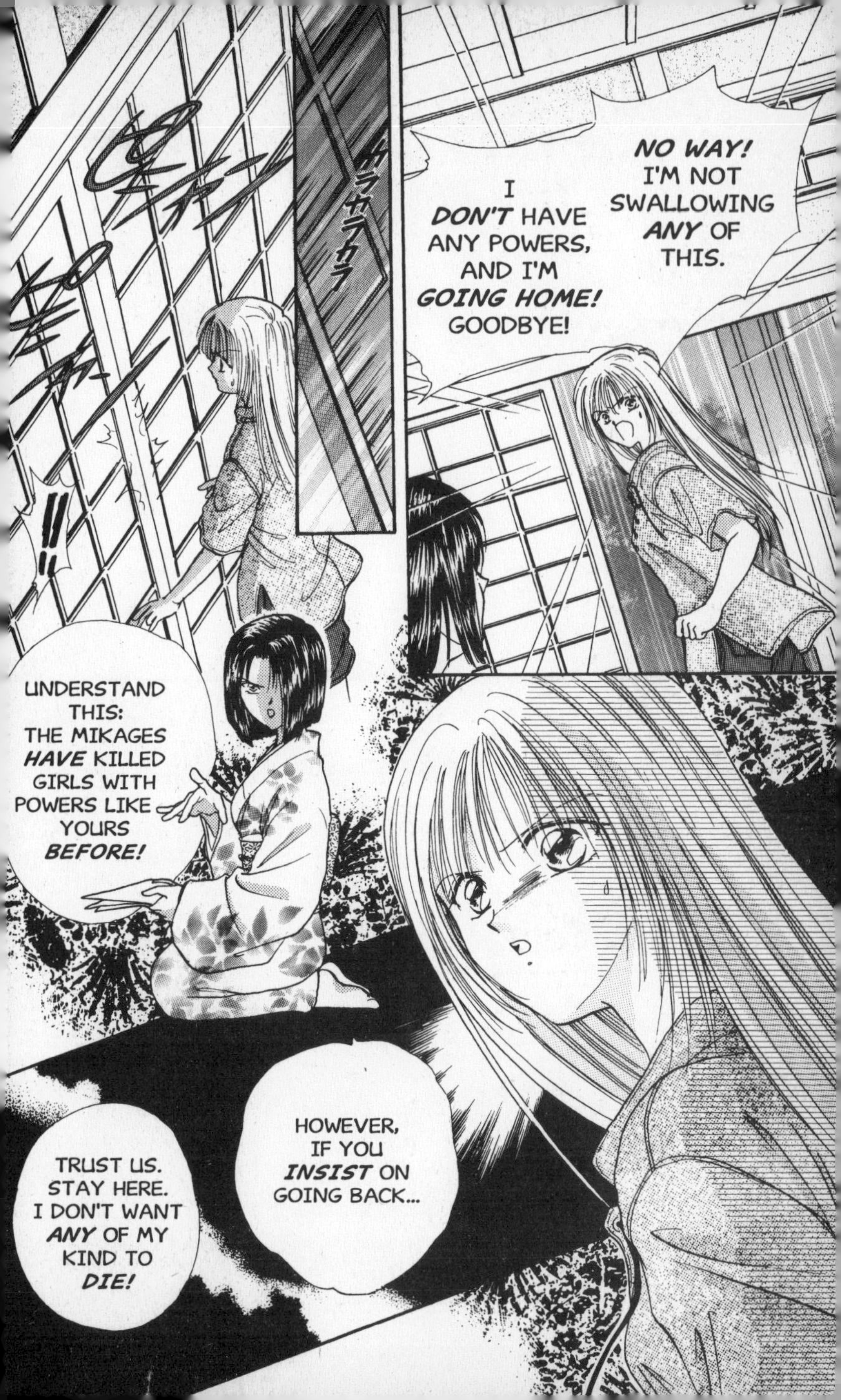
NO WAY! I'M NOT SWALLOWING ANY OF THIS.
I DON'T HAVE ANY POWERS, AND I'M GOING HOME! GOODBYE!
!!
UNDERSTAND THIS: THE MIKAGES HAVE KILLED GIRLS WITH POWERS LIKE YOURS BEFORE!
HOWEVER, IF YOU INSIST ON GOING BACK...
TRUST US. STAY HERE. I DON'T WANT ANY OF MY KIND TO DIE!

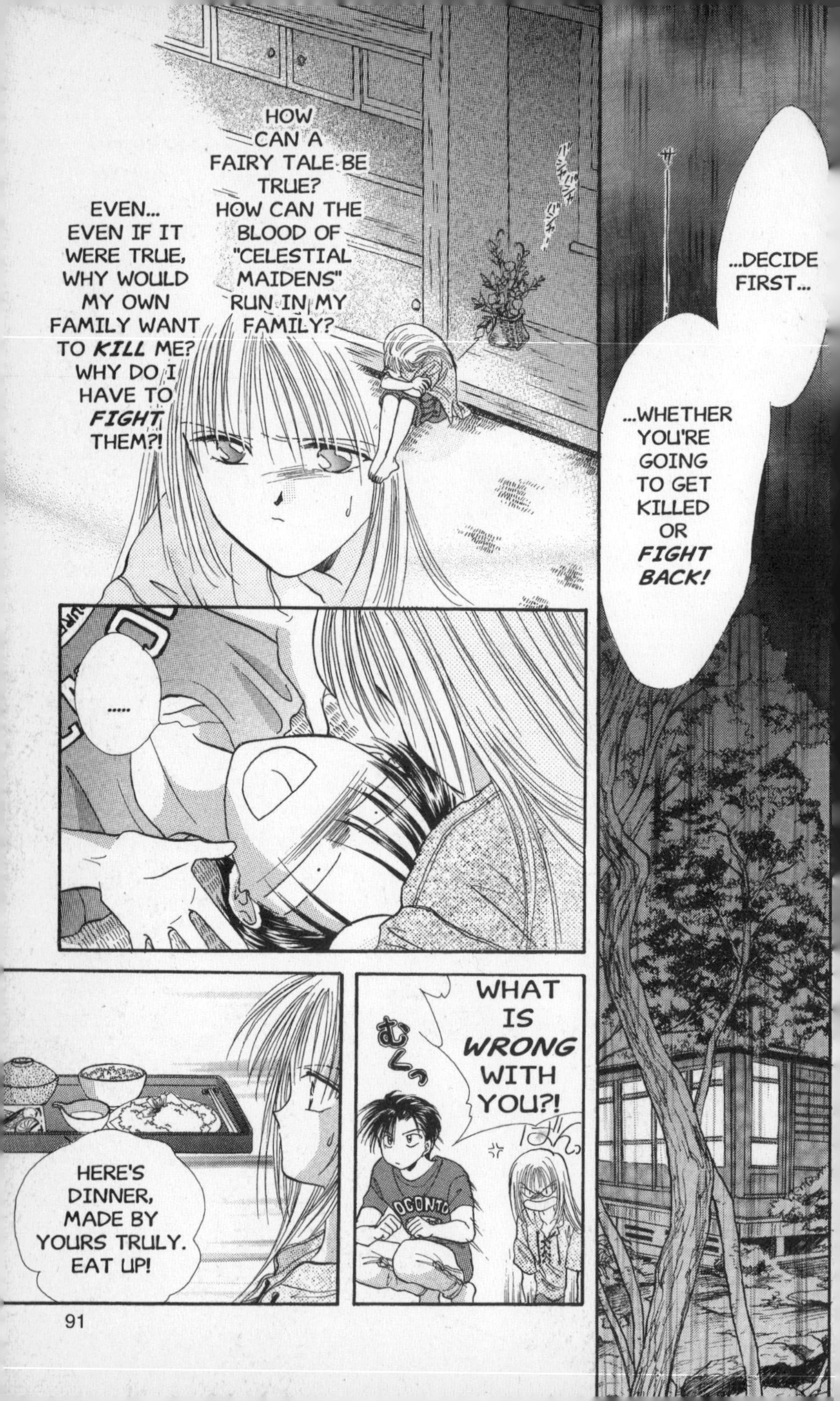
...DECIDE FIRST...
...WHETHER YOU'RE GOING TO GET KILLED OR FIGHT BACK!
HOW CAN A FAIRY TALE BE TRUE? HOW CAN THE BLOOD OF "CELESTIAL MAIDENS" RUN IN MY FAMILY?
EVEN... EVEN IF IT WERE TRUE, WHY WOULD MY OWN FAMILY WANT TO KILL ME? WHY DO I HAVE TO FIGHT THEM?!
.....
WHAT IS WRONG WITH YOU?!
HERE'S DINNER, MADE BY YOURS TRULY. EAT UP!

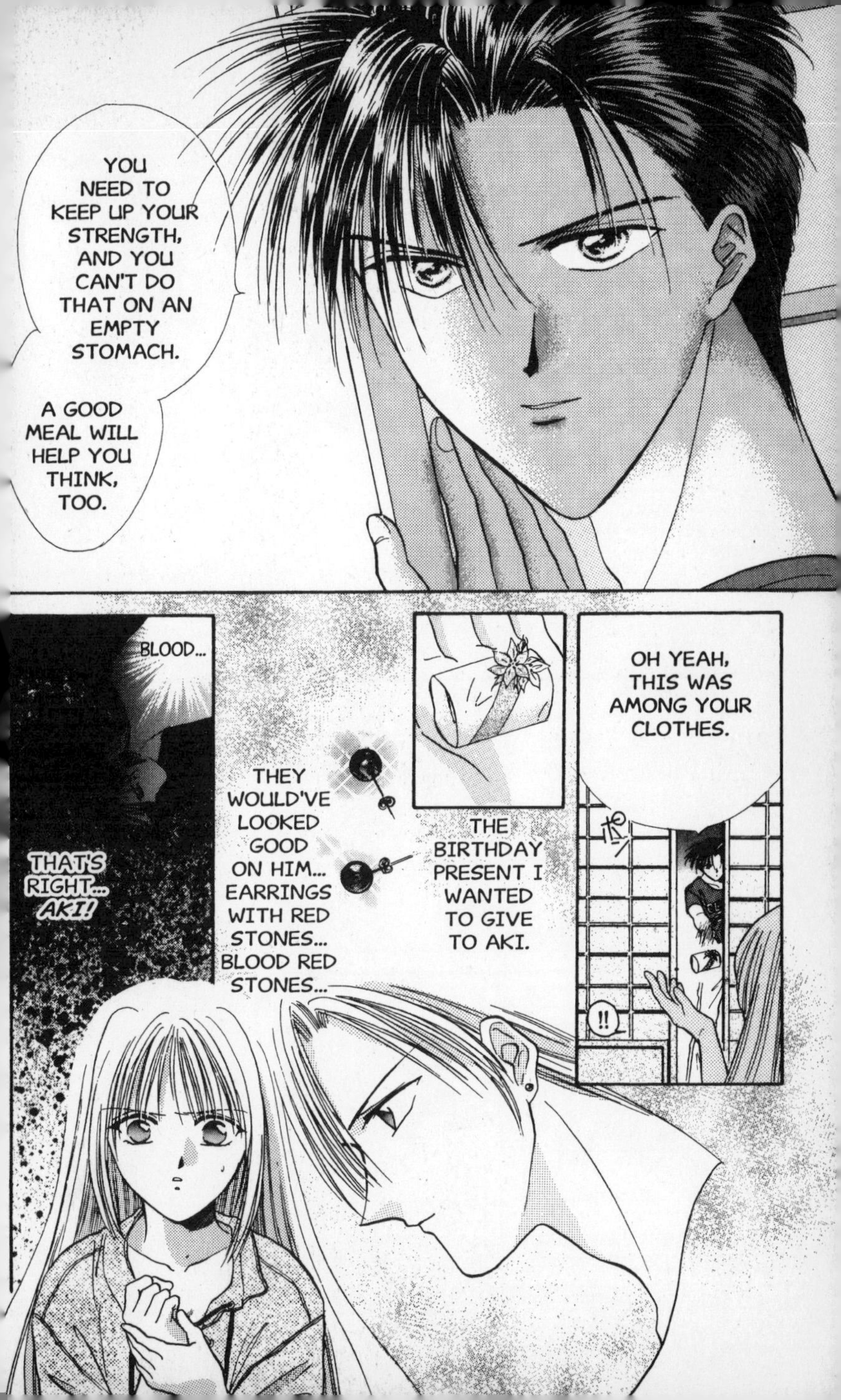
YOU NEED TO KEEP UP YOUR STRENGTH, AND YOU CAN'T DO THAT ON AN EMPTY STOMACH.
A GOOD MEAL WILL HELP YOU THINK, TOO.
OH YEAH, THIS WAS AMONG YOUR CLOTHES.
!!
THE BIRTHDAY PRESENT I WANTED TO GIVE TO AKI.
THEY WOULD'VE LOOKED GOOD ON HIM... EARRINGS WITH RED STONES... BLOOD RED STONES...
BLOOD...
THAT'S RIGHT... AKI!

◆ Aya ◆

But really, voice actors are funny. They're great entertainers. Oh, the theater announcements (before the event started) were done by Tamahome in Osaka, and Chichiri in Tokyo, and Mr. Seki said stuff like, "please, no flash photography-no da," just like Chichiri! I laughed at the end when he mumbled, "oh, i'm pooped-no da." It made me happy that it sounded like it was the characters talking. In Tokyo, at the Q&A session, there were some impromptu questions from the audience as well, which made me nervous. When they asked, "Isn't there going to be any more FY manga" and I answered something like "basically," some voices piped up that said "novels!" Wow, you hadn't forgotten! But it was awesome to see the first OAV episode on the big screen and with surround sound -- just like in the movies! Mr. Motohashi had shown it to me before on a TVset, but I was still oohing and ahhing. By the way, while it was playing, my editor and I sneaked into the back of the audience and watched it along with everyone else! ~♫ Bet nobody noticed. But the parts where the audience reacted were different in Tokyo and Osaka. Episode 1 is full of mysteries, so I was wondering what they'd think. The murmuring at the end was louder in Osaka.

In any case, even though I'm the creator, I did nothing for this OAV. The director had made up the story, so I felt relieved that I wasn't responsible of anything! ~♫ But in the new ending credits, there were all these embarrassing drawings I've done! Even some old ones. And on the big screen! (whaahh!)

Oh, the ending sequence is different from the one shown to the one sold on video.

There were even more illustrations in the video!

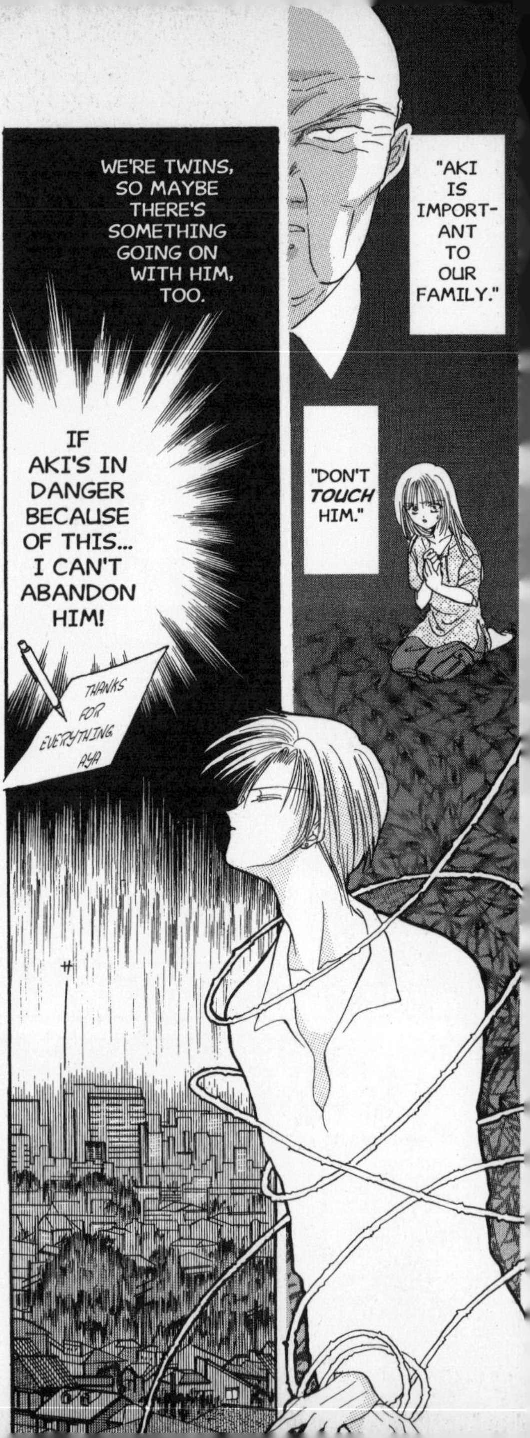
"AKI IS IMPORTANT TO OUR FAMILY."
"DON'T *TOUCH* HIM."
WE'RE TWINS, SO MAYBE THERE'S SOMETHING GOING ON WITH HIM, TOO.
IF AKI'S IN DANGER BECAUSE OF THIS... I CAN'T ABANDON HIM!
THANKS FOR EVERYTHING. AYA

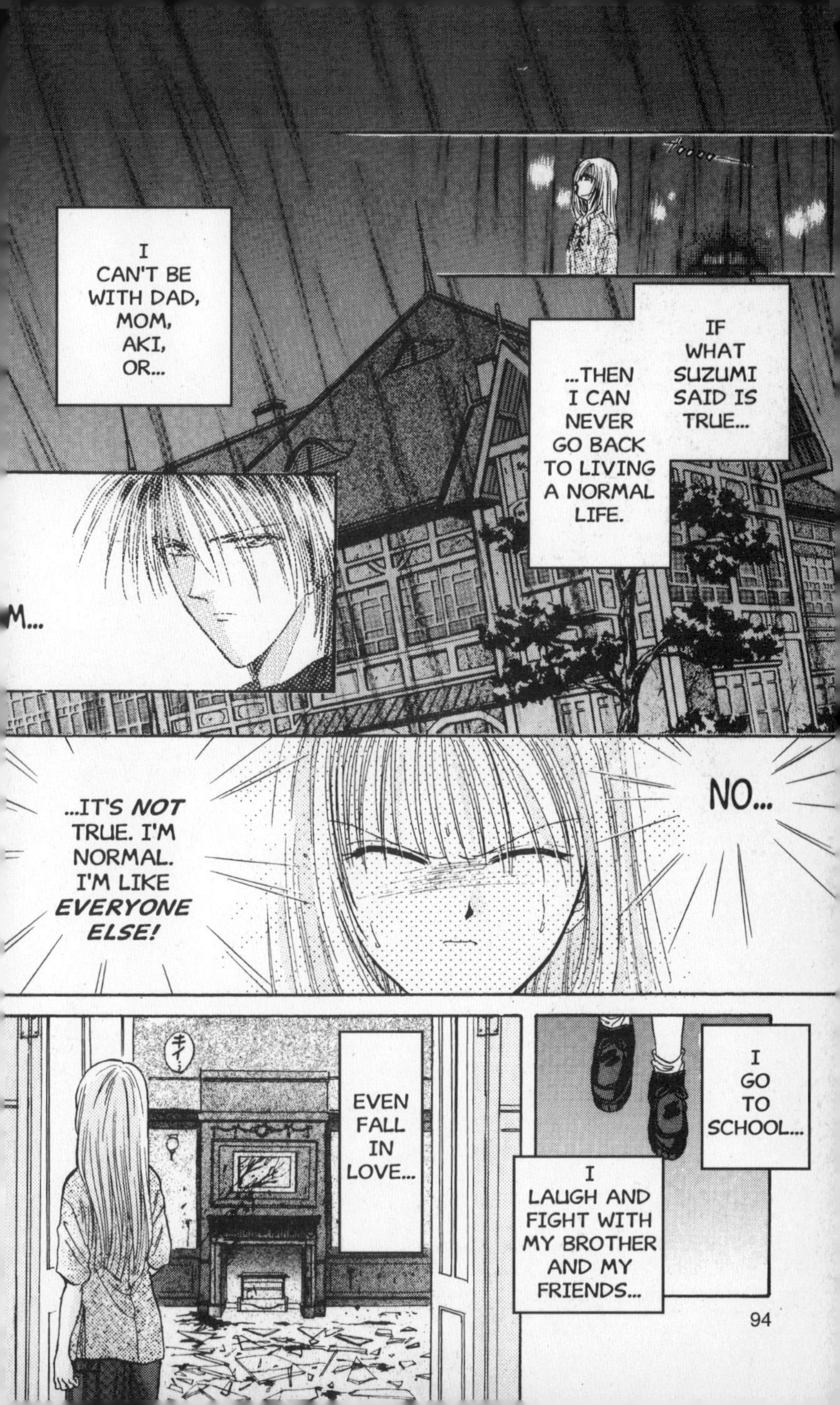

IF WHAT SUZUMI SAID IS TRUE...
...THEN I CAN NEVER GO BACK TO LIVING A NORMAL LIFE.
I CAN'T BE WITH DAD, MOM, AKI, OR...
M...
NO...
...IT'S *NOT* TRUE. I'M NORMAL. I'M LIKE *EVERYONE ELSE!*
I GO TO SCHOOL...
I LAUGH AND FIGHT WITH MY BROTHER AND MY FRIENDS...
キイ
EVEN FALL IN LOVE...

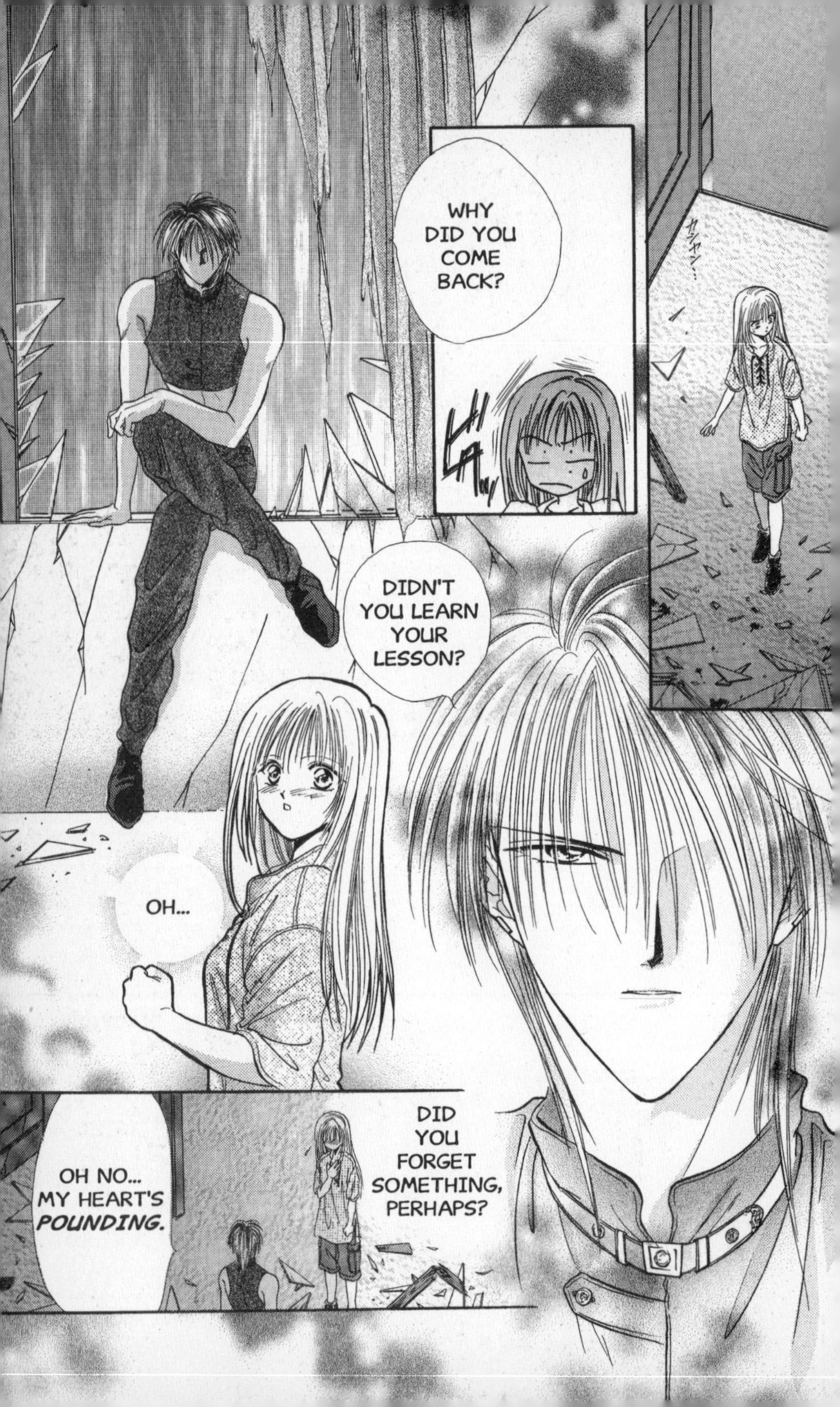
WHY DID YOU COME BACK?
DIDN'T YOU LEARN YOUR LESSON?
OH...
DID YOU FORGET SOMETHING, PERHAPS?
OH NO... MY HEART'S *POUNDING.*

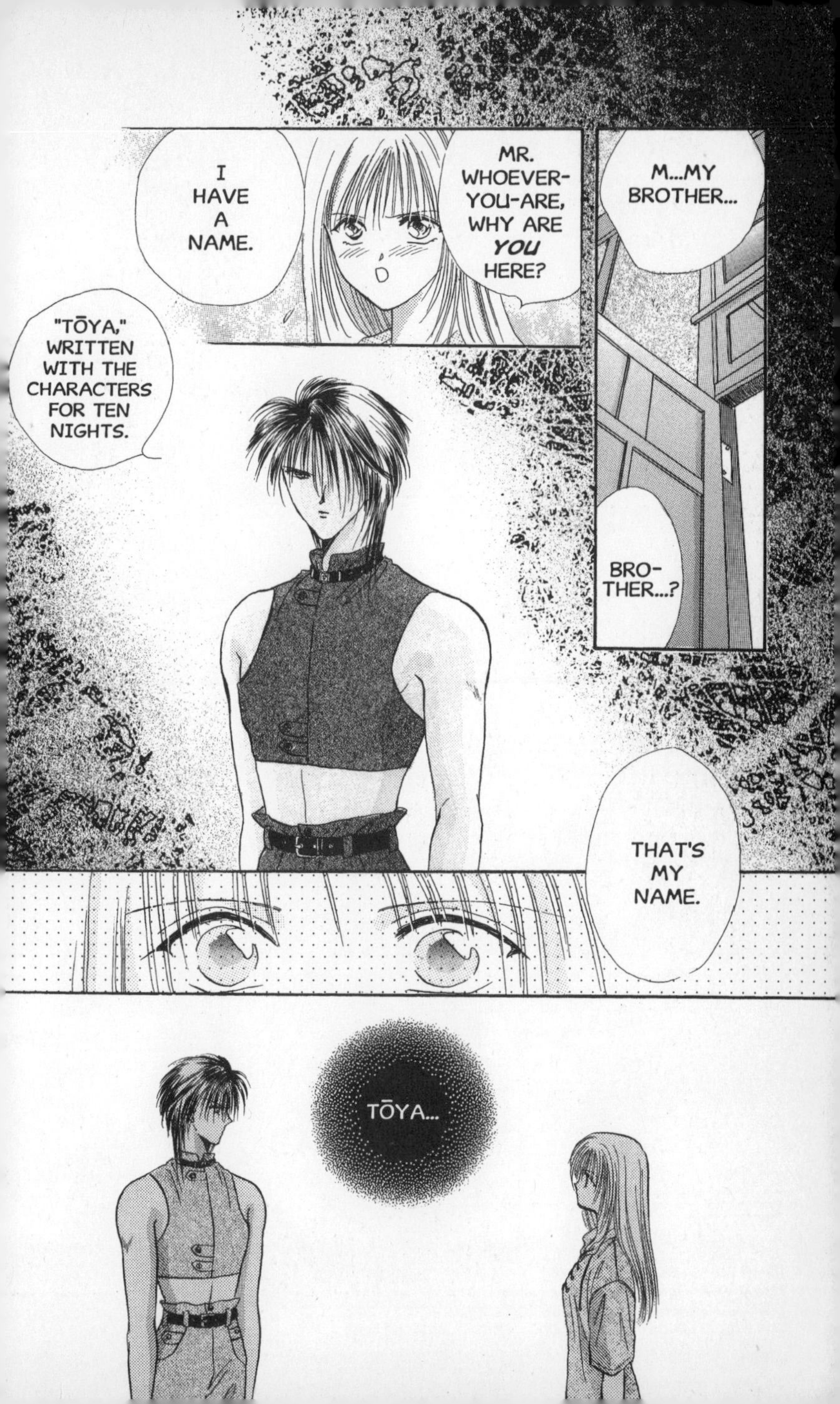
M...MY BROTHER...
BRO-THER...?
MR. WHOEVER-YOU-ARE, WHY ARE *YOU* HERE?
I HAVE A NAME.
"TŌYA," WRITTEN WITH THE CHARACTERS FOR TEN NIGHTS.
THAT'S MY NAME.
TŌYA...

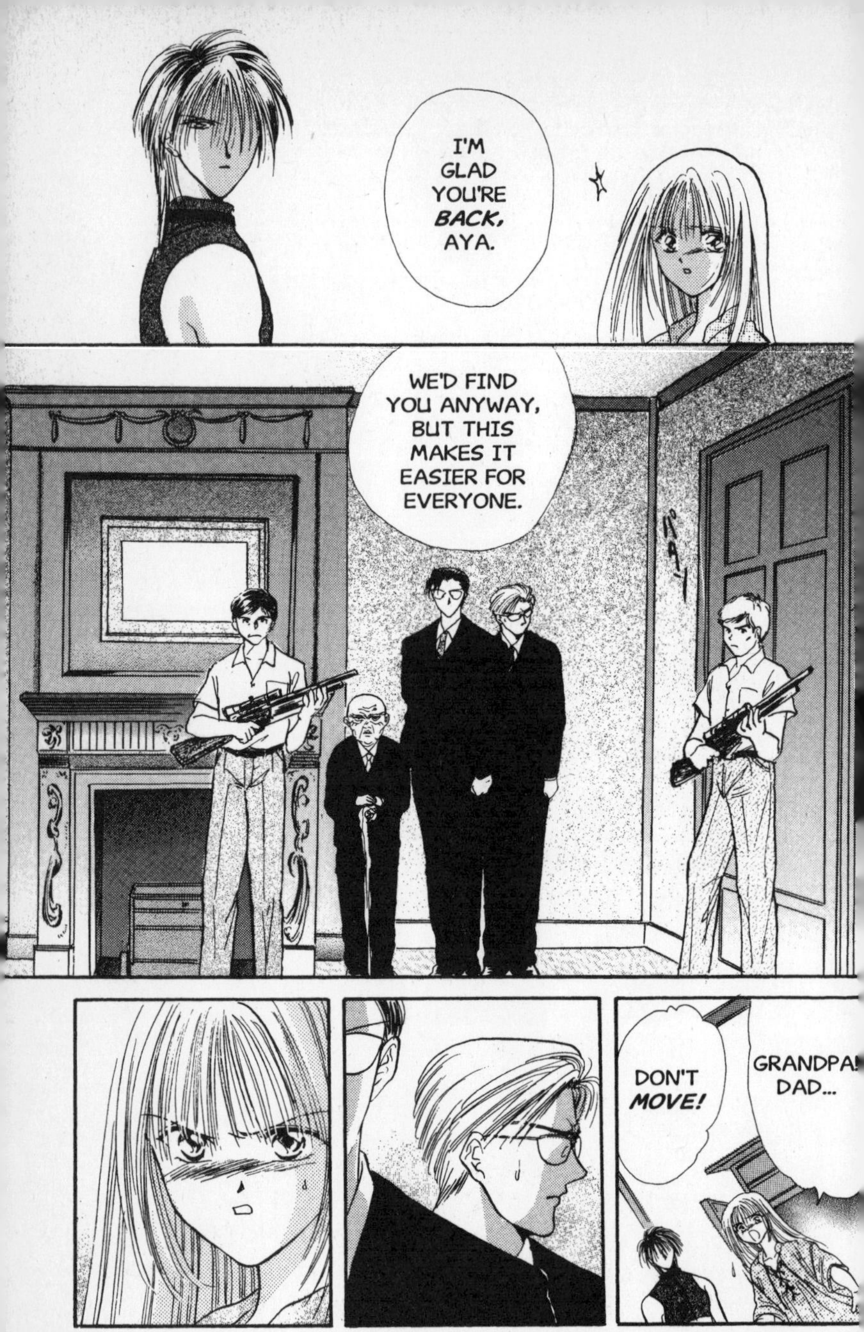
I'M GLAD YOU'RE BACK, AYA.
WE'D FIND YOU ANYWAY, BUT THIS MAKES IT EASIER FOR EVERYONE.
GRANDPA! DAD...
DON'T MOVE!

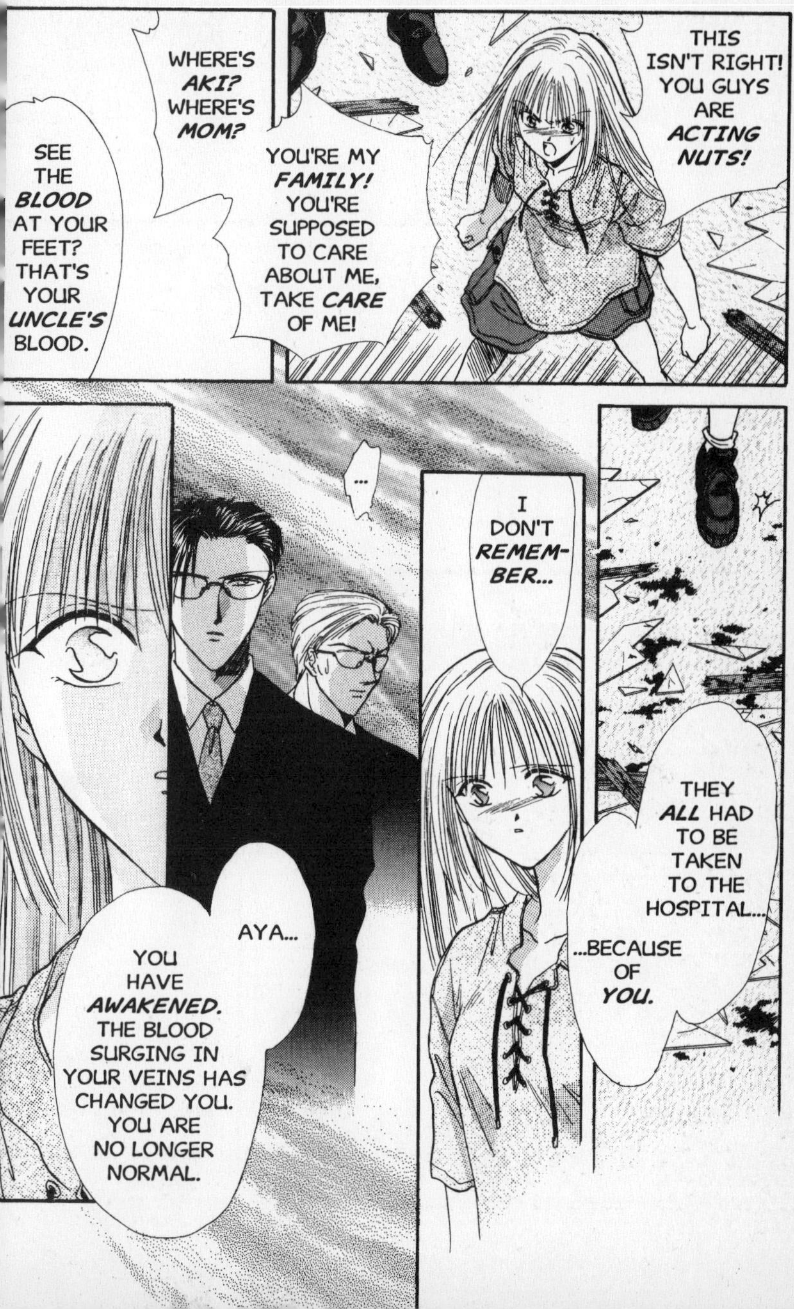
THIS ISN'T RIGHT! YOU GUYS ARE ACTING NUTS!
YOU'RE MY FAMILY! YOU'RE SUPPOSED TO CARE ABOUT ME, TAKE CARE OF ME!
WHERE'S AKI? WHERE'S MOM?
SEE THE BLOOD AT YOUR FEET? THAT'S YOUR UNCLE'S BLOOD.
THEY ALL HAD TO BE TAKEN TO THE HOSPITAL...
...BECAUSE OF YOU.
I DON'T REMEMBER...
...
AYA... YOU HAVE AWAKENED. THE BLOOD SURGING IN YOUR VEINS HAS CHANGED YOU. YOU ARE NO LONGER NORMAL.

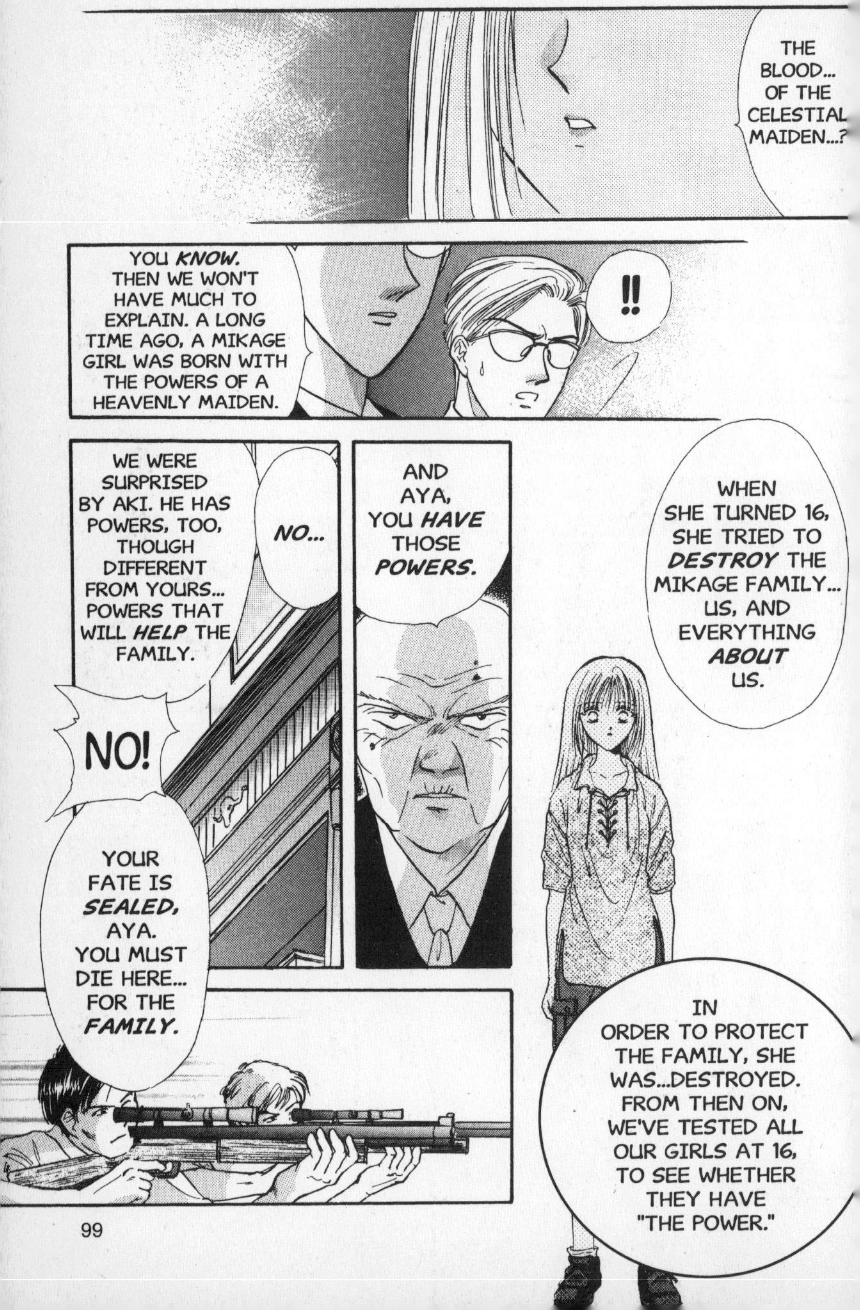
THE BLOOD... OF THE CELESTIAL MAIDEN...?
!!
YOU KNOW. THEN WE WON'T HAVE MUCH TO EXPLAIN. A LONG TIME AGO, A MIKAGE GIRL WAS BORN WITH THE POWERS OF A HEAVENLY MAIDEN.
WHEN SHE TURNED 16, SHE TRIED TO DESTROY THE MIKAGE FAMILY... US, AND EVERYTHING ABOUT US.
IN ORDER TO PROTECT THE FAMILY, SHE WAS...DESTROYED. FROM THEN ON, WE'VE TESTED ALL OUR GIRLS AT 16, TO SEE WHETHER THEY HAVE "THE POWER."
AND AYA, YOU HAVE THOSE POWERS.
NO...
WE WERE SURPRISED BY AKI. HE HAS POWERS, TOO, THOUGH DIFFERENT FROM YOURS... POWERS THAT WILL HELP THE FAMILY.
NO!
YOUR FATE IS SEALED, AYA. YOU MUST DIE HERE... FOR THE FAMILY.

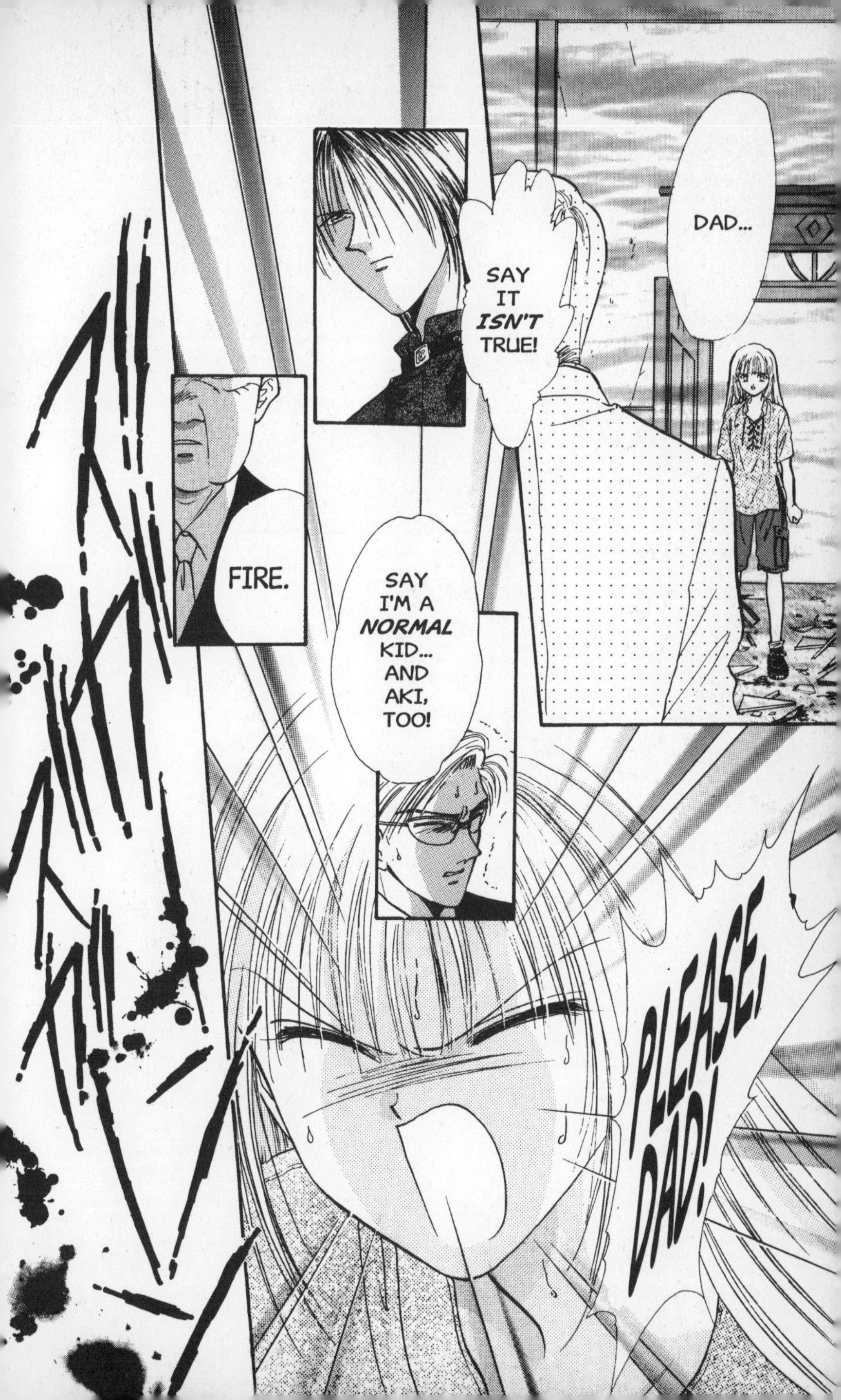
DAD...
SAY IT *ISN'T* TRUE!
SAY I'M A *NORMAL* KID... AND AKI, TOO!
PLEASE, DAD!
FIRE.

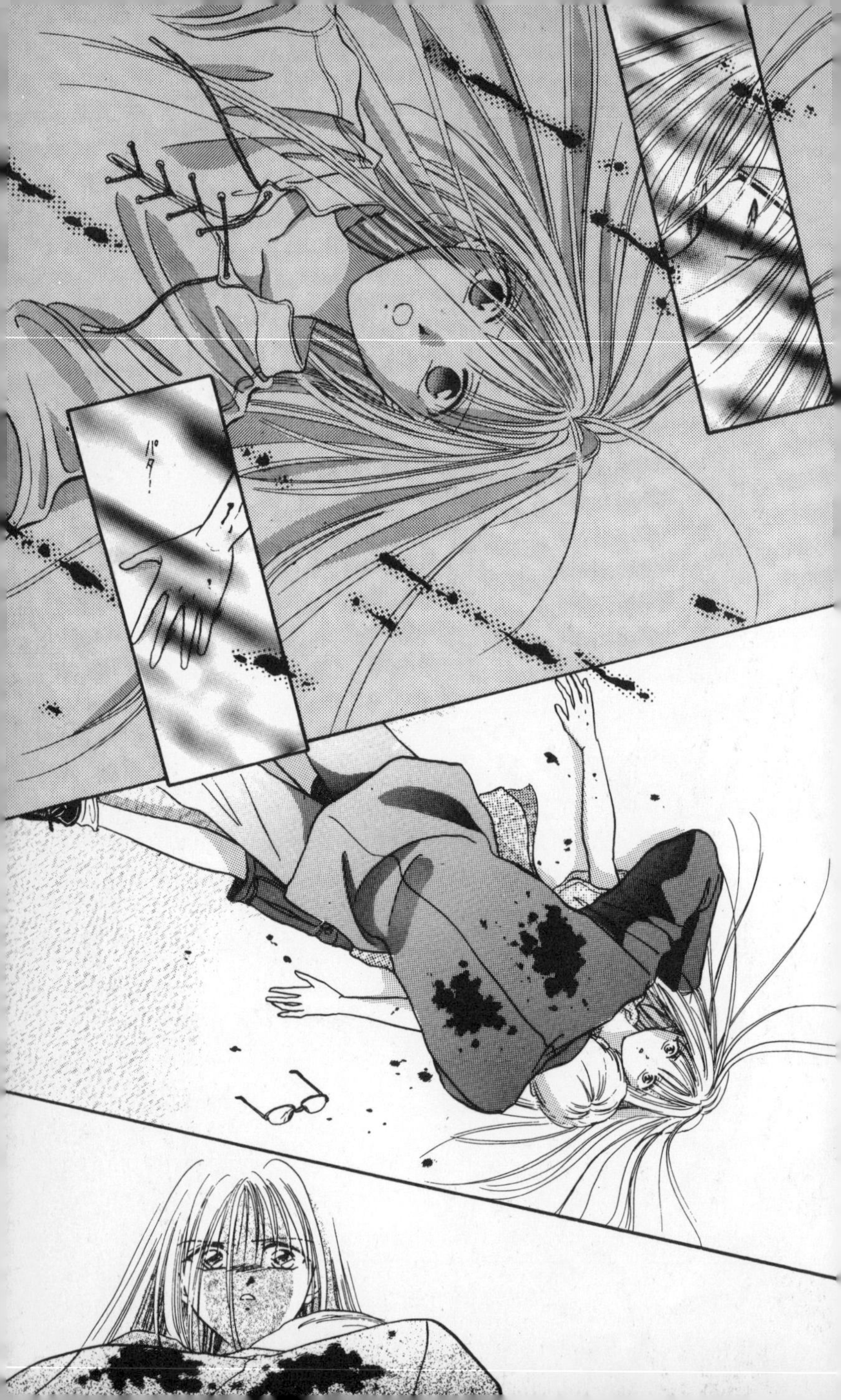
パタ！

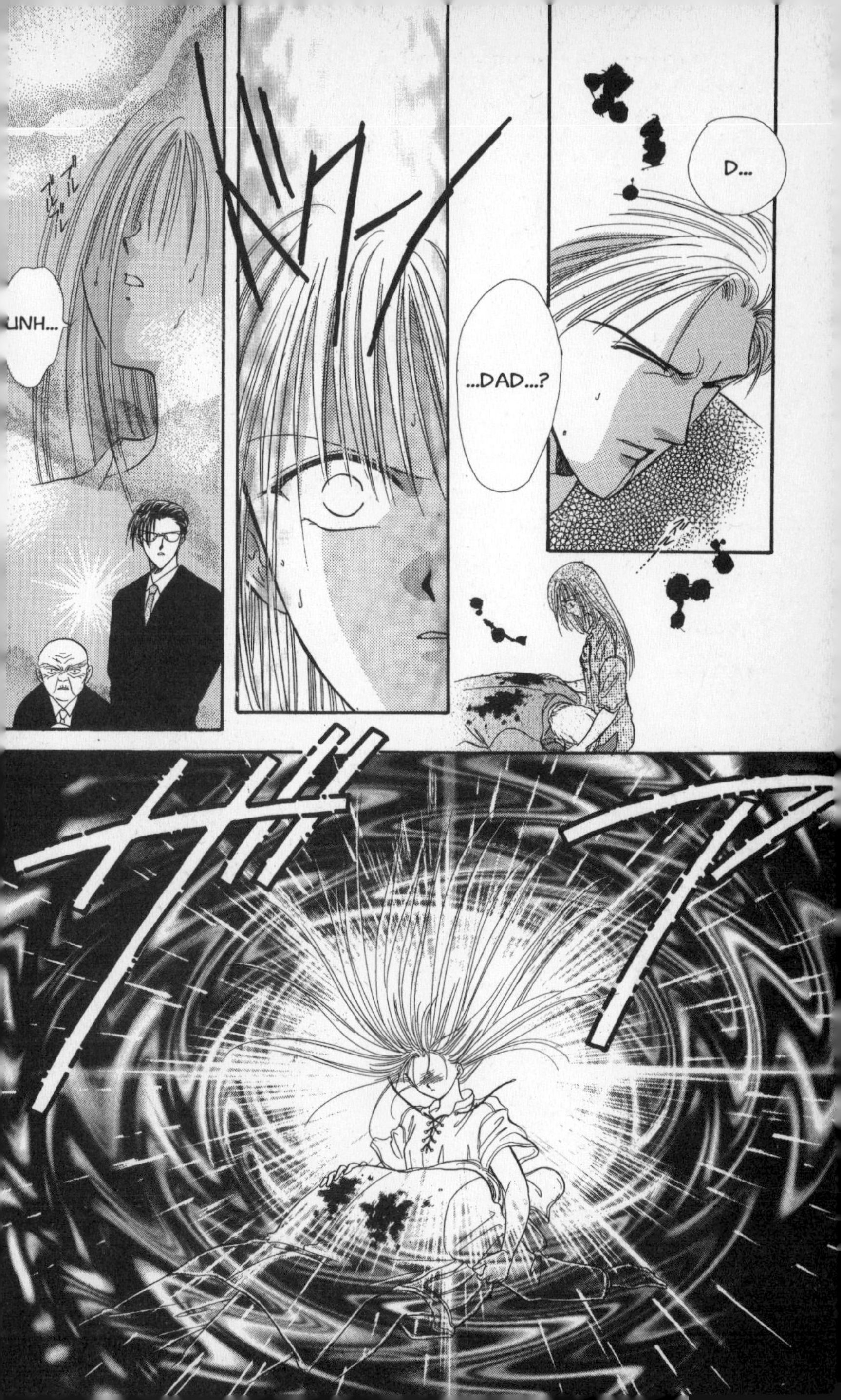
D...
...DAD...?
UNH...
ブルブル

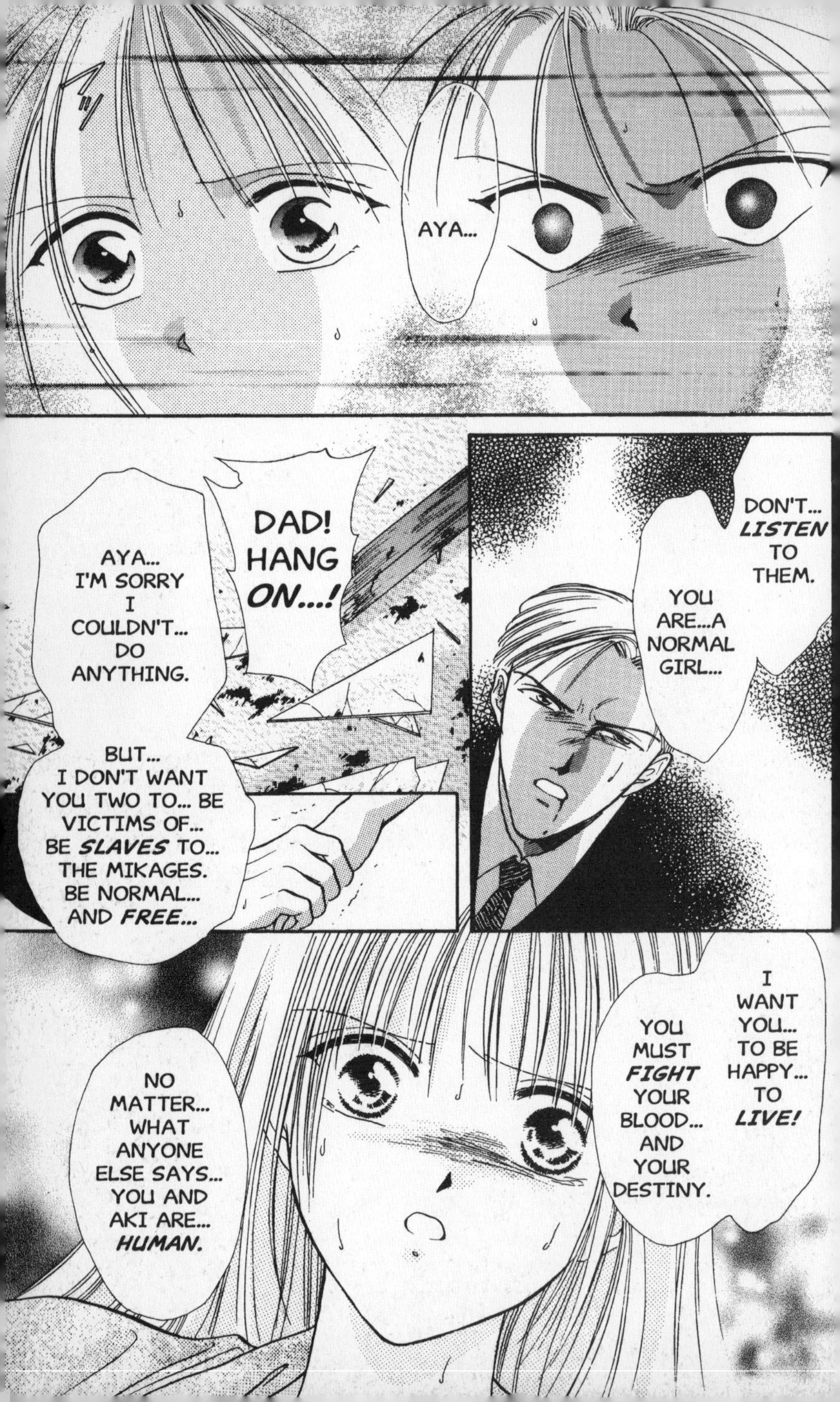
AYA...
DON'T... LISTEN TO THEM.
YOU ARE...A NORMAL GIRL...
DAD! HANG ON...!
AYA... I'M SORRY I COULDN'T... DO ANYTHING.
BUT... I DON'T WANT YOU TWO TO... BE VICTIMS OF... BE SLAVES TO... THE MIKAGES. BE NORMAL... AND FREE...
I WANT YOU... TO BE HAPPY... TO LIVE!
YOU MUST FIGHT YOUR BLOOD... AND YOUR DESTINY.
NO MATTER... WHAT ANYONE ELSE SAYS... YOU AND AKI ARE... HUMAN.

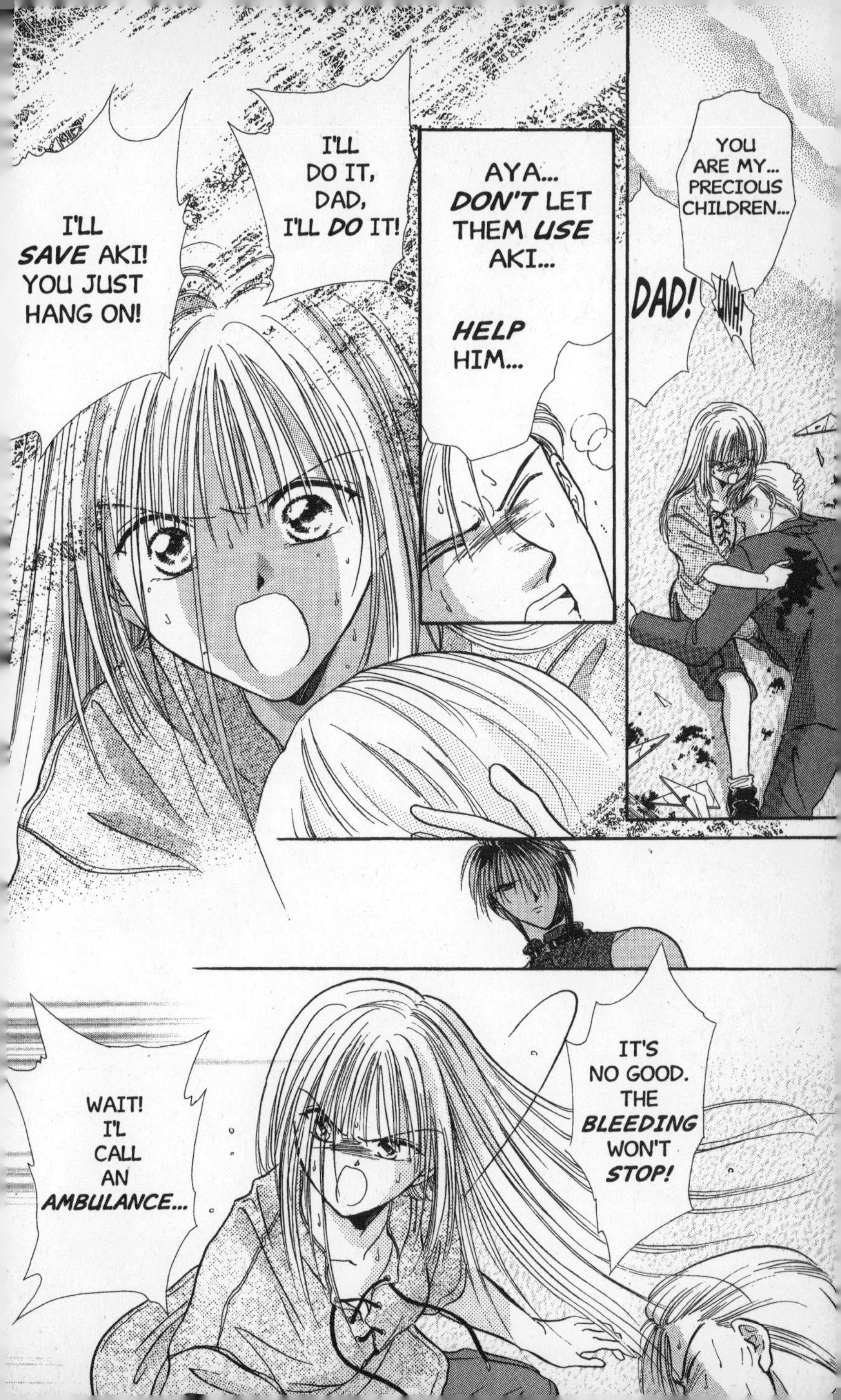
YOU ARE MY... PRECIOUS CHILDREN...
UNH!
DAD!
AYA... *DON'T* LET THEM *USE* AKI...
HELP HIM...
I'LL DO IT, DAD, I'LL *DO* IT!
I'LL *SAVE* AKI! YOU JUST HANG ON!
IT'S NO GOOD. THE *BLEEDING* WON'T *STOP!*
WAIT! I'L CALL AN *AMBULANCE...*

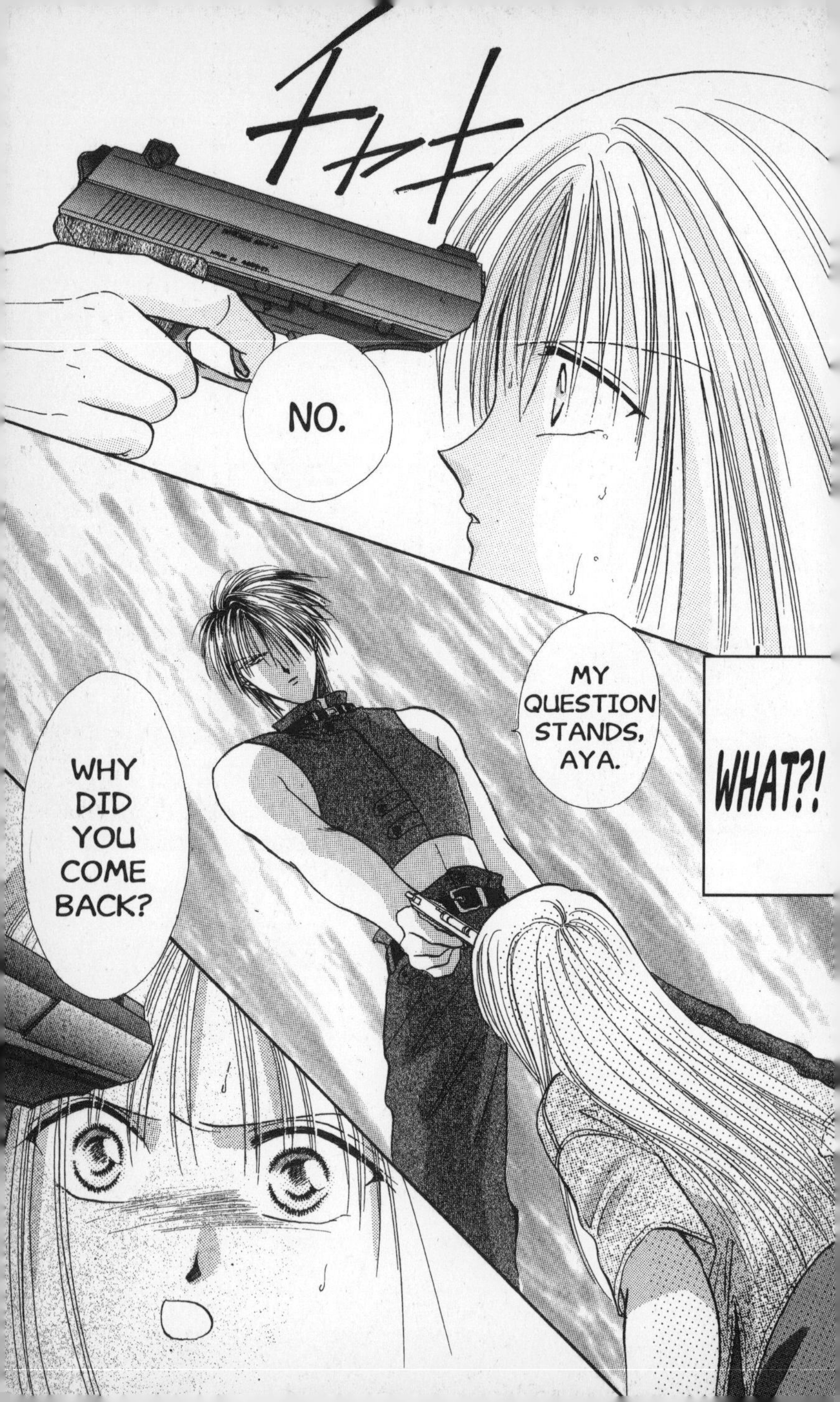
チャキ
NO.
WHAT?!
MY QUESTION STANDS, AYA.
WHY DID YOU COME BACK?

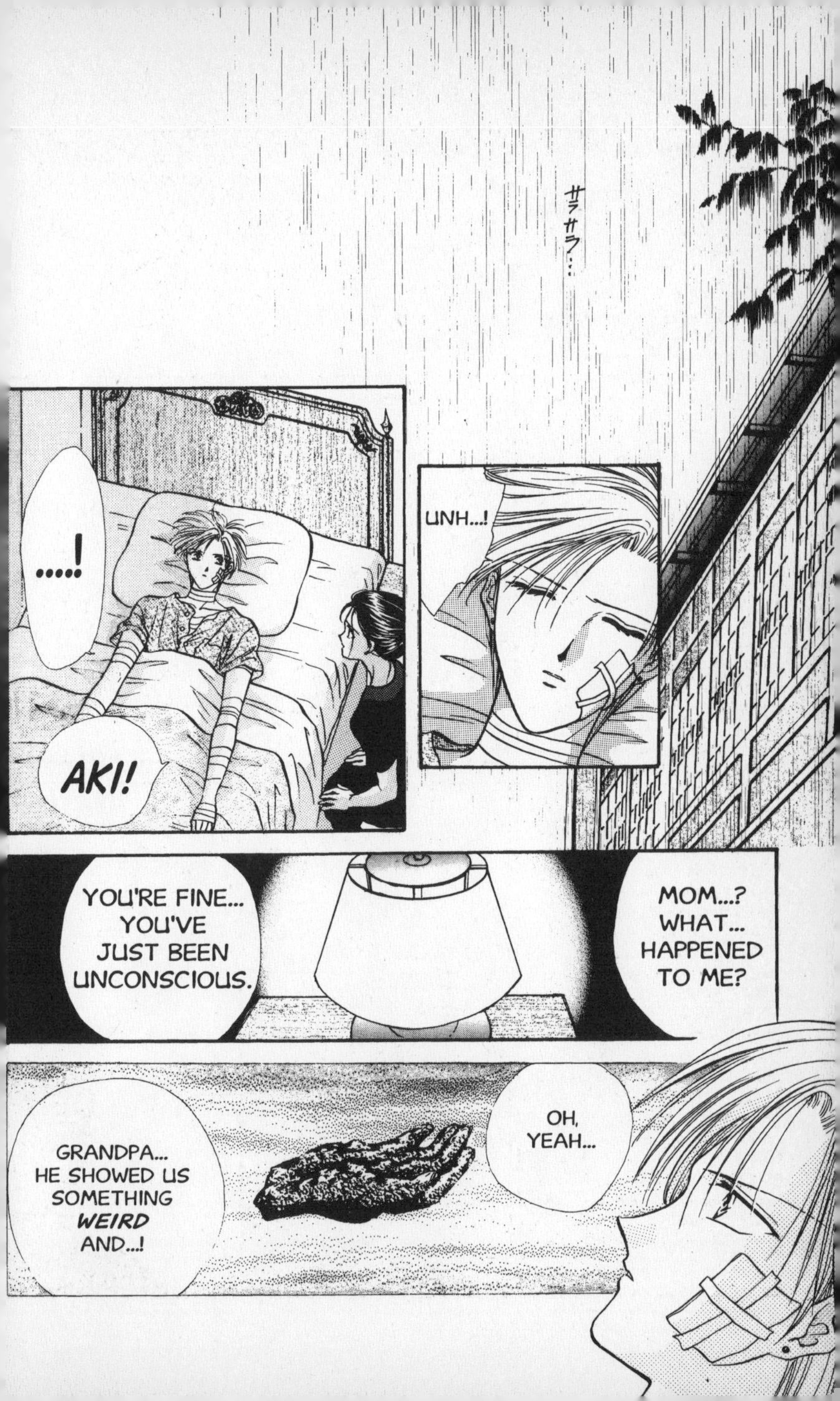
サラサラ…
UNH...!
....!
AKI!
MOM...? WHAT... HAPPENED TO ME?
YOU'RE FINE... YOU'VE JUST BEEN UNCONSCIOUS.
OH, YEAH...
GRANDPA... HE SHOWED US SOMETHING *WEIRD* AND...!

And before the event started, I was watching what everyone was doing on the monitor in the waiting room! Saying things like "Ooh, look at them run!" while scarfing the box lunch they had for me...
In Tokyo, there were several cosplayers, so it was fun. When it was over, I was told I could have one of the cels (and get it signed by Mr. Motohashi!), so I dashed out to choose from among the display in the lobby, which they were cleaning up. I remember there were some cosplayers gathered around the entrance who saw me and waved, squealing. Oh, at the autograph session over the summer, there were also about 10 of them, and it was funny that it became an impromptu photo session. (And several impromptu autograph sessions popped up... 💧💧) Their costumes are amazing. It's so nice when they put so much love into it. I got some dojinshi (some? I have almost 100!) (Um, aren't I the creator...? 💧 Well, they were gifts), but I can really see a difference between superficial ones and ones that are made with love. (Oh! Does that sound self-congratulatory?) If there is love--I write it as "love," but read it as "heart"-- then I don't mind what you do with my stories (within limits). Man, have I digressed! Right. What was exhausting at the event was-- what you'd expect. "The first 100 people who reserve OAV vol. 1 on site get the promotional poster signed by Watase and Mr. Motohashi!" That. It was basically an autograph session, and my old, old back can't stand the strain anymore. Did you get one, everybody? The omake anime was so funny! Suboshi is so cute. Actually I got vol. 2 the other day... Everyone--I mean FY fans-- you gotta see it! R-Really!

urk!

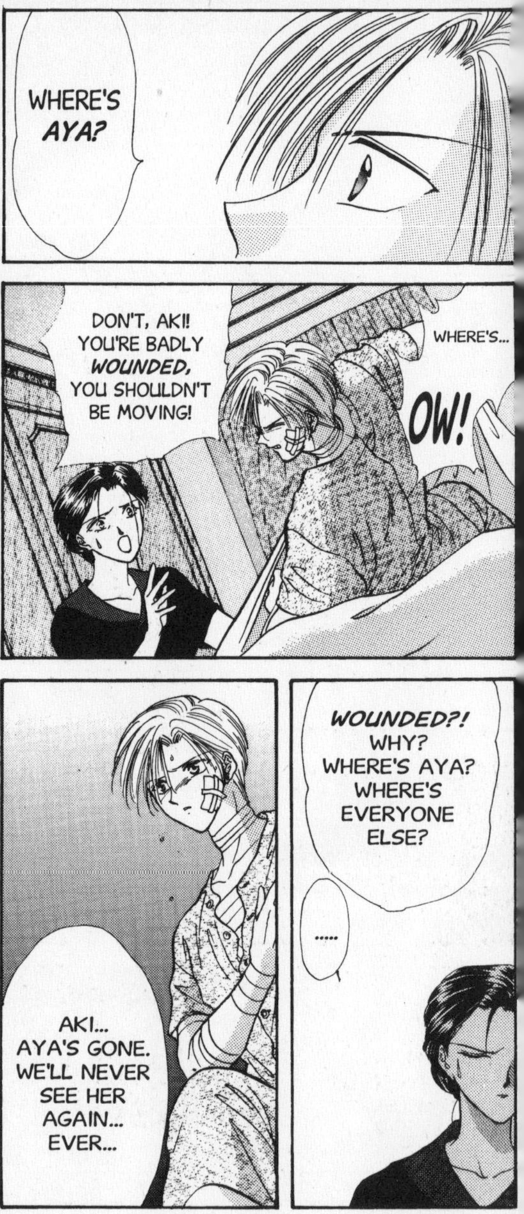
WHERE'S AYA?
WHERE'S...
OW!
DON'T, AKI! YOU'RE BADLY WOUNDED, YOU SHOULDN'T BE MOVING!
WOUNDED?! WHY? WHERE'S AYA? WHERE'S EVERYONE ELSE?
.....
AKI... AYA'S GONE. WE'LL NEVER SEE HER AGAIN... EVER...

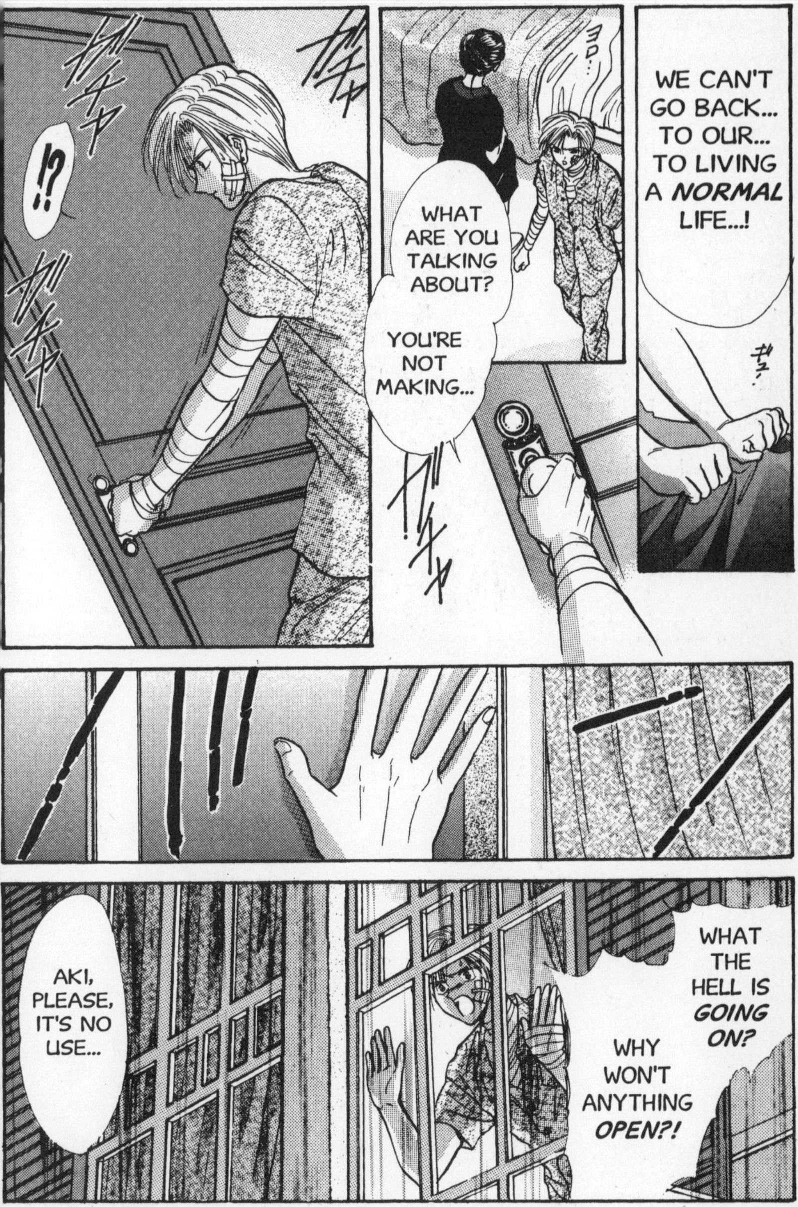
WE CAN'T GO BACK... TO OUR... TO LIVING A *NORMAL* LIFE...!
WHAT ARE YOU TALKING ABOUT?
YOU'RE NOT MAKING...
!?
WHAT THE HELL IS *GOING ON?*
WHY WON'T ANYTHING *OPEN?!*
AKI, PLEASE, IT'S NO USE...

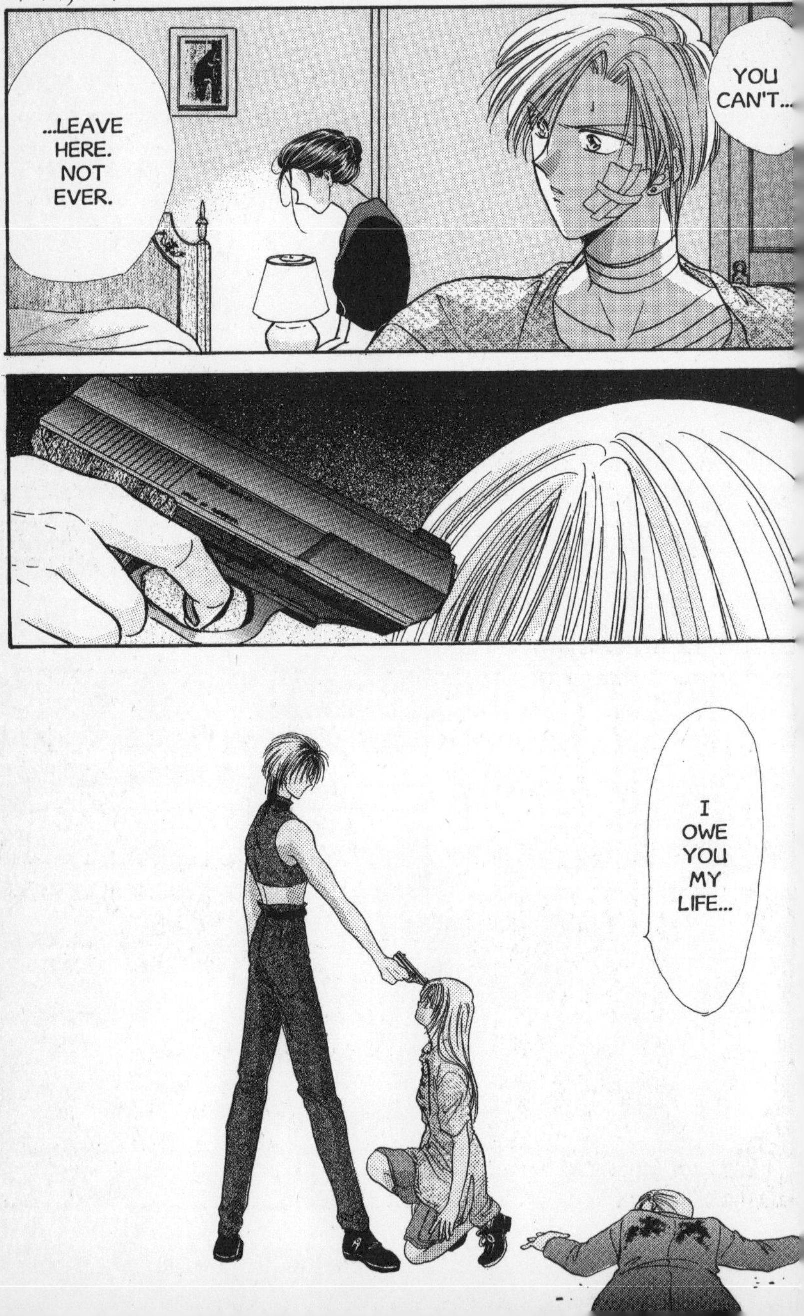
YOU CAN'T...
...LEAVE HERE. NOT EVER.
I OWE YOU MY LIFE...

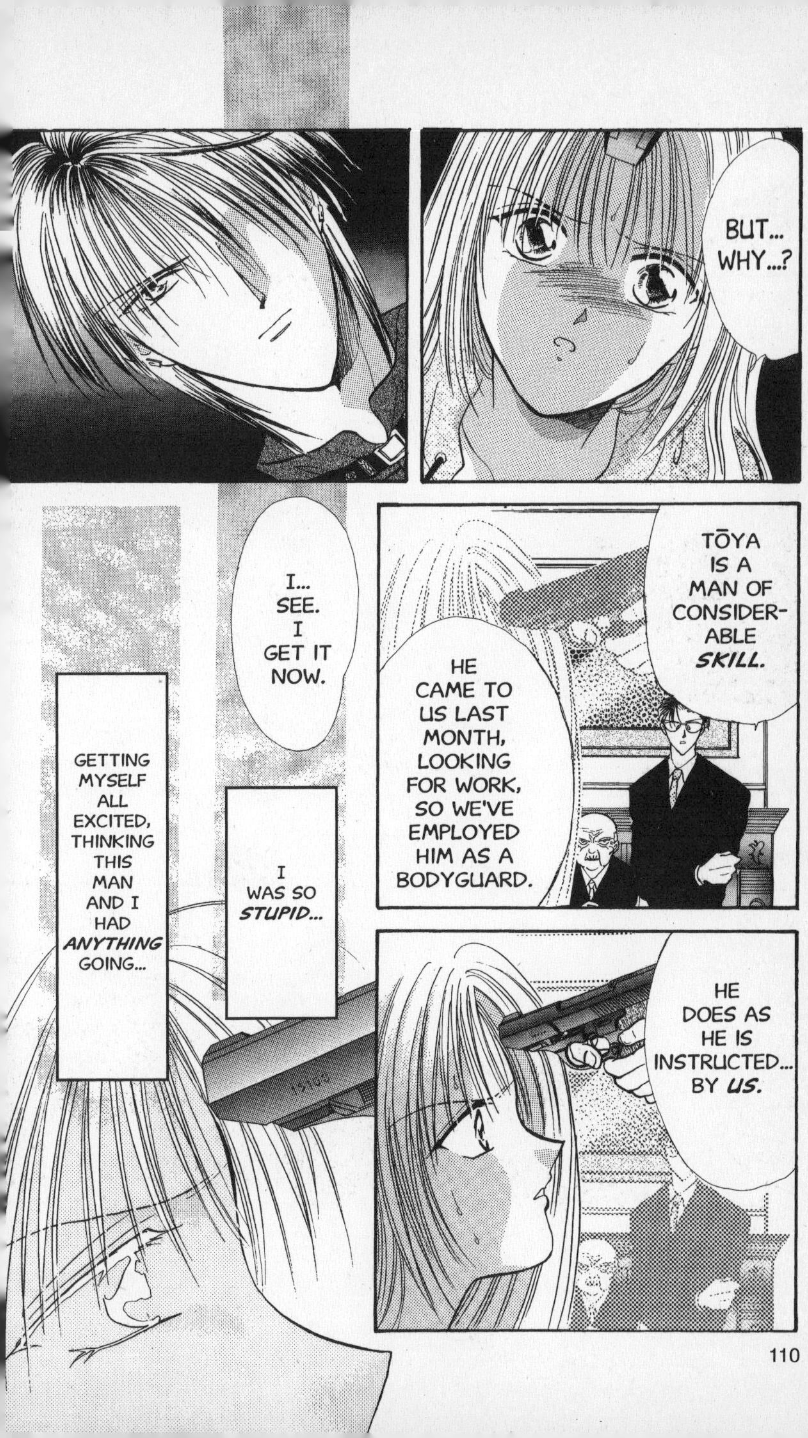
BUT... WHY...?
TŌYA IS A MAN OF CONSIDERABLE-ABLE SKILL.
HE CAME TO US LAST MONTH, LOOKING FOR WORK, SO WE'VE EMPLOYED HIM AS A BODYGUARD.
I... SEE. I GET IT NOW.
HE DOES AS HE IS INSTRUCTED... BY US.
I WAS SO STUPID...
GETTING MYSELF ALL EXCITED, THINKING THIS MAN AND I HAD ANYTHING GOING...

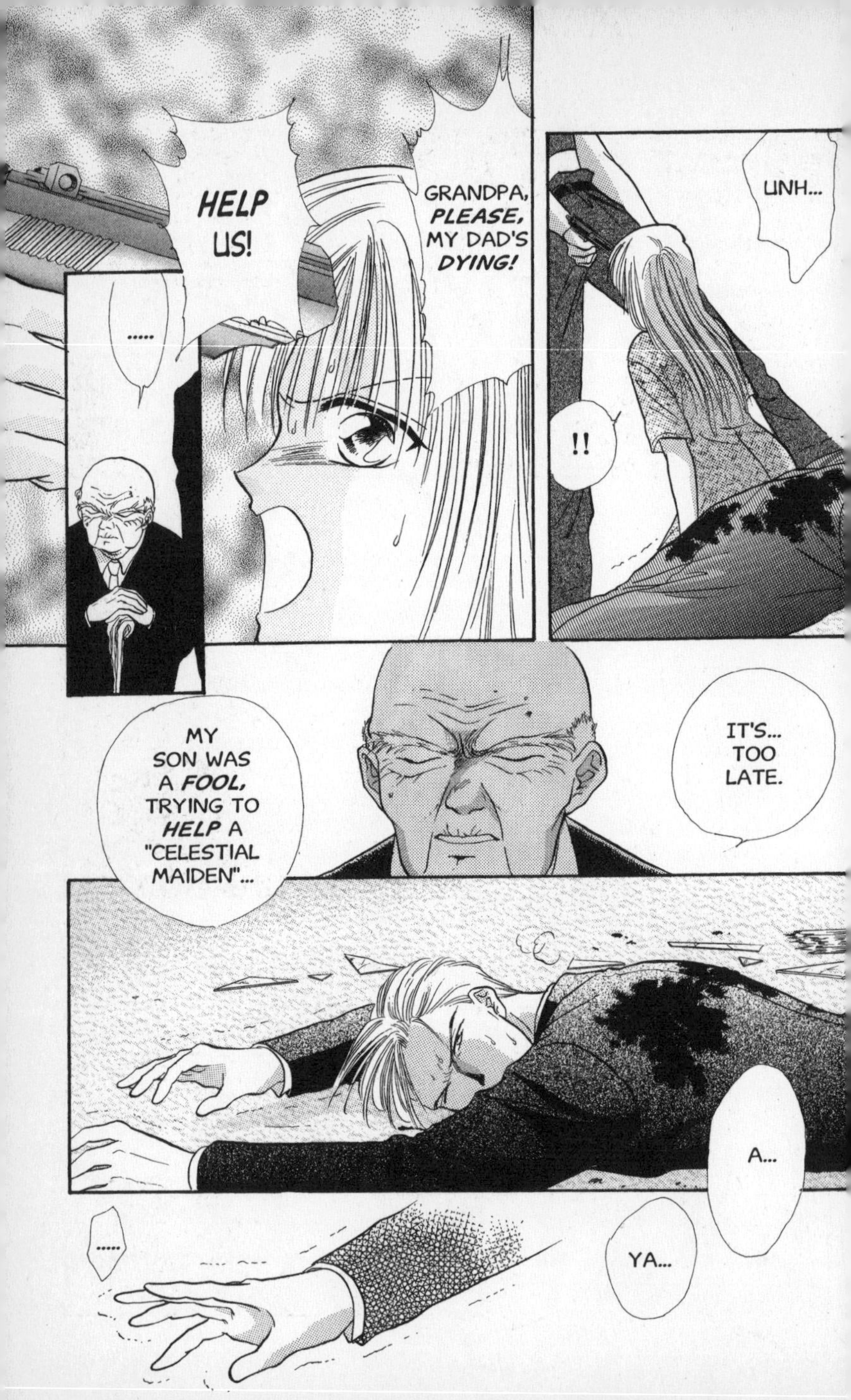

UNH...
!!
GRANDPA, PLEASE, MY DAD'S DYING!
HELP US!
.....
IT'S... TOO LATE.
MY SON WAS A FOOL, TRYING TO HELP A "CELESTIAL MAIDEN"...
A...
YA...
.....

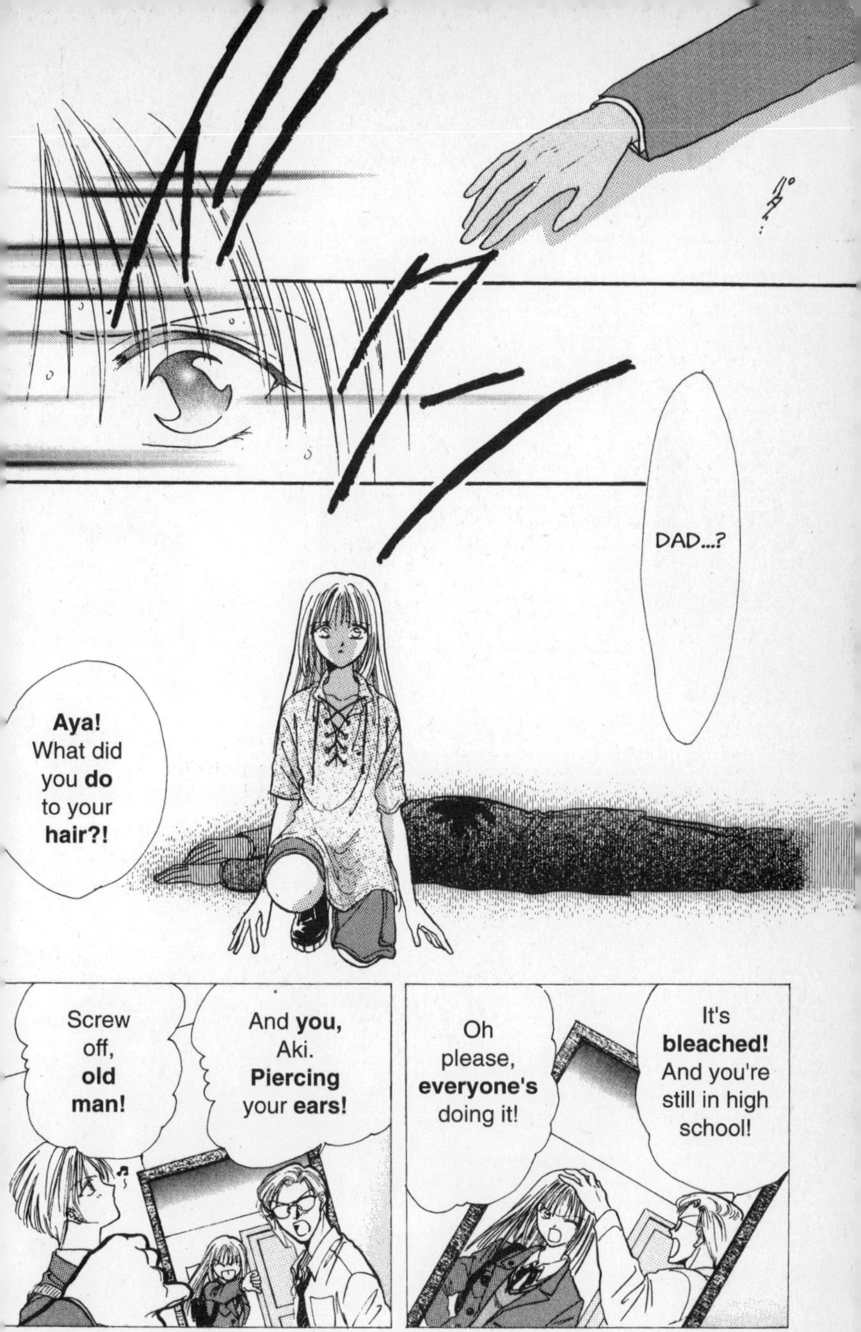
DAD...?
Aya! What did you do to your hair?!
It's bleached! And you're still in high school!
Oh please, everyone's doing it!
And you, Aki. Piercing your ears!
Screw off, old man!

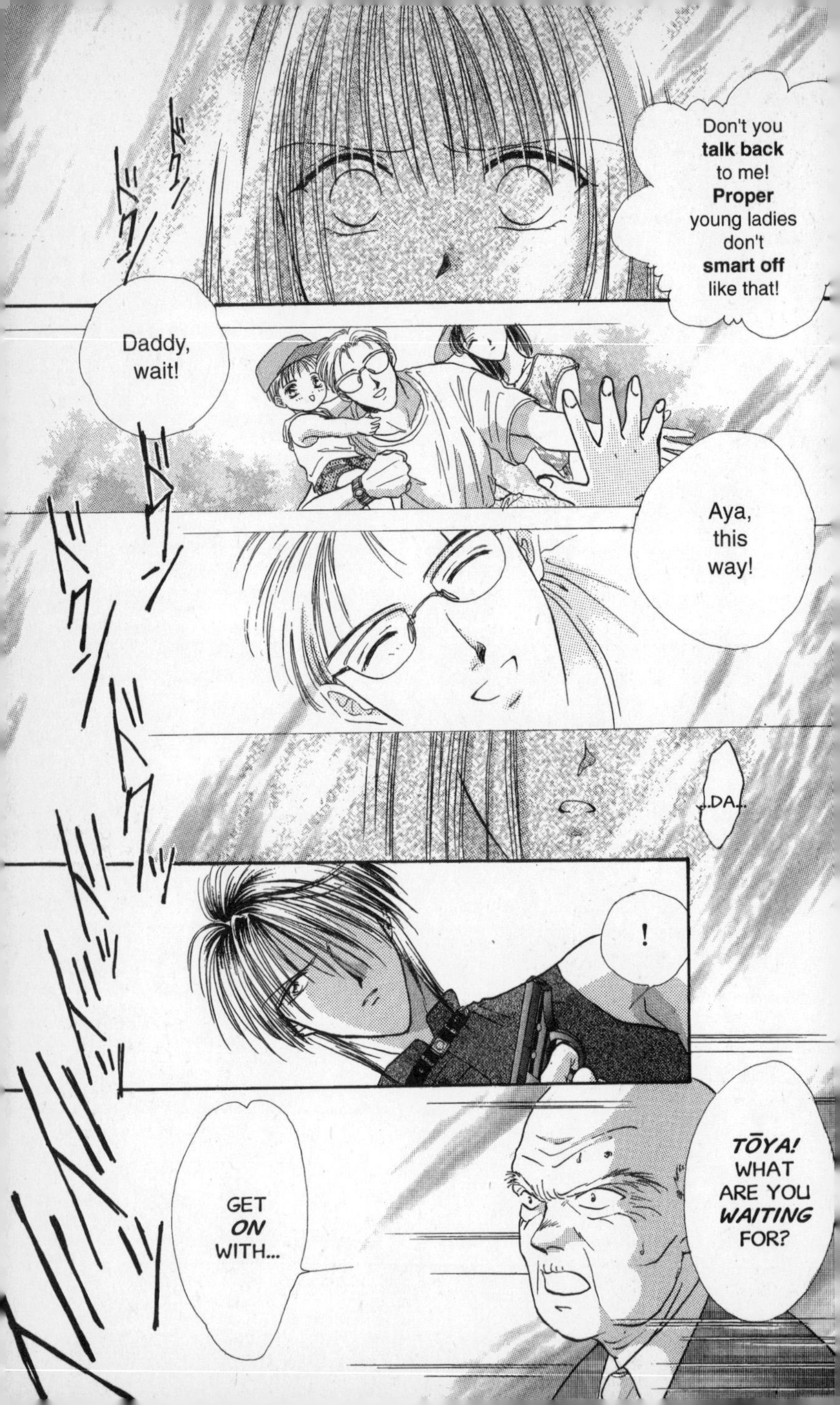

Don't you **talk back** to me! **Proper** young ladies don't **smart off** like that!
Daddy, wait!
Aya, this way!
...DA...
!
TŌYA! WHAT ARE YOU *WAITING* FOR?
GET *ON* WITH...

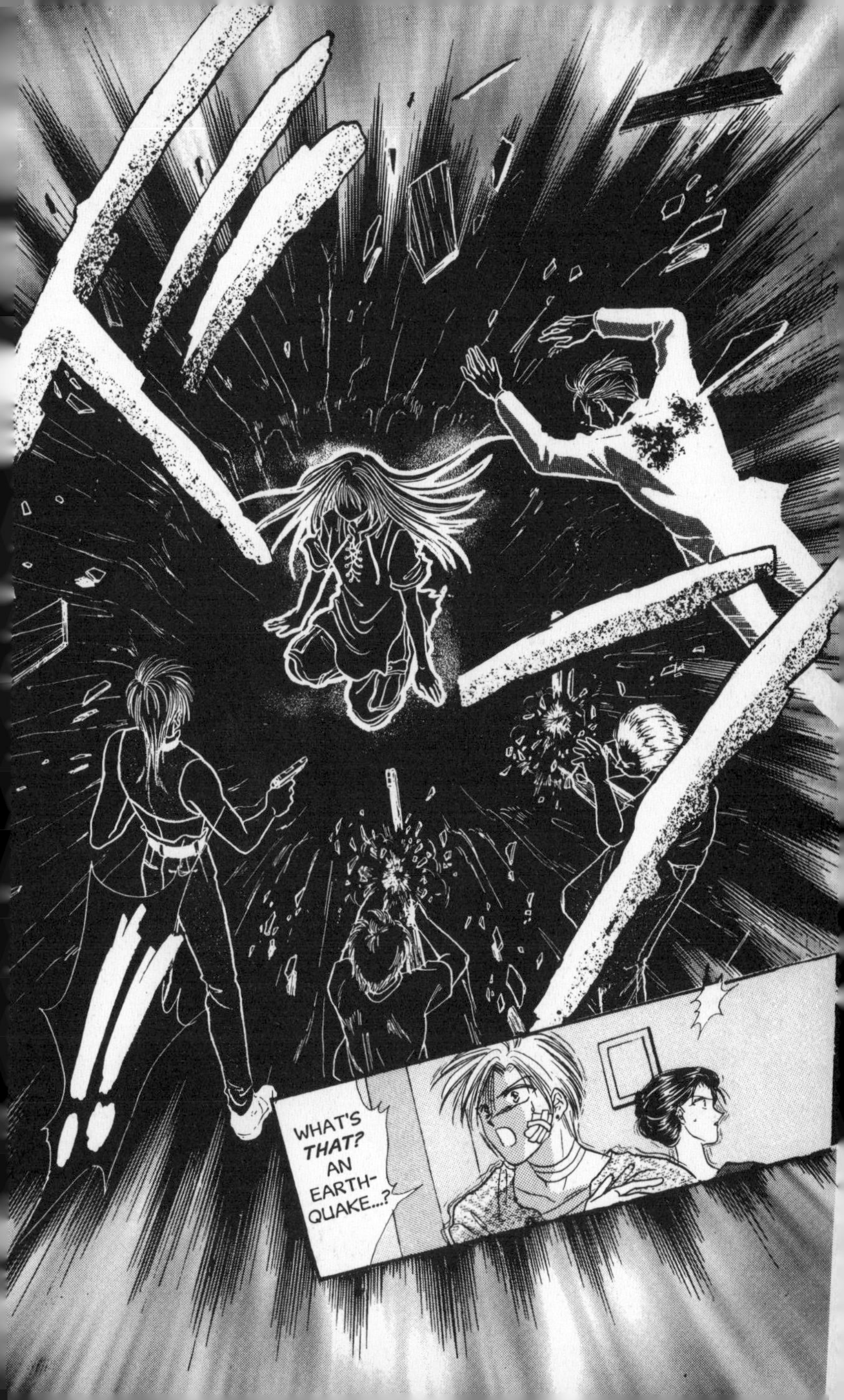
WHAT'S *THAT?* AN EARTH-QUAKE...?

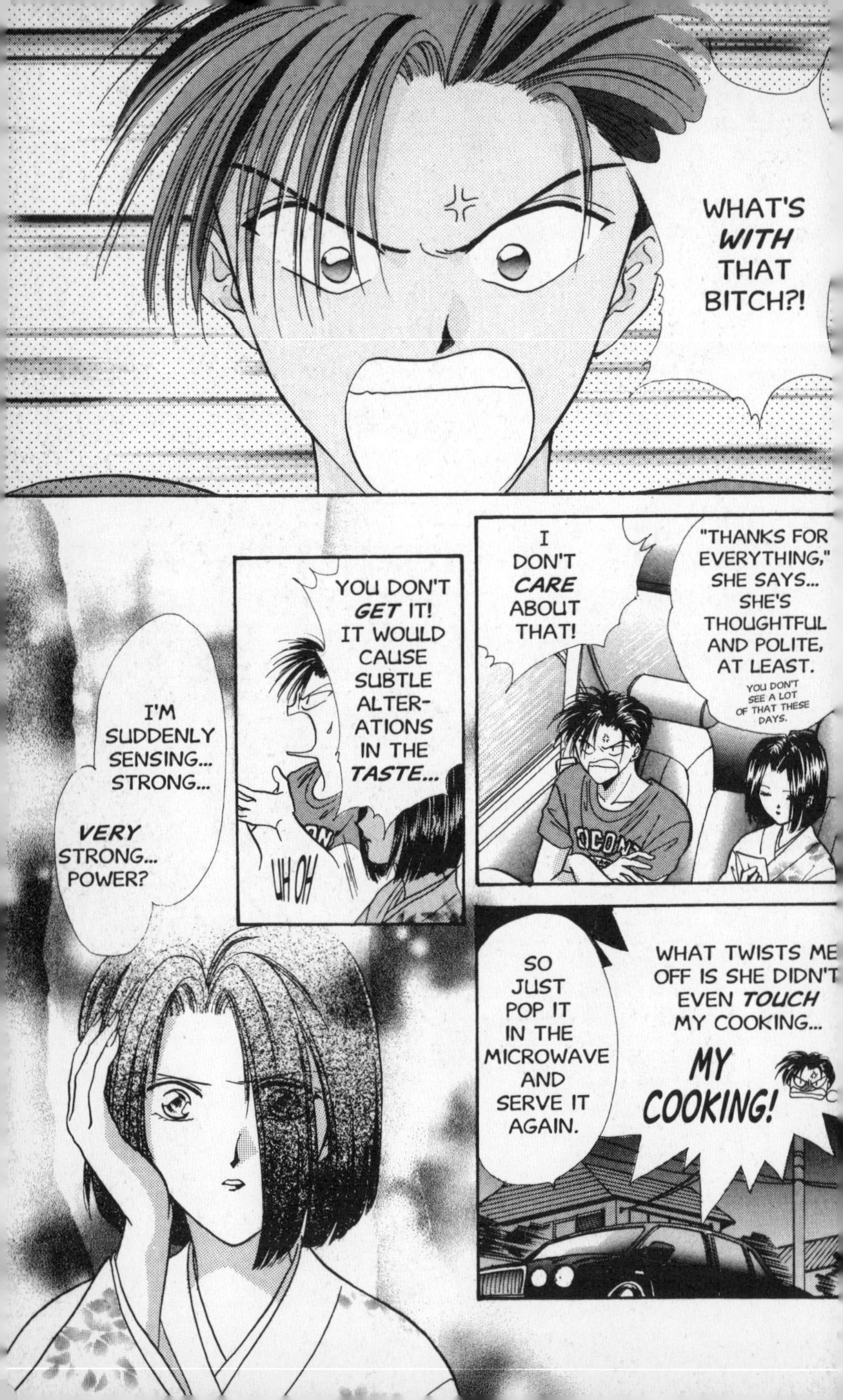
WHAT'S WITH THAT BITCH?!
"THANKS FOR EVERYTHING," SHE SAYS... SHE'S THOUGHTFUL AND POLITE, AT LEAST.
YOU DON'T SEE A LOT OF THAT THESE DAYS.
I DON'T CARE ABOUT THAT!
WHAT TWISTS ME OFF IS SHE DIDN'T EVEN TOUCH MY COOKING...
MY COOKING!
SO JUST POP IT IN THE MICROWAVE AND SERVE IT AGAIN.
YOU DON'T GET IT! IT WOULD CAUSE SUBTLE ALTER-ATIONS IN THE TASTE...
UH OH
I'M SUDDENLY SENSING... STRONG...
VERY STRONG... POWER?

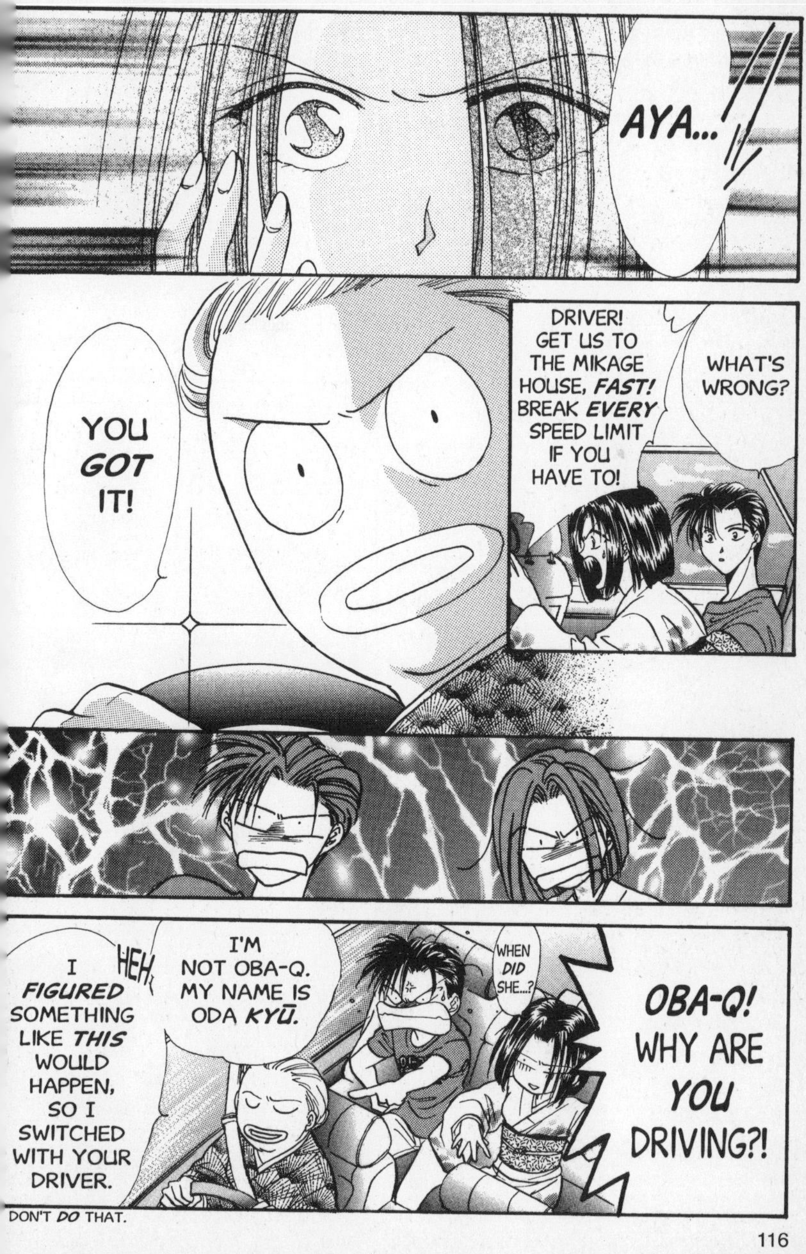
AYA...
WHAT'S WRONG?
DRIVER! GET US TO THE MIKAGE HOUSE, *FAST!* BREAK *EVERY* SPEED LIMIT IF YOU HAVE TO!
YOU *GOT* IT!
OBA-Q! WHY ARE *YOU* DRIVING?!
WHEN *DID* SHE...?
I'M NOT OBA-Q. MY NAME IS ODA *KYŪ.*
HEH,
I *FIGURED* SOMETHING LIKE *THIS* WOULD HAPPEN, SO I SWITCHED WITH YOUR DRIVER.

DON'T *DO* THAT.

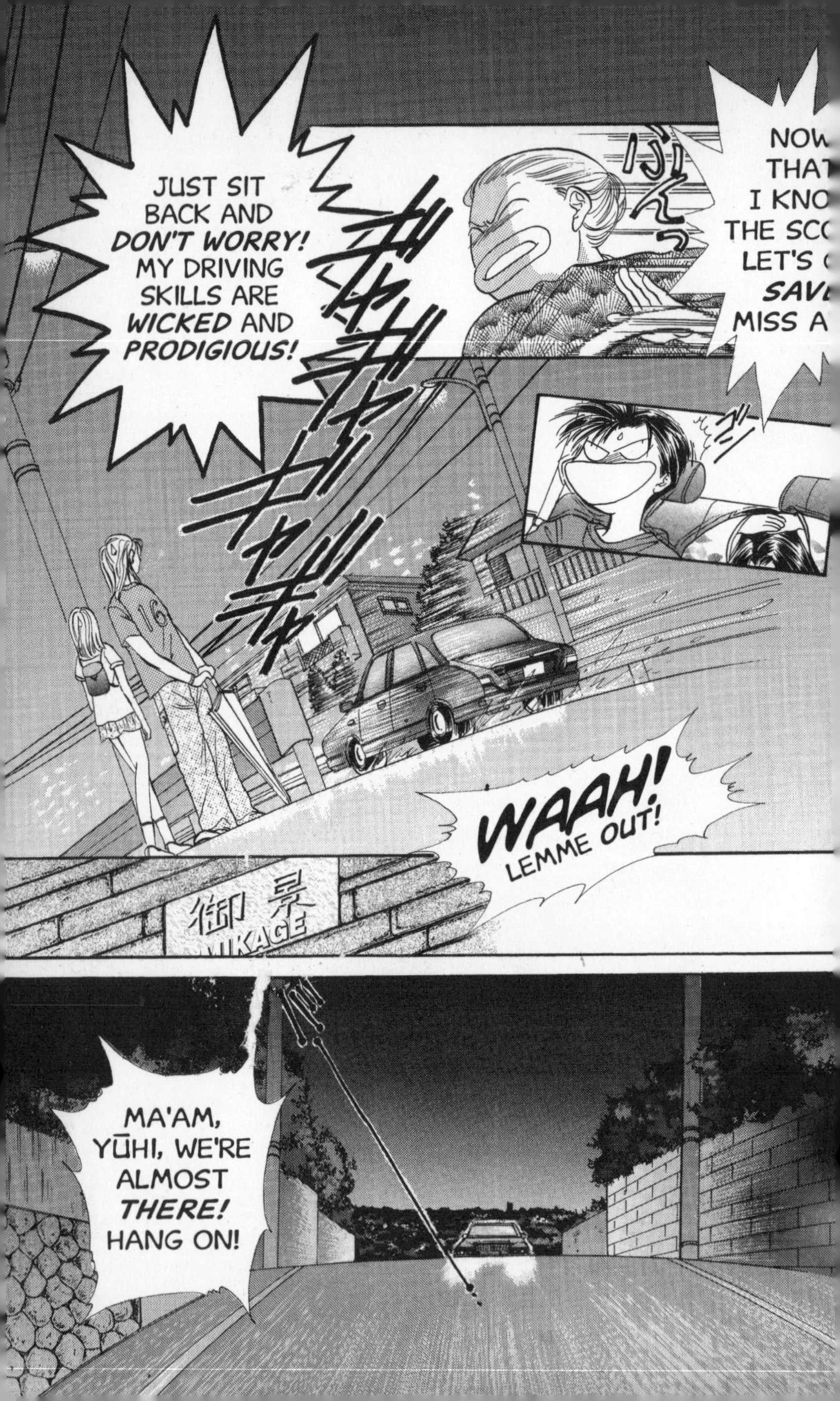

NOW THAT I KNO THE SC LET'S SAV MISS A
JUST SIT BACK AND DON'T WORRY! MY DRIVING SKILLS ARE WICKED AND PRODIGIOUS!
WAAH! LEMME OUT!
御影
MA'AM, YŪHI, WE'RE ALMOST THERE! HANG ON!

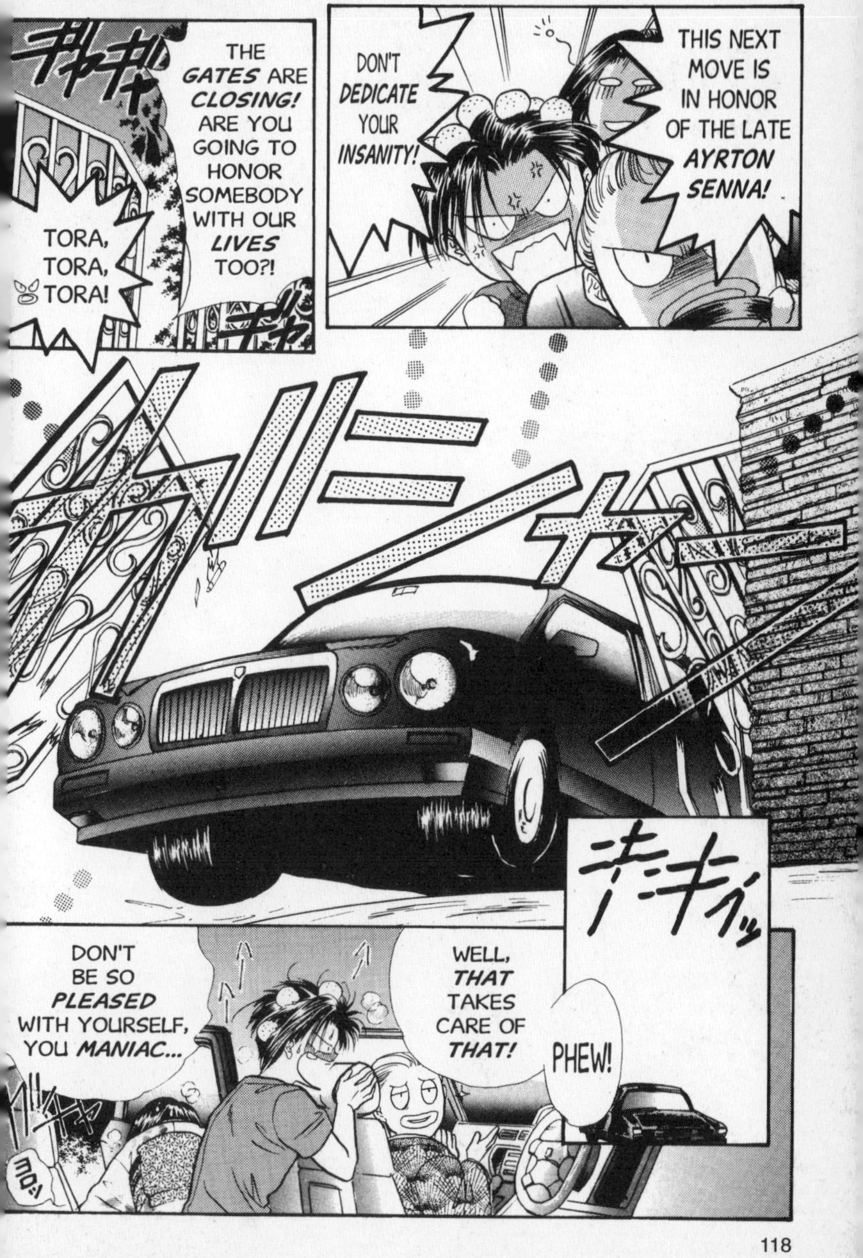
THIS NEXT MOVE IS IN HONOR OF THE LATE AYRTON SENNA!
DON'T DEDICATE YOUR INSANITY!
THE GATES ARE CLOSING! ARE YOU GOING TO HONOR SOMEBODY WITH OUR LIVES TOO?!
TORA, TORA, TORA!
WELL, THAT TAKES CARE OF THAT!
PHEW!
DON'T BE SO PLEASED WITH YOURSELF, YOU MANIAC...

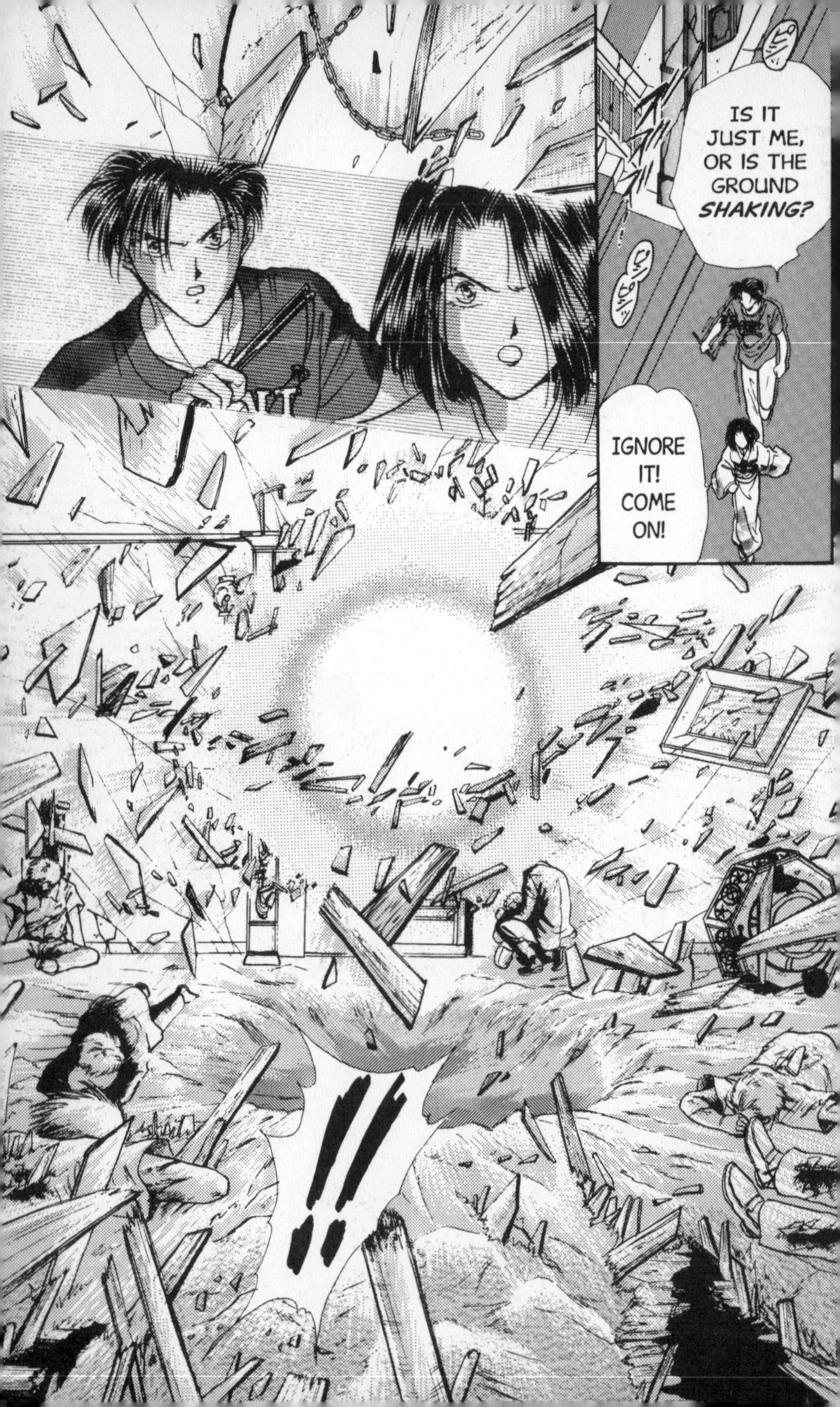
IS IT JUST ME, OR IS THE GROUND *SHAKING?*
IGNORE IT! COME ON!

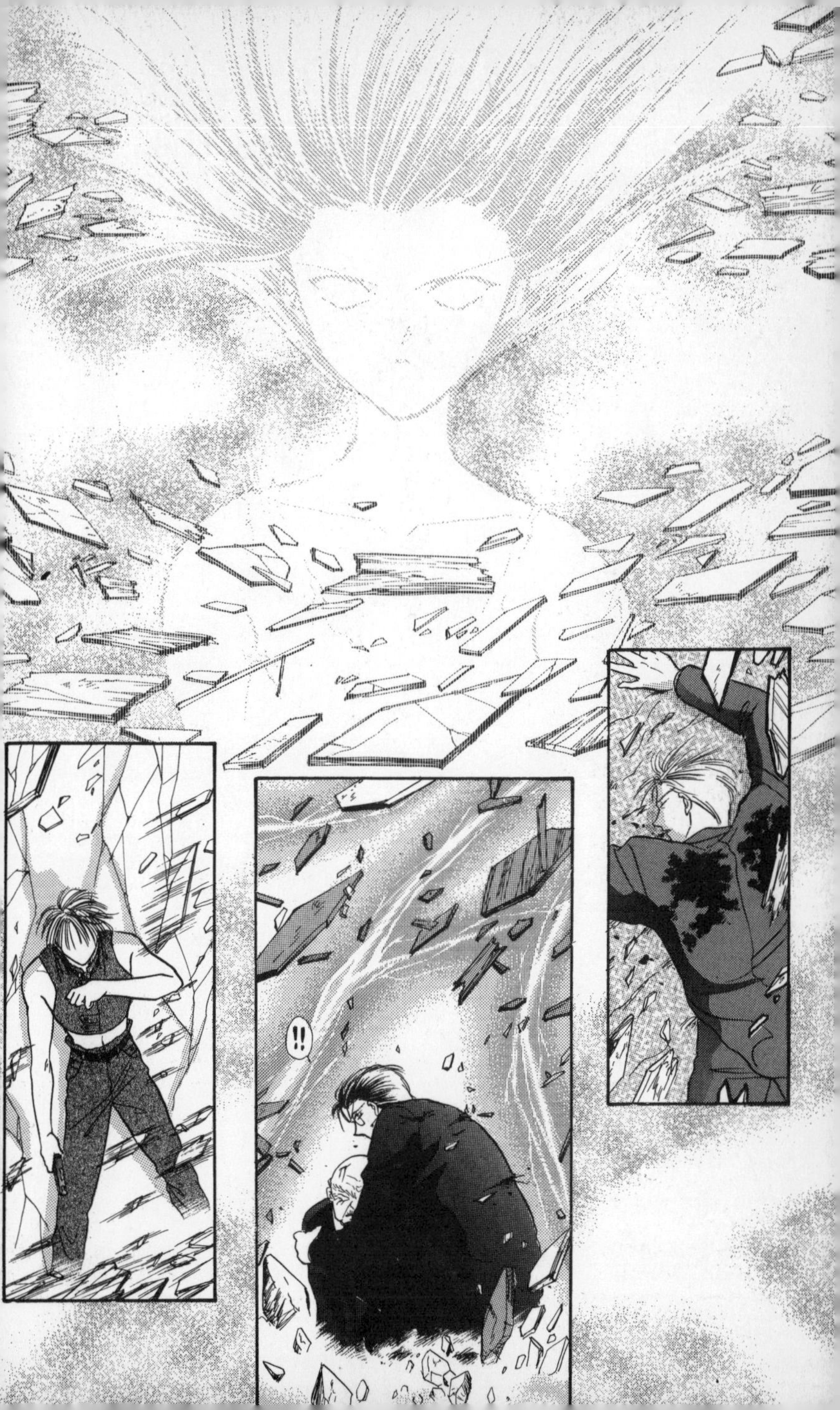
!!

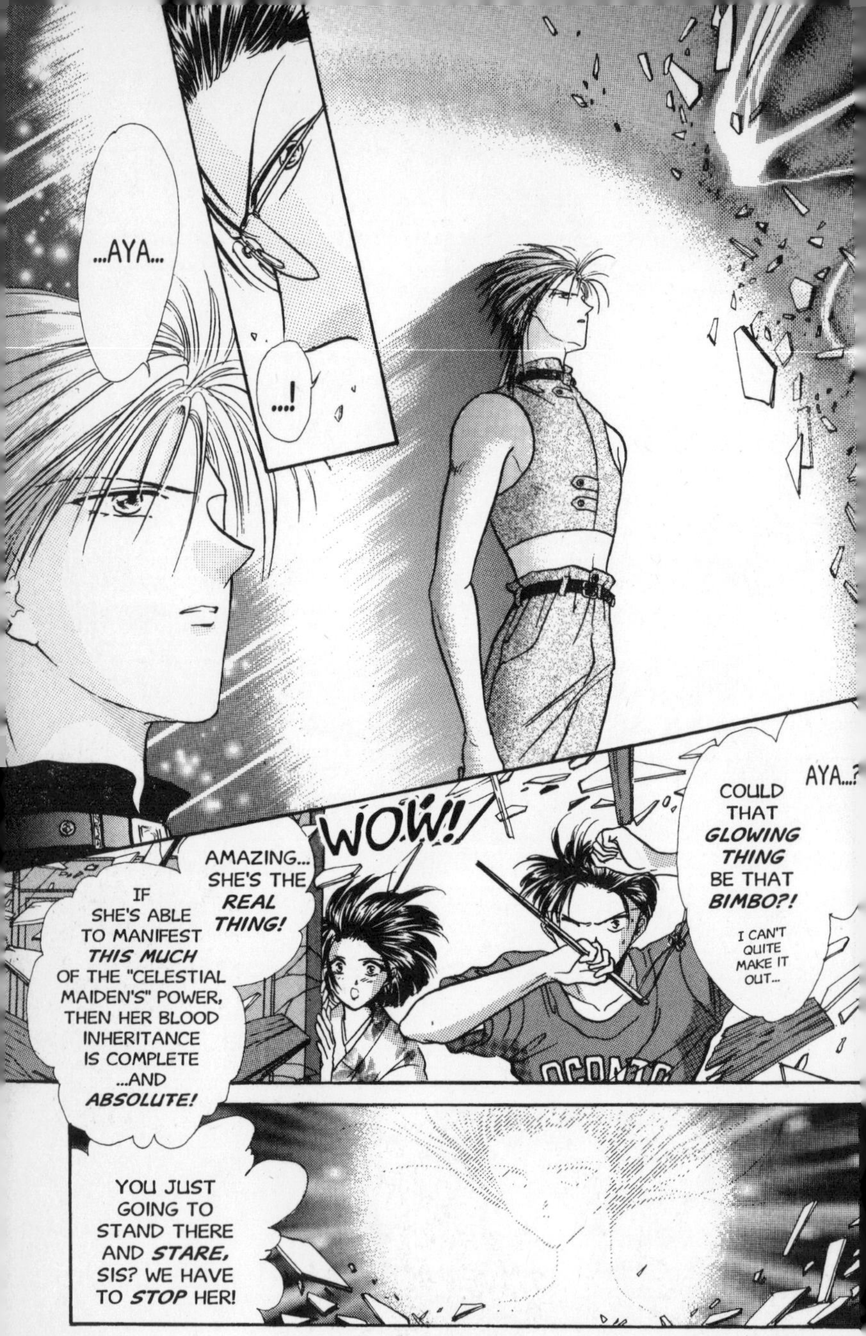

...!
...AYA...
AYA...?
COULD THAT GLOWING THING BE THAT BIMBO?!
I CAN'T QUITE MAKE IT OUT...
WOW!
AMAZING... SHE'S THE REAL THING!
IF SHE'S ABLE TO MANIFEST THIS MUCH OF THE "CELESTIAL MAIDEN'S" POWER, THEN HER BLOOD INHERITANCE IS COMPLETE ...AND ABSOLUTE!
YOU JUST GOING TO STAND THERE AND STARE, SIS? WE HAVE TO STOP HER!

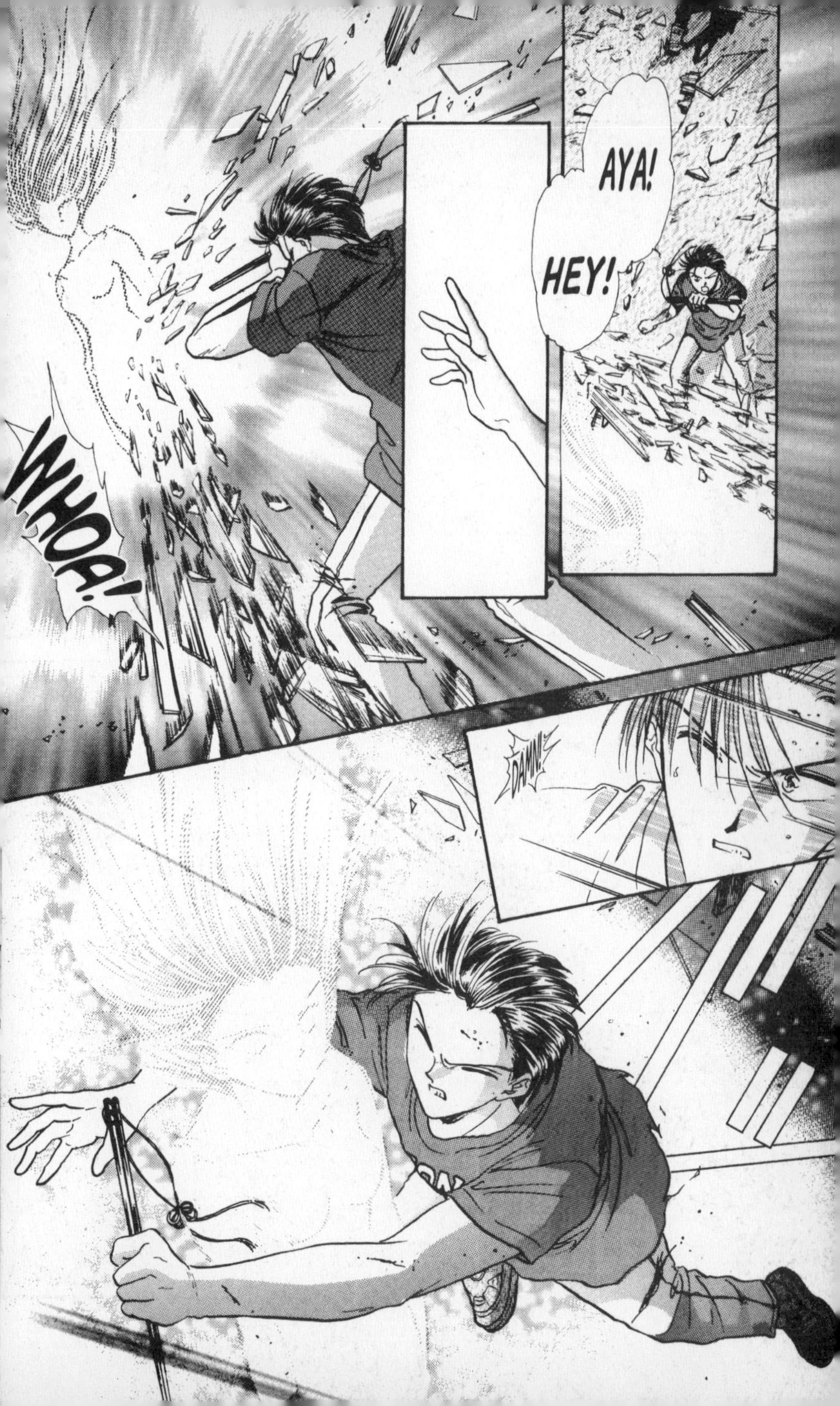
AYA!
HEY!
WHOA!
DAMN!

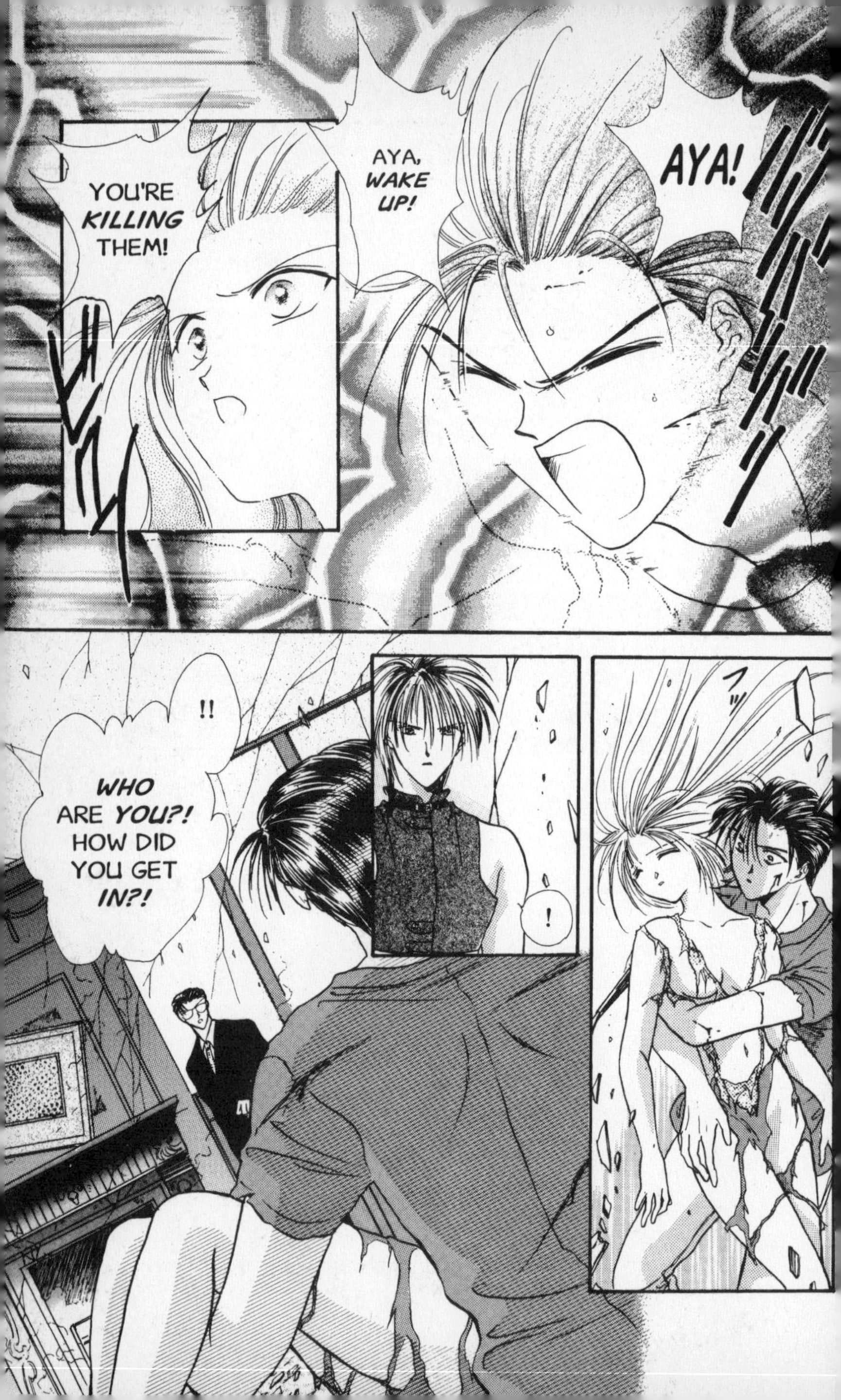
AYA!
AYA, WAKE UP!
YOU'RE KILLING THEM!
フッ
!
!!
WHO ARE YOU?! HOW DID YOU GET IN?!

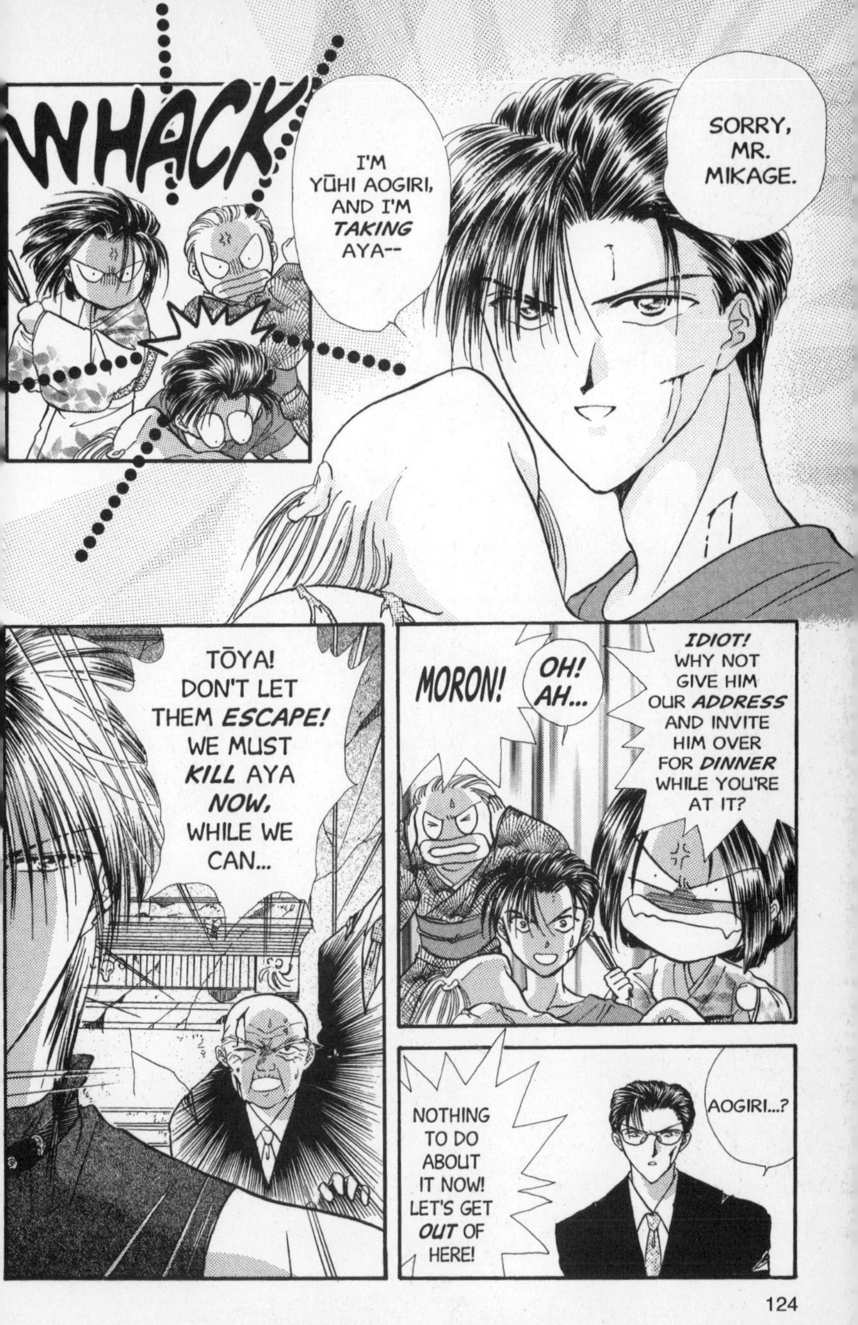
SORRY, MR. MIKAGE.
I'M YŪHI AOGIRI, AND I'M *TAKING* AYA--
WHACK
IDIOT! WHY NOT GIVE HIM OUR *ADDRESS* AND INVITE HIM OVER FOR *DINNER* WHILE YOU'RE AT IT?
OH! AH...
MORON!
AOGIRI...?
NOTHING TO DO ABOUT IT NOW! LET'S GET *OUT* OF HERE!
TŌYA! DON'T LET THEM *ESCAPE!* WE MUST *KILL* AYA *NOW,* WHILE WE CAN...

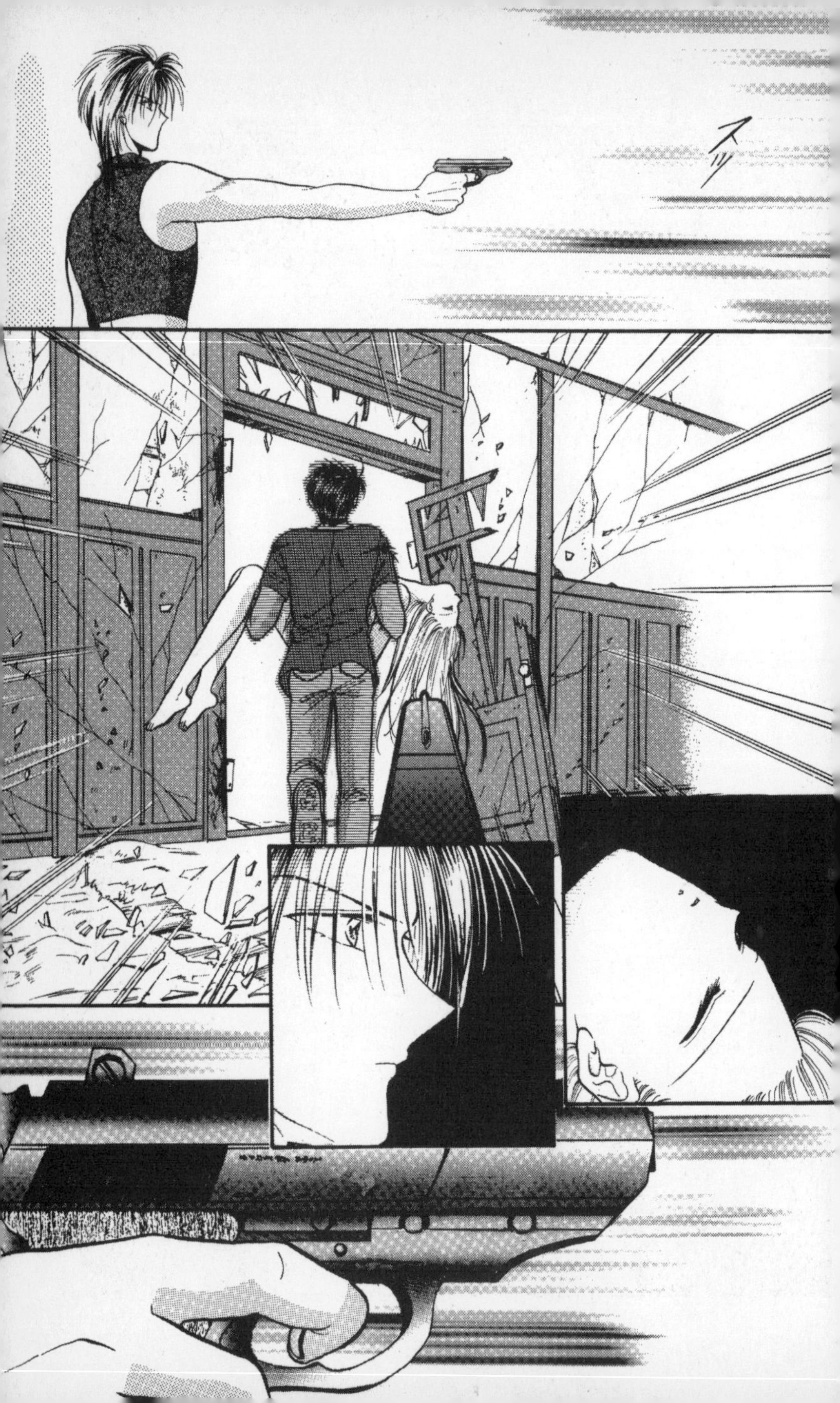
スッ

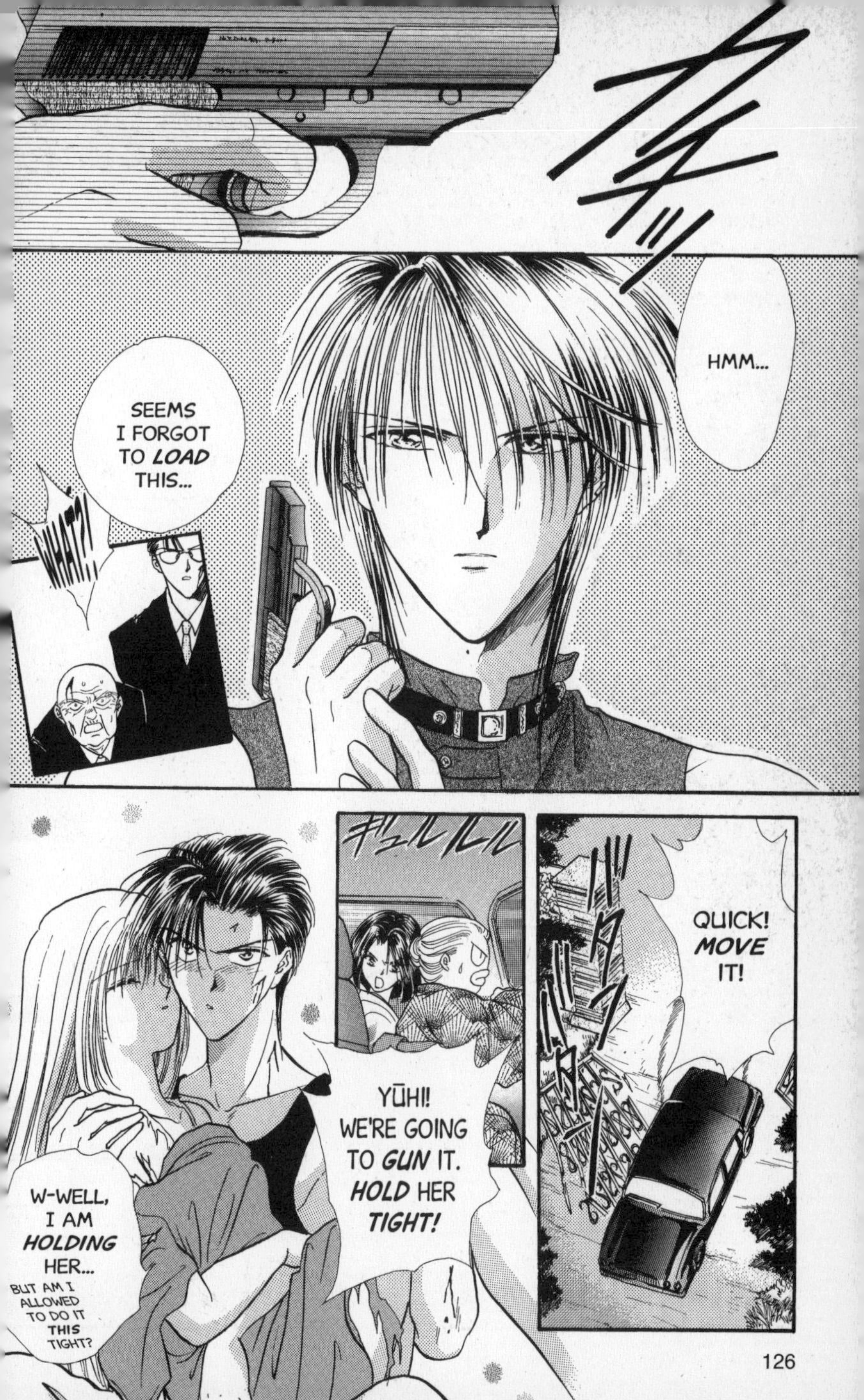
HMM...
SEEMS I FORGOT TO *LOAD* THIS...
WHAT?!
QUICK! *MOVE* IT!
YŪHI! WE'RE GOING TO *GUN* IT. *HOLD* HER *TIGHT!*
W-WELL, I AM *HOLDING* HER...
BUT AM I ALLOWED TO DO IT **THIS** TIGHT?

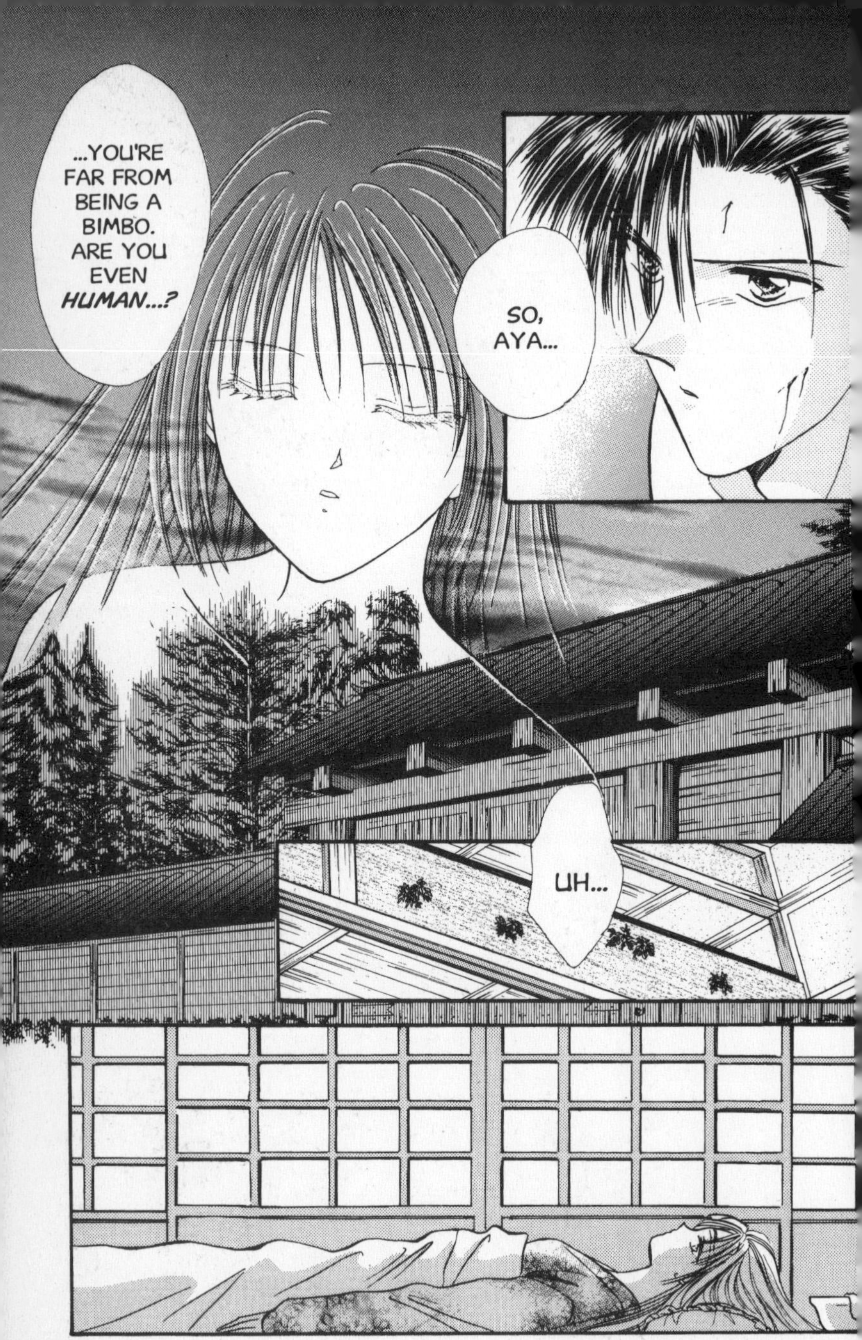
SO, AYA...
...YOU'RE FAR FROM BEING A BIMBO. ARE YOU EVEN *HUMAN...?*
UH...

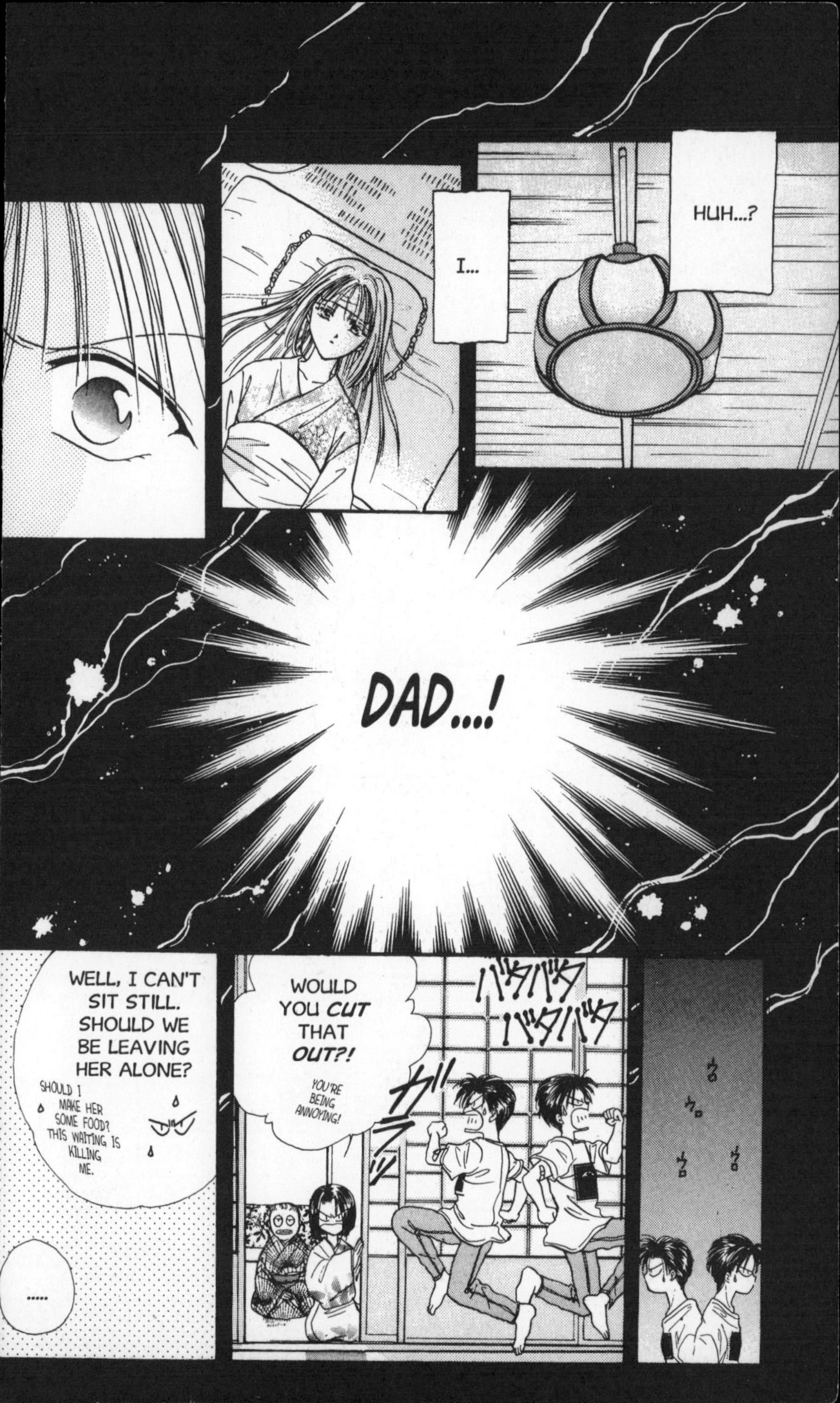
HUH...?
I...
DAD...!
WOULD YOU *CUT* THAT *OUT?!*
YOU'RE BEING ANNOYING!
バタバタ
バタバタ
ガラッ
WELL, I CAN'T SIT STILL. SHOULD WE BE LEAVING HER ALONE?
SHOULD I MAKE HER SOME FOOD? THIS WAITING IS KILLING ME.
......

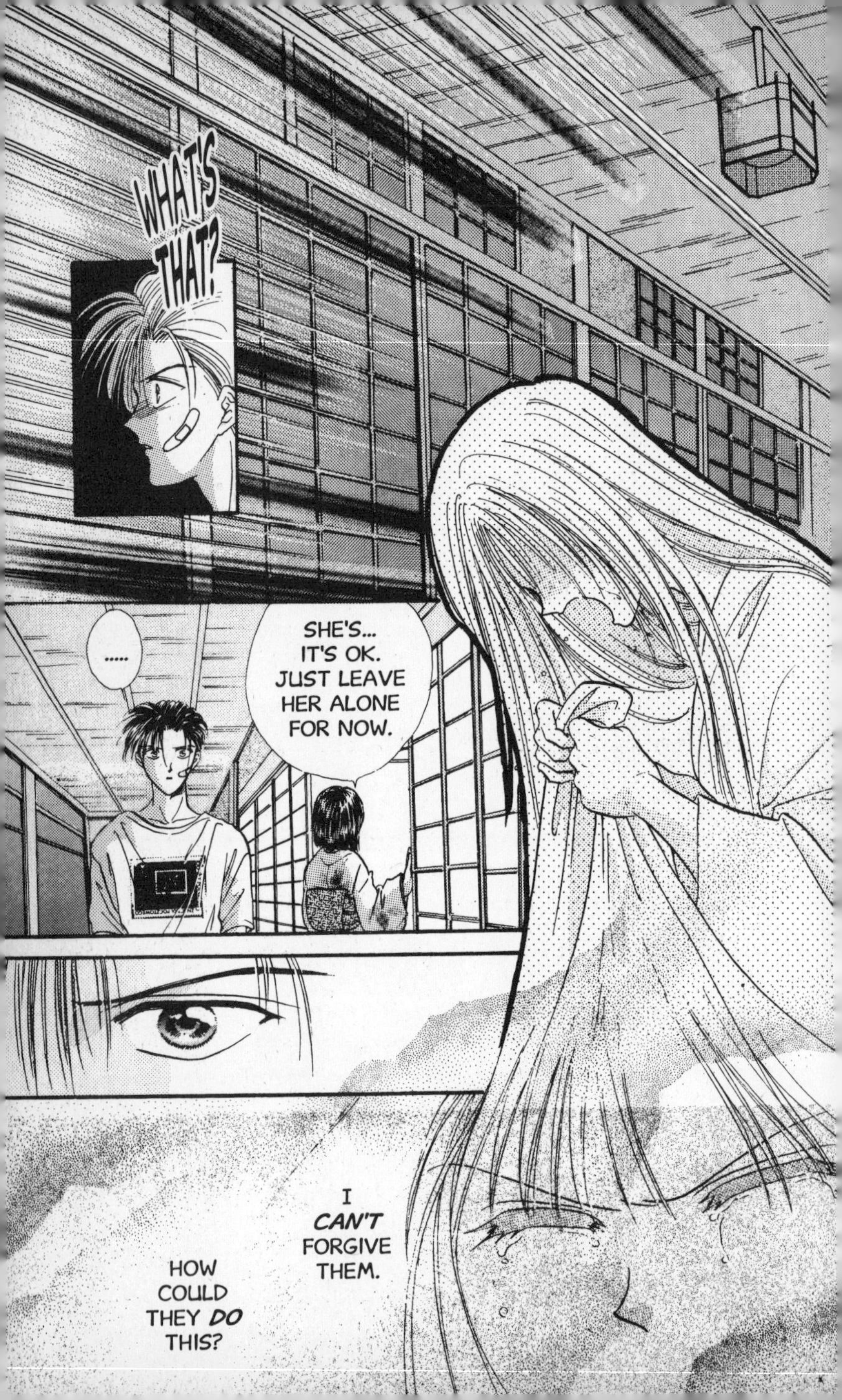
WHAT'S THAT?
SHE'S... IT'S OK. JUST LEAVE HER ALONE FOR NOW.
......
I *CAN'T* FORGIVE THEM.
HOW COULD THEY *DO* THIS?

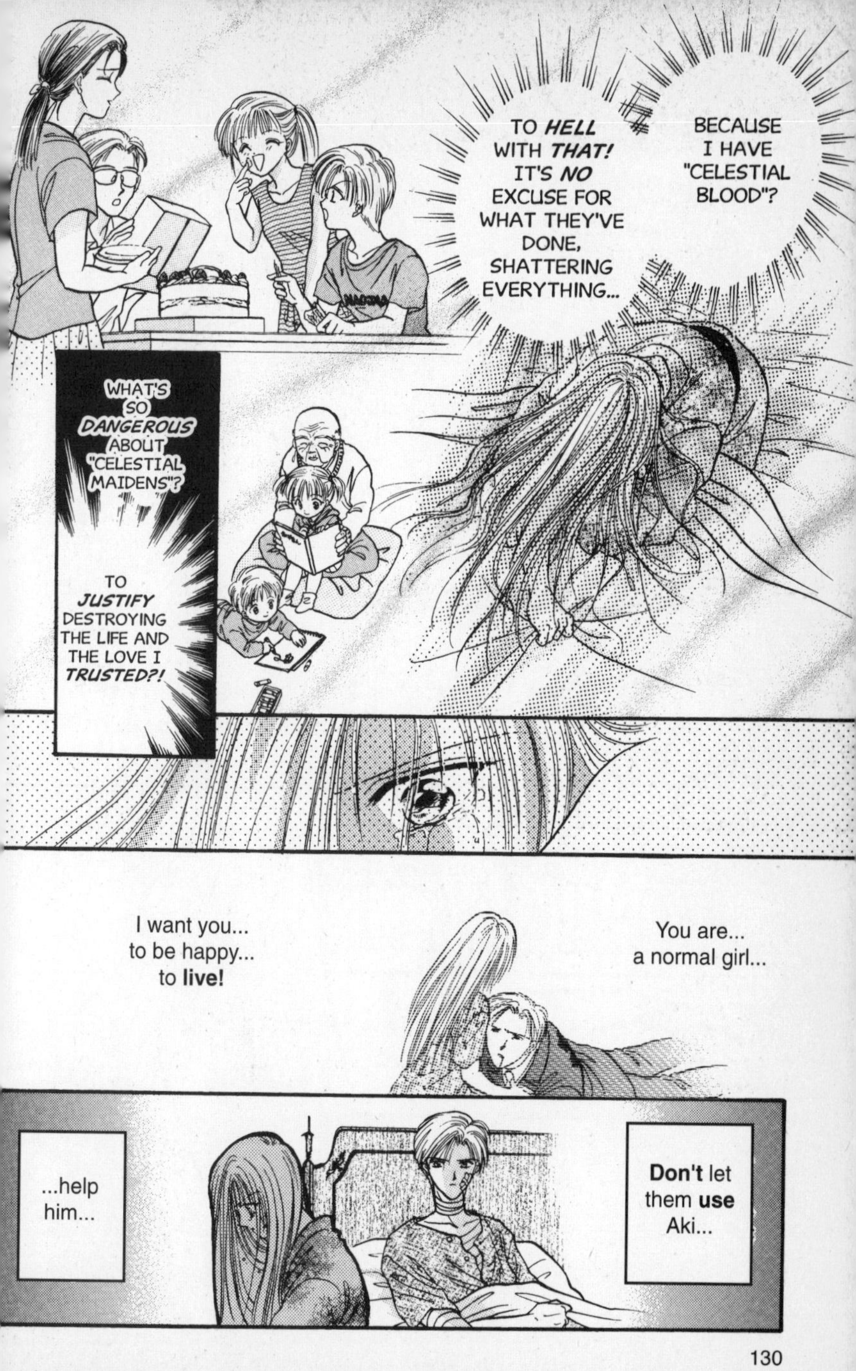

BECAUSE I HAVE "CELESTIAL BLOOD"?
TO HELL WITH THAT! IT'S NO EXCUSE FOR WHAT THEY'VE DONE, SHATTERING EVERYTHING...
WHAT'S SO DANGEROUS ABOUT "CELESTIAL MAIDENS"?
TO JUSTIFY DESTROYING THE LIFE AND THE LOVE I TRUSTED?!
You are... a normal girl...
I want you... to be happy... to live!
Don't let them use Aki...
...help him...

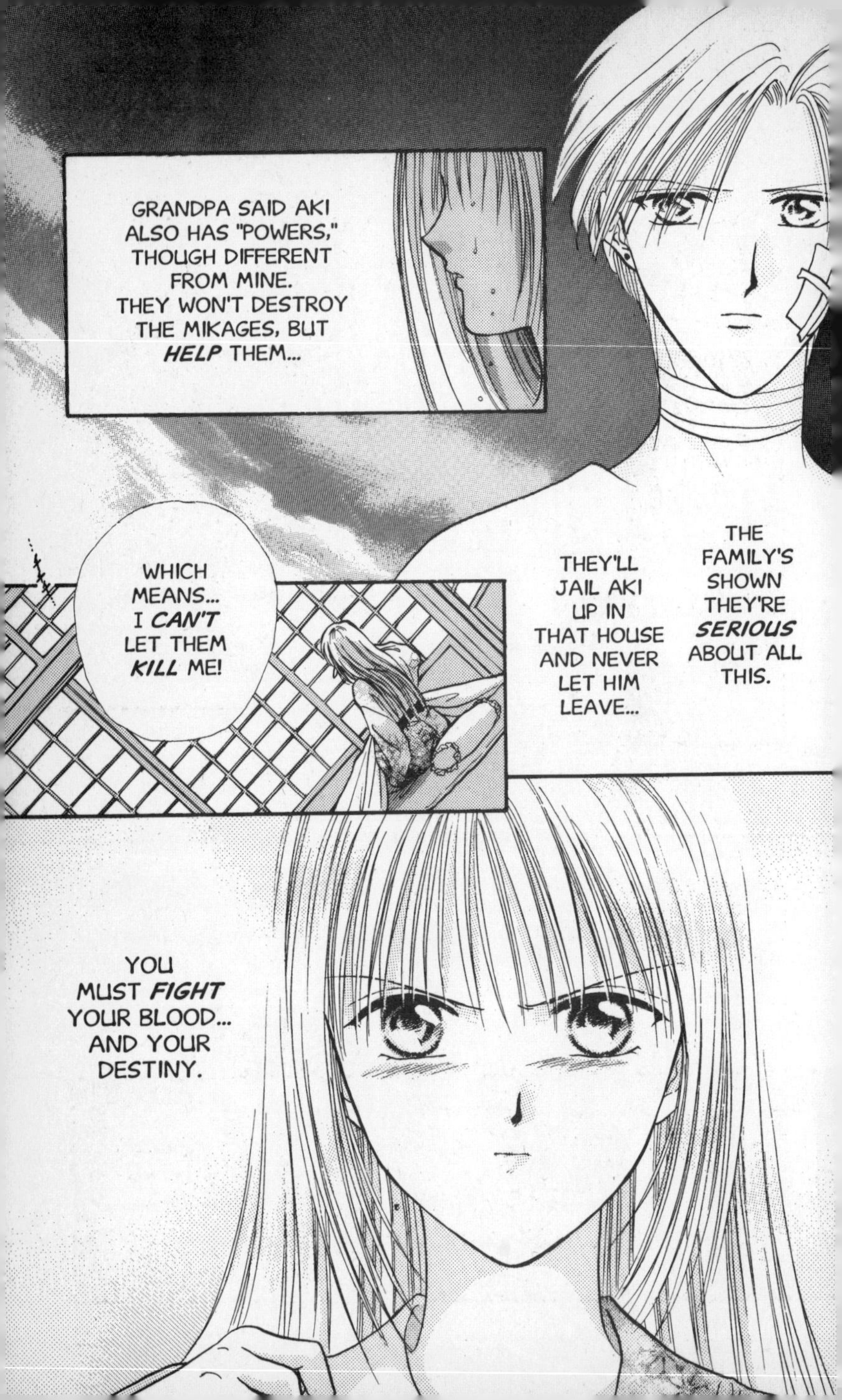

GRANDPA SAID AKI ALSO HAS "POWERS," THOUGH DIFFERENT FROM MINE. THEY WON'T DESTROY THE MIKAGES, BUT *HELP* THEM...
THE FAMILY'S SHOWN THEY'RE *SERIOUS* ABOUT ALL THIS.
THEY'LL JAIL AKI UP IN THAT HOUSE AND NEVER LET HIM LEAVE...
WHICH MEANS... I *CAN'T* LET THEM *KILL* ME!
YOU MUST *FIGHT* YOUR BLOOD... AND YOUR DESTINY.

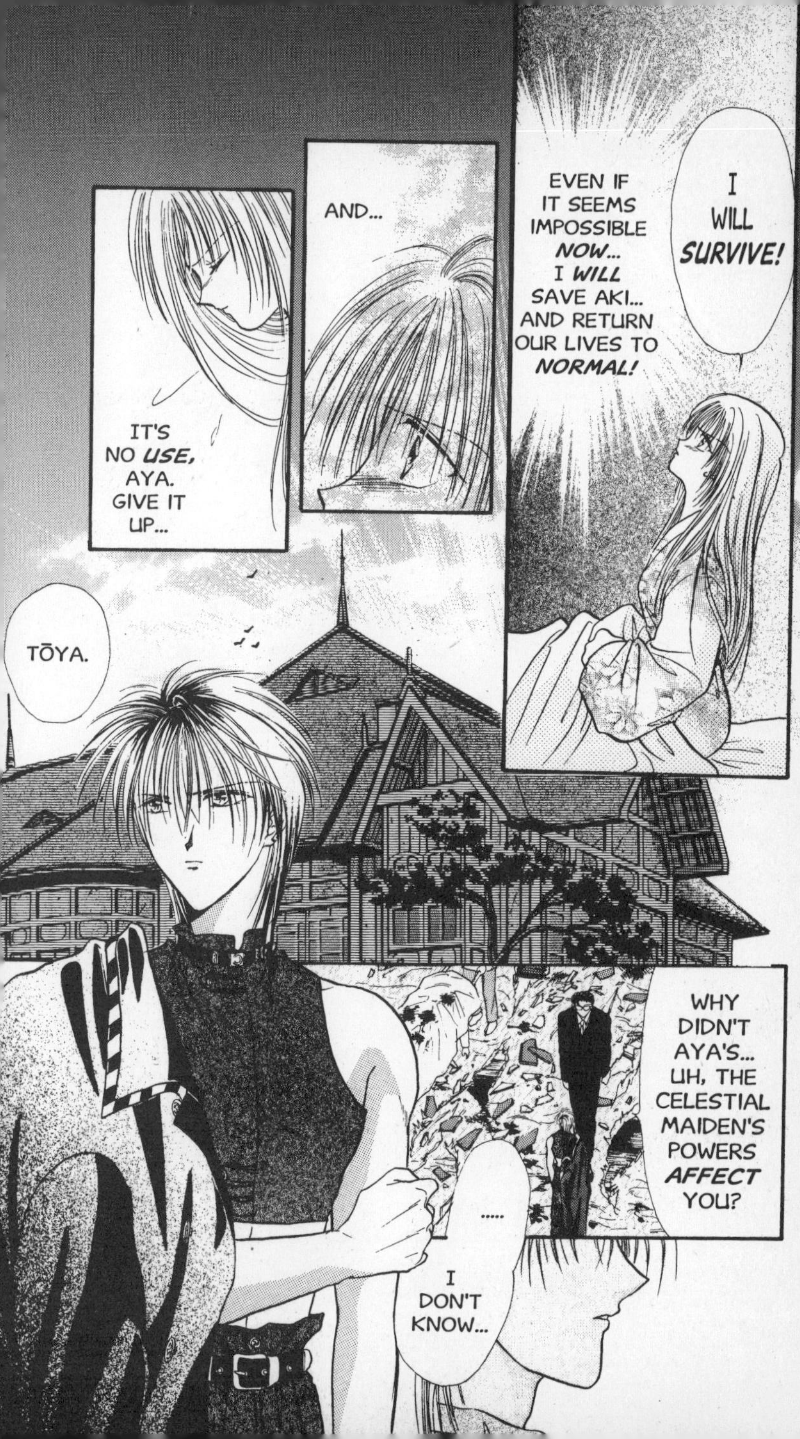
IT'S NO *USE,* AYA. GIVE IT UP...
AND...
EVEN IF IT SEEMS IMPOSSIBLE *NOW*... I *WILL* SAVE AKI... AND RETURN OUR LIVES TO *NORMAL!*
I WILL *SURVIVE!*
TŌYA.
WHY DIDN'T AYA'S... UH, THE CELESTIAL MAIDEN'S POWERS *AFFECT* YOU?
.....
I DON'T KNOW...

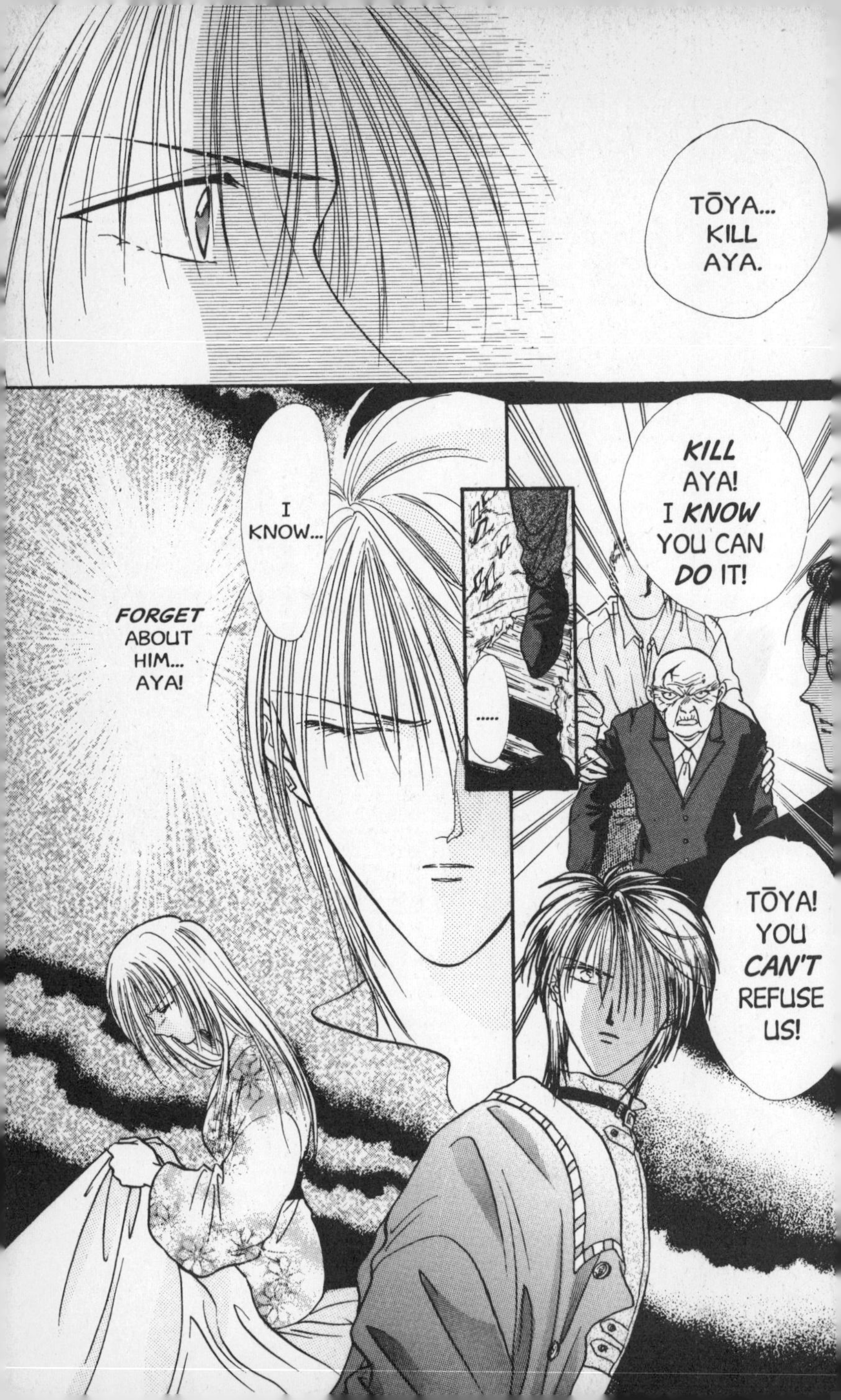
TŌYA... KILL AYA.
KILL AYA! I *KNOW* YOU CAN *DO* IT!
TŌYA! YOU *CAN'T* REFUSE US!
.....
I KNOW...
FORGET ABOUT HIM... AYA!

BIRTHDAY: September 24, Libra

BLOOD TYPE: O

HEIGHT: ? BUST: ? WAIST: ? HIPS: ?

HOBBY: Collecting CDs I want my own computer!

SPECIAL TALENT: Conversational English

AKI MIKAGE

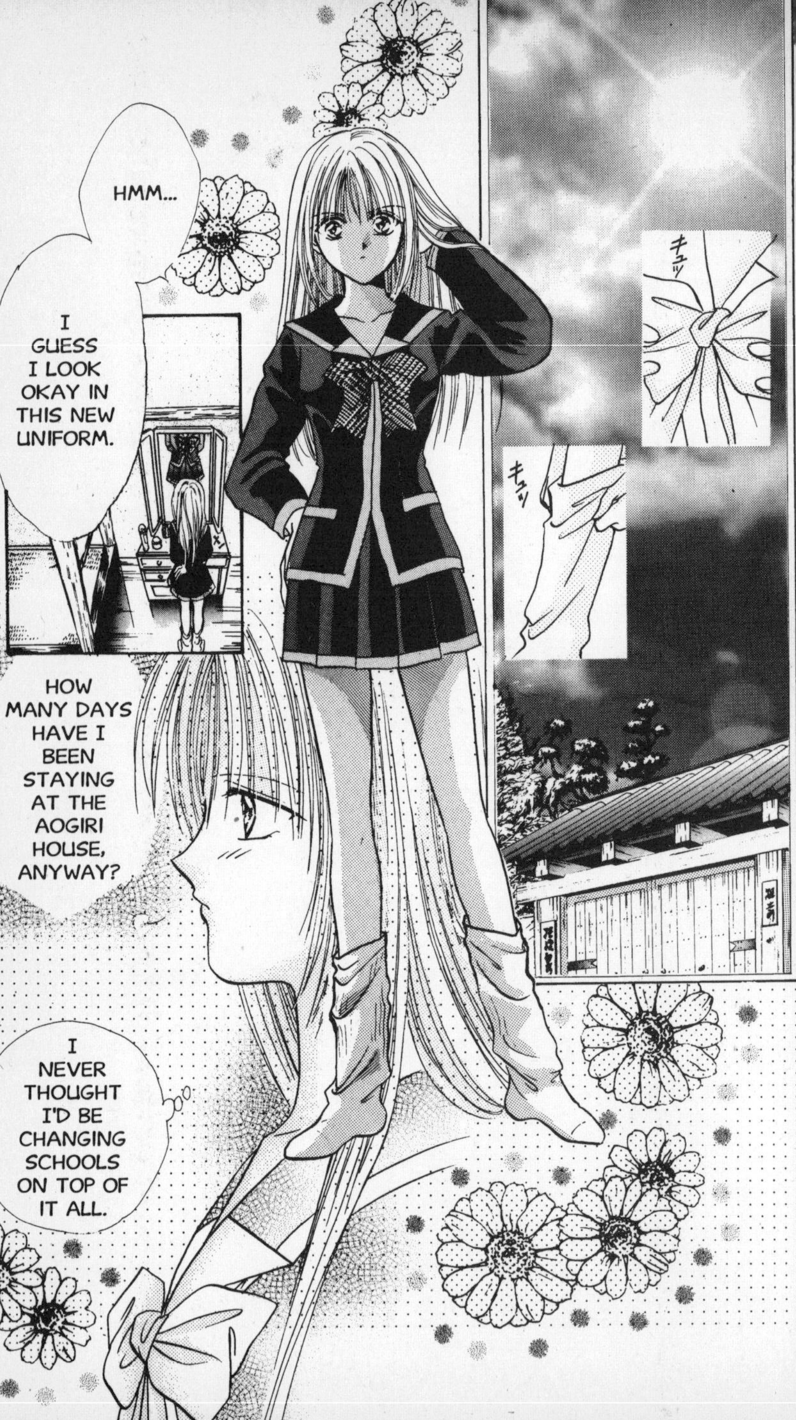
キュッ
キュッ
HMM...
I GUESS I LOOK OKAY IN THIS NEW UNIFORM.
HOW MANY DAYS HAVE I BEEN STAYING AT THE AOGIRI HOUSE, ANYWAY?
I NEVER THOUGHT I'D BE CHANGING SCHOOLS ON TOP OF IT ALL.

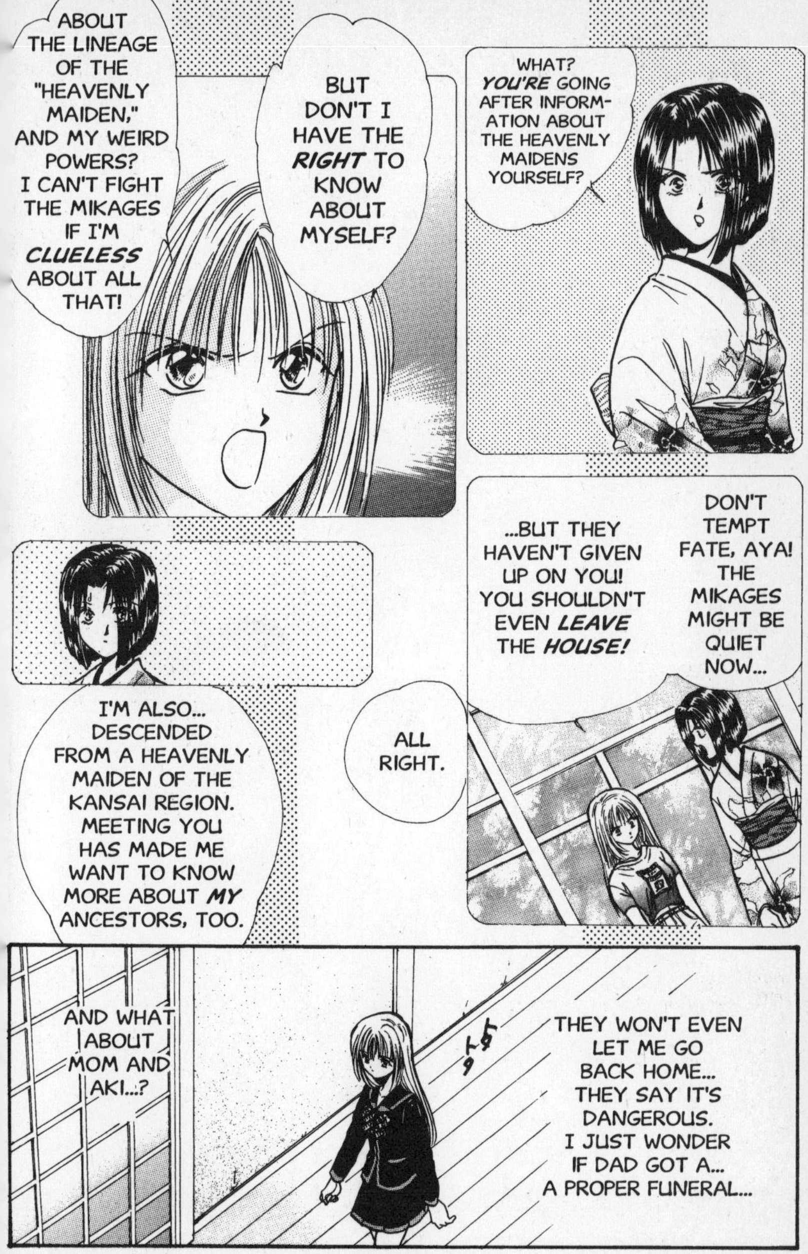
WHAT? *YOU'RE* GOING AFTER INFORMATION ABOUT THE HEAVENLY MAIDENS YOURSELF?
BUT DON'T I HAVE THE *RIGHT* TO KNOW ABOUT MYSELF?
ABOUT THE LINEAGE OF THE "HEAVENLY MAIDEN," AND MY WEIRD POWERS? I CAN'T FIGHT THE MIKAGES IF I'M *CLUELESS* ABOUT ALL THAT!
DON'T TEMPT FATE, AYA! THE MIKAGES MIGHT BE QUIET NOW...
...BUT THEY HAVEN'T GIVEN UP ON YOU! YOU SHOULDN'T EVEN *LEAVE* THE *HOUSE!*
ALL RIGHT.
I'M ALSO... DESCENDED FROM A HEAVENLY MAIDEN OF THE KANSAI REGION. MEETING YOU HAS MADE ME WANT TO KNOW MORE ABOUT *MY* ANCESTORS, TOO.
THEY WON'T EVEN LET ME GO BACK HOME... THEY SAY IT'S DANGEROUS. I JUST WONDER IF DAD GOT A... A PROPER FUNERAL...
AND WHAT ABOUT MOM AND AKI...?

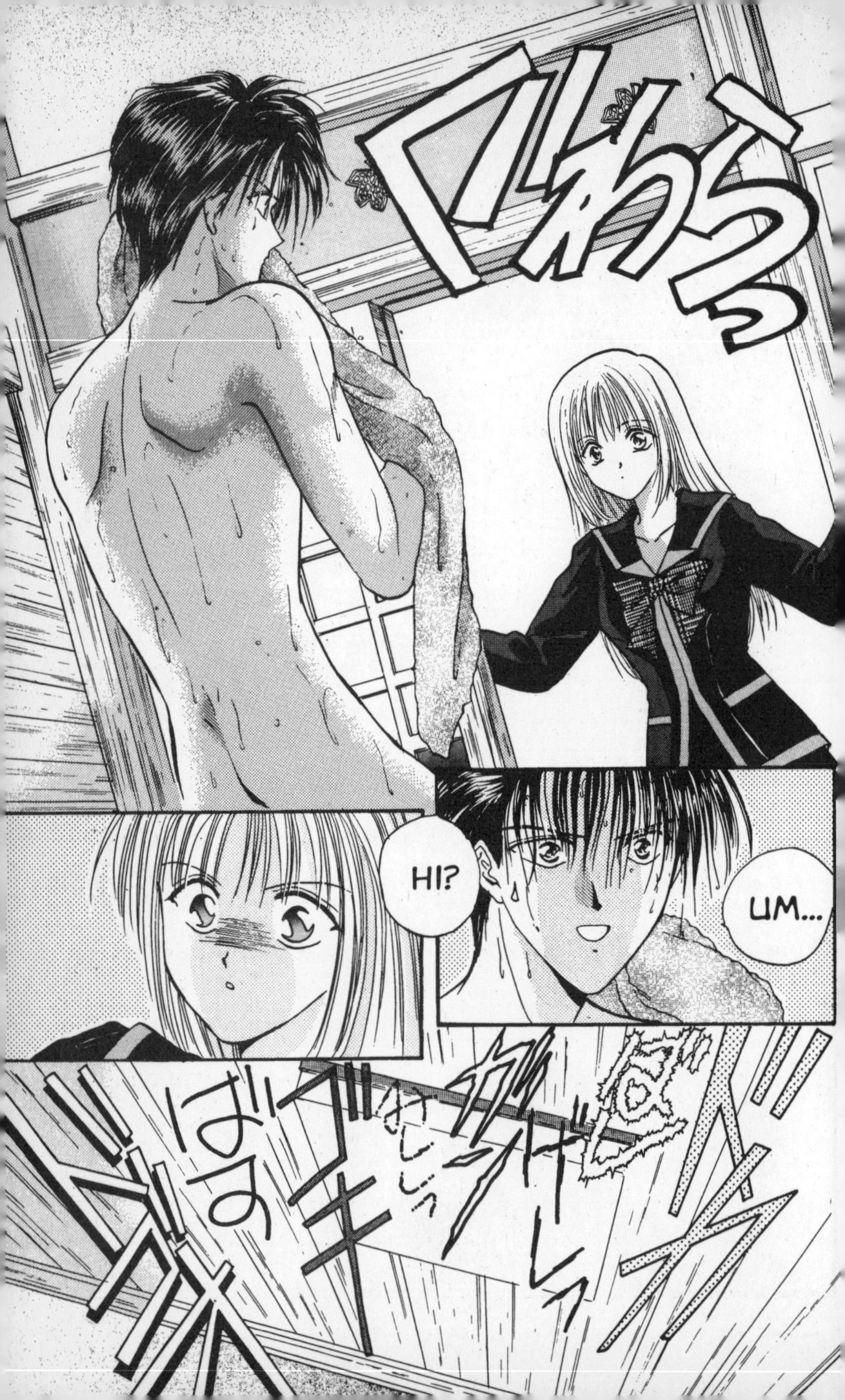
UM...
HI?

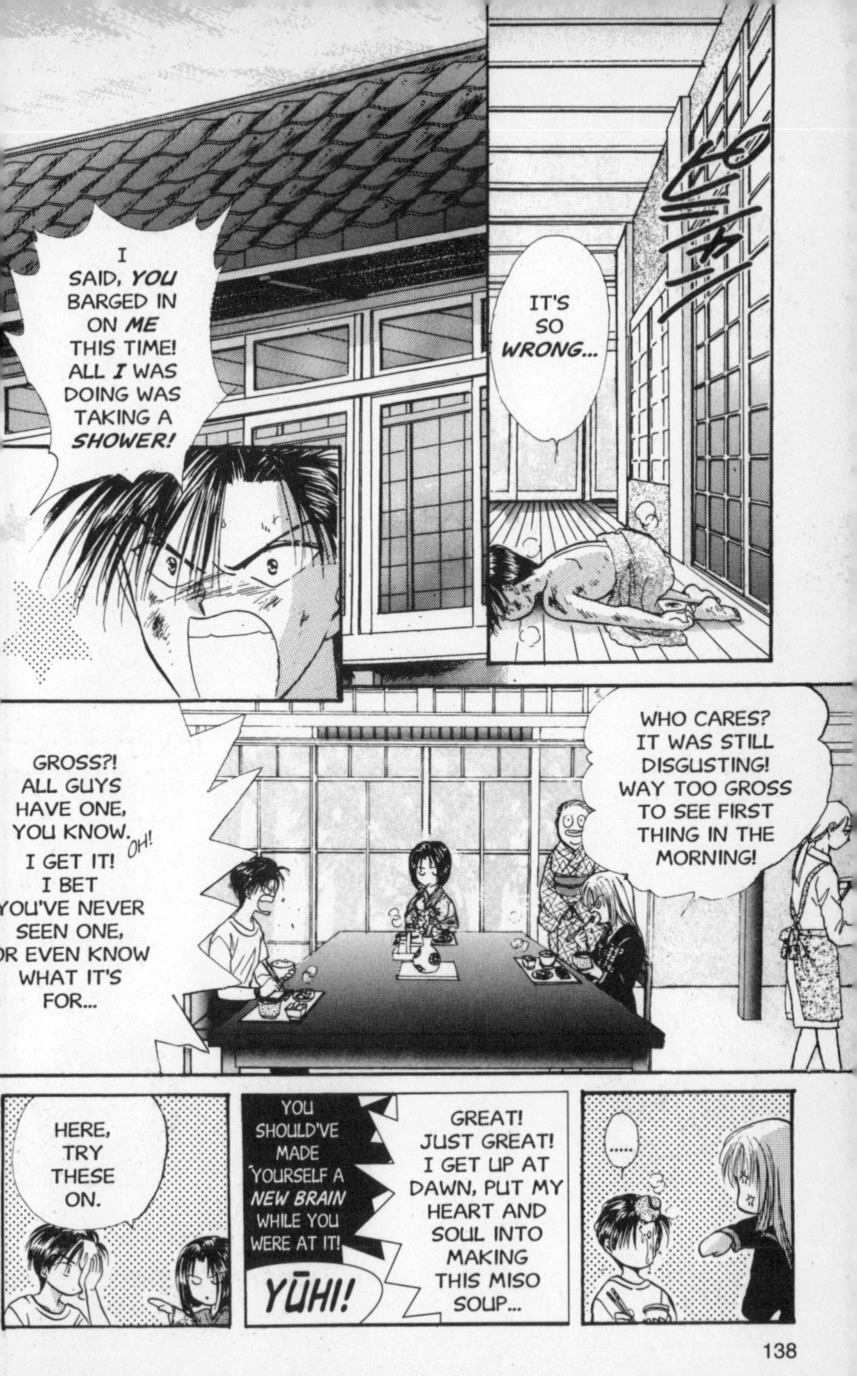

IT'S SO *WRONG*...
I SAID, *YOU* BARGED IN ON *ME* THIS TIME! ALL *I* WAS DOING WAS TAKING A *SHOWER!*
WHO CARES? IT WAS STILL DISGUSTING! WAY TOO GROSS TO SEE FIRST THING IN THE MORNING!
GROSS?! ALL GUYS HAVE ONE, YOU KNOW.
OH!
I GET IT! I BET YOU'VE NEVER SEEN ONE, OR EVEN KNOW WHAT IT'S FOR...
......
GREAT! JUST GREAT! I GET UP AT DAWN, PUT MY HEART AND SOUL INTO MAKING THIS MISO SOUP...
YOU SHOULD'VE MADE YOURSELF A *NEW BRAIN* WHILE YOU WERE AT IT!
YŪHI!
HERE, TRY THESE ON.

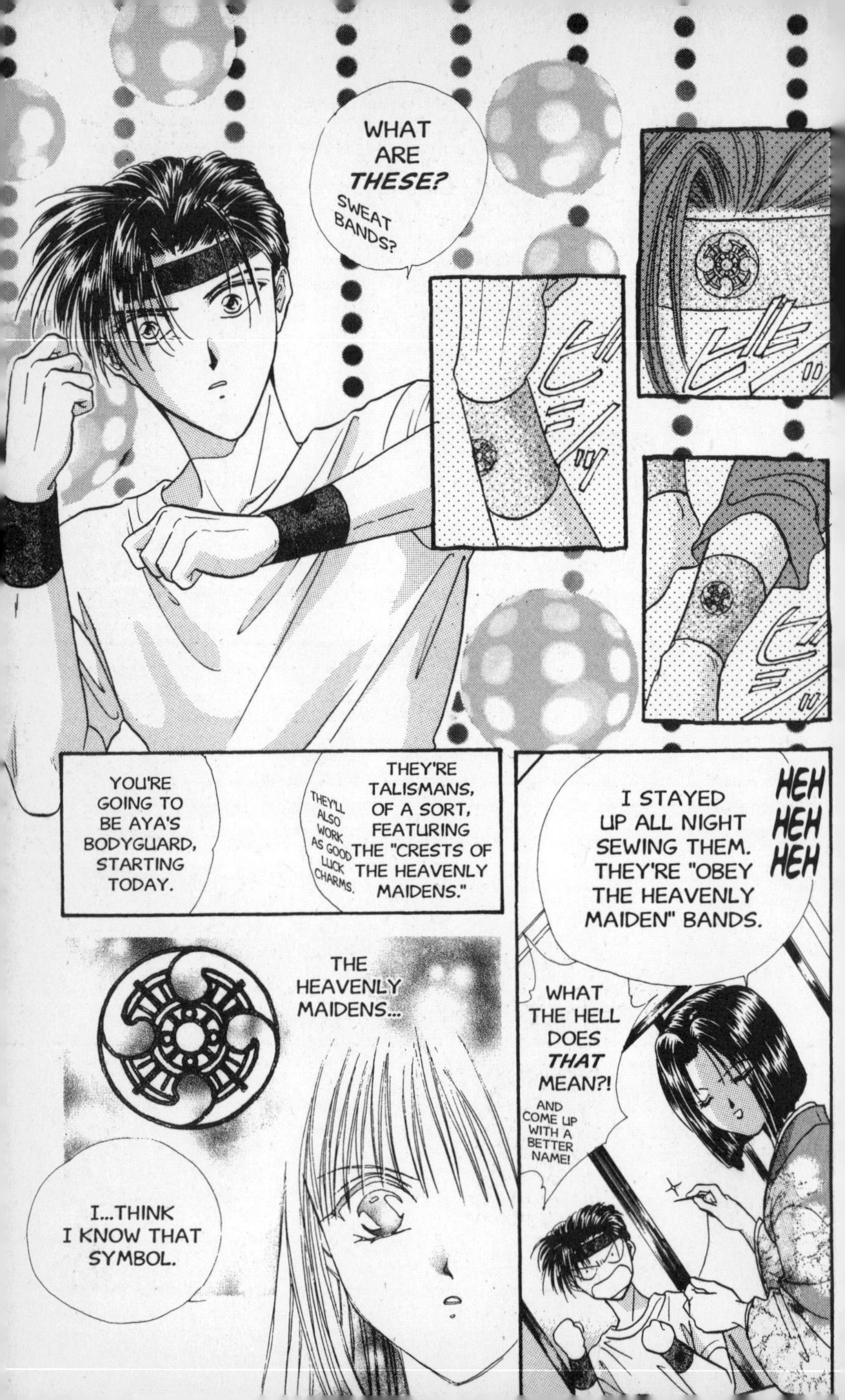
WHAT ARE *THESE?*
SWEAT BANDS?
HEH HEH HEH
I STAYED UP ALL NIGHT SEWING THEM. THEY'RE "OBEY THE HEAVENLY MAIDEN" BANDS.
WHAT THE HELL DOES *THAT* MEAN?!
AND COME UP WITH A BETTER NAME!
THEY'RE TALISMANS, OF A SORT, FEATURING THE "CRESTS OF THE HEAVENLY MAIDENS."
THEY'LL ALSO WORK AS GOOD LUCK CHARMS.
YOU'RE GOING TO BE AYA'S BODYGUARD, STARTING TODAY.
THE HEAVENLY MAIDENS...
I...THINK I KNOW THAT SYMBOL.

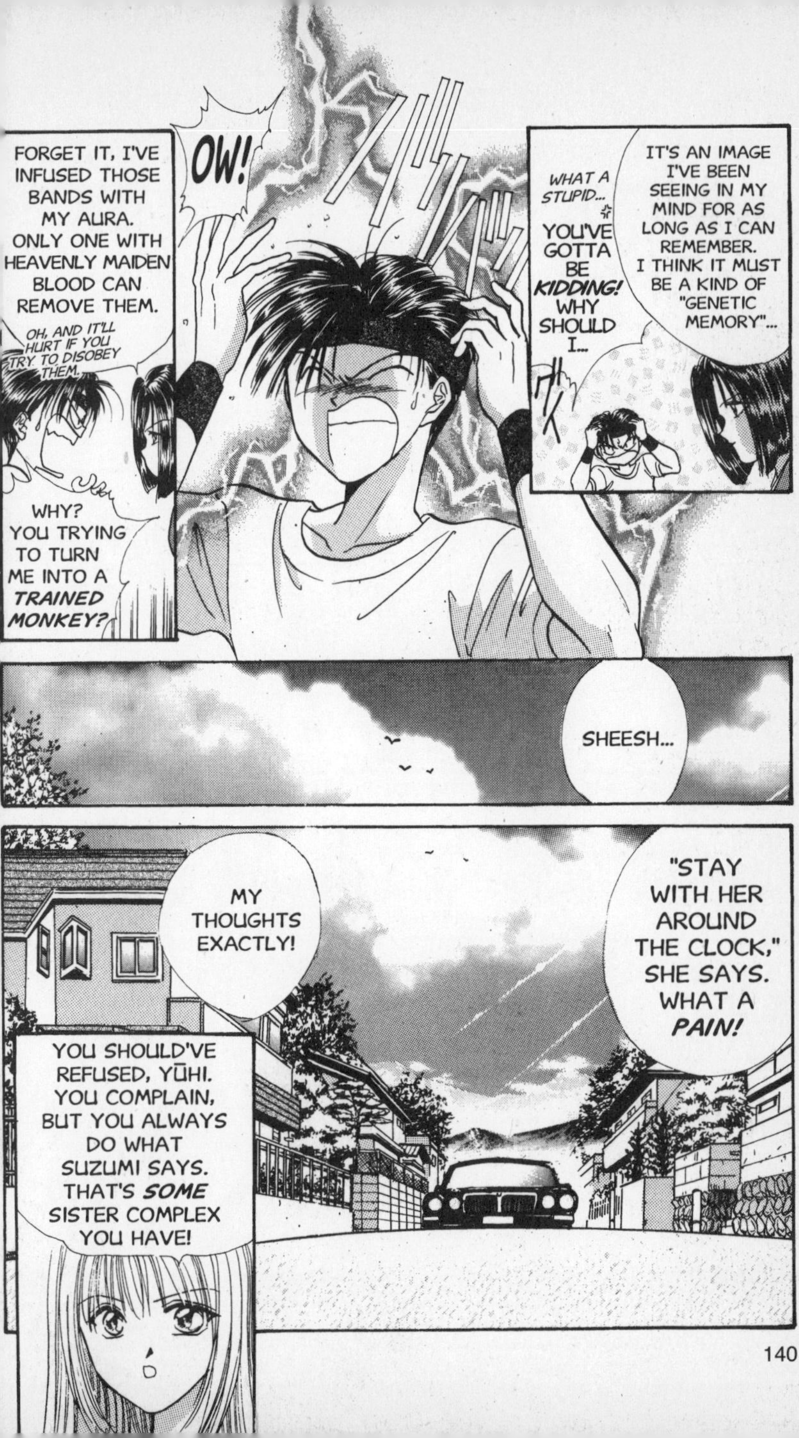
IT'S AN IMAGE I'VE BEEN SEEING IN MY MIND FOR AS LONG AS I CAN REMEMBER. I THINK IT MUST BE A KIND OF "GENETIC MEMORY"...
WHAT A STUPID...
YOU'VE GOTTA BE *KIDDING!* WHY SHOULD I...
OW!
FORGET IT, I'VE INFUSED THOSE BANDS WITH MY AURA. ONLY ONE WITH HEAVENLY MAIDEN BLOOD CAN REMOVE THEM.
OH, AND IT'LL HURT IF YOU TRY TO DISOBEY THEM.
WHY? YOU TRYING TO TURN ME INTO A *TRAINED MONKEY?*
SHEESH...
"STAY WITH HER AROUND THE CLOCK," SHE SAYS. WHAT A *PAIN!*
MY THOUGHTS EXACTLY!
YOU SHOULD'VE REFUSED, YŪHI. YOU COMPLAIN, BUT YOU ALWAYS DO WHAT SUZUMI SAYS. THAT'S *SOME* SISTER COMPLEX YOU HAVE!

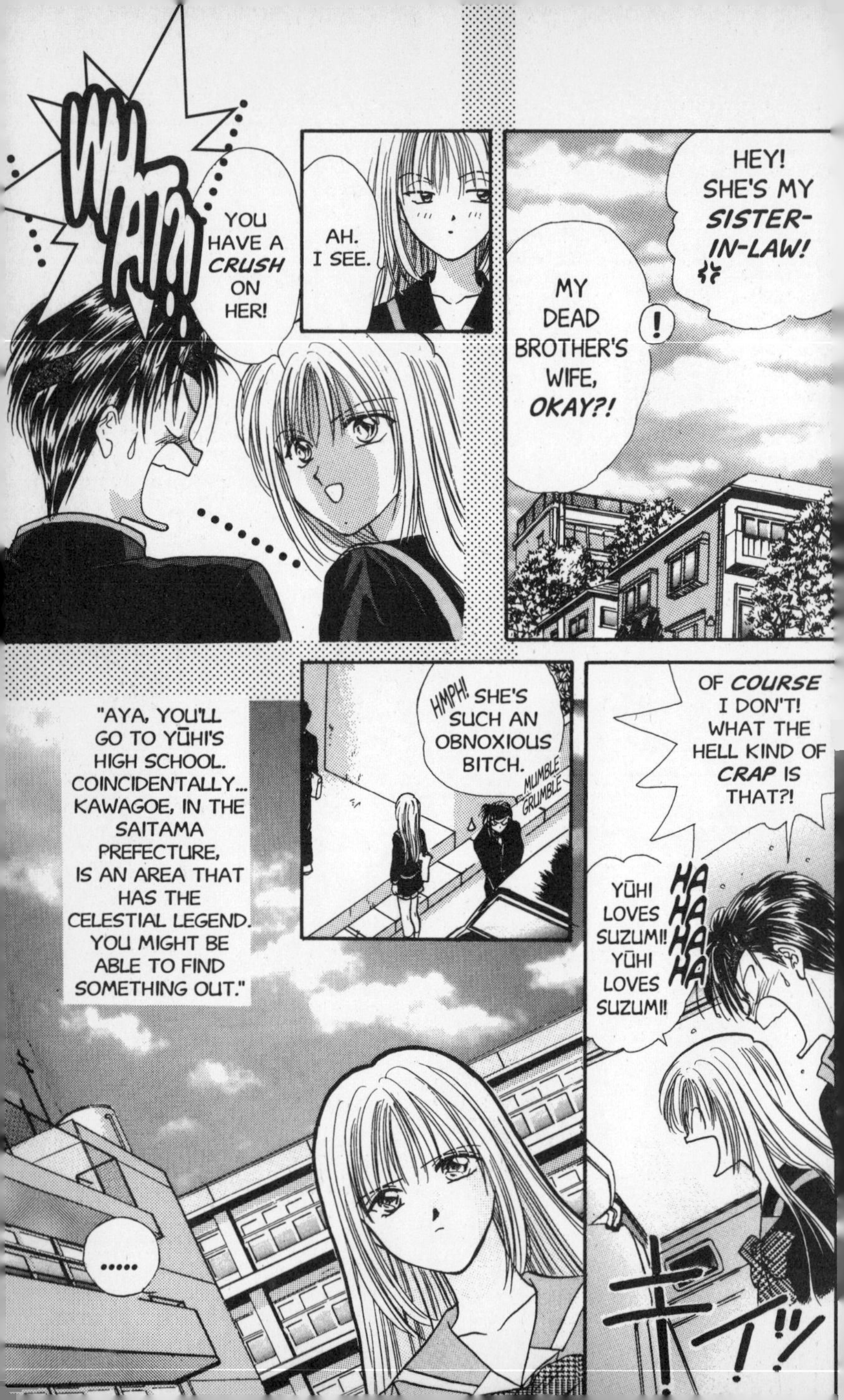
HEY! SHE'S MY SISTER-IN-LAW!
MY DEAD BROTHER'S WIFE, OKAY?!
!
AH. I SEE.
YOU HAVE A CRUSH ON HER!
WHAT?!
......
OF COURSE I DON'T! WHAT THE HELL KIND OF CRAP IS THAT?!
HAHAHAHA
YŪHI LOVES SUZUMI!! YŪHI LOVES SUZUMI!!
HMPH! SHE'S SUCH AN OBNOXIOUS BITCH.
MUMBLE GRUMBLE
"AYA, YOU'LL GO TO YŪHI'S HIGH SCHOOL. COINCIDENTALLY... KAWAGOE, IN THE SAITAMA PREFECTURE, IS AN AREA THAT HAS THE CELESTIAL LEGEND. YOU MIGHT BE ABLE TO FIND SOMETHING OUT."
.....

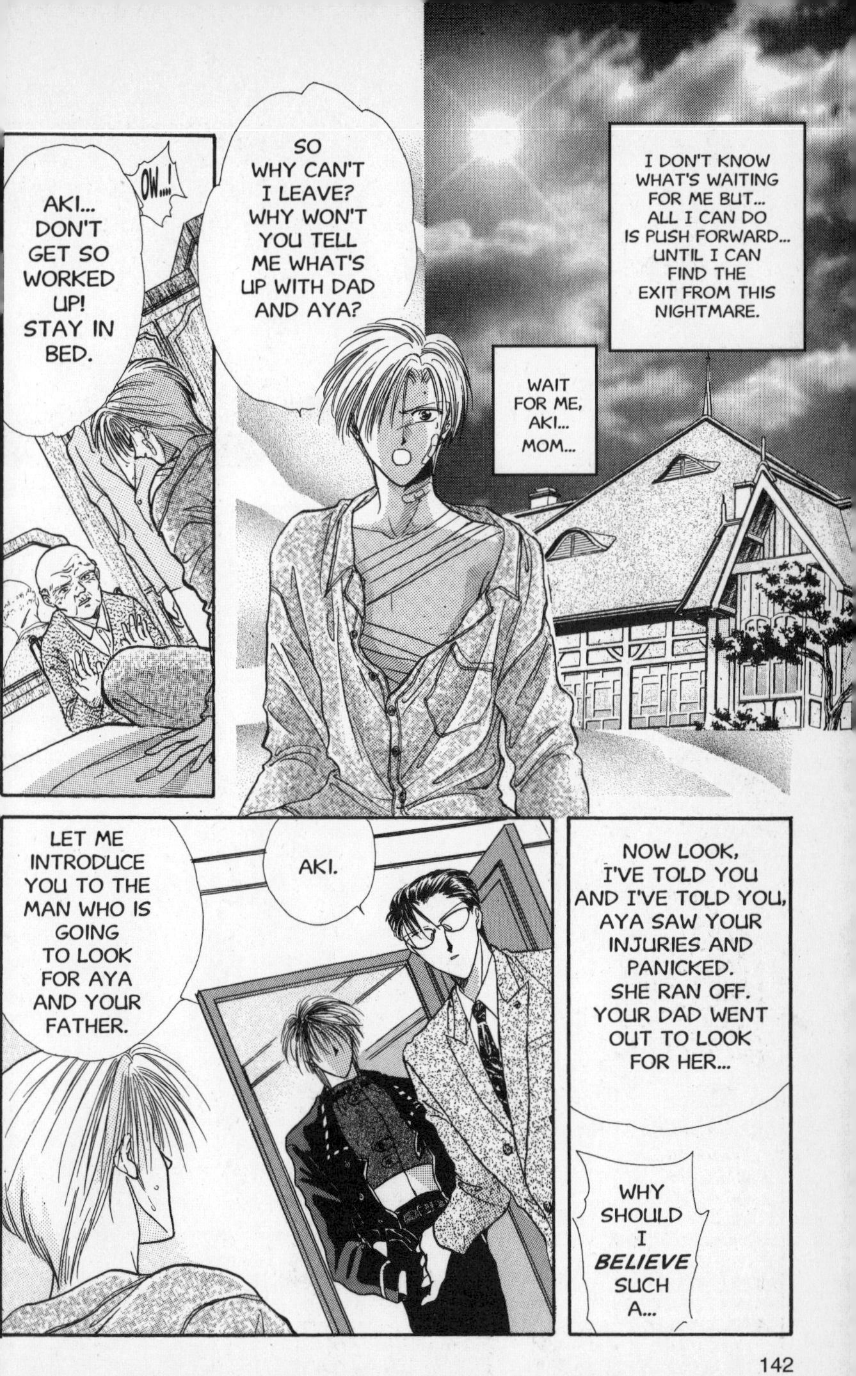
I DON'T KNOW WHAT'S WAITING FOR ME BUT... ALL I CAN DO IS PUSH FORWARD... UNTIL I CAN FIND THE EXIT FROM THIS NIGHTMARE.
WAIT FOR ME, AKI... MOM...
SO WHY CAN'T I LEAVE? WHY WON'T YOU TELL ME WHAT'S UP WITH DAD AND AYA?
OW...!
AKI... DON'T GET SO WORKED UP! STAY IN BED.
NOW LOOK, I'VE TOLD YOU AND I'VE TOLD YOU, AYA SAW YOUR INJURIES AND PANICKED. SHE RAN OFF. YOUR DAD WENT OUT TO LOOK FOR HER...
WHY SHOULD I *BELIEVE* SUCH A...
AKI.
LET ME INTRODUCE YOU TO THE MAN WHO IS GOING TO LOOK FOR AYA AND YOUR FATHER.

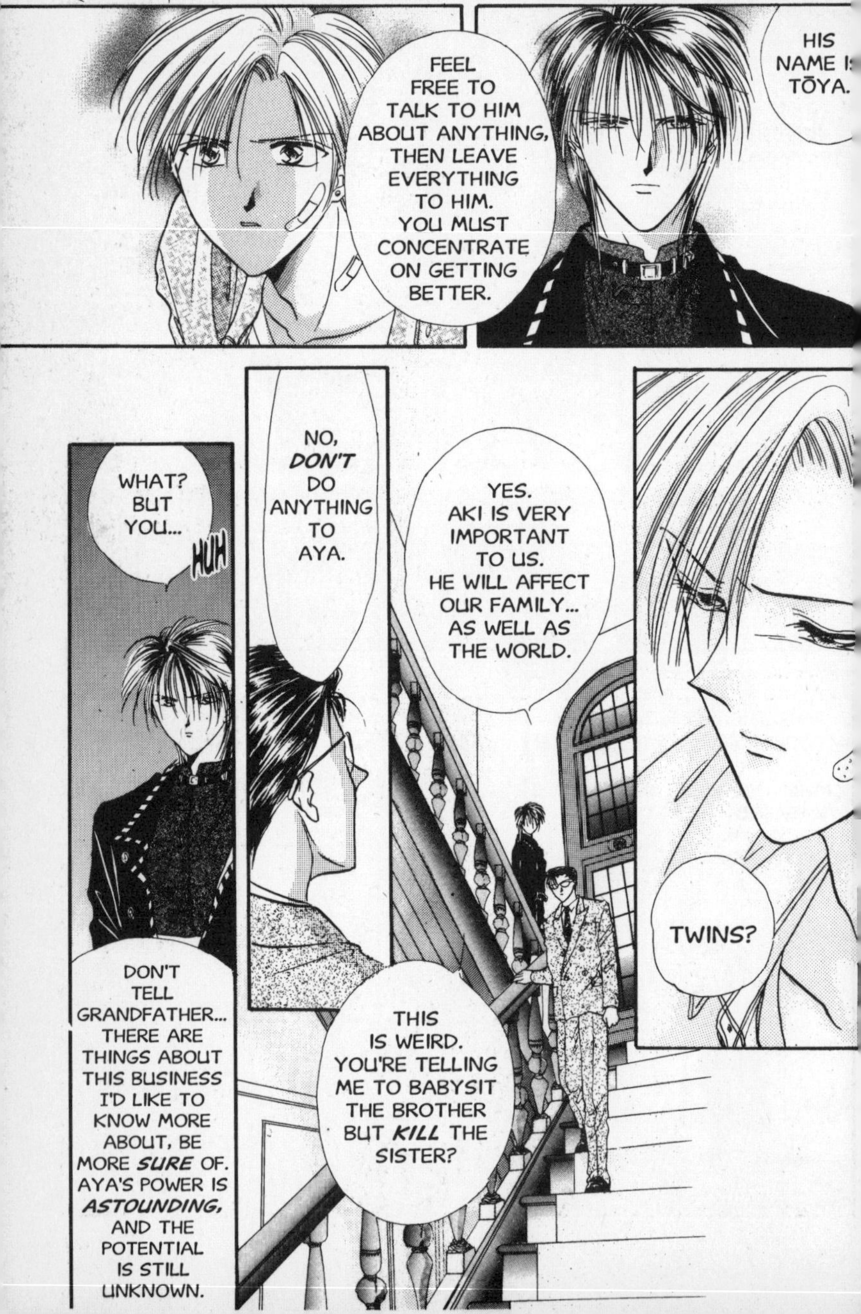
HIS NAME IS TŌYA.
FEEL FREE TO TALK TO HIM ABOUT ANYTHING, THEN LEAVE EVERYTHING TO HIM. YOU MUST CONCENTRATE ON GETTING BETTER.
TWINS?
YES. AKI IS VERY IMPORTANT TO US. HE WILL AFFECT OUR FAMILY... AS WELL AS THE WORLD.
THIS IS WEIRD. YOU'RE TELLING ME TO BABYSIT THE BROTHER BUT KILL THE SISTER?
NO, DON'T DO ANYTHING TO AYA.
WHAT? BUT YOU...
HUH
DON'T TELL GRANDFATHER... THERE ARE THINGS ABOUT THIS BUSINESS I'D LIKE TO KNOW MORE ABOUT, BE MORE SURE OF. AYA'S POWER IS ASTOUNDING, AND THE POTENTIAL IS STILL UNKNOWN.

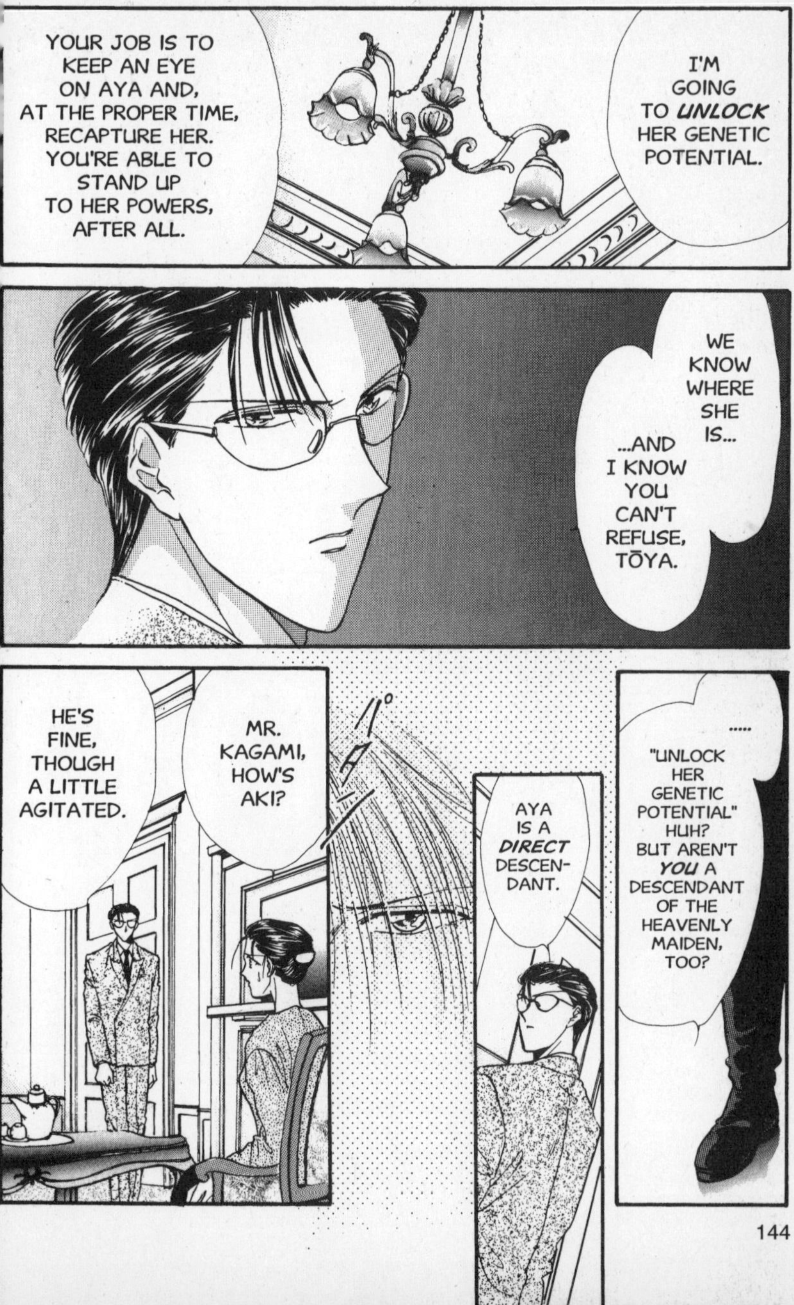
I'M GOING TO *UNLOCK* HER GENETIC POTENTIAL.
YOUR JOB IS TO KEEP AN EYE ON AYA AND, AT THE PROPER TIME, RECAPTURE HER. YOU'RE ABLE TO STAND UP TO HER POWERS, AFTER ALL.
WE KNOW WHERE SHE IS...
...AND I KNOW YOU CAN'T REFUSE, TŌYA.
.....
"UNLOCK HER GENETIC POTENTIAL" HUH? BUT AREN'T *YOU* A DESCENDANT OF THE HEAVENLY MAIDEN, TOO?
AYA IS A *DIRECT* DESCENDANT.
MR. KAGAMI, HOW'S AKI?
HE'S FINE, THOUGH A LITTLE AGITATED.

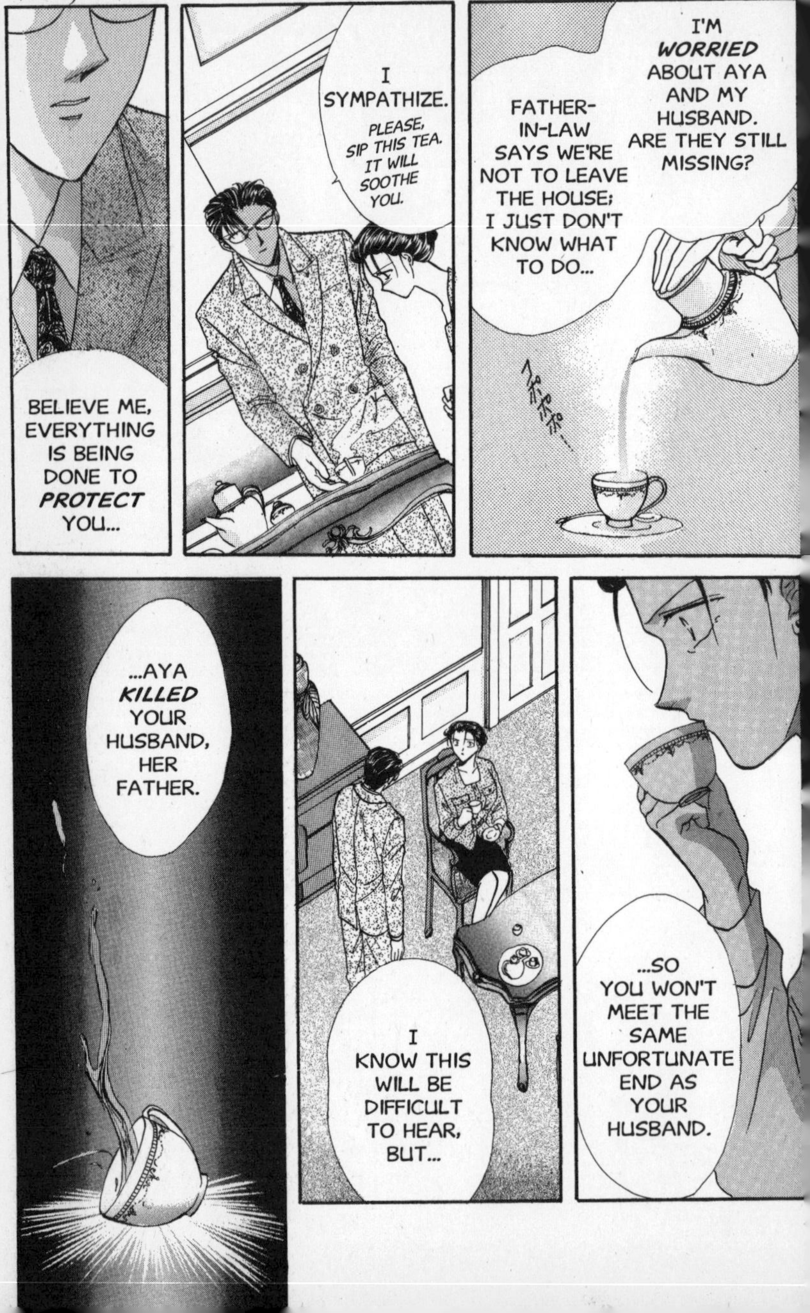
I'M WORRIED ABOUT AYA AND MY HUSBAND. ARE THEY STILL MISSING?
FATHER-IN-LAW SAYS WE'RE NOT TO LEAVE THE HOUSE; I JUST DON'T KNOW WHAT TO DO...
I SYMPATHIZE.
PLEASE, SIP THIS TEA. IT WILL SOOTHE YOU.
BELIEVE ME, EVERYTHING IS BEING DONE TO PROTECT YOU...
...SO YOU WON'T MEET THE SAME UNFORTUNATE END AS YOUR HUSBAND.
I KNOW THIS WILL BE DIFFICULT TO HEAR, BUT...
...AYA KILLED YOUR HUSBAND, HER FATHER.

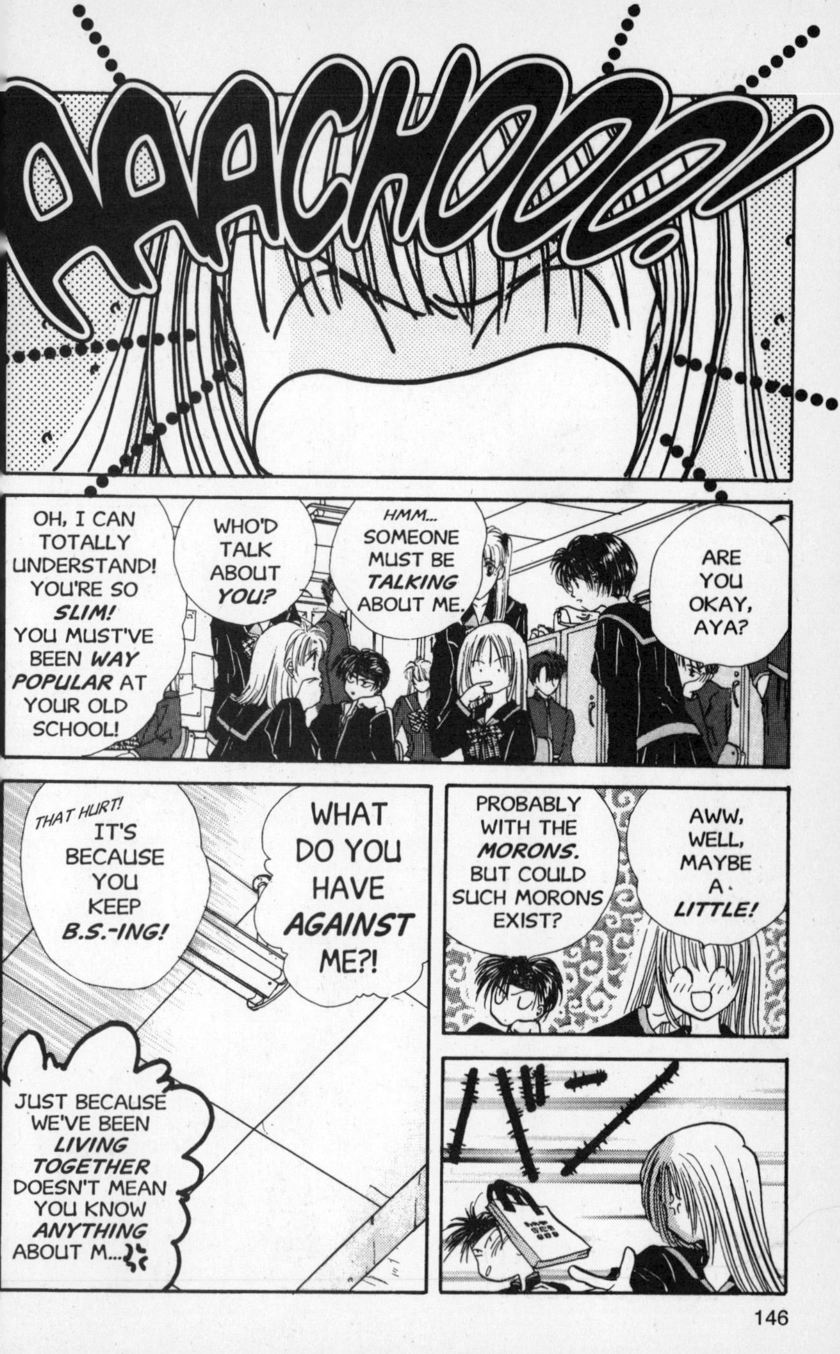
AACHOO!!
ARE YOU OKAY, AYA?
HMM... SOMEONE MUST BE TALKING ABOUT ME.
WHO'D TALK ABOUT YOU?
OH, I CAN TOTALLY UNDERSTAND! YOU'RE SO SLIM! YOU MUST'VE BEEN WAY POPULAR AT YOUR OLD SCHOOL!
AWW, WELL, MAYBE A LITTLE!
PROBABLY WITH THE MORONS. BUT COULD SUCH MORONS EXIST?
WHAT DO YOU HAVE AGAINST ME?!
THAT HURT! IT'S BECAUSE YOU KEEP B.S.-ING!
JUST BECAUSE WE'VE BEEN LIVING TOGETHER DOESN'T MEAN YOU KNOW ANYTHING ABOUT M...

Ceres: 1

Nah, I'm not gonna tell!
But this time I hadn't seen the storyboard beforehand, so it was really exciting! Watching it alone in the middle of the night, I kept shouting out (I can be such an idiot). "Ooh!" "Tama's so cool!" "Whoa?!" "Tasuki! Nicely done!" "Ack!" "Ooh! Amiboshi's so cute!" "Gack!" "Hey!" "Eek!" "Er?!" (I'm getting further removed from human speech) . . . And at the end, "Aww!" -- ♡ such a girlie sound, so out of character for me. . . . Why? You'll have to see for yourself. It's great! It goes on sale Dec. 18th. . . I think? The new song and the soundtrack are on sale too. In vol. 3 everything will become clear. The director and the staff are amazing. I really recommend it.
The art is so beautiful! I'd like to learn from it. . . ~♪
But that scene in vol. 2 is dirty. . .

So! Enough advertising, and back to the topic. I think "Ceres" has a lot of my personal tastes in it. Ms. (Naoko) Takeuchi wrote me in her letter that "it has a lot of female fan service," and I was like, "gasp!" Really? Maybe a little? Well, maybe. Yeah, sure! Over and above "Ceres," I'm. . . obsessed with erotic beauty. Good-looking guys and slightly twisted forbidden love. There'd be some blood flying, and a melancholy mood, and there would be expressions of love that are totally over the top. And it would all be linked to "death." The BGM would have to be classical! My works are said to be "positive and enthusiastic," but there's actually another side to it. . . Even if it's over-the-top, there would have to be "love!" Don't you get enraptured listening to Buck-Tick's Misshitsu ("Behind Closed Doors") from the album Six/Nine. . .? Don't you? I'd like to draw all these things, but then I'd be excluded from shojo comics!
My innocent readers are going to run away. Darn!

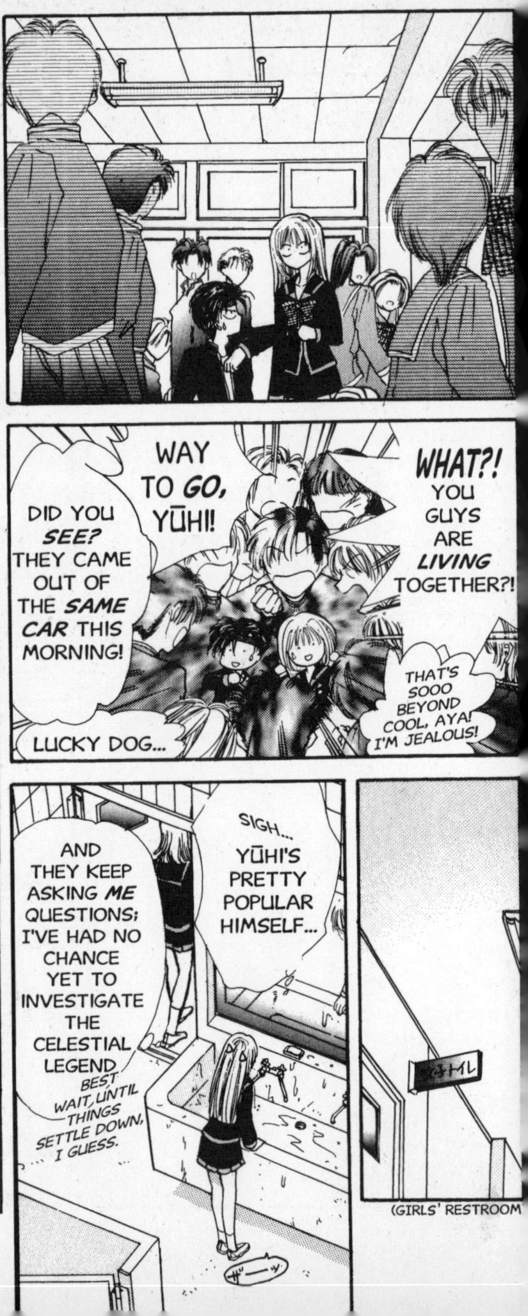
WHAT?! YOU GUYS ARE LIVING TOGETHER?!
THAT'S SOOO BEYOND COOL, AYA! I'M JEALOUS!
WAY TO GO, YŪHI!
DID YOU SEE? THEY CAME OUT OF THE SAME CAR THIS MORNING!
LUCKY DOG...
(GIRLS' RESTROOM)
SIGH... YŪHI'S PRETTY POPULAR HIMSELF...
AND THEY KEEP ASKING ME QUESTIONS; I'VE HAD NO CHANCE YET TO INVESTIGATE THE CELESTIAL LEGEND
BEST WAIT, UNTIL THINGS SETTLE DOWN, I GUESS.

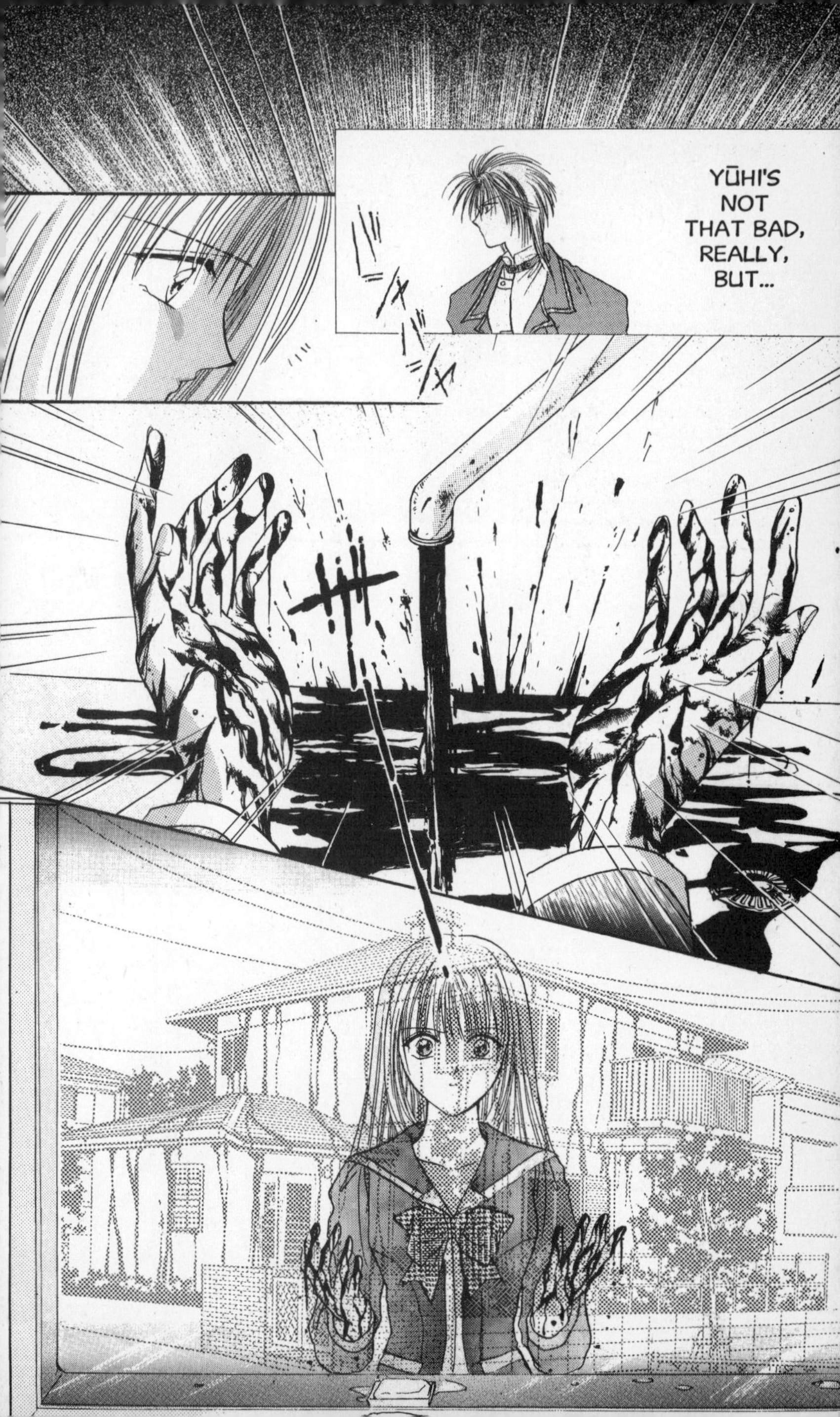
YŪHI'S NOT THAT BAD, REALLY, BUT...

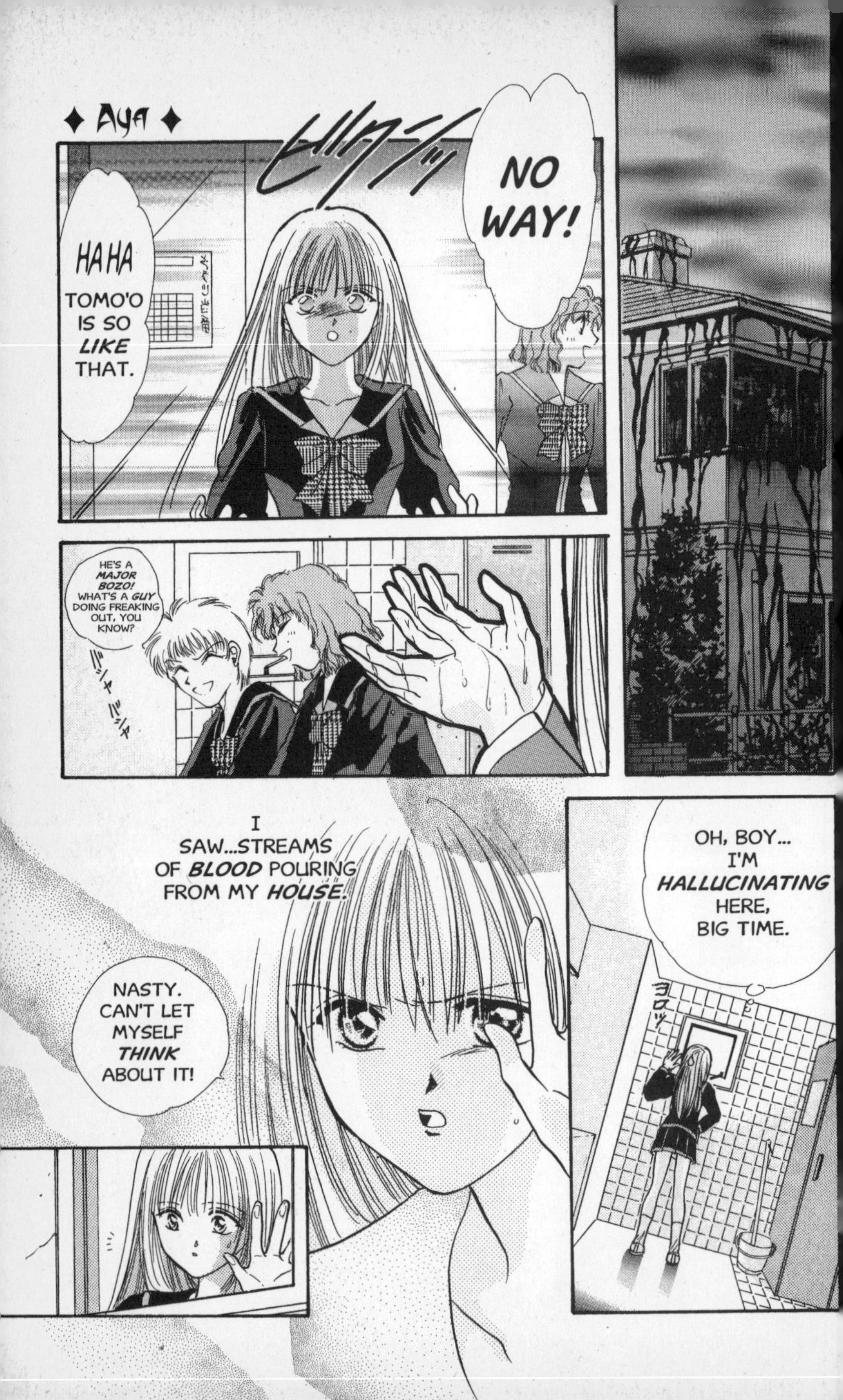
NO WAY!
HA HA TOMO'O IS SO *LIKE* THAT.
HE'S A *MAJOR BOZO!* WHAT'S A *GUY* DOING FREAKING OUT, YOU KNOW?
OH, BOY... I'M *HALLUCINATING* HERE, BIG TIME.
I SAW...STREAMS OF *BLOOD* POURING FROM MY *HOUSE.*
NASTY. CAN'T LET MYSELF *THINK* ABOUT IT!

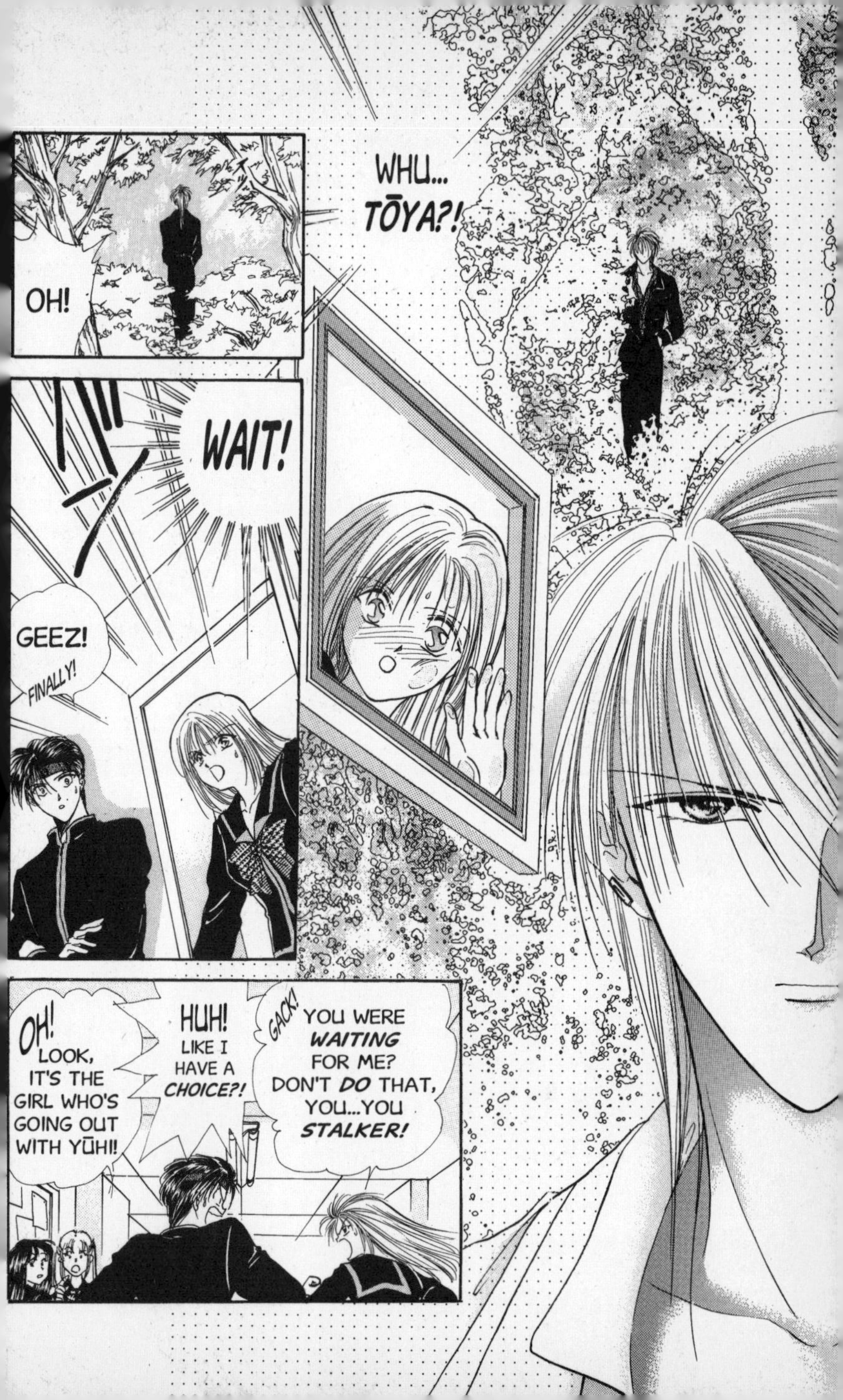
WHU... TŌYA?!
OH!
WAIT!
GEEZ!
FINALLY!
GACK!
YOU WERE WAITING FOR ME? DON'T DO THAT, YOU...YOU STALKER!
HUH! LIKE I HAVE A CHOICE?!
OH! LOOK, IT'S THE GIRL WHO'S GOING OUT WITH YŪHI!

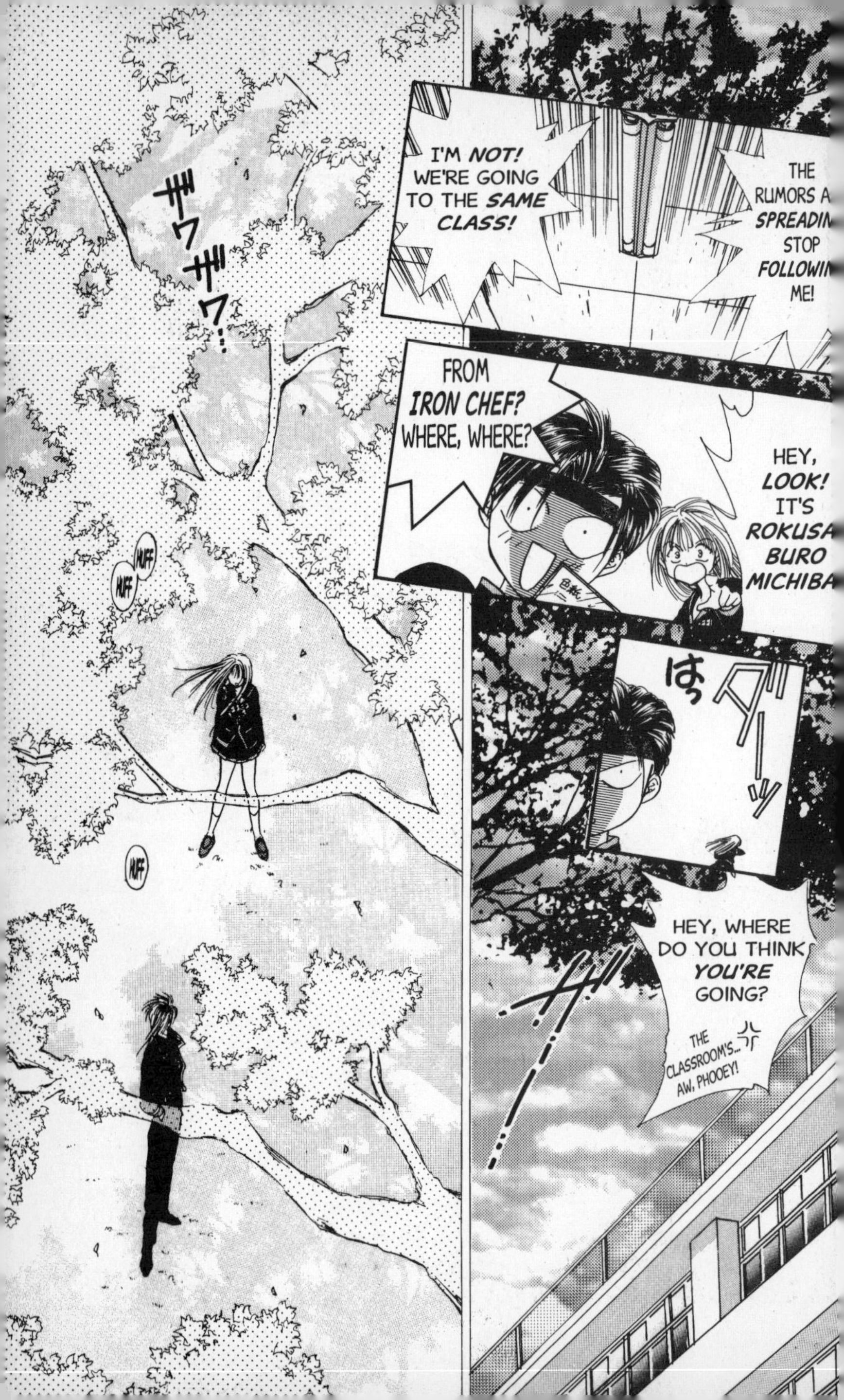
THE RUMORS A SPREADIN STOP FOLLOWIN ME!
I'M NOT! WE'RE GOING TO THE SAME CLASS!
HEY, LOOK! IT'S ROKUSA BURO MICHIBA
FROM IRON CHEF? WHERE, WHERE?
はっ
ダーッ
HEY, WHERE DO YOU THINK YOU'RE GOING?
THE CLASSROOM'S... AW, PHOOEY!
ザワザワ‥
HUFF
HUFF
HUFF

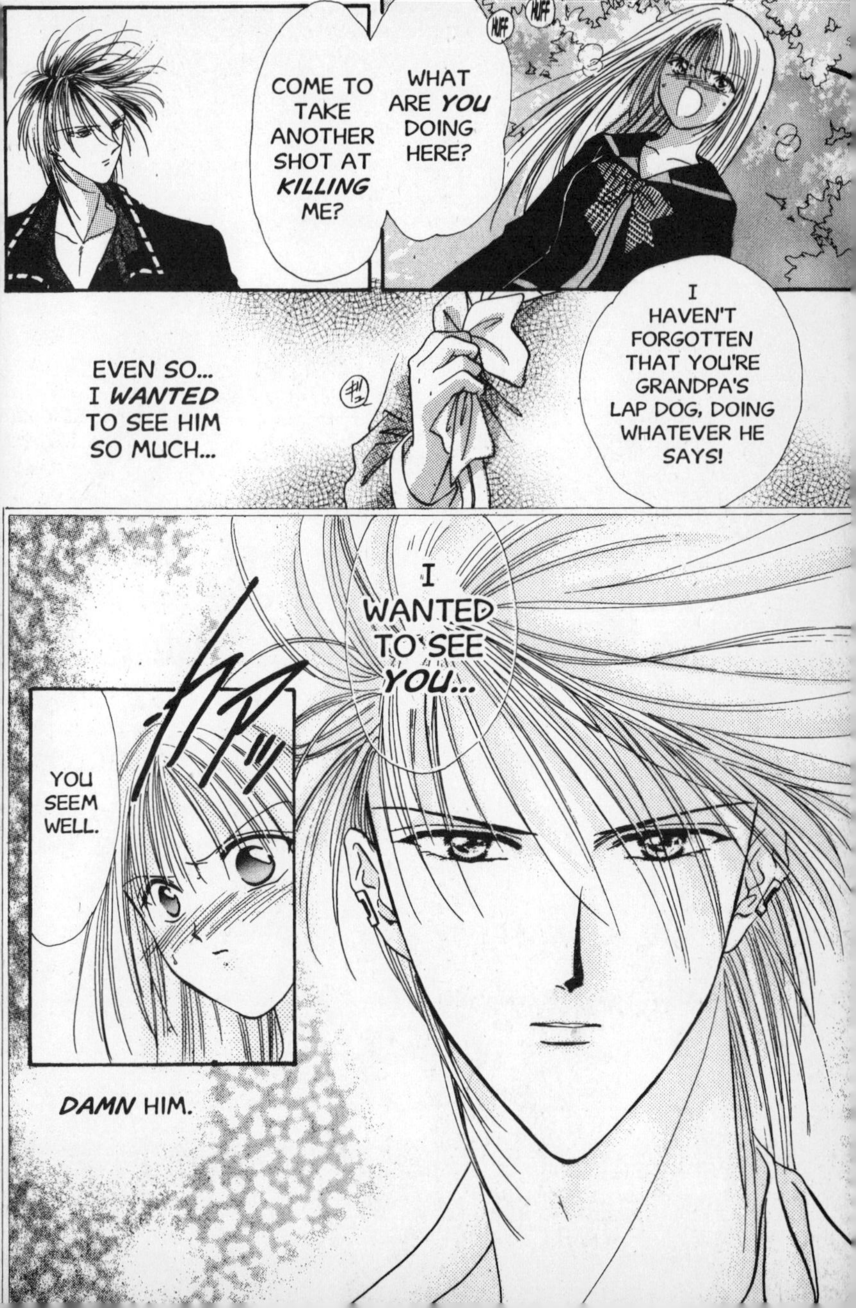
HUFF
HUFF
WHAT ARE YOU DOING HERE?
COME TO TAKE ANOTHER SHOT AT KILLING ME?
I HAVEN'T FORGOTTEN THAT YOU'RE GRANDPA'S LAP DOG, DOING WHATEVER HE SAYS!
EVEN SO... I WANTED TO SEE HIM SO MUCH...
I WANTED TO SEE YOU...
YOU SEEM WELL.
DAMN HIM.

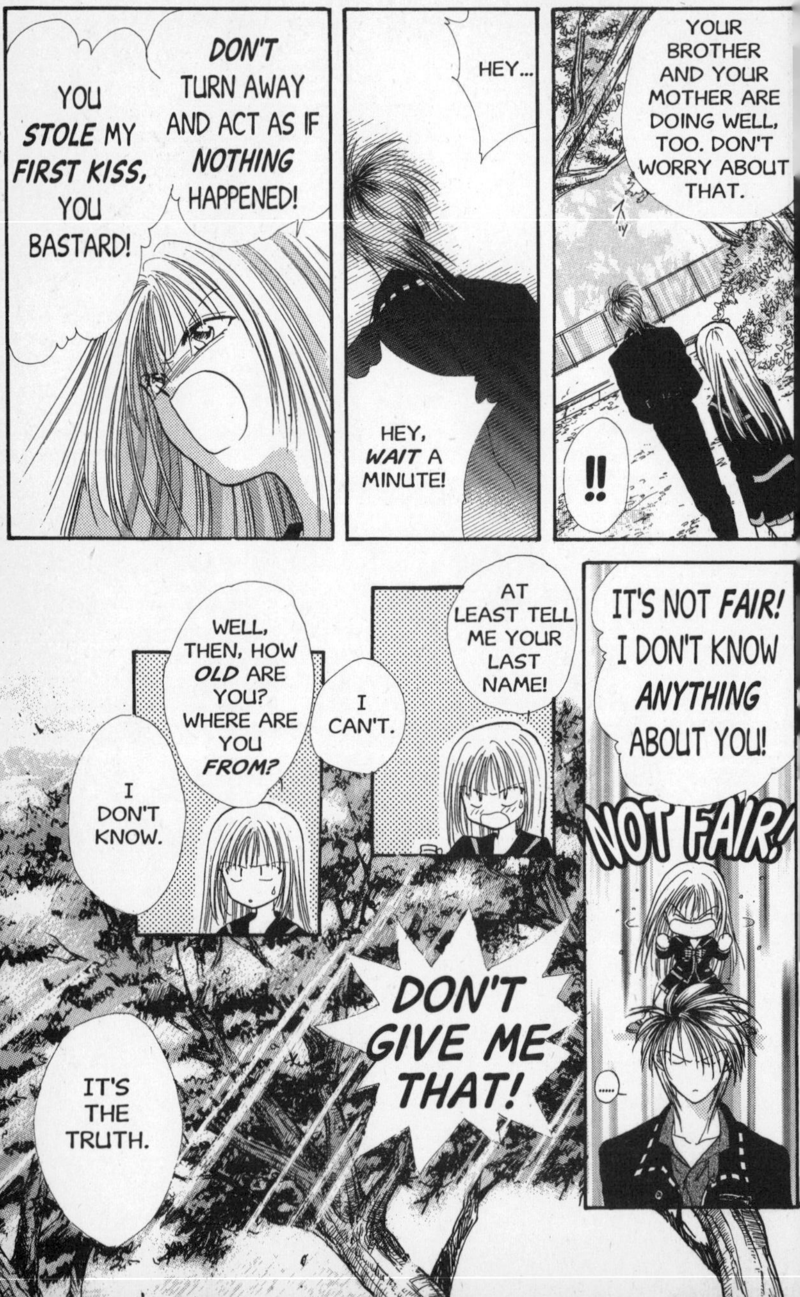
YOUR BROTHER AND YOUR MOTHER ARE DOING WELL, TOO. DON'T WORRY ABOUT THAT.
!!
HEY...
HEY, WAIT A MINUTE!
DON'T TURN AWAY AND ACT AS IF NOTHING HAPPENED!
YOU STOLE MY FIRST KISS, YOU BASTARD!
IT'S NOT FAIR! I DON'T KNOW ANYTHING ABOUT YOU!
NOT FAIR!
......
AT LEAST TELL ME YOUR LAST NAME!
I CAN'T.
WELL, THEN, HOW OLD ARE YOU? WHERE ARE YOU FROM?
I DON'T KNOW.
DON'T GIVE ME THAT!
IT'S THE TRUTH.

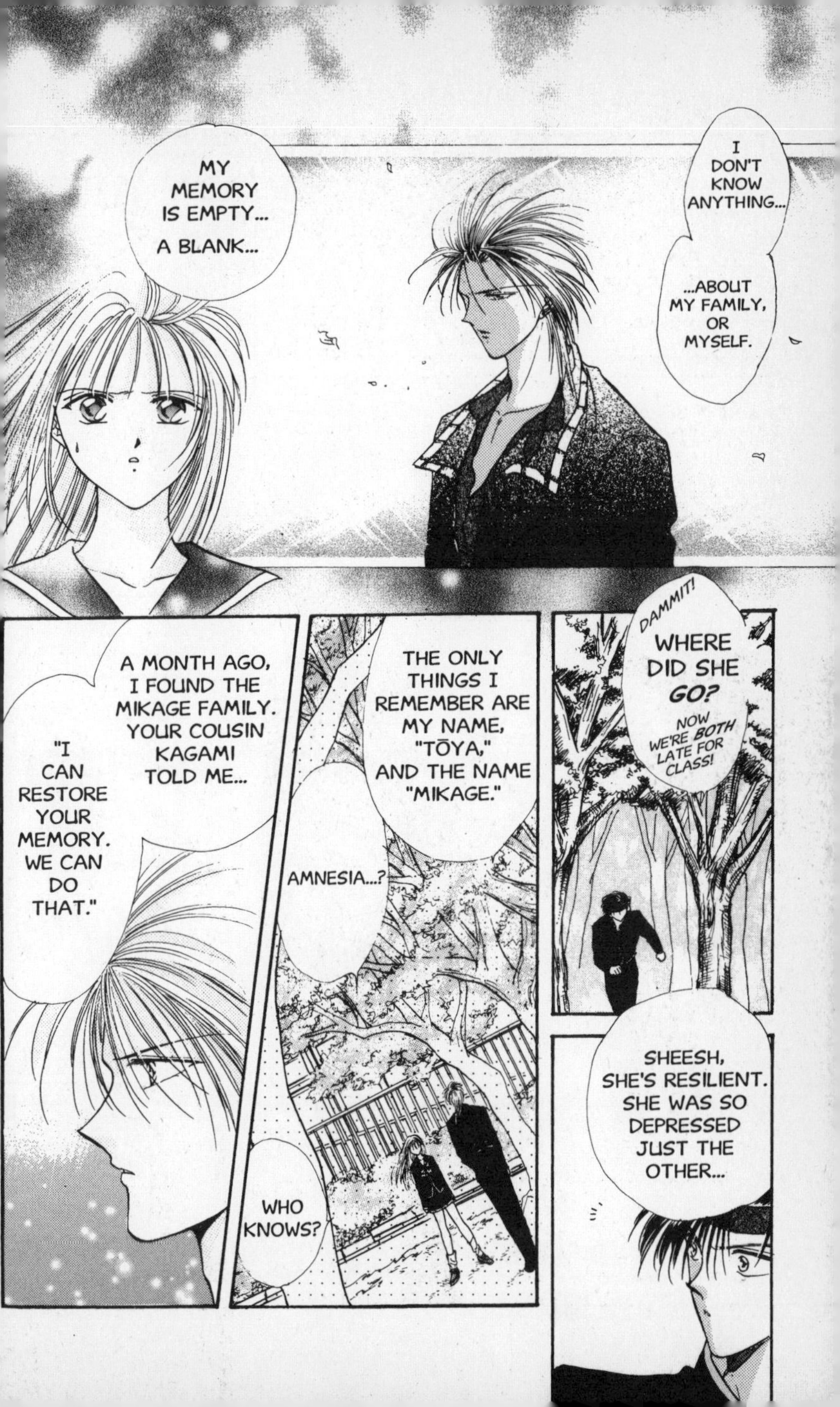
I DON'T KNOW ANYTHING...
...ABOUT MY FAMILY, OR MYSELF.
MY MEMORY IS EMPTY...
A BLANK...
DAMMIT!
WHERE DID SHE GO?
NOW WE'RE BOTH LATE FOR CLASS!
SHEESH, SHE'S RESILIENT. SHE WAS SO DEPRESSED JUST THE OTHER...
THE ONLY THINGS I REMEMBER ARE MY NAME, "TŌYA," AND THE NAME "MIKAGE."
AMNESIA...?
WHO KNOWS?
A MONTH AGO, I FOUND THE MIKAGE FAMILY. YOUR COUSIN KAGAMI TOLD ME...
"I CAN RESTORE YOUR MEMORY. WE CAN DO THAT."

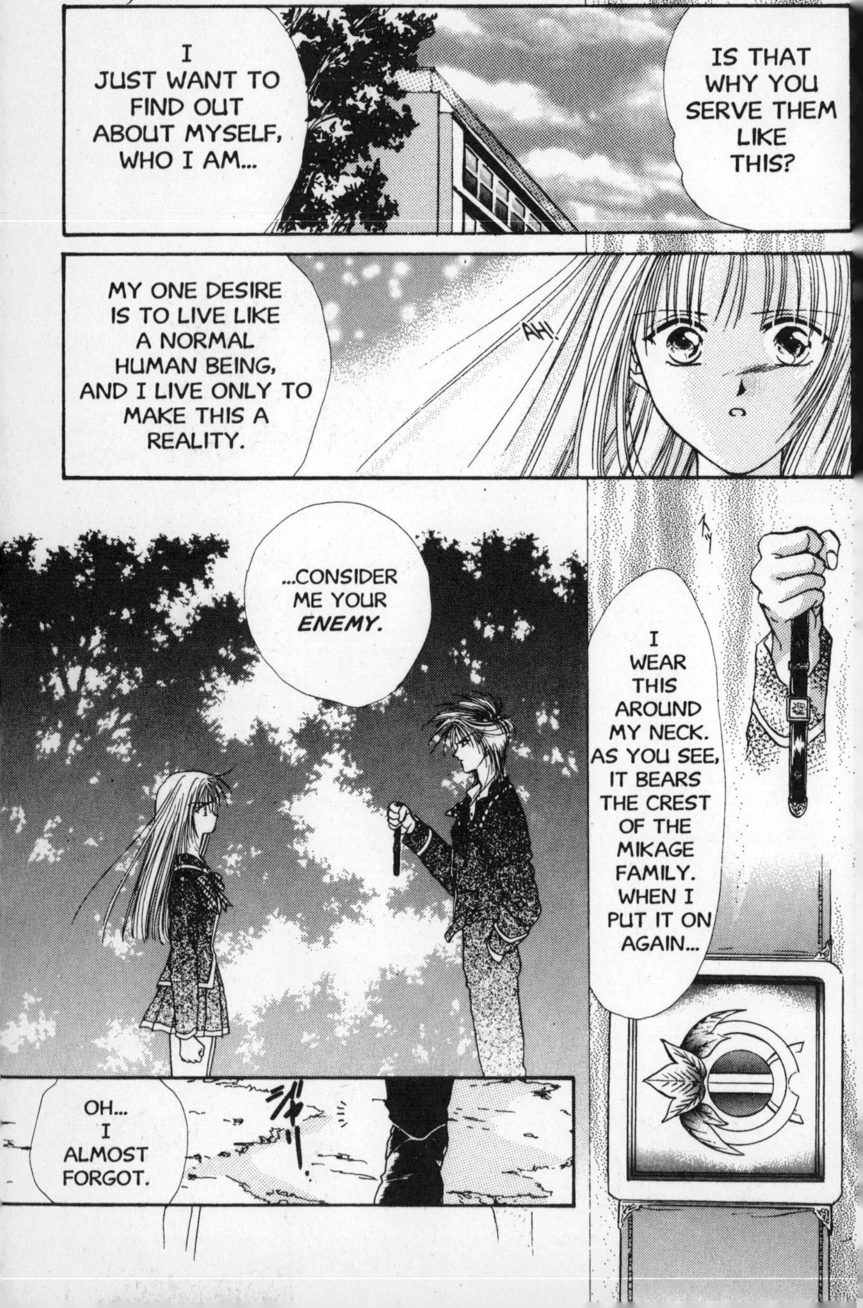
IS THAT WHY YOU SERVE THEM LIKE THIS?
I JUST WANT TO FIND OUT ABOUT MYSELF, WHO I AM...
MY ONE DESIRE IS TO LIVE LIKE A NORMAL HUMAN BEING, AND I LIVE ONLY TO MAKE THIS A REALITY.
AH!
I WEAR THIS AROUND MY NECK. AS YOU SEE, IT BEARS THE CREST OF THE MIKAGE FAMILY. WHEN I PUT IT ON AGAIN...
...CONSIDER ME YOUR *ENEMY.*
OH... I ALMOST FORGOT.

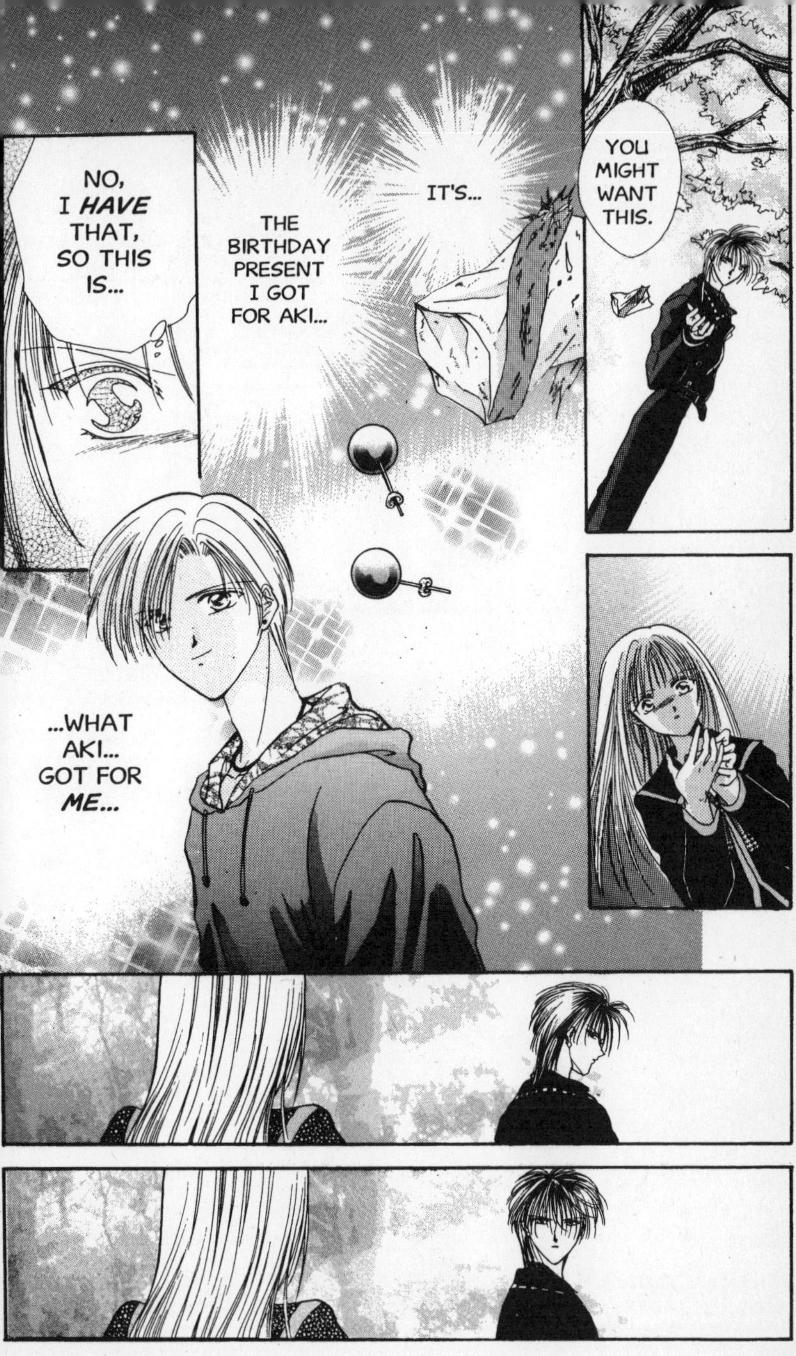
YOU MIGHT WANT THIS.
IT'S...
THE BIRTHDAY PRESENT I GOT FOR AKI...
NO, I *HAVE* THAT, SO THIS IS...
...WHAT AKI... GOT FOR *ME*...

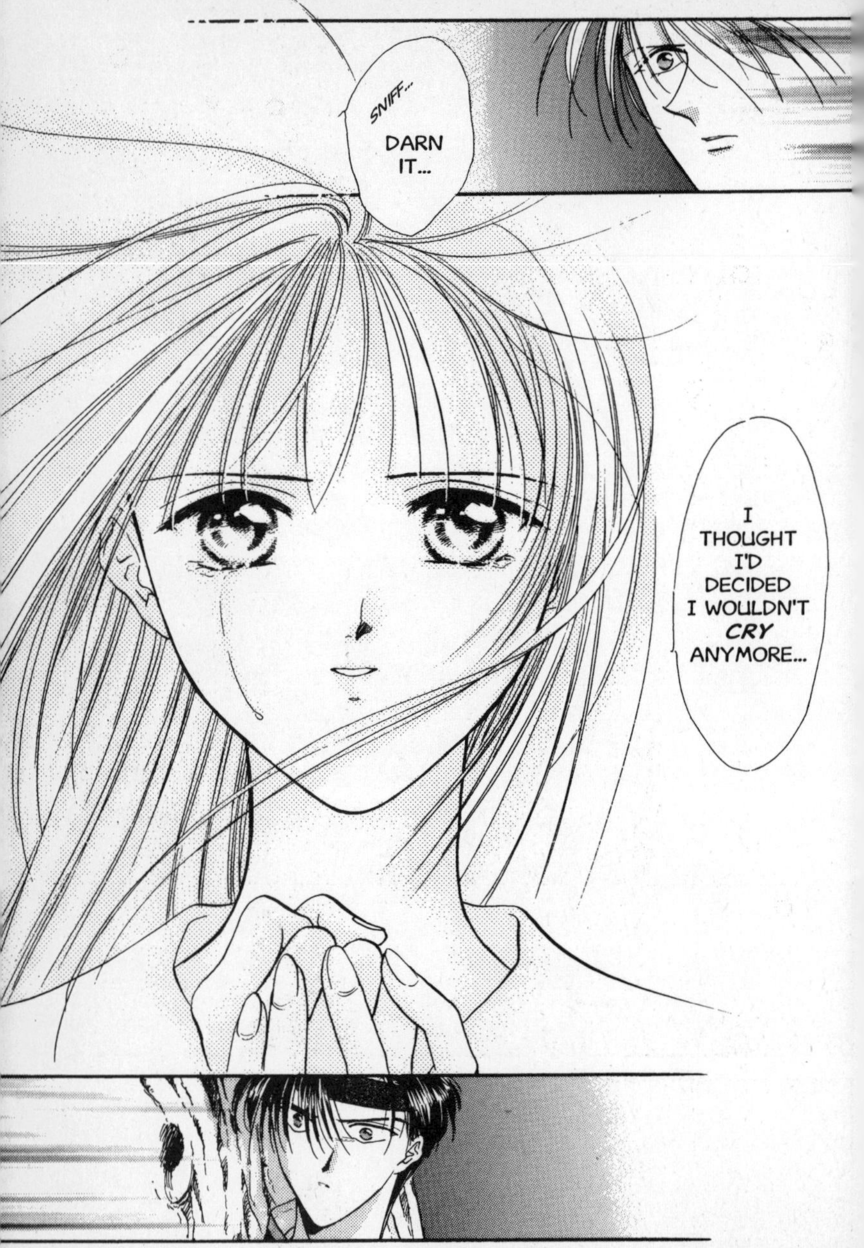
SNIFF... DARN IT...
I THOUGHT I'D DECIDED I WOULDN'T CRY ANYMORE...

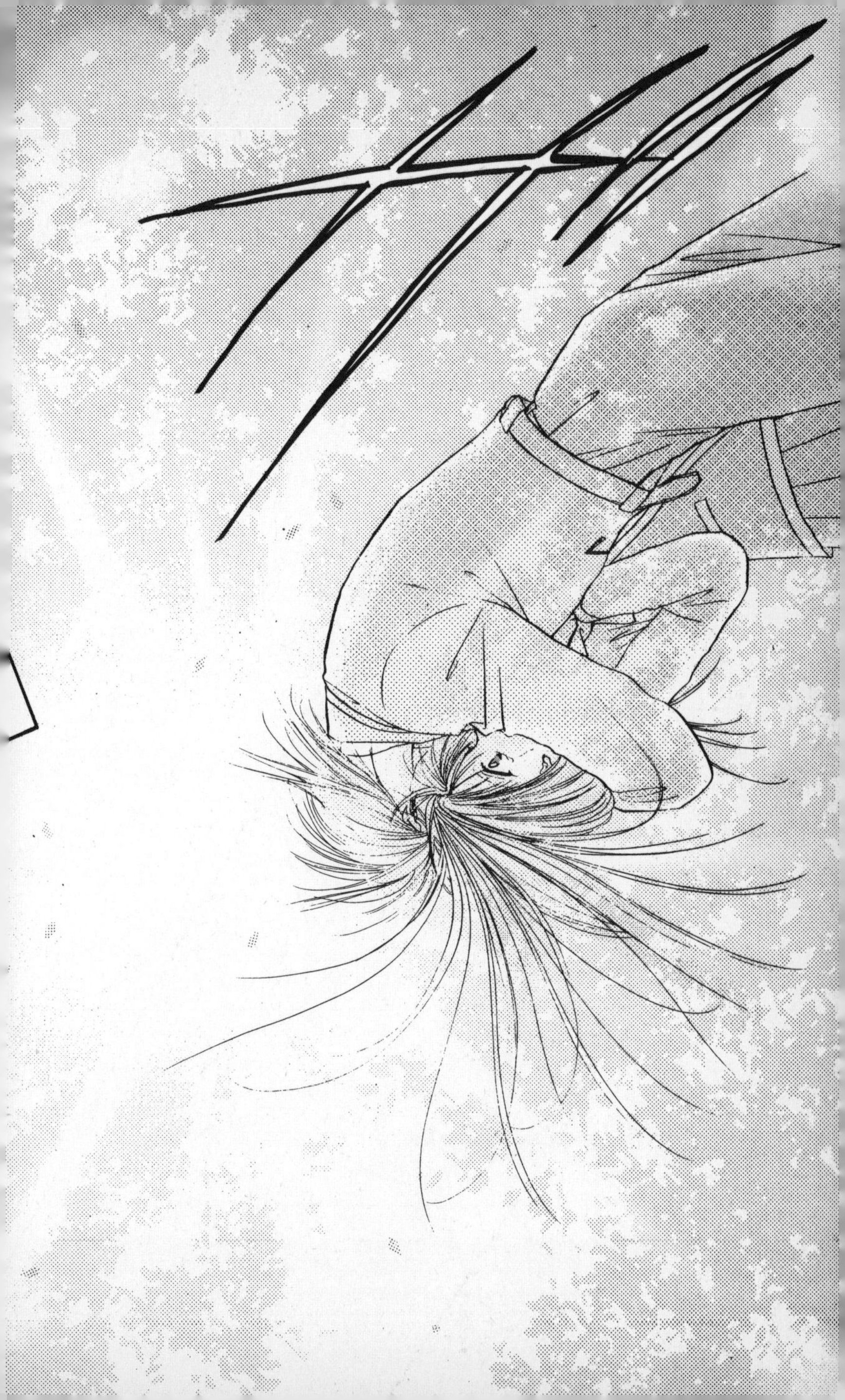

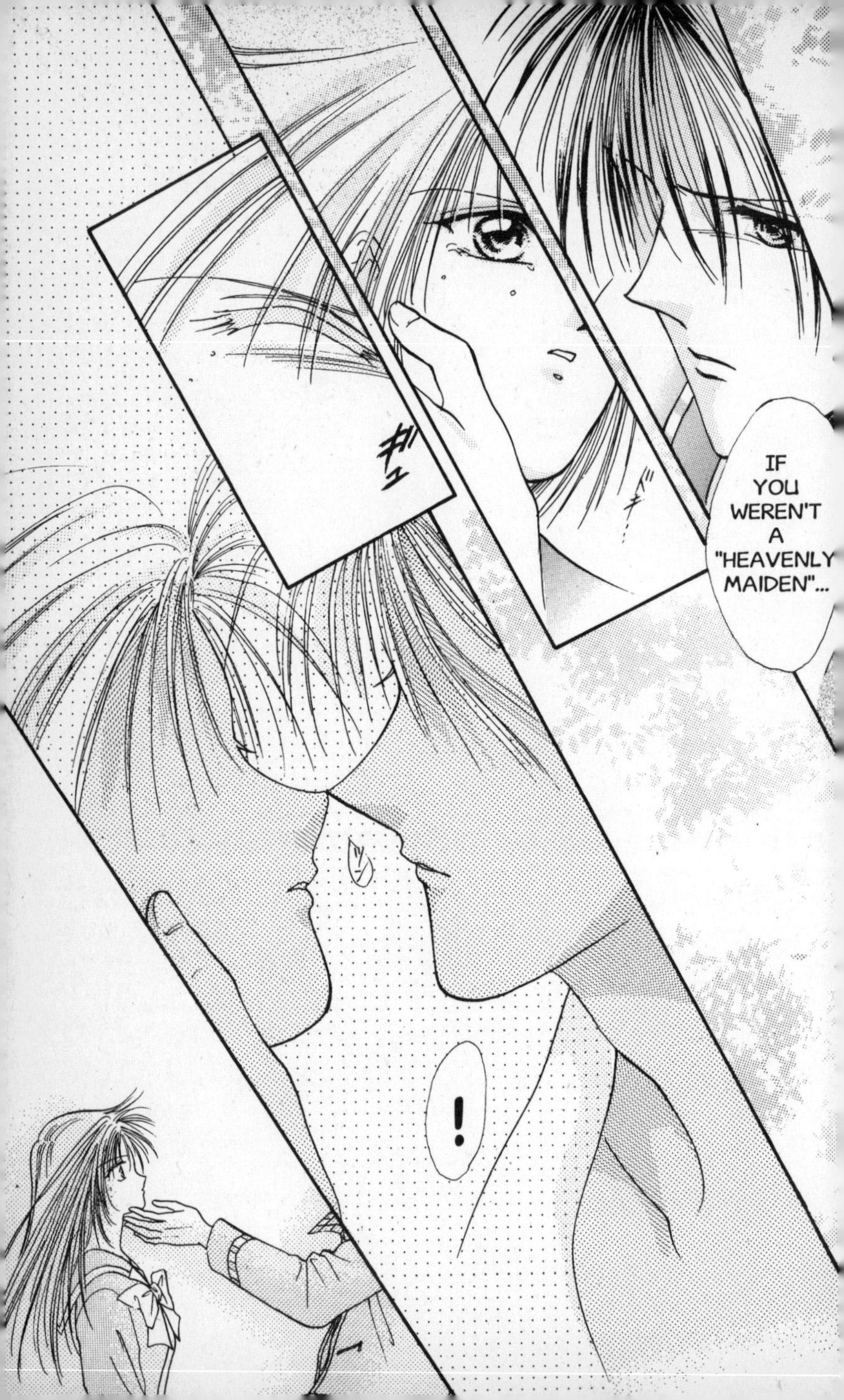
IF YOU WEREN'T A "HEAVENLY MAIDEN"...
!

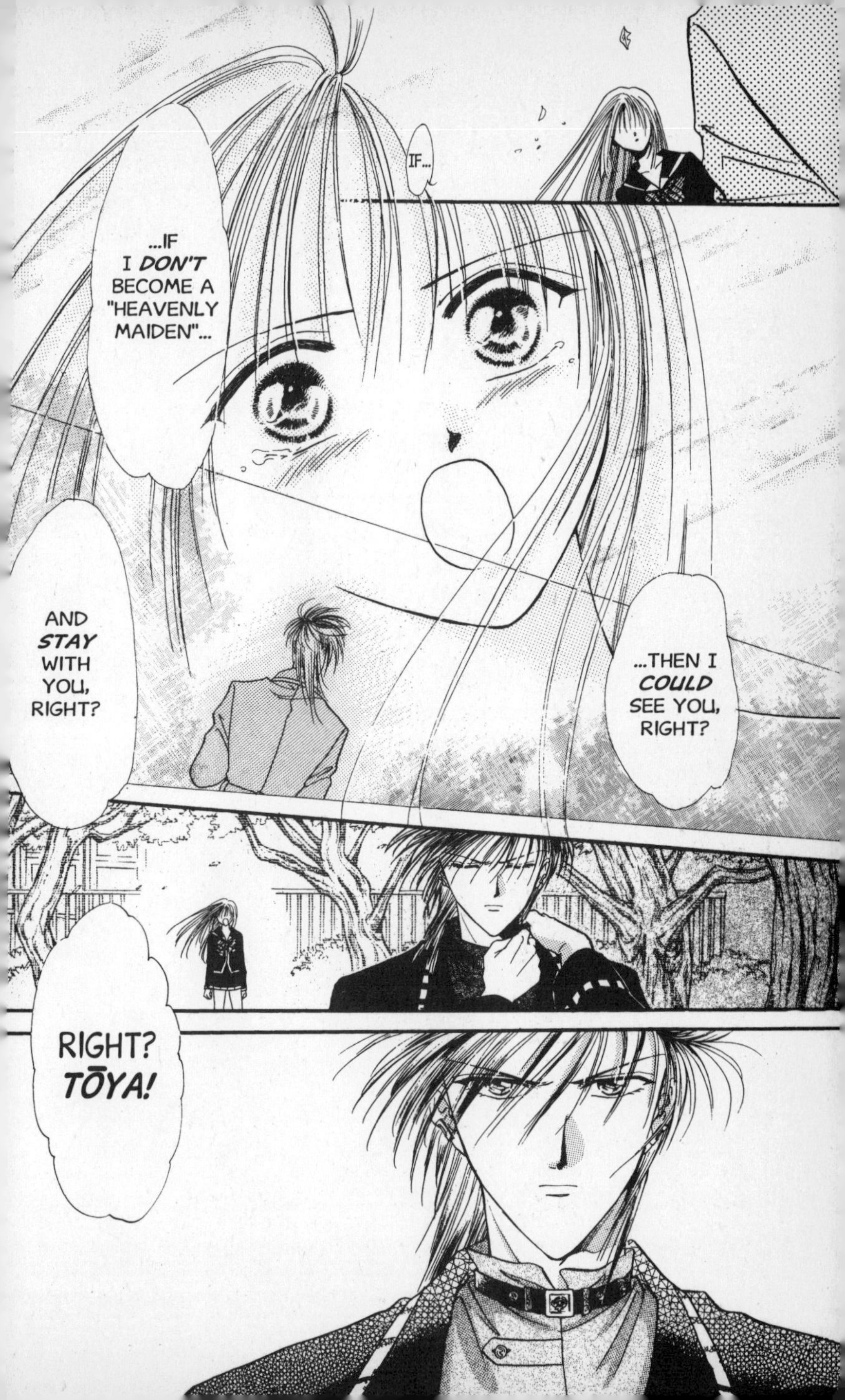

IF...
...IF I DON'T BECOME A "HEAVENLY MAIDEN"...
...THEN I COULD SEE YOU, RIGHT?
AND STAY WITH YOU, RIGHT?
RIGHT? TŌYA!

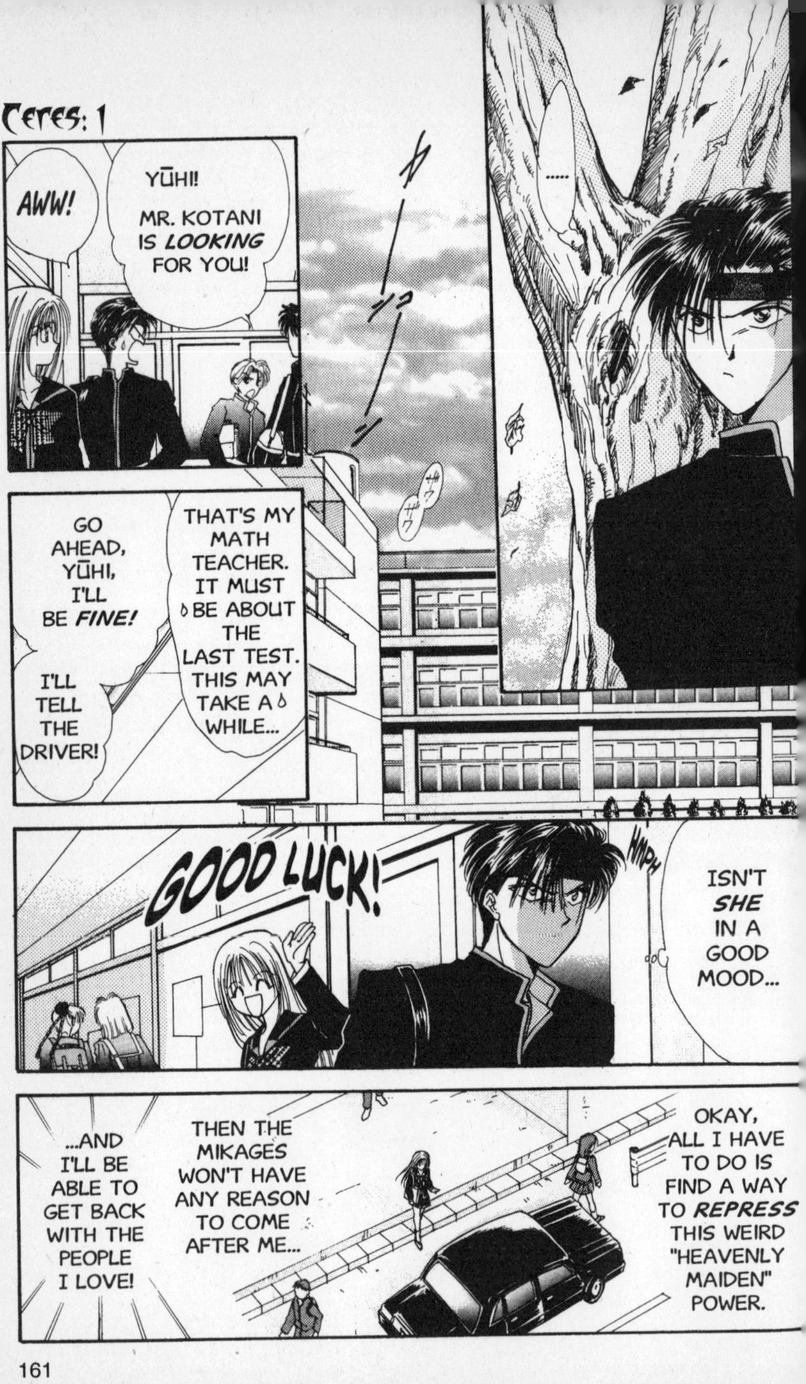
.....
YŪHI!
MR. KOTANI IS *LOOKING* FOR YOU!
AWW!
ザワ ザワ
THAT'S MY MATH TEACHER. IT MUST BE ABOUT THE LAST TEST. THIS MAY TAKE A WHILE...
GO AHEAD, YŪHI, I'LL BE *FINE!*
I'LL TELL THE DRIVER!
HMPH
ISN'T *SHE* IN A GOOD MOOD...
GOOD LUCK!
OKAY, ALL I HAVE TO DO IS FIND A WAY TO *REPRESS* THIS WEIRD "HEAVENLY MAIDEN" POWER.
THEN THE MIKAGES WON'T HAVE ANY REASON TO COME AFTER ME...
...AND I'LL BE ABLE TO GET BACK WITH THE PEOPLE I LOVE!

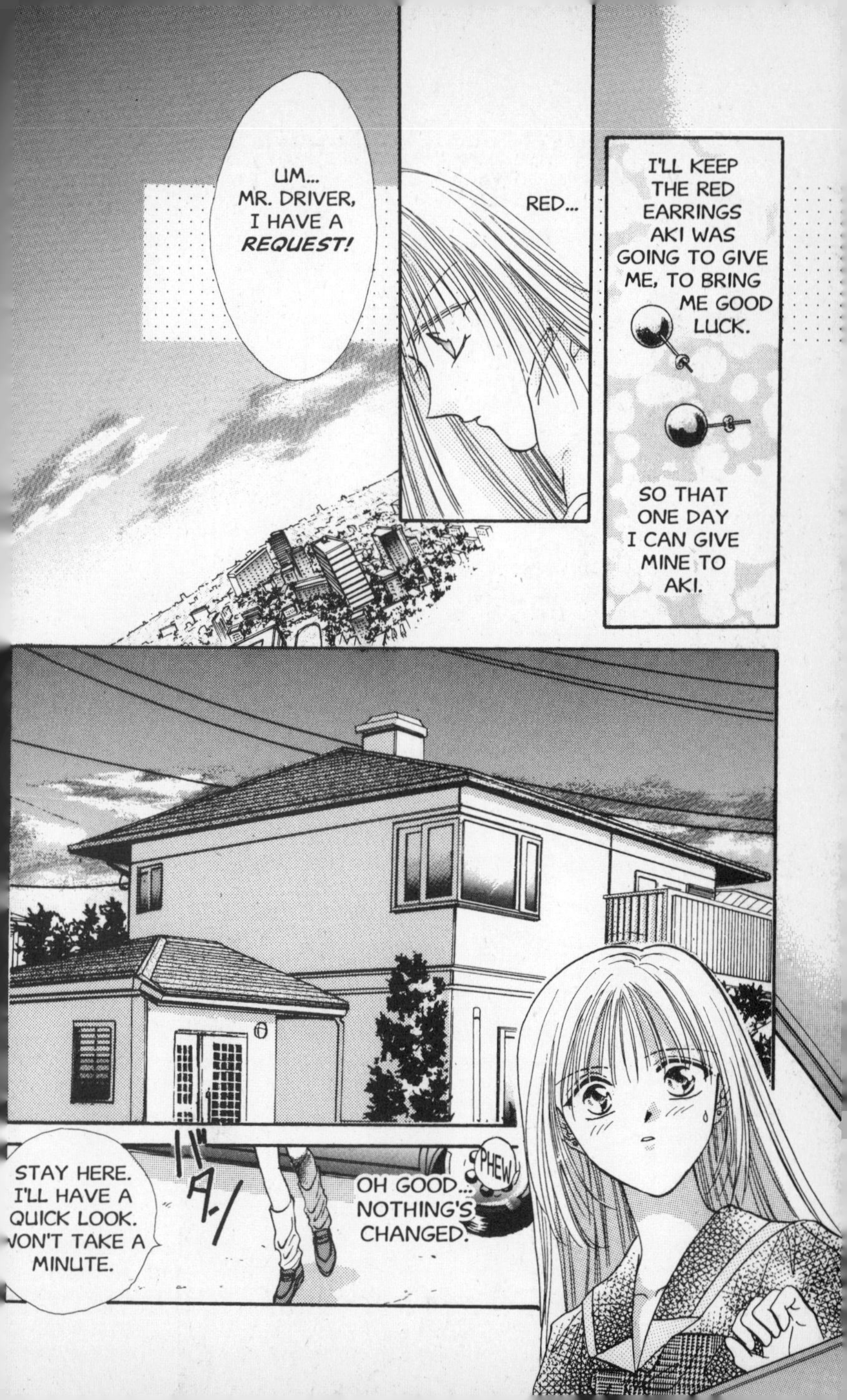

I'LL KEEP THE RED EARRINGS AKI WAS GOING TO GIVE ME, TO BRING ME GOOD LUCK.
SO THAT ONE DAY I CAN GIVE MINE TO AKI.
RED...
UM... MR. DRIVER, I HAVE A *REQUEST!*
PHEW
OH GOOD... NOTHING'S CHANGED.
STAY HERE. I'LL HAVE A QUICK LOOK. WON'T TAKE A MINUTE.

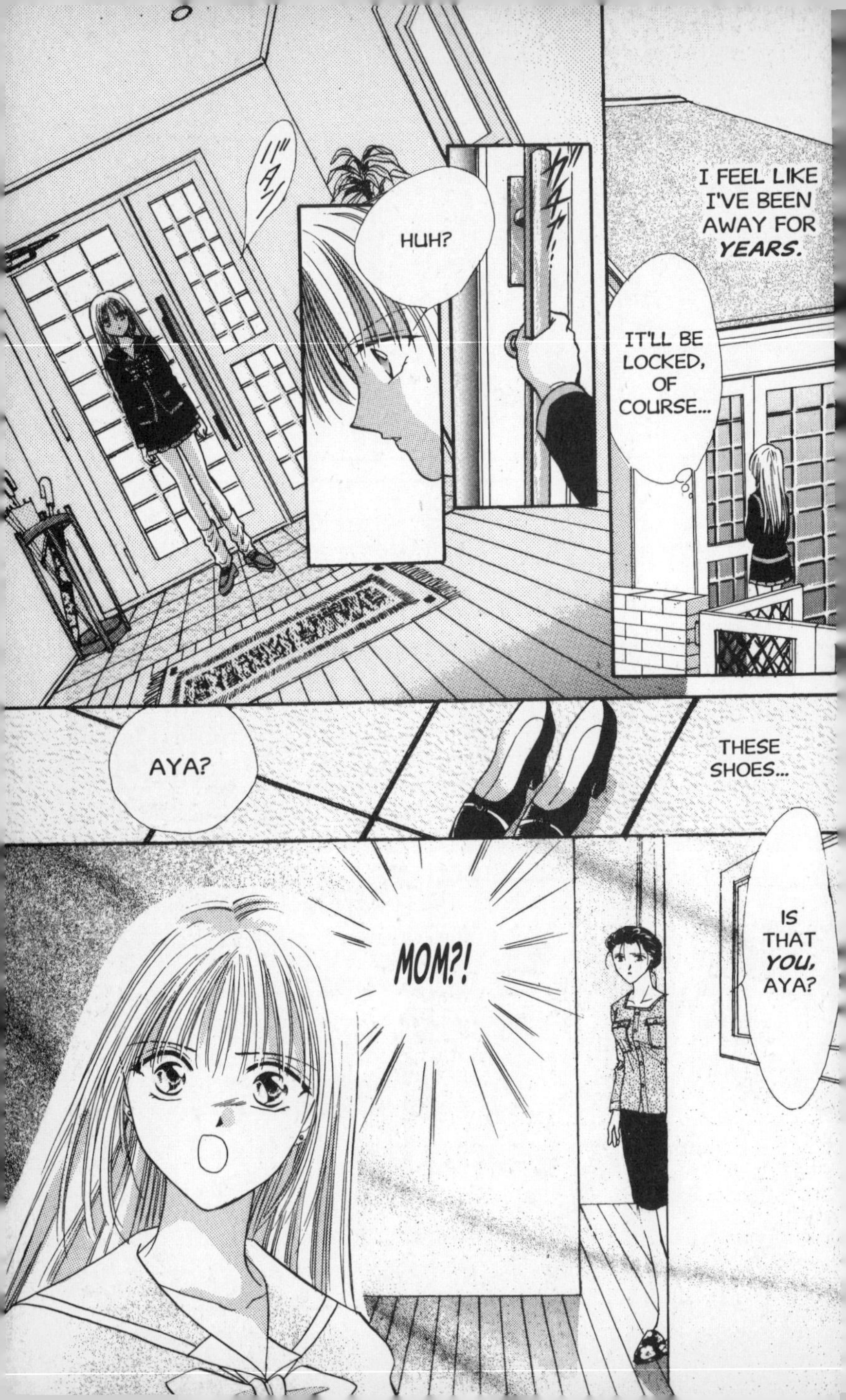

I FEEL LIKE I'VE BEEN AWAY FOR *YEARS.*
IT'LL BE LOCKED, OF COURSE...
ガチャ!!
HUH?
バタン
THESE SHOES...
AYA?
IS THAT *YOU,* AYA?
MOM?!

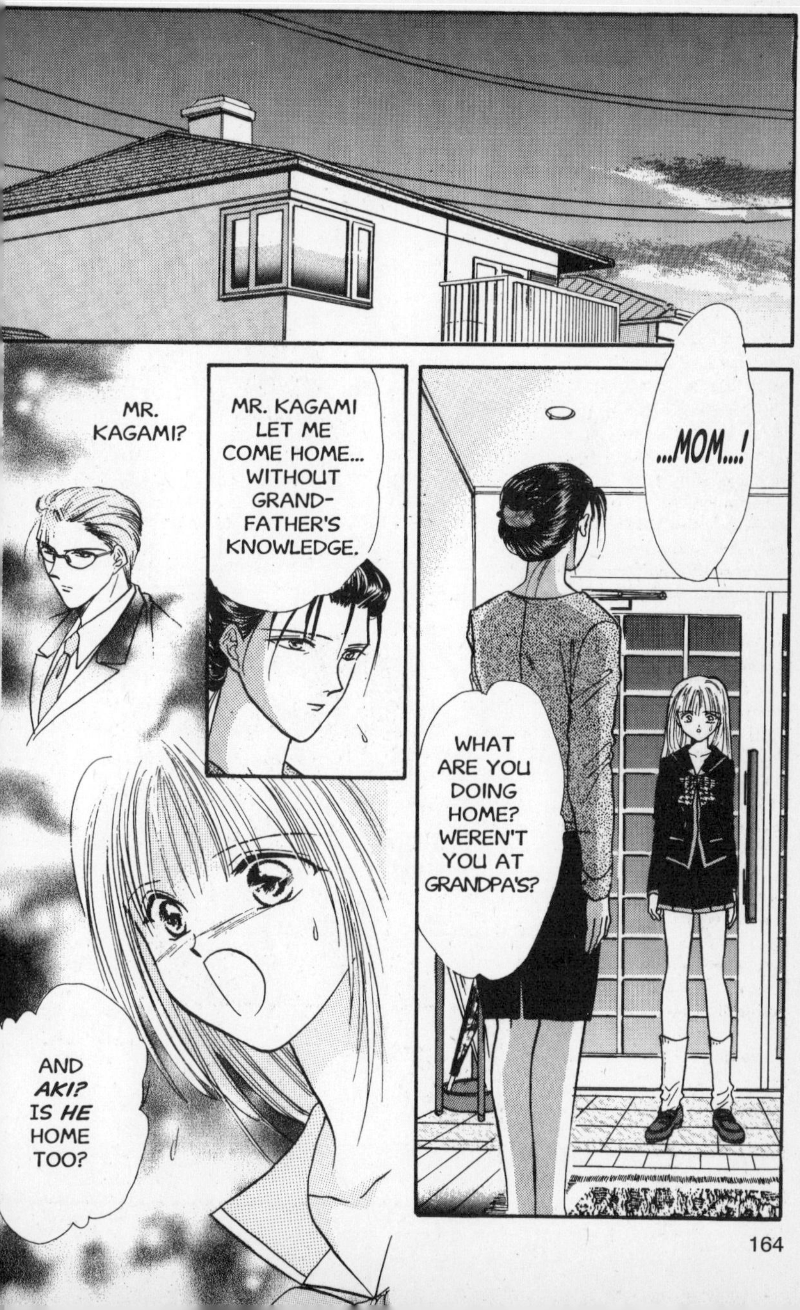
...MOM...!
WHAT ARE YOU DOING HOME? WEREN'T YOU AT GRANDPA'S?
MR. KAGAMI LET ME COME HOME... WITHOUT GRAND-FATHER'S KNOWLEDGE.
MR. KAGAMI?
AND *AKI?* IS *HE* HOME TOO?

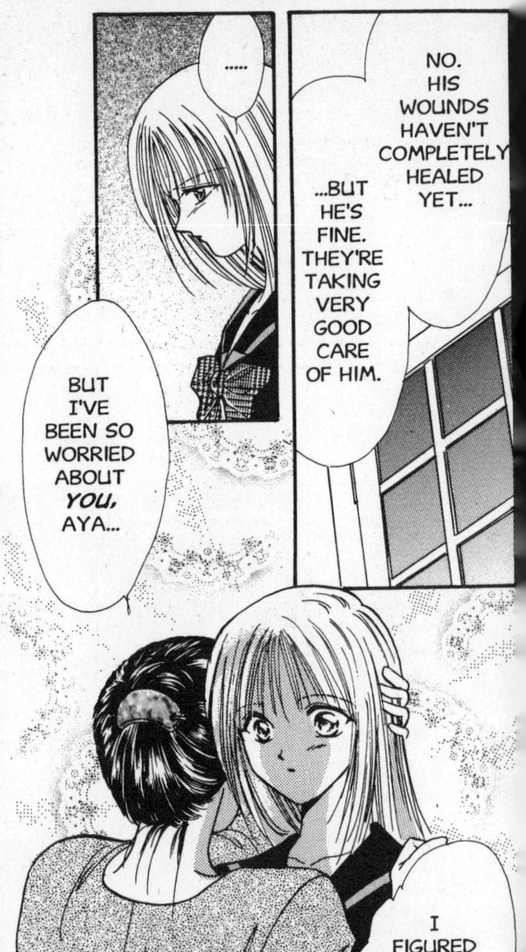
NO. HIS WOUNDS HAVEN'T COMPLETELY HEALED YET...
...BUT HE'S FINE. THEY'RE TAKING VERY GOOD CARE OF HIM.
.....
BUT I'VE BEEN SO WORRIED ABOUT *YOU,* AYA...
I FIGURED YOU WOULD COME HOME. I'M GLAD, SO GLAD YOU'RE *SAFE...!*

♦ Aya ♦

But I think "love that's gone just short of insanity" is really sublime in some respects. Eros and Thanatos... There could be a dark side to it too, so I know that there's danger in depicting it.
But I also love the warm and fuzzy world. ...Well, more than the other. But still... So human psychology, and everything in the world, is made up of two opposite facets, two sides of the same coin. Part and counterpart.
I think the world of "Ceres," while the theme is different, is also modeled after this idea of "pairs." Man and woman, love and hate, light and shadow, good and evil, past and future, etc. Among all pairs, "twins" are really interesting. And Aya and Aki are a twin girl and boy. Fraternal twins. You could say that's a key point of this story. Yūhi and Tōya are total opposites too. We'll see which one Aya is going to end up with. If there were a thousand people, there would be a thousand different forms of love, so there are no answers... So how will Aya love, and be loved? And what's more, the near-absent love from her family. You never know, dear readers. Just in case, you should get to know your parents, and the relationships your relatives have... You never know to whom your ancestors are connected. Maybe one day there'll be a revelation. Like Aki said, you never know when normal life is going to fall apart. After all, humanity is always living side by side with the "pair" called "life and death." ...What am I doing, scaring you!
Well, see you in vol. 2.

Come to think of it, genes are "paired" too.
'96.10.

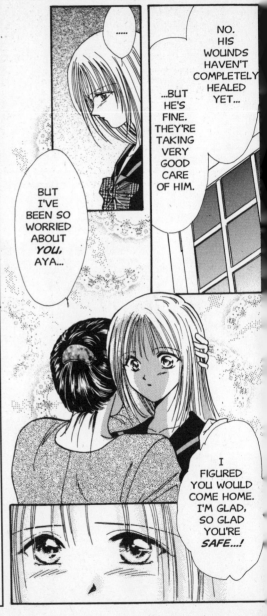

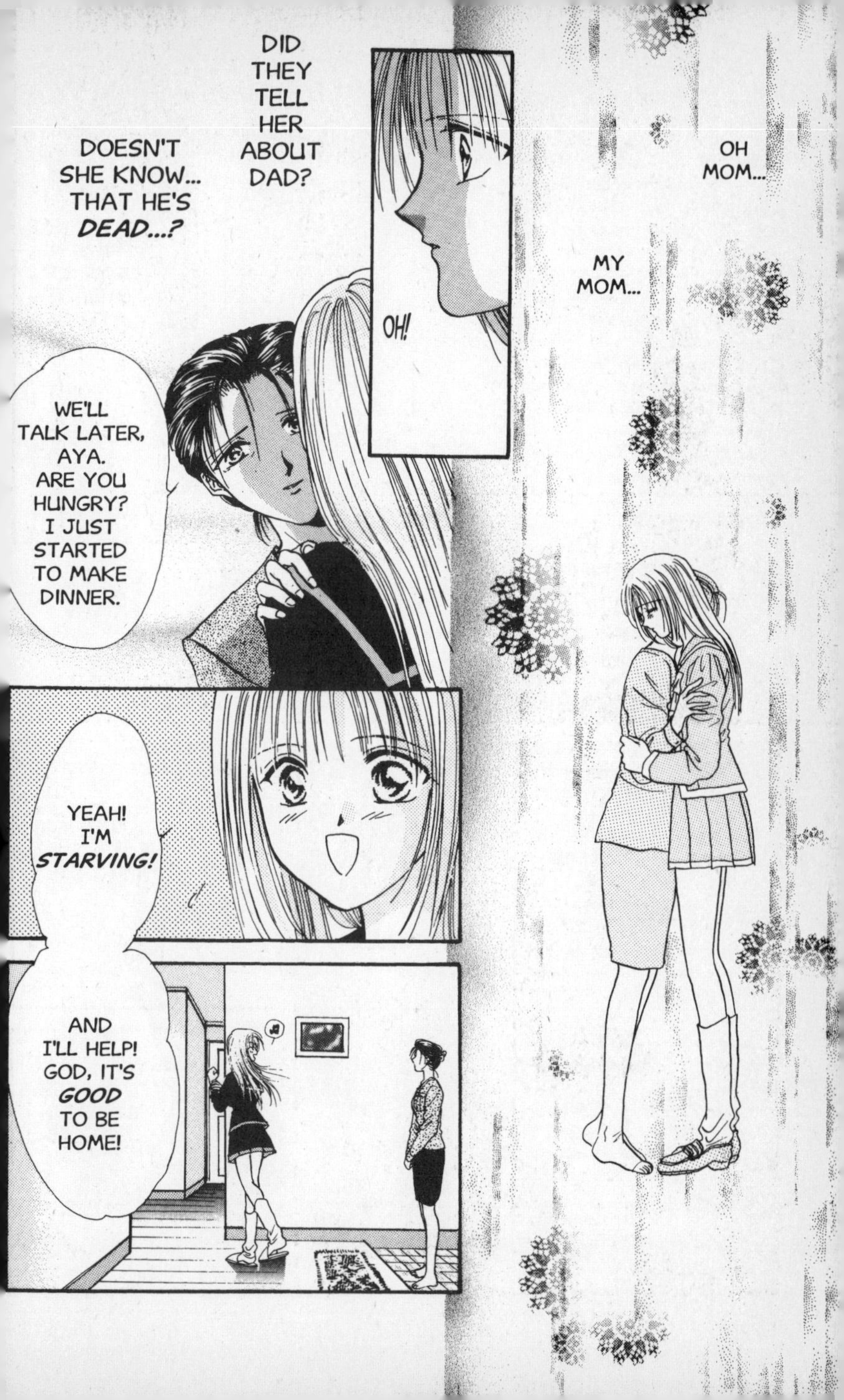

OH MOM...
MY MOM...
DID THEY TELL HER ABOUT DAD?
DOESN'T SHE KNOW... THAT HE'S DEAD...?
OH!
WE'LL TALK LATER, AYA. ARE YOU HUNGRY? I JUST STARTED TO MAKE DINNER.
YEAH! I'M STARVING!
AND I'LL HELP! GOD, IT'S GOOD TO BE HOME!

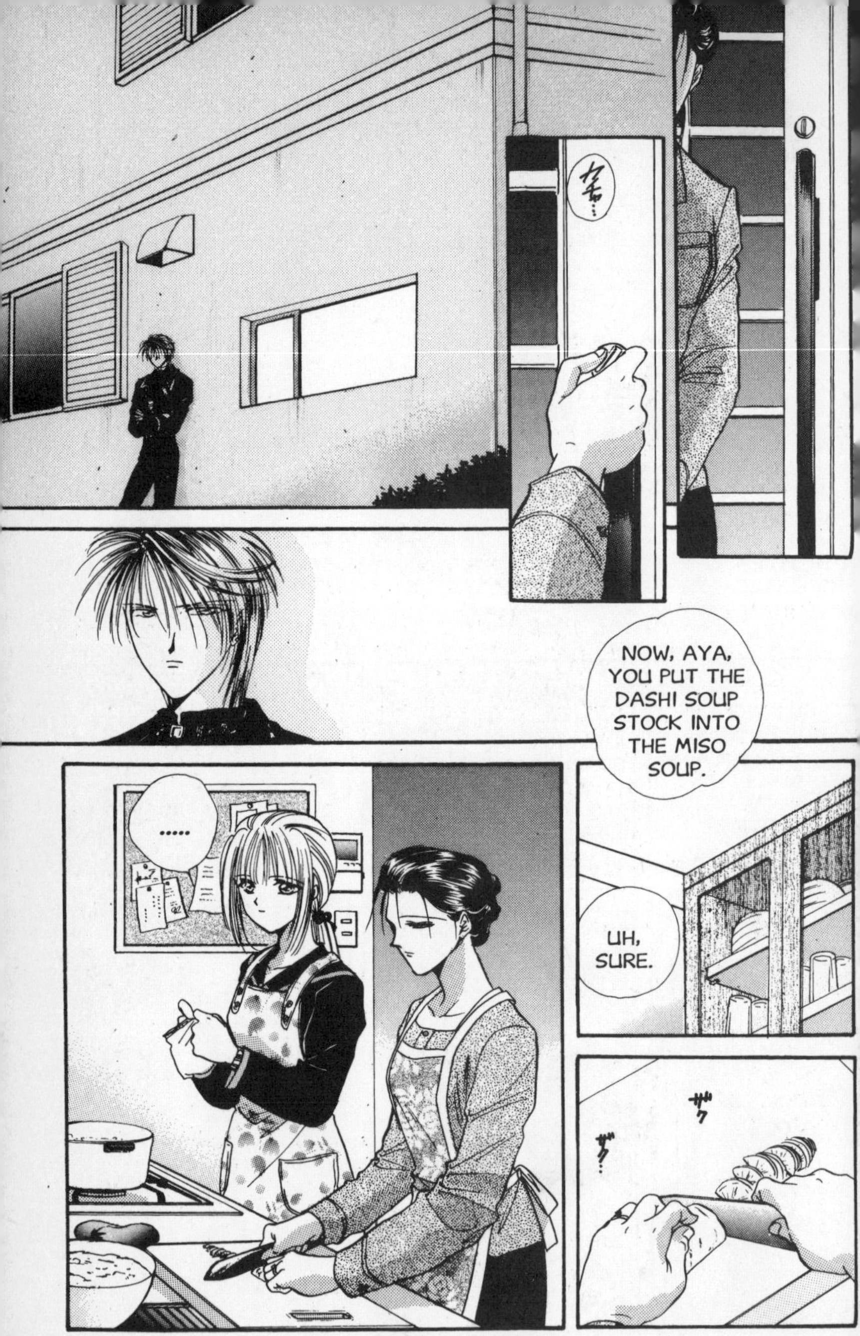
カチャ…
NOW, AYA, YOU PUT THE DASHI SOUP STOCK INTO THE MISO SOUP.
UH, SURE.
ザク
ザク…
......

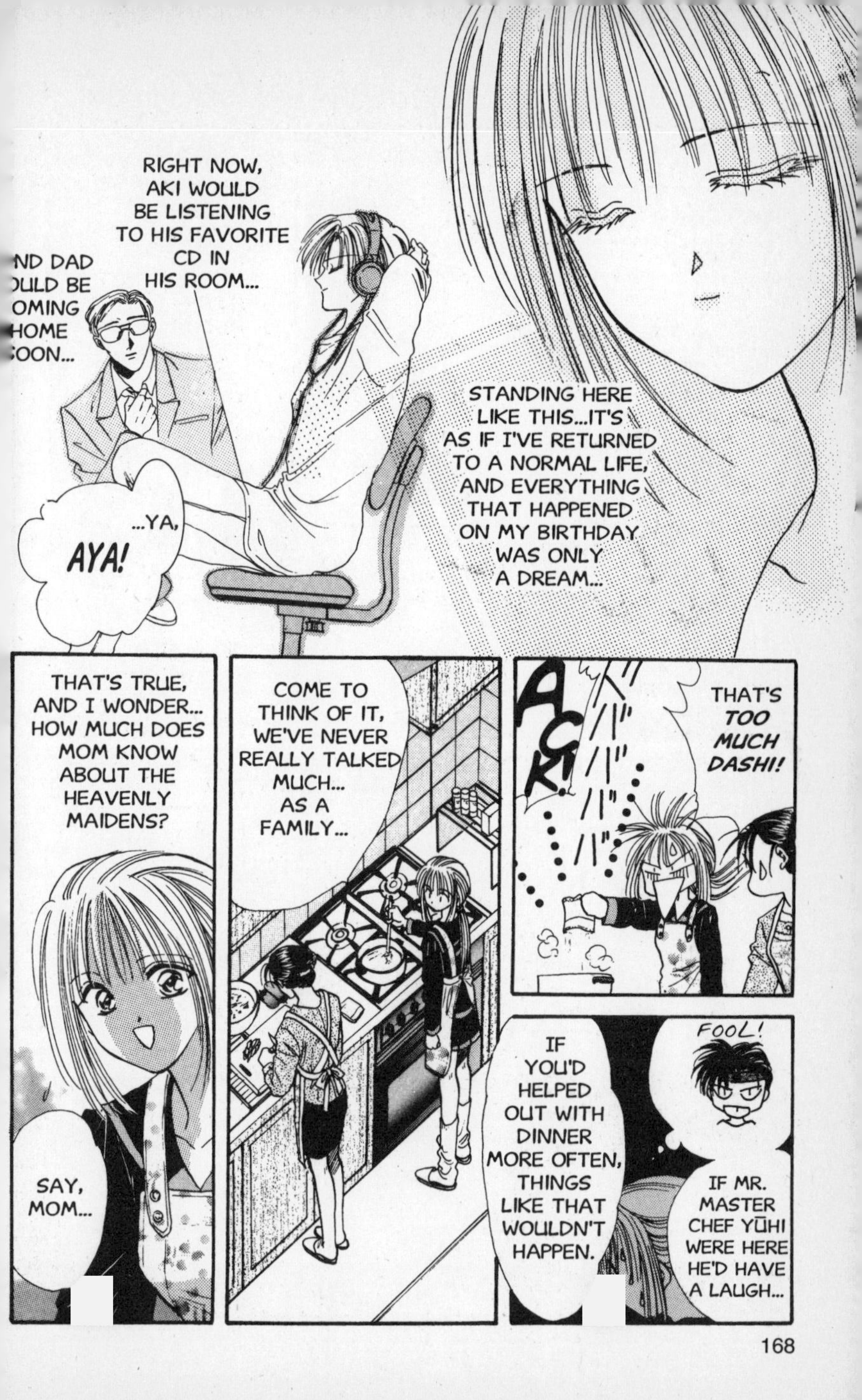
STANDING HERE LIKE THIS...IT'S AS IF I'VE RETURNED TO A NORMAL LIFE, AND EVERYTHING THAT HAPPENED ON MY BIRTHDAY WAS ONLY A DREAM...
RIGHT NOW, AKI WOULD BE LISTENING TO HIS FAVORITE CD IN HIS ROOM...
ND DAD OULD BE OMING HOME OON...
...YA,
AYA!
THAT'S TOO MUCH DASHI!
ACK!
FOOL!
IF MR. MASTER CHEF YŪHI WERE HERE HE'D HAVE A LAUGH...
IF YOU'D HELPED OUT WITH DINNER MORE OFTEN, THINGS LIKE THAT WOULDN'T HAPPEN.
COME TO THINK OF IT, WE'VE NEVER REALLY TALKED MUCH... AS A FAMILY...
THAT'S TRUE, AND I WONDER... HOW MUCH DOES MOM KNOW ABOUT THE HEAVENLY MAIDENS?
SAY, MOM...

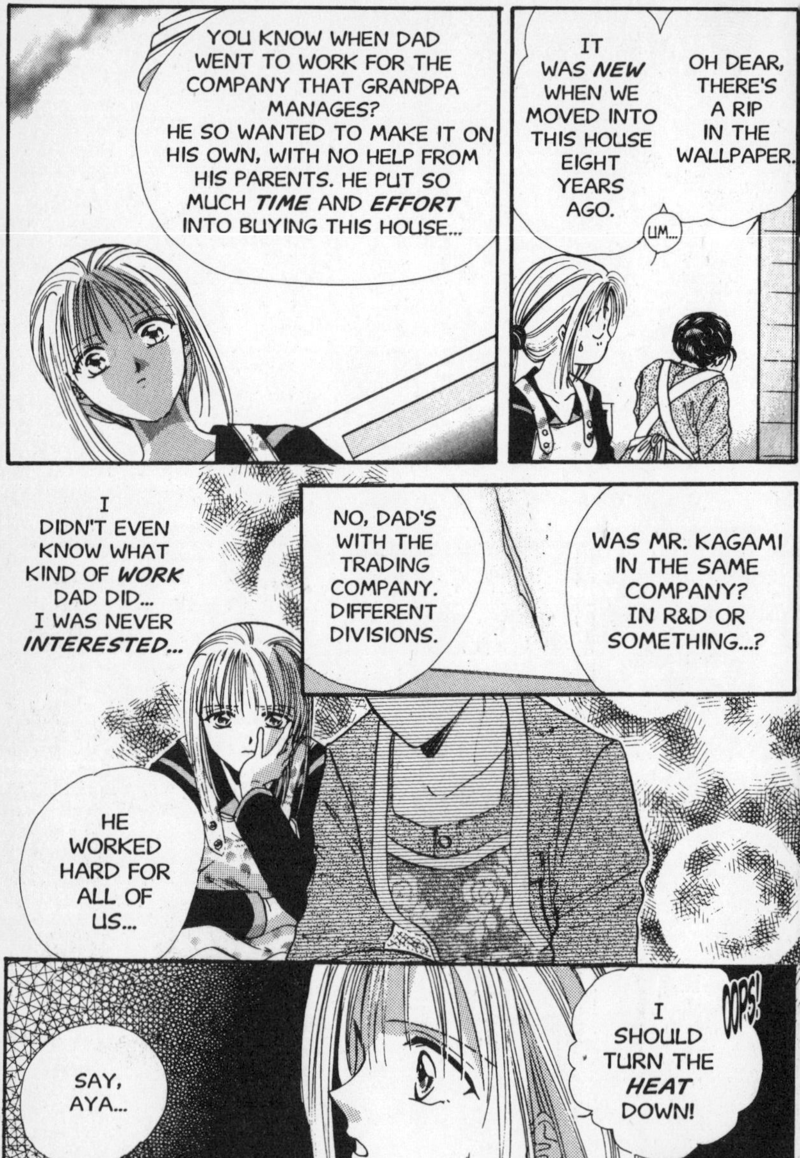
OH DEAR, THERE'S A RIP IN THE WALLPAPER.
IT WAS *NEW* WHEN WE MOVED INTO THIS HOUSE EIGHT YEARS AGO.
UM...
YOU KNOW WHEN DAD WENT TO WORK FOR THE COMPANY THAT GRANDPA MANAGES? HE SO WANTED TO MAKE IT ON HIS OWN, WITH NO HELP FROM HIS PARENTS. HE PUT SO MUCH *TIME* AND *EFFORT* INTO BUYING THIS HOUSE...
WAS MR. KAGAMI IN THE SAME COMPANY? IN R&D OR SOMETHING...?
NO, DAD'S WITH THE TRADING COMPANY. DIFFERENT DIVISIONS.
I DIDN'T EVEN KNOW WHAT KIND OF *WORK* DAD DID... I WAS NEVER *INTERESTED...*
HE WORKED HARD FOR ALL OF US...
OOPS!
I SHOULD TURN THE *HEAT* DOWN!
SAY, AYA...

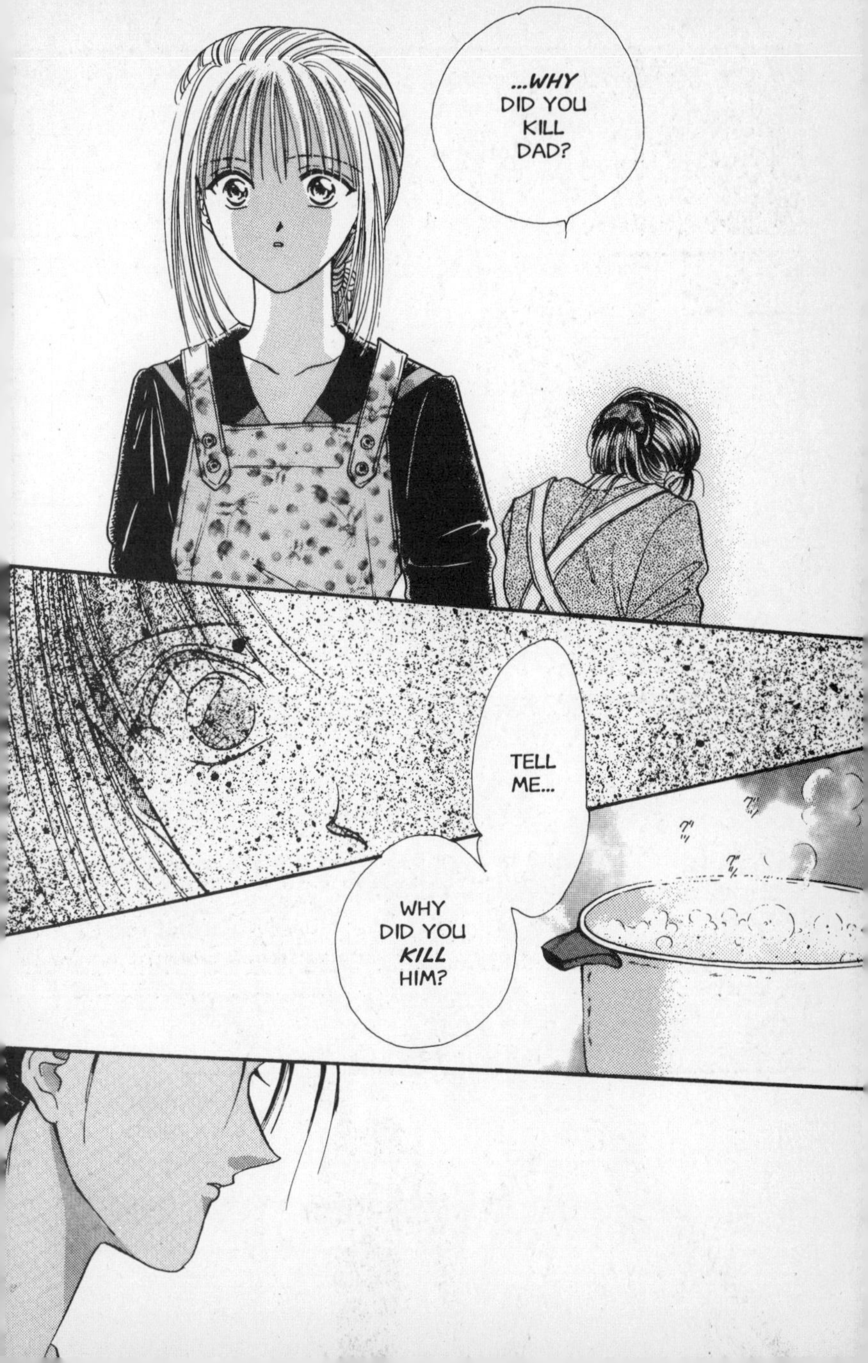
...WHY DID YOU KILL DAD?
TELL ME...
WHY DID YOU KILL HIM?

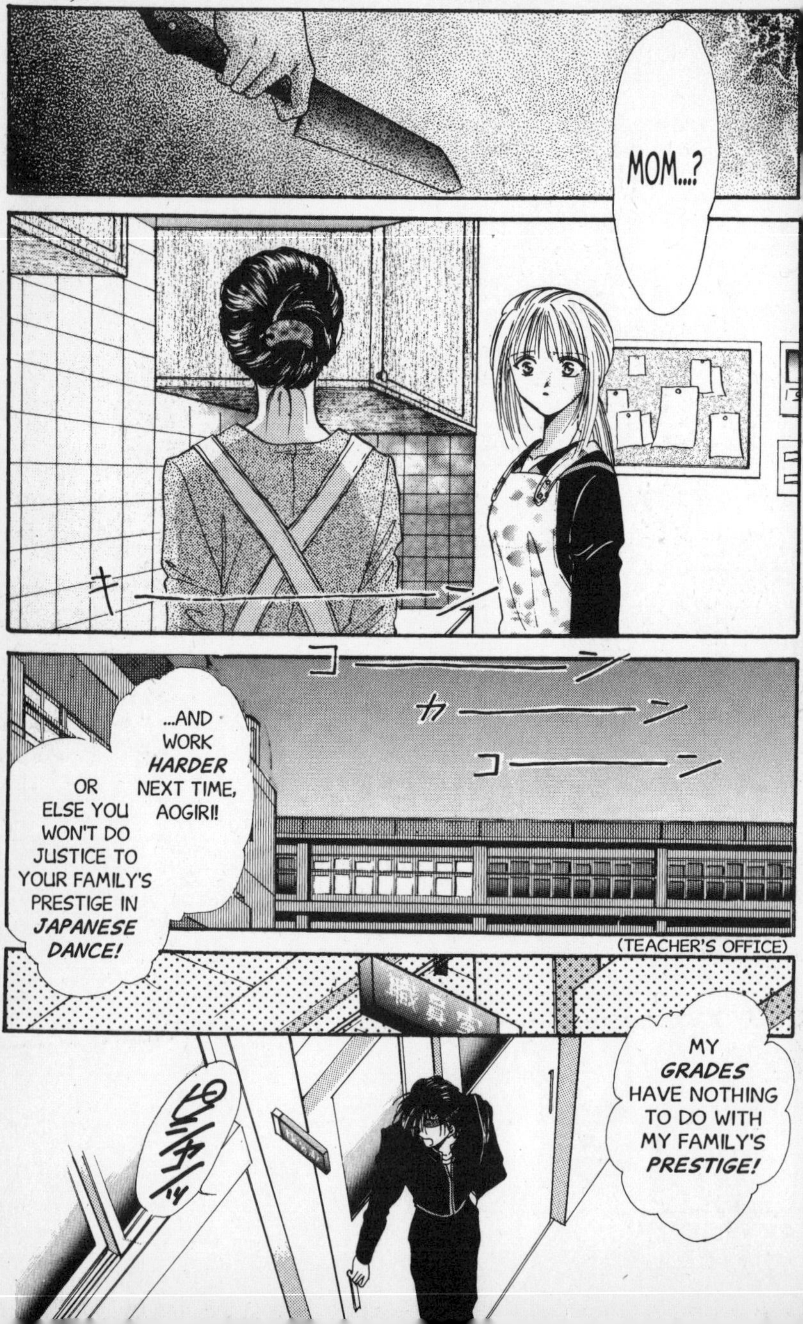
MOM...?
キーーン
コーーン
カーーン
コーーン
...AND WORK HARDER NEXT TIME, AOGIRI!
OR ELSE YOU WON'T DO JUSTICE TO YOUR FAMILY'S PRESTIGE IN JAPANESE DANCE!
(TEACHER'S OFFICE)
職員室
MY GRADES HAVE NOTHING TO DO WITH MY FAMILY'S PRESTIGE!

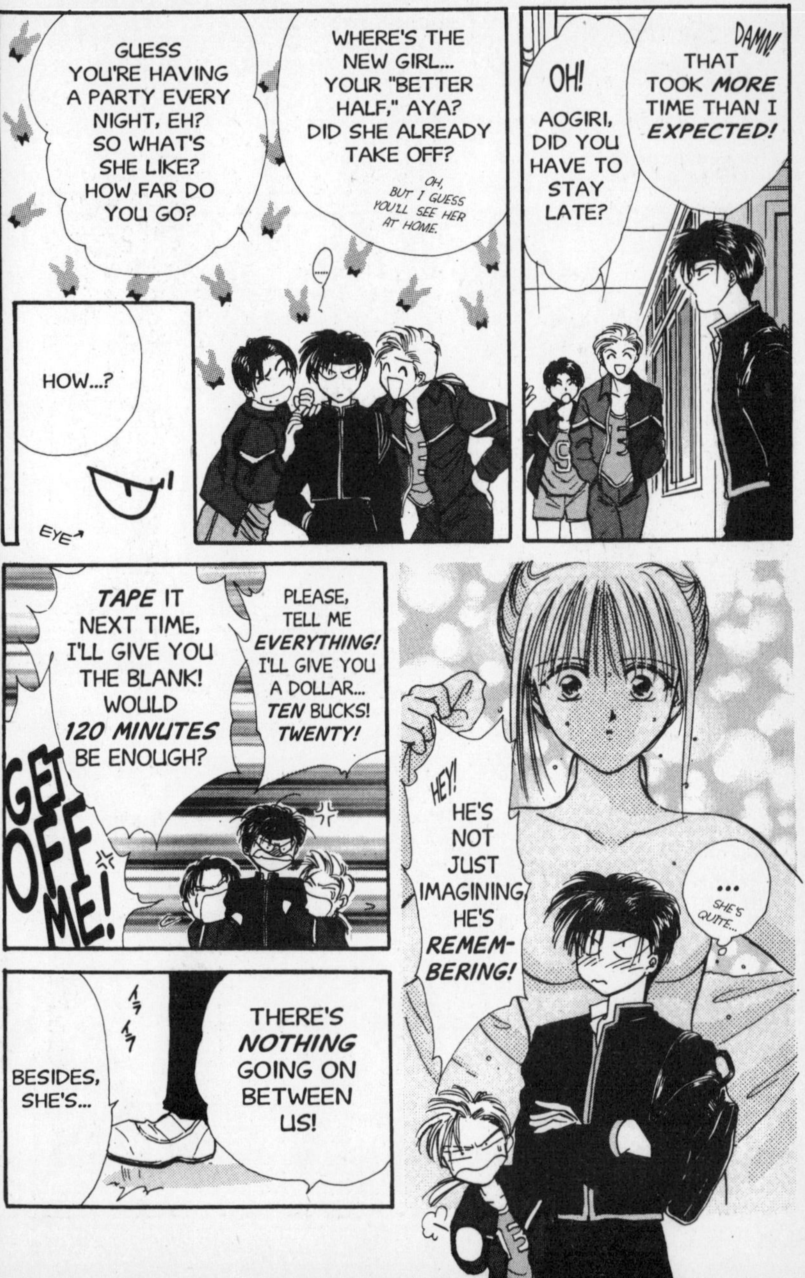
DAMN!
THAT TOOK MORE TIME THAN I EXPECTED!
OH!
AOGIRI, DID YOU HAVE TO STAY LATE?
WHERE'S THE NEW GIRL... YOUR "BETTER HALF," AYA? DID SHE ALREADY TAKE OFF?
OH, BUT I GUESS YOU'LL SEE HER AT HOME.
GUESS YOU'RE HAVING A PARTY EVERY NIGHT, EH? SO WHAT'S SHE LIKE? HOW FAR DO YOU GO?
.....
HOW...?
EYE
...
SHE'S QUITE...
HEY!
HE'S NOT JUST IMAGINING HE'S REMEMBERING!
PLEASE, TELL ME EVERYTHING! I'LL GIVE YOU A DOLLAR... TEN BUCKS! TWENTY!
TAPE IT NEXT TIME, I'LL GIVE YOU THE BLANK! WOULD 120 MINUTES BE ENOUGH?
GET OFF ME!
THERE'S NOTHING GOING ON BETWEEN US!
BESIDES, SHE'S...

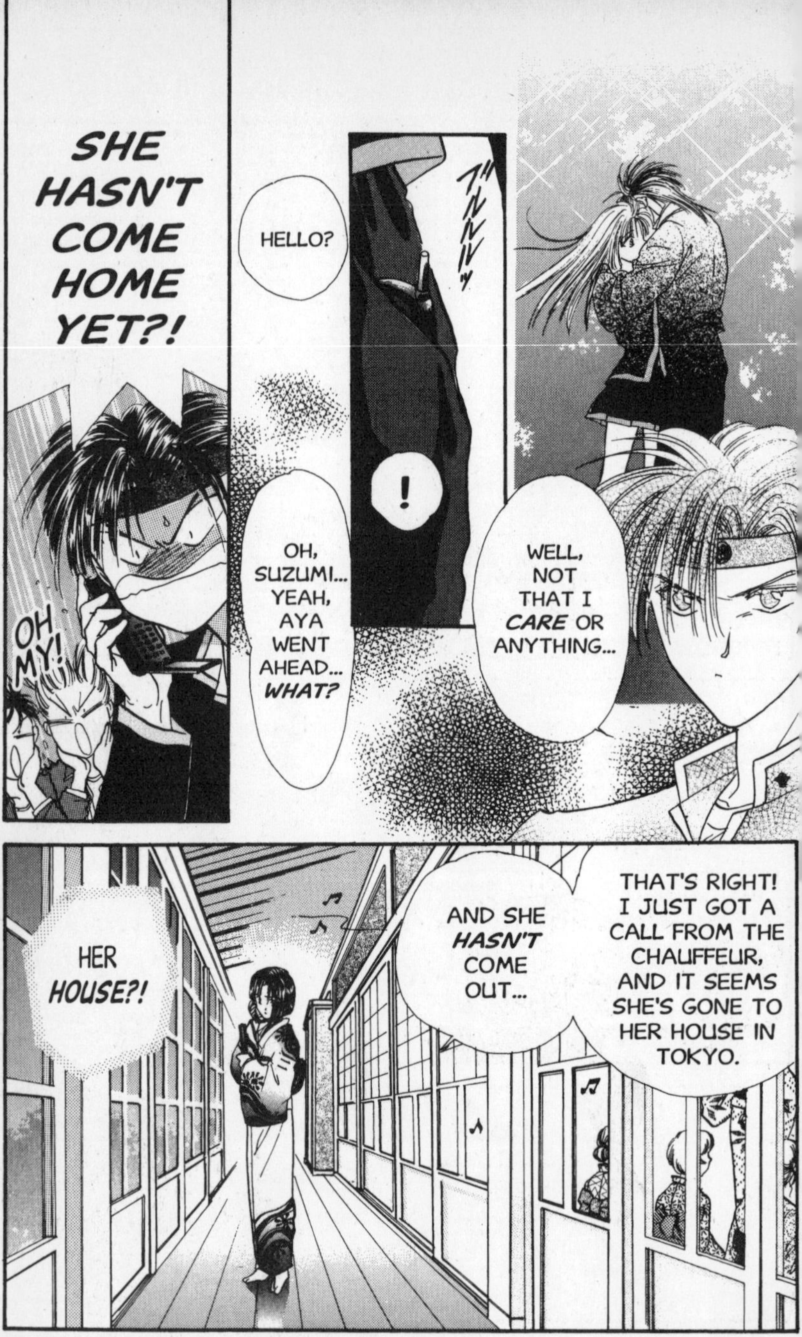
WELL, NOT THAT I *CARE* OR ANYTHING...
ブルルルッ
HELLO?
OH, SUZUMI... YEAH, AYA WENT AHEAD... *WHAT?*
!
SHE HASN'T COME HOME YET?!
OH MY!
THAT'S RIGHT! I JUST GOT A CALL FROM THE CHAUFFEUR, AND IT SEEMS SHE'S GONE TO HER HOUSE IN TOKYO.
AND SHE *HASN'T* COME OUT...
HER *HOUSE?!*

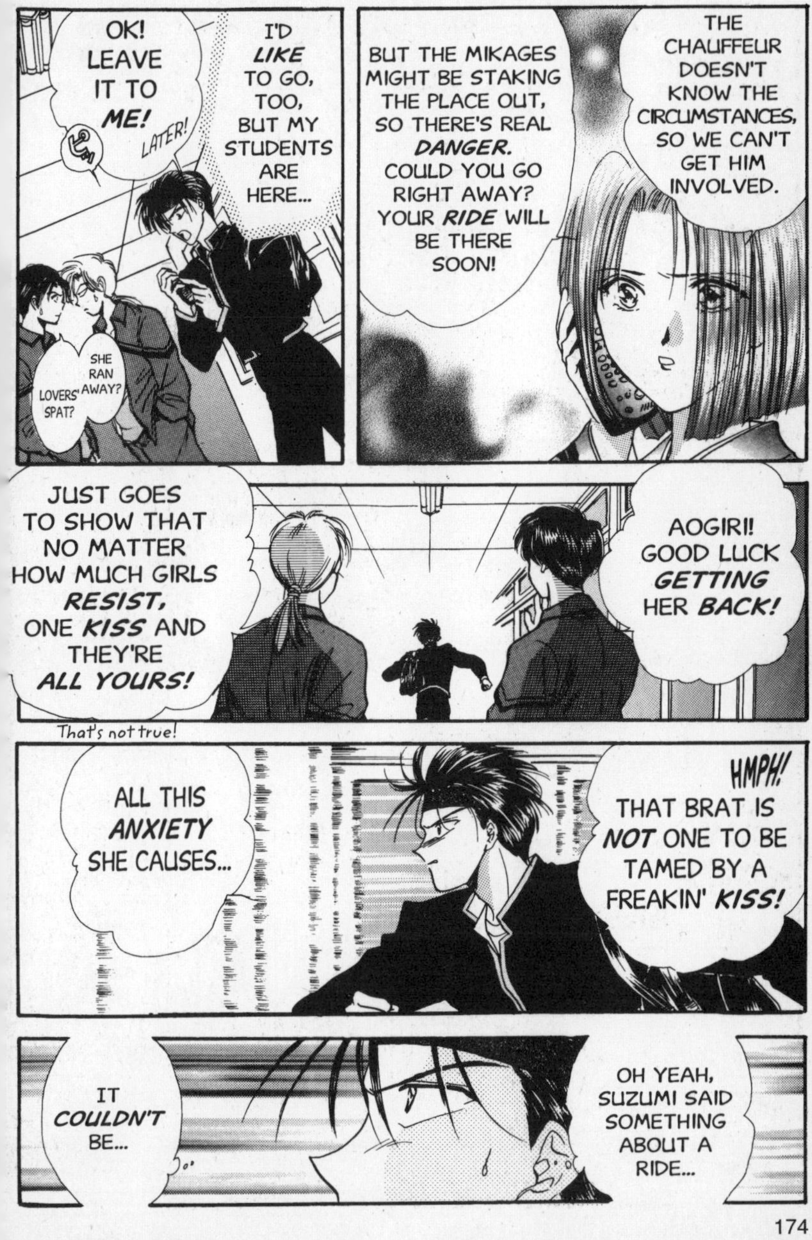
THE CHAUFFEUR DOESN'T KNOW THE CIRCUMSTANCES, SO WE CAN'T GET HIM INVOLVED.
BUT THE MIKAGES MIGHT BE STAKING THE PLACE OUT, SO THERE'S REAL DANGER. COULD YOU GO RIGHT AWAY? YOUR RIDE WILL BE THERE SOON!
I'D LIKE TO GO, TOO, BUT MY STUDENTS ARE HERE...
OK! LEAVE IT TO ME!
LATER!
SHE RAN AWAY?
LOVERS' SPAT?
AOGIRI! GOOD LUCK GETTING HER BACK!
JUST GOES TO SHOW THAT NO MATTER HOW MUCH GIRLS RESIST, ONE KISS AND THEY'RE ALL YOURS!
That's not true!
HMPH!
THAT BRAT IS NOT ONE TO BE TAMED BY A FREAKIN' KISS!
ALL THIS ANXIETY SHE CAUSES...
OH YEAH, SUZUMI SAID SOMETHING ABOUT A RIDE...
IT COULDN'T BE...

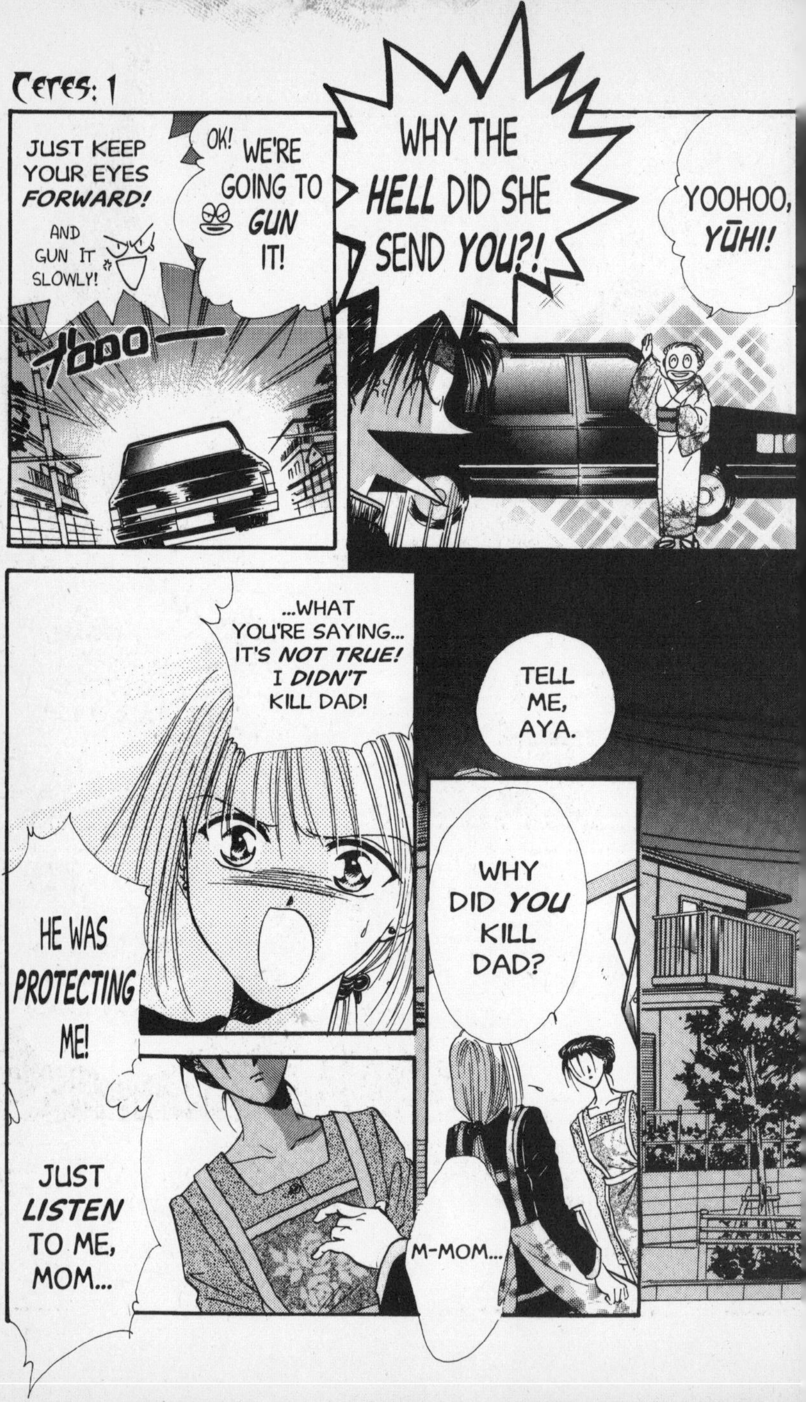
YOOHOO, YŪHI!
WHY THE HELL DID SHE SEND YOU?!
OK! WE'RE GOING TO GUN IT!
JUST KEEP YOUR EYES FORWARD!
AND GUN IT SLOWLY!
TOOO—
TELL ME, AYA.
WHY DID YOU KILL DAD?
M-MOM...
...WHAT YOU'RE SAYING... IT'S NOT TRUE! I DIDN'T KILL DAD!
HE WAS PROTECTING ME!
JUST LISTEN TO ME, MOM...

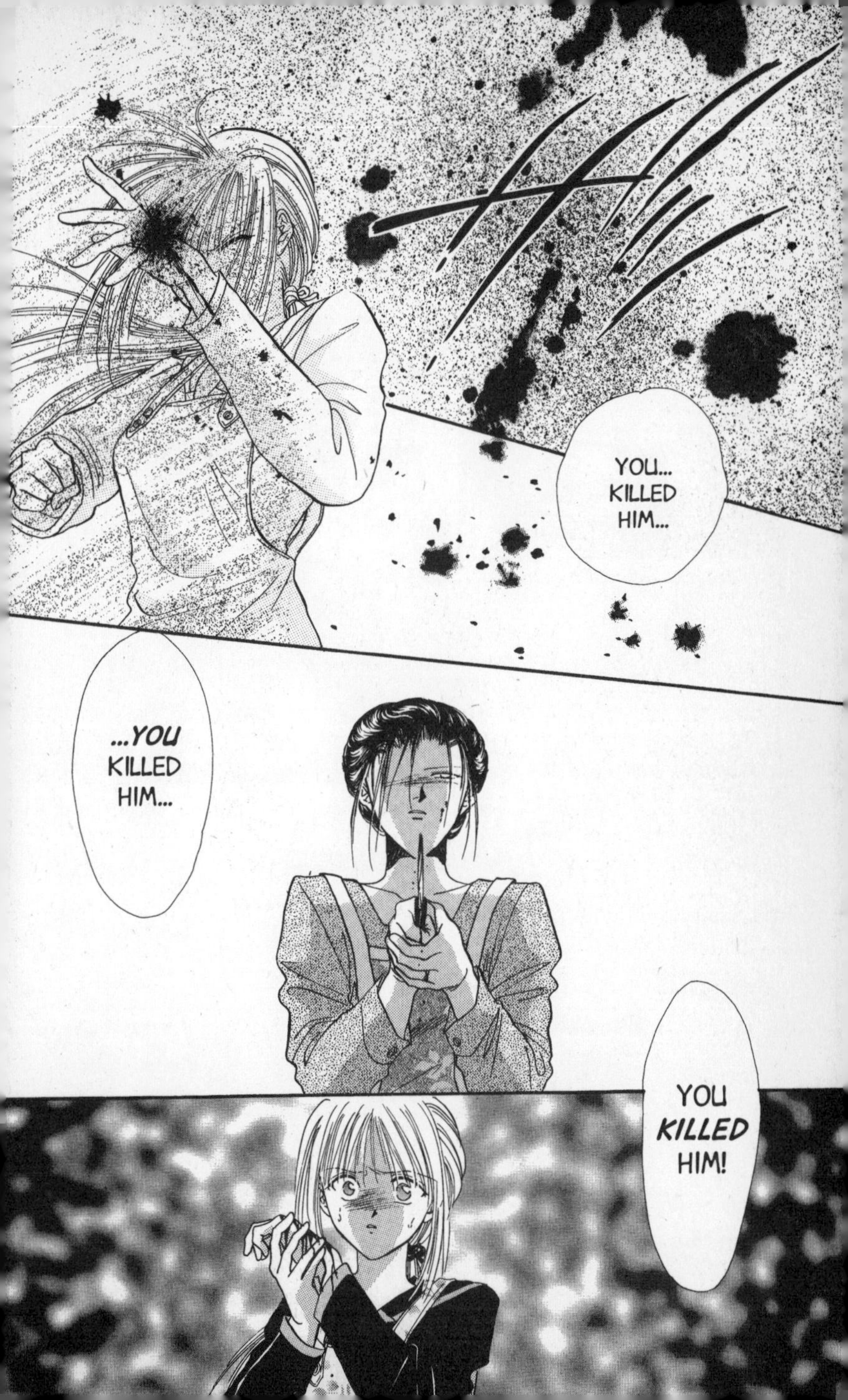
YOU... KILLED HIM...
...YOU KILLED HIM...
YOU KILLED HIM!

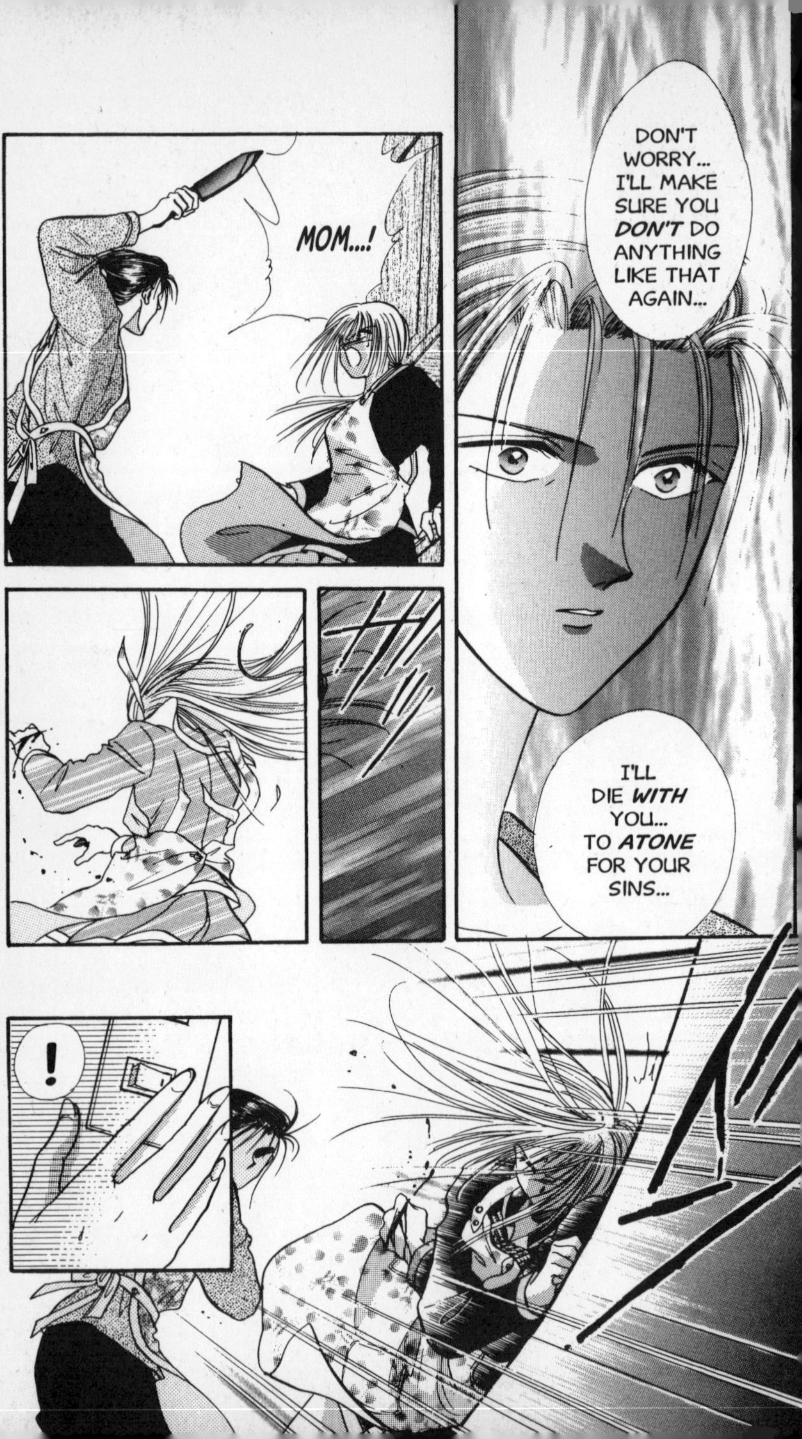
DON'T WORRY... I'LL MAKE SURE YOU *DON'T* DO ANYTHING LIKE THAT AGAIN...
I'LL DIE *WITH* YOU... TO *ATONE* FOR YOUR SINS...
MOM...!
!

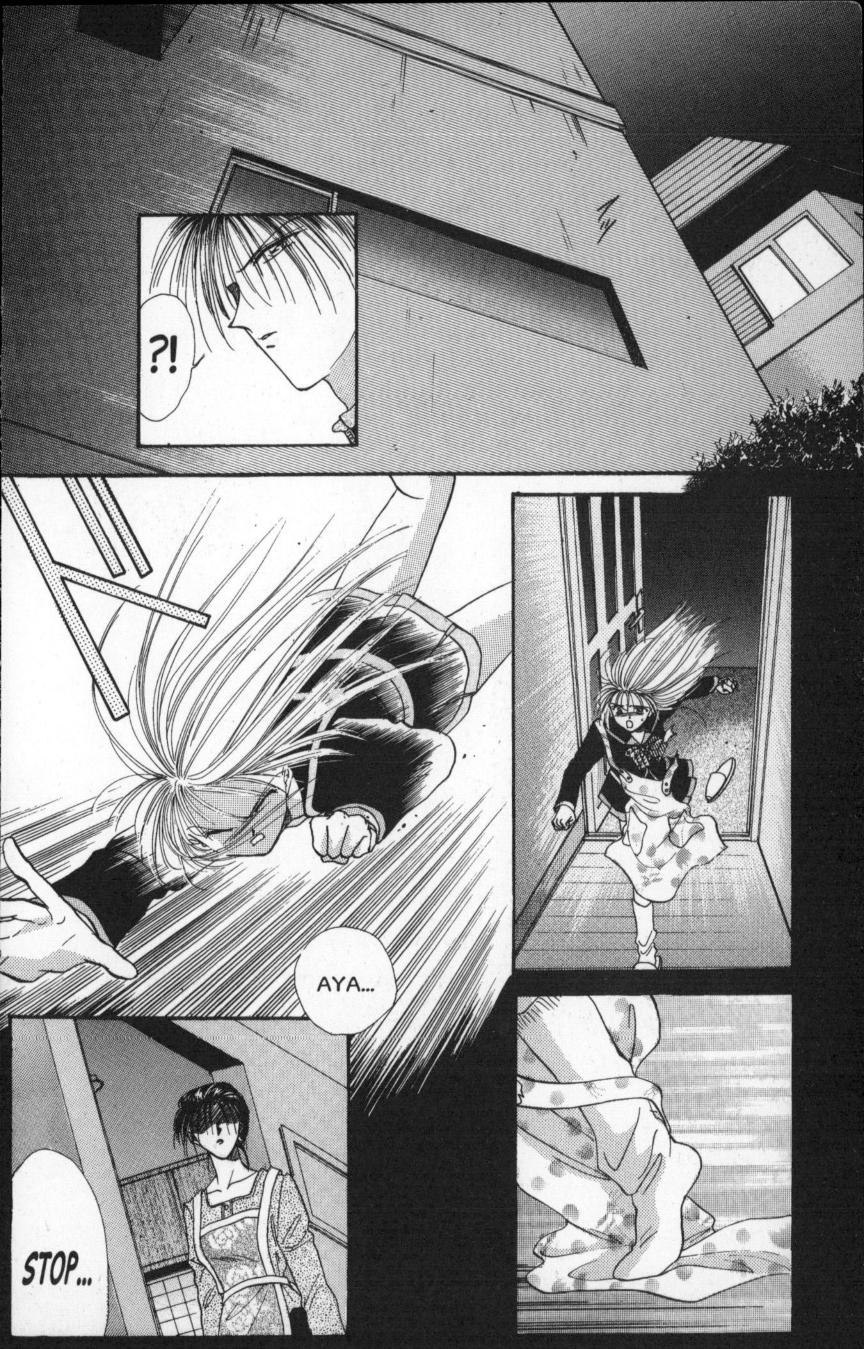
?!
AYA...
STOP...

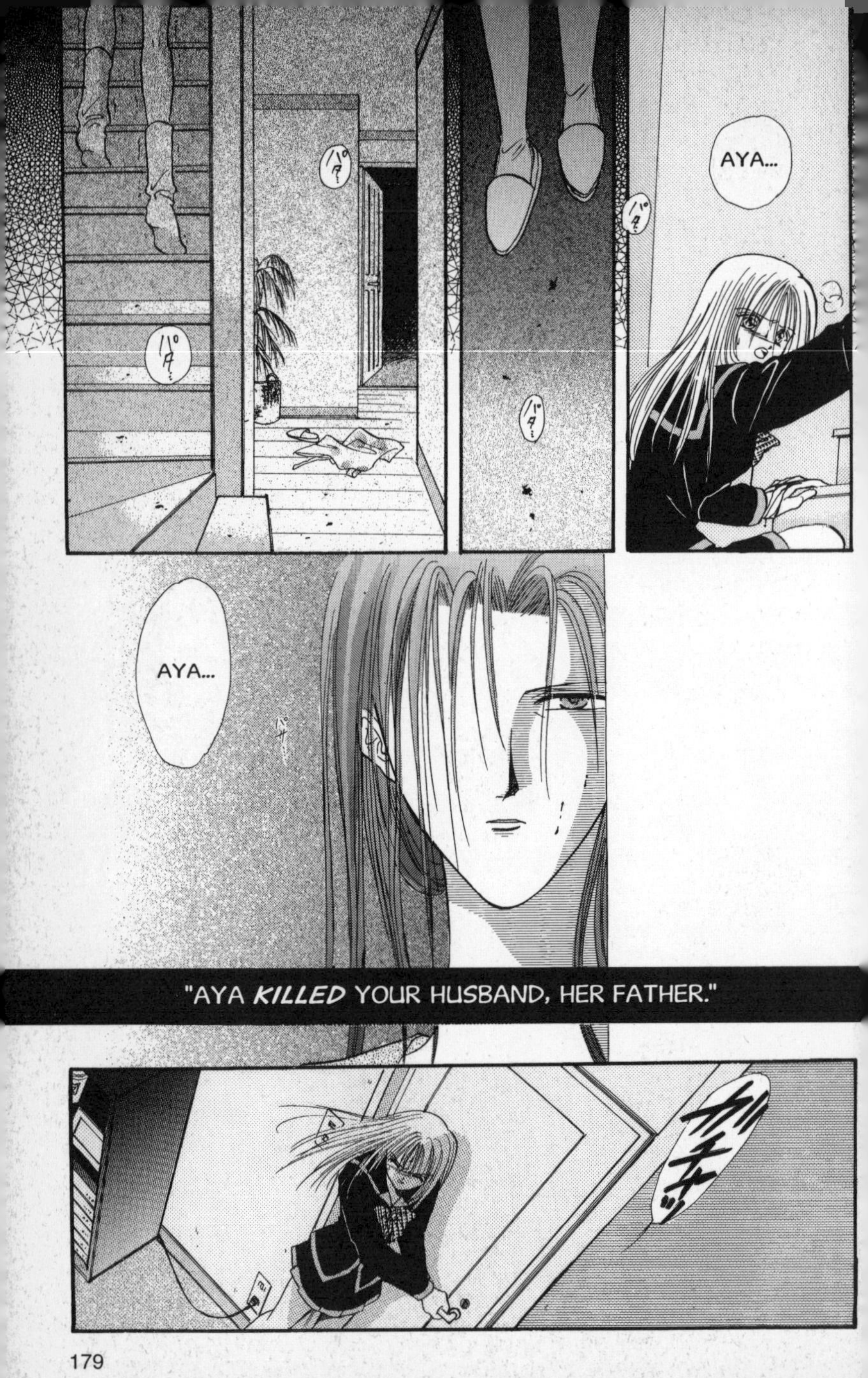
AYA...
パタ
パタ
パタ
パタ
AYA...
"AYA KILLED YOUR HUSBAND, HER FATHER."

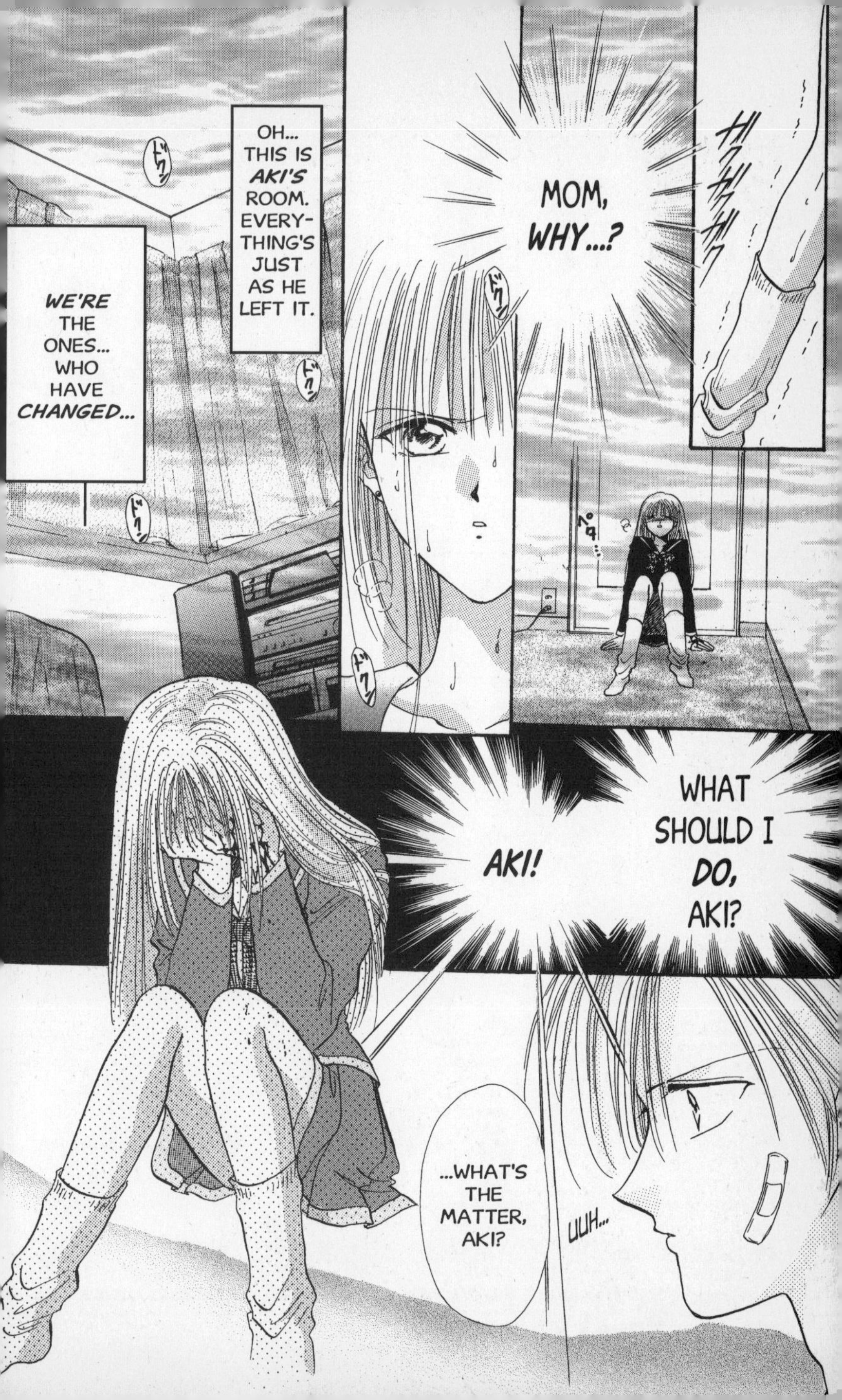
MOM, WHY...?
OH... THIS IS AKI'S ROOM. EVERYTHING'S JUST AS HE LEFT IT.
WE'RE THE ONES... WHO HAVE CHANGED...
WHAT SHOULD I DO, AKI?
AKI!
UUH...
...WHAT'S THE MATTER, AKI?

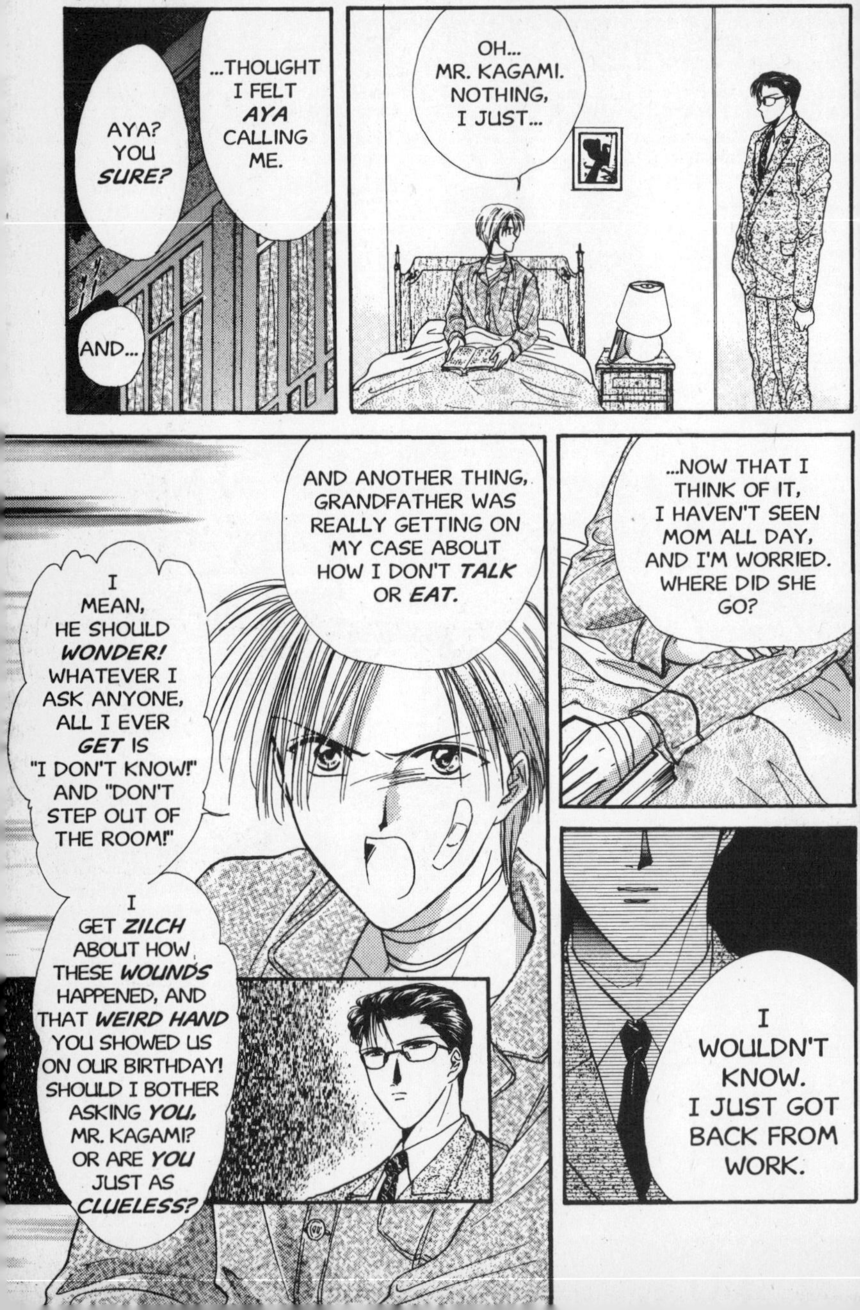
OH... MR. KAGAMI. NOTHING, I JUST...
...THOUGHT I FELT AYA CALLING ME.
AYA? YOU SURE?
AND...
...NOW THAT I THINK OF IT, I HAVEN'T SEEN MOM ALL DAY, AND I'M WORRIED. WHERE DID SHE GO?
I WOULDN'T KNOW. I JUST GOT BACK FROM WORK.
AND ANOTHER THING, GRANDFATHER WAS REALLY GETTING ON MY CASE ABOUT HOW I DON'T TALK OR EAT.
I MEAN, HE SHOULD WONDER! WHATEVER I ASK ANYONE, ALL I EVER GET IS "I DON'T KNOW!" AND "DON'T STEP OUT OF THE ROOM!"
I GET ZILCH ABOUT HOW THESE WOUNDS HAPPENED, AND THAT WEIRD HAND YOU SHOWED US ON OUR BIRTHDAY! SHOULD I BOTHER ASKING YOU, MR. KAGAMI? OR ARE YOU JUST AS CLUELESS?

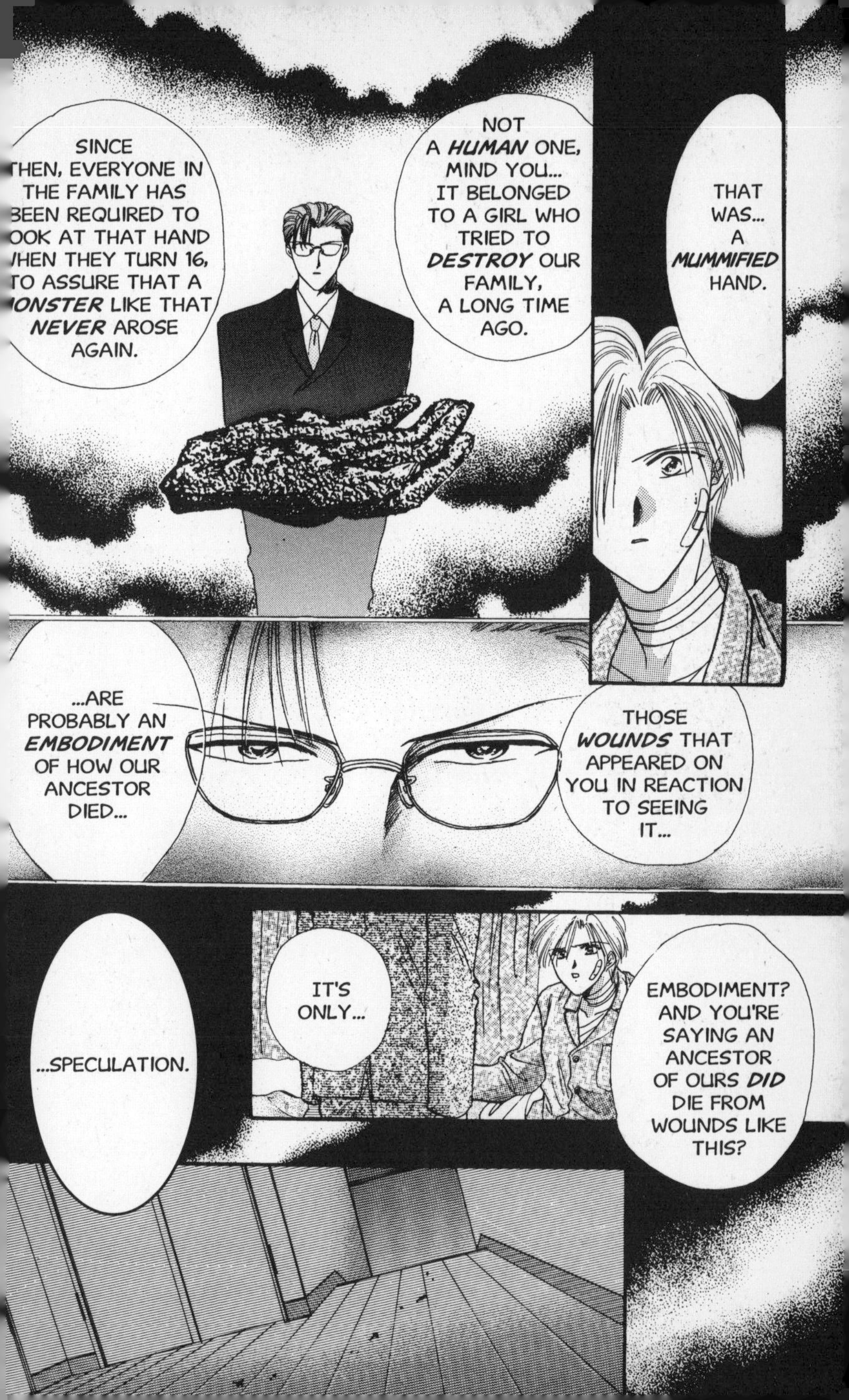
THAT WAS... A MUMMIFIED HAND.
NOT A HUMAN ONE, MIND YOU... IT BELONGED TO A GIRL WHO TRIED TO DESTROY OUR FAMILY, A LONG TIME AGO.
SINCE THEN, EVERYONE IN THE FAMILY HAS BEEN REQUIRED TO OOK AT THAT HAND HEN THEY TURN 16, TO ASSURE THAT A ONSTER LIKE THAT NEVER AROSE AGAIN.
THOSE WOUNDS THAT APPEARED ON YOU IN REACTION TO SEEING IT...
...ARE PROBABLY AN EMBODIMENT OF HOW OUR ANCESTOR DIED...
EMBODIMENT? AND YOU'RE SAYING AN ANCESTOR OF OURS DID DIE FROM WOUNDS LIKE THIS?
IT'S ONLY...
...SPECULATION.

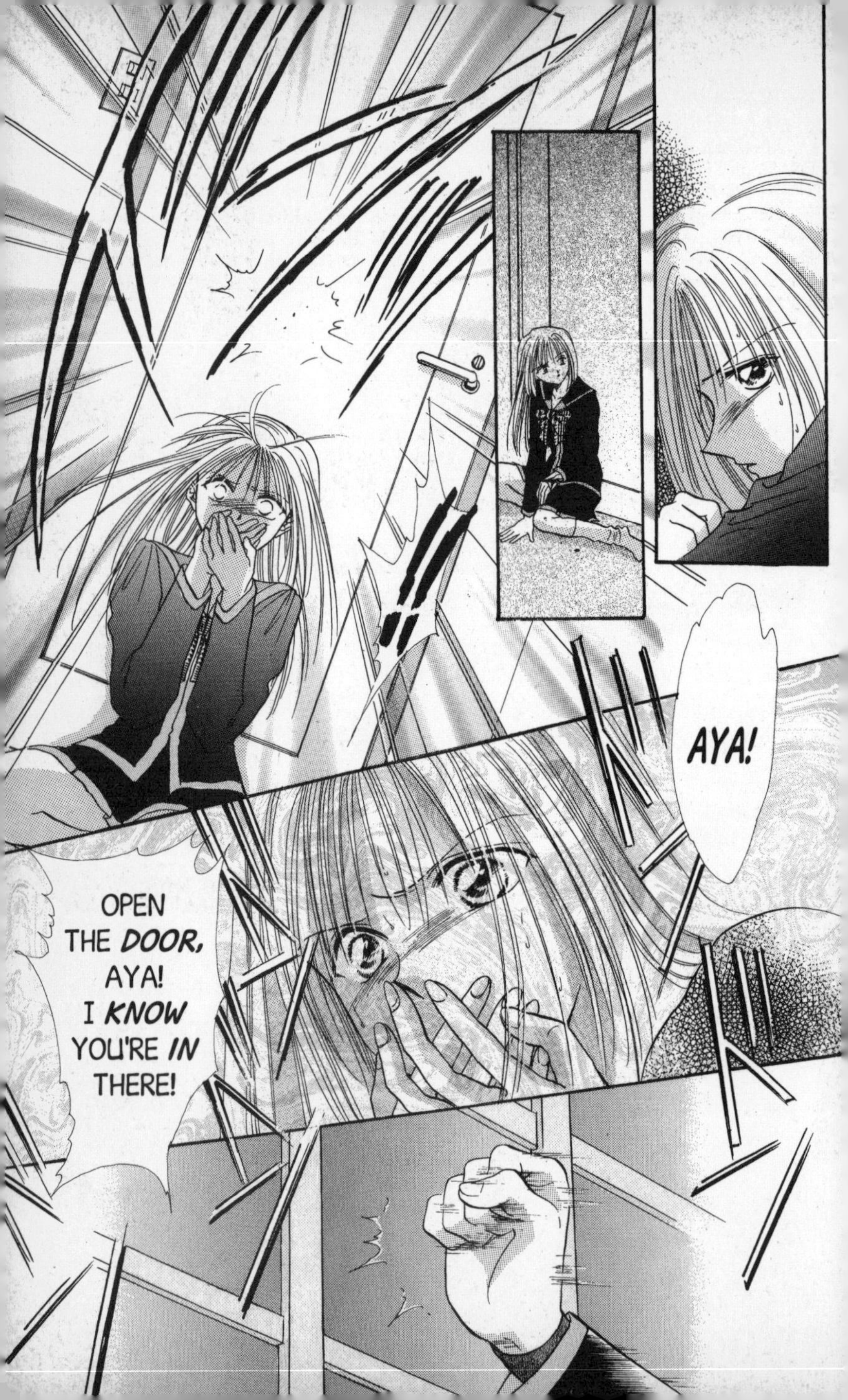
AYA!
OPEN THE DOOR, AYA! I KNOW YOU'RE IN THERE!

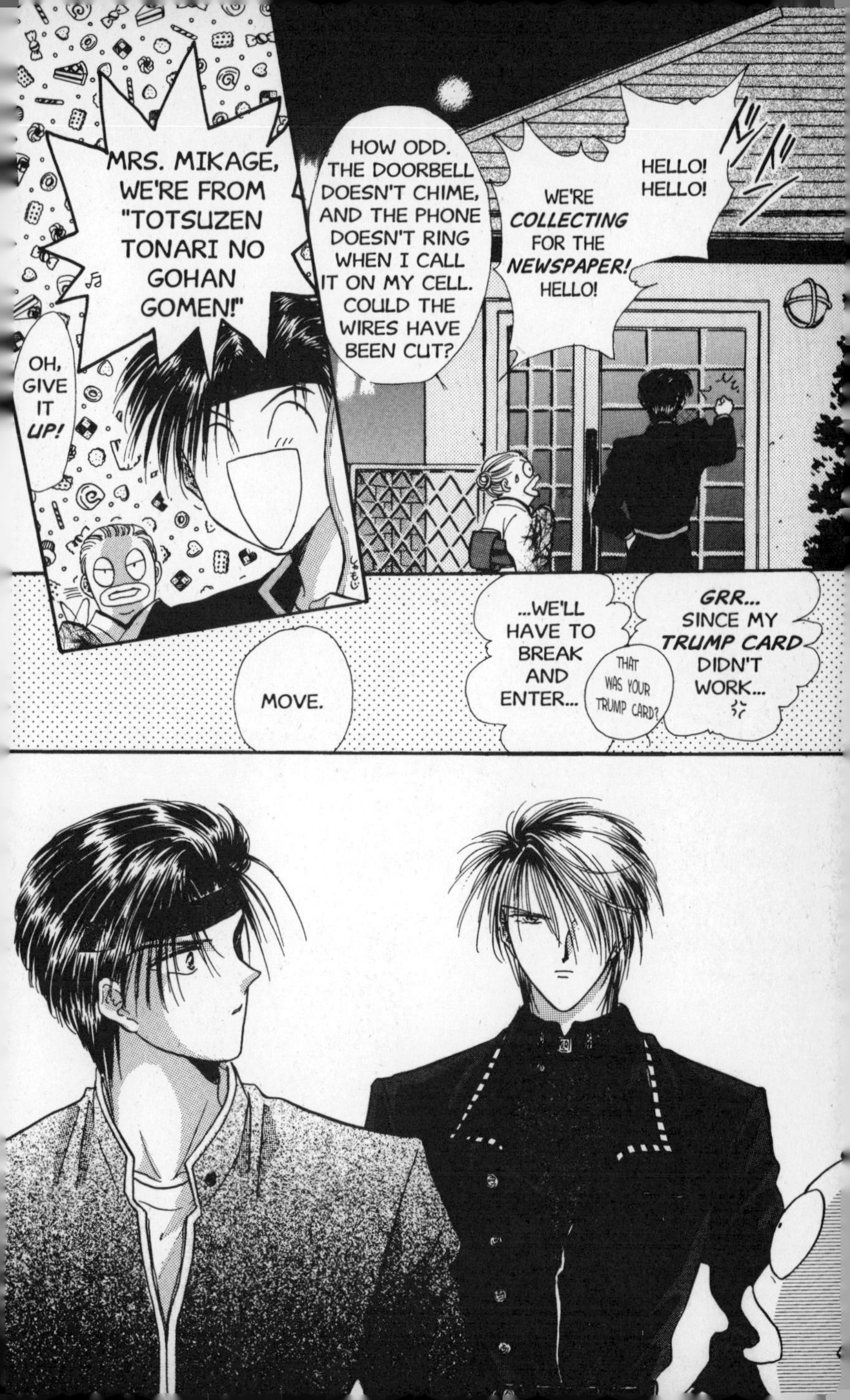
HELLO! HELLO!
WE'RE *COLLECTING* FOR THE *NEWSPAPER!* HELLO!
HOW ODD. THE DOORBELL DOESN'T CHIME, AND THE PHONE DOESN'T RING WHEN I CALL IT ON MY CELL. COULD THE WIRES HAVE BEEN CUT?
MRS. MIKAGE, WE'RE FROM "TOTSUZEN TONARI NO GOHAN GOMEN!"
OH, GIVE IT *UP!*
GRR... SINCE MY *TRUMP CARD* DIDN'T WORK...
THAT WAS YOUR TRUMP CARD?
...WE'LL HAVE TO BREAK AND ENTER...
MOVE.

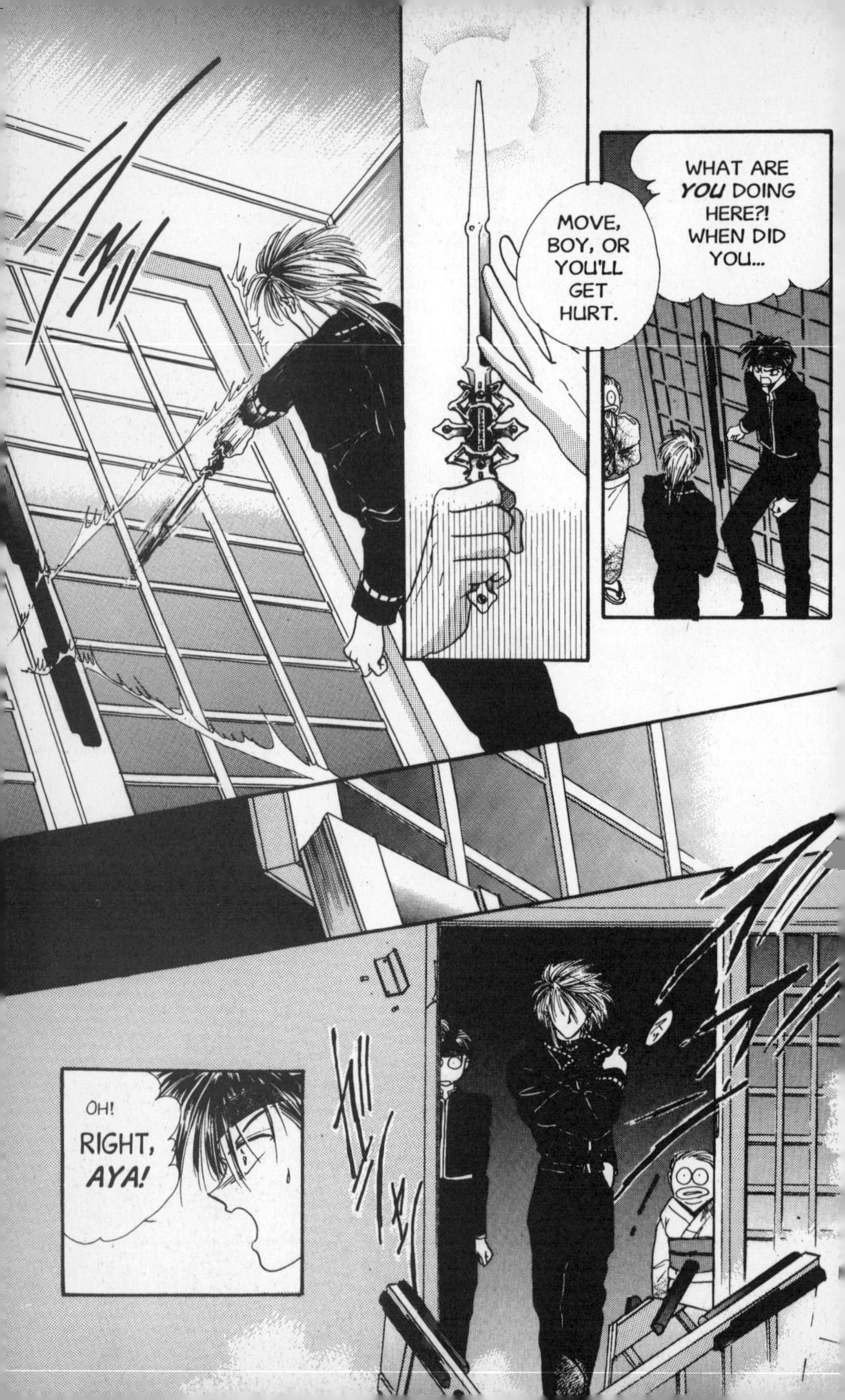
WHAT ARE YOU DOING HERE?! WHEN DID YOU...
MOVE, BOY, OR YOU'LL GET HURT.
OH!
RIGHT, AYA!

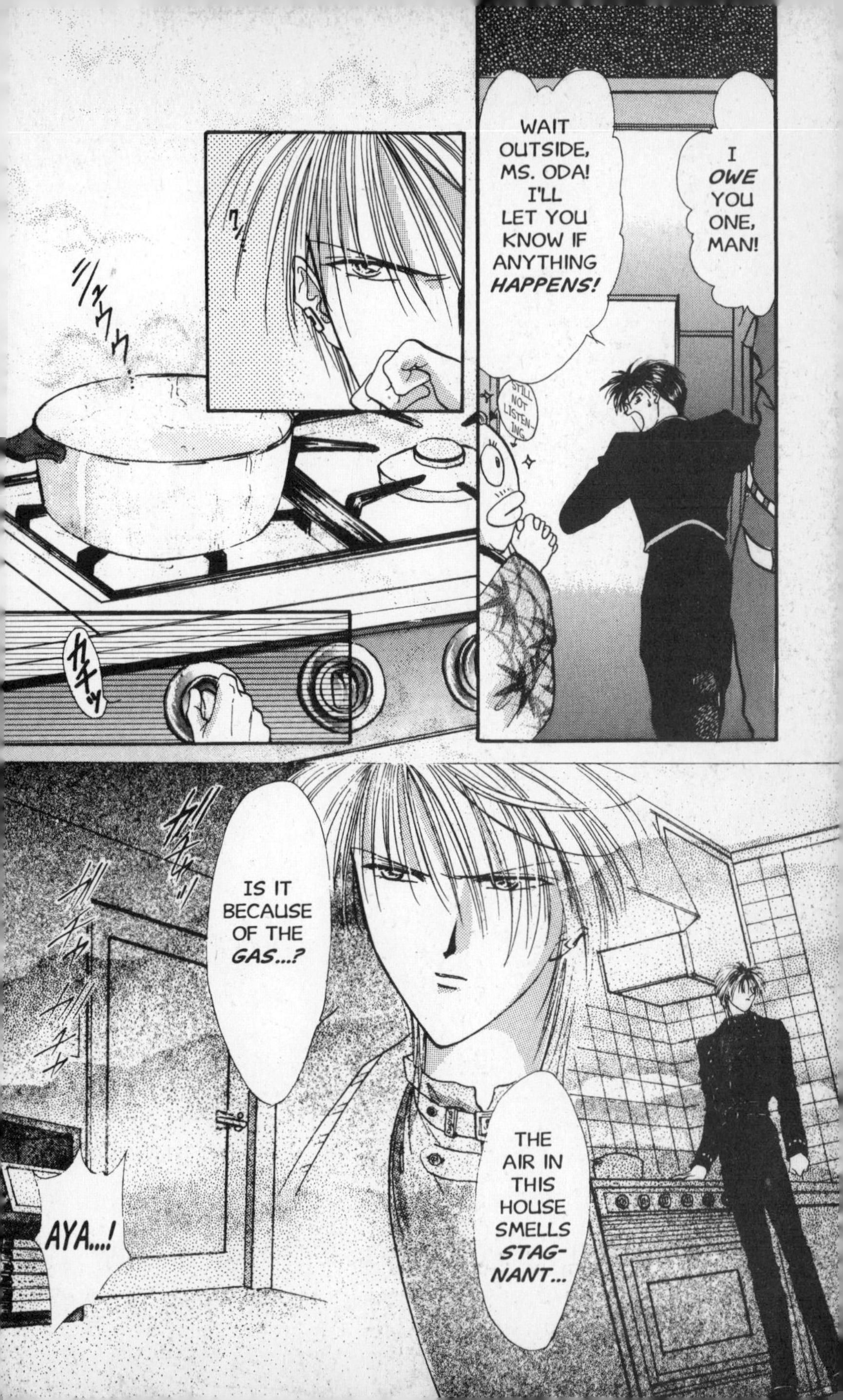
I OWE YOU ONE, MAN!
WAIT OUTSIDE, MS. ODA! I'LL LET YOU KNOW IF ANYTHING HAPPENS!
STILL NOT LISTEN-ING.
IS IT BECAUSE OF THE GAS...?
THE AIR IN THIS HOUSE SMELLS STAG-NANT...
AYA...!

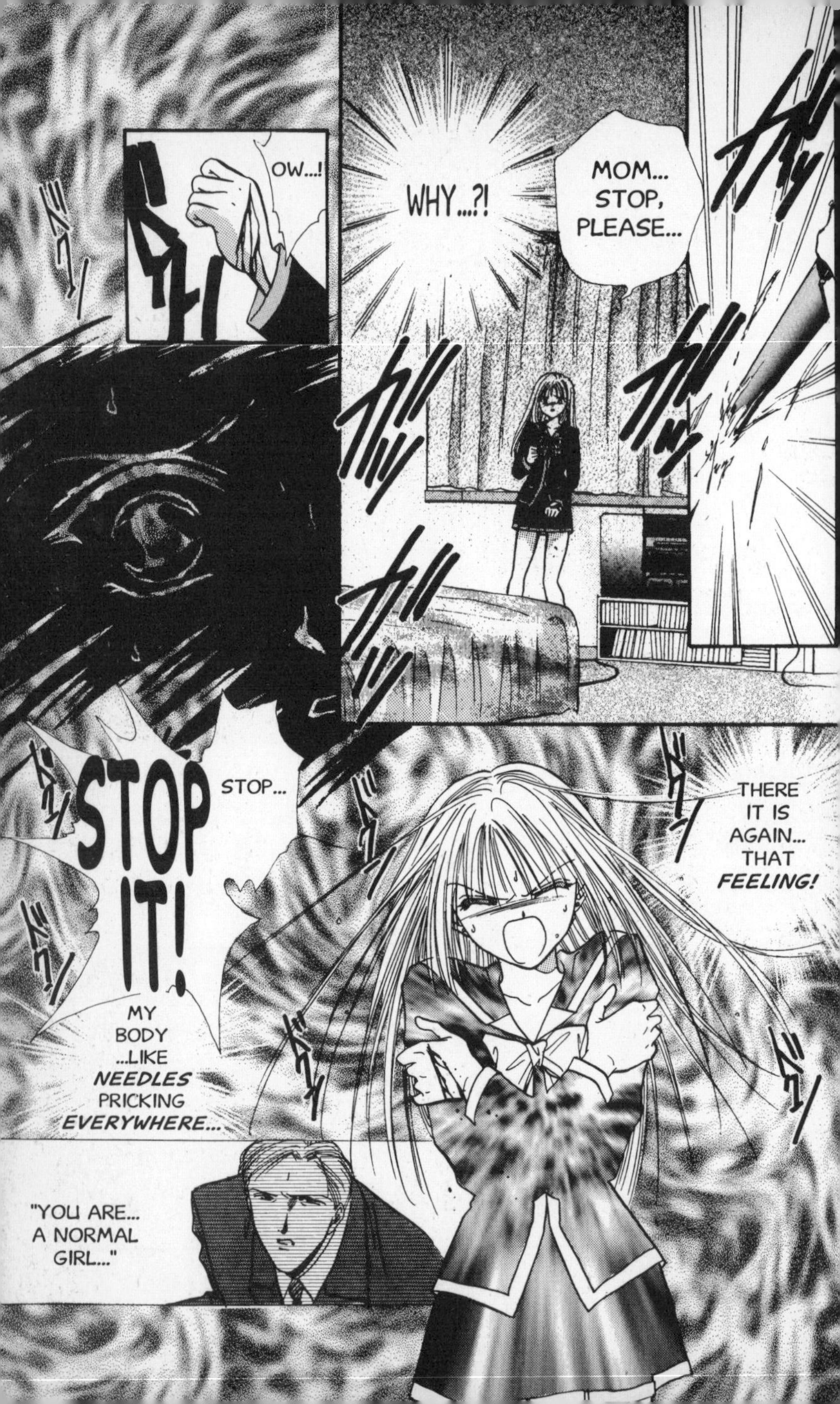
MOM... STOP, PLEASE...
WHY...?!
OW...!
THERE IT IS AGAIN... THAT *FEELING!*
STOP...
STOP IT!
MY BODY ...LIKE *NEEDLES* PRICKING *EVERYWHERE...*
"YOU ARE... A NORMAL GIRL..."

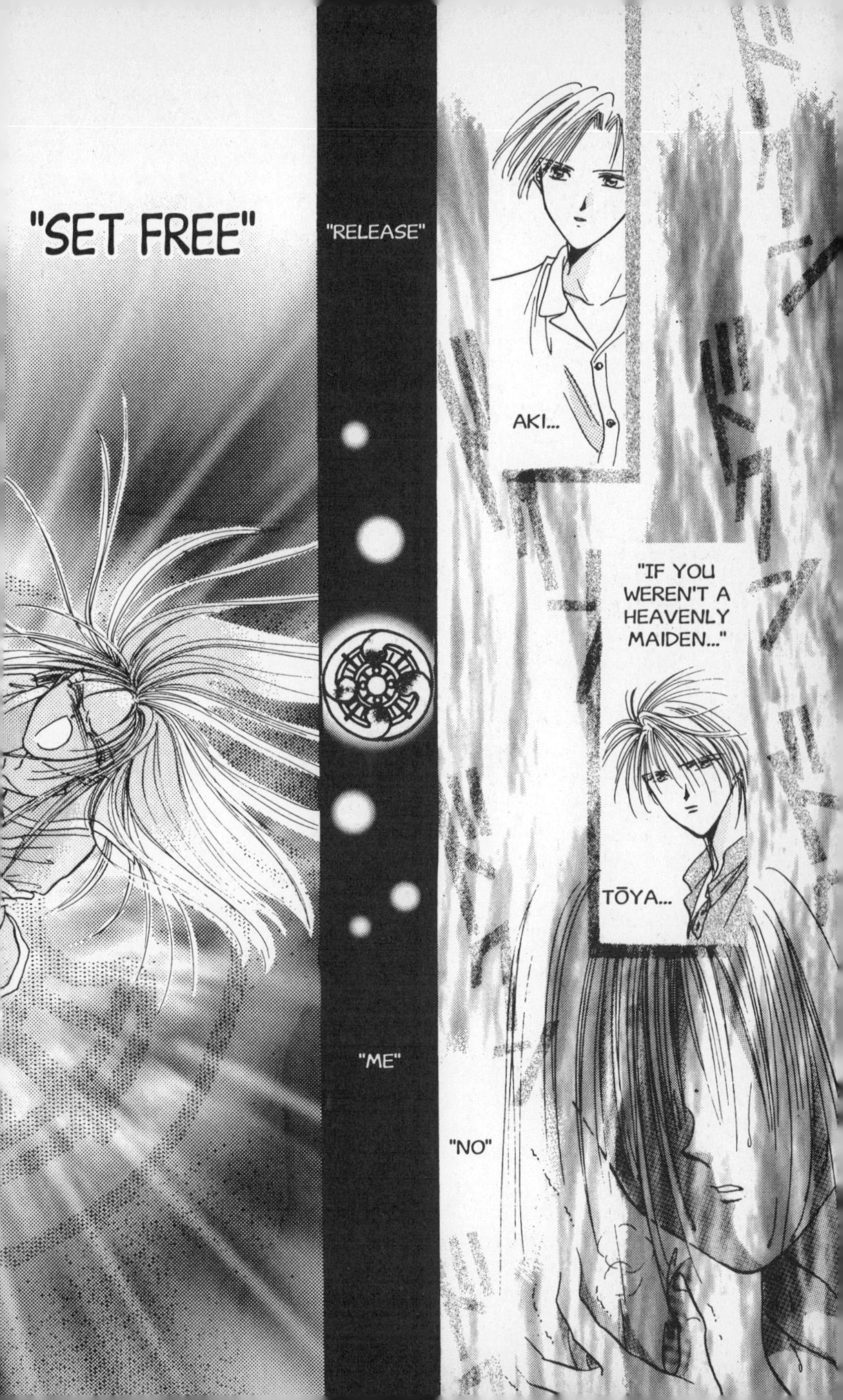
AKI...
"IF YOU WEREN'T A HEAVENLY MAIDEN..."
TŌYA...
"NO"
"RELEASE"
"ME"
"SET FREE"

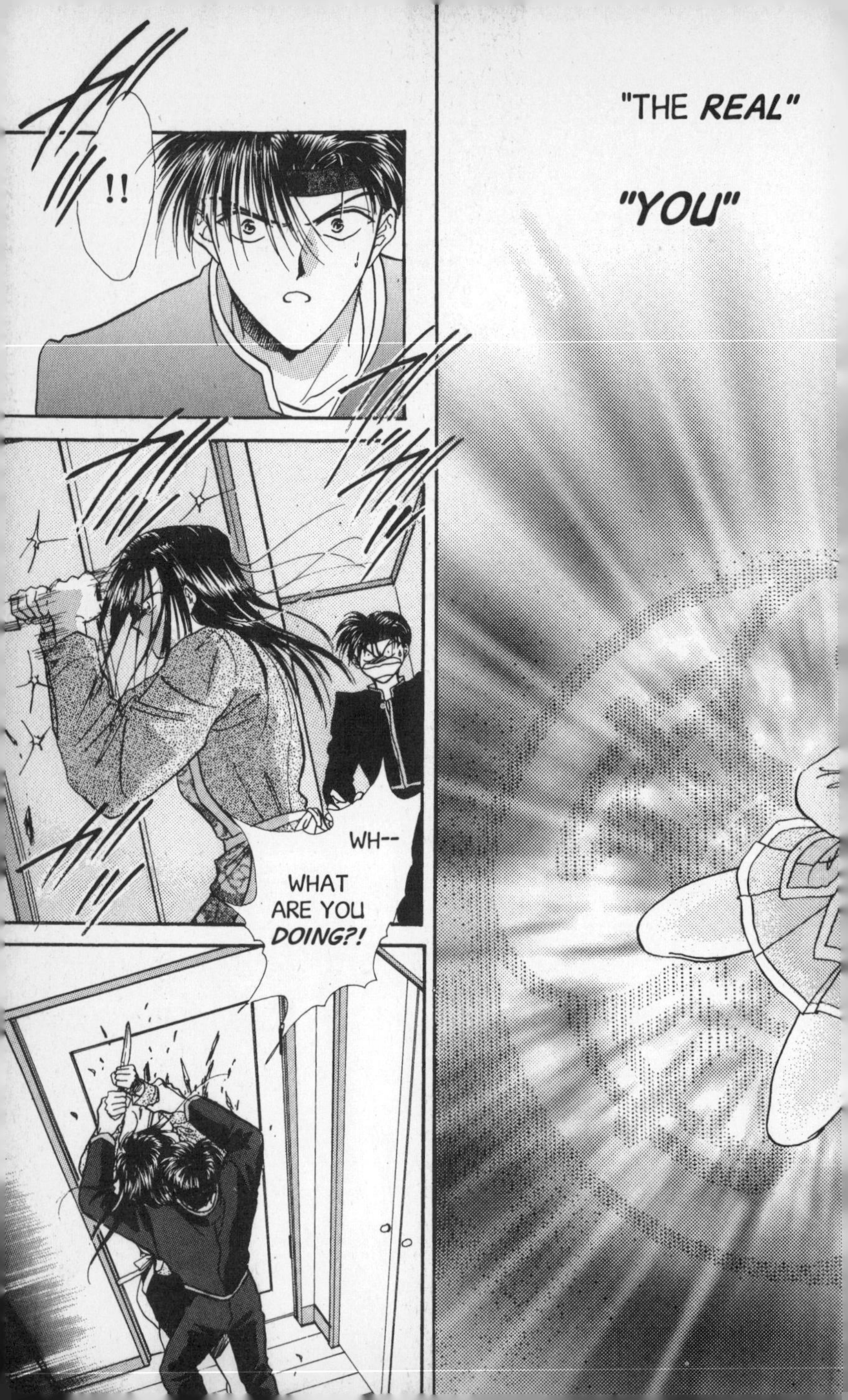
"THE *REAL*"
"YOU"
!!
WH--
WHAT ARE YOU *DOING?!*

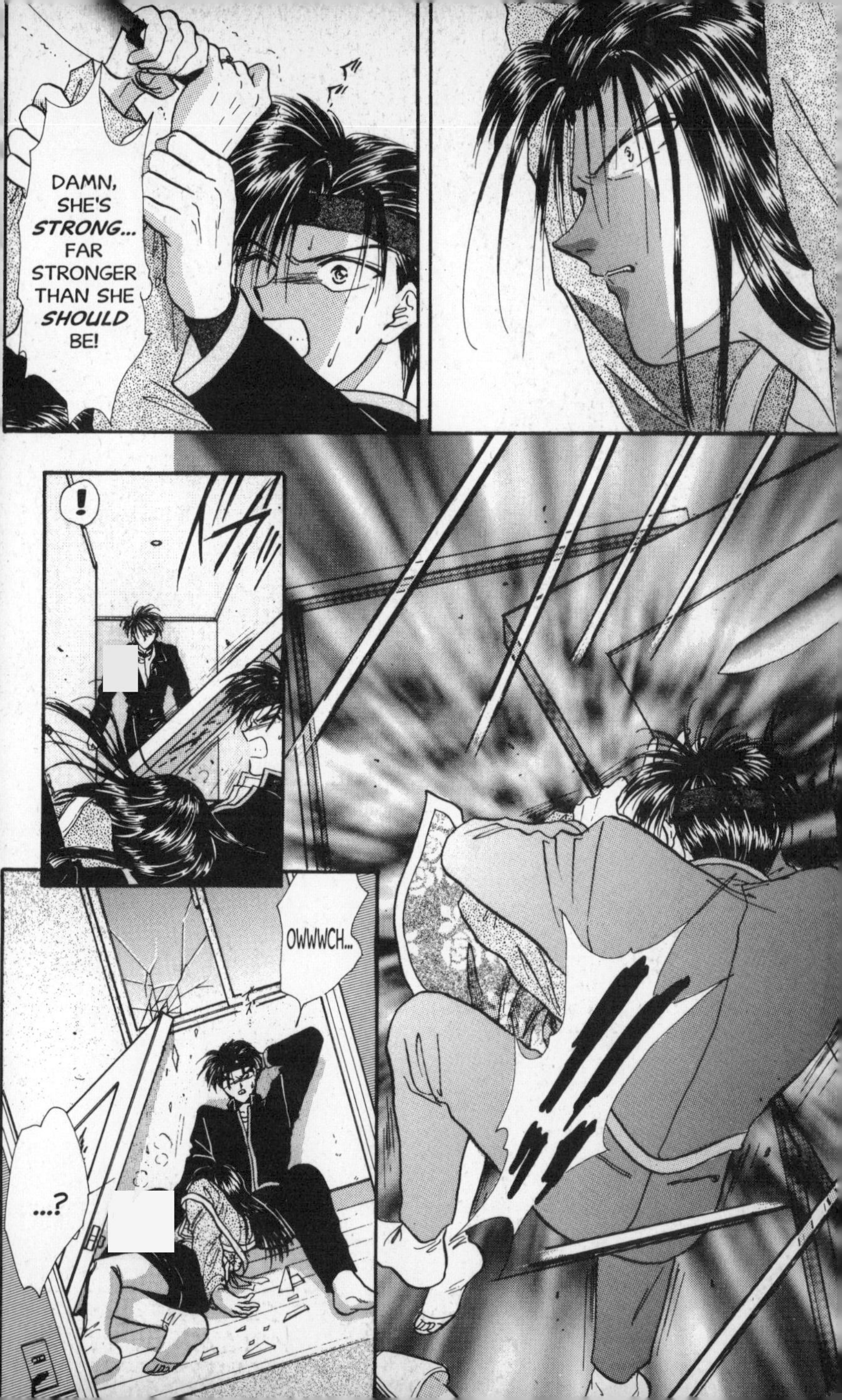
DAMN, SHE'S STRONG... FAR STRONGER THAN SHE SHOULD BE!
!
OWWWCH...
...?

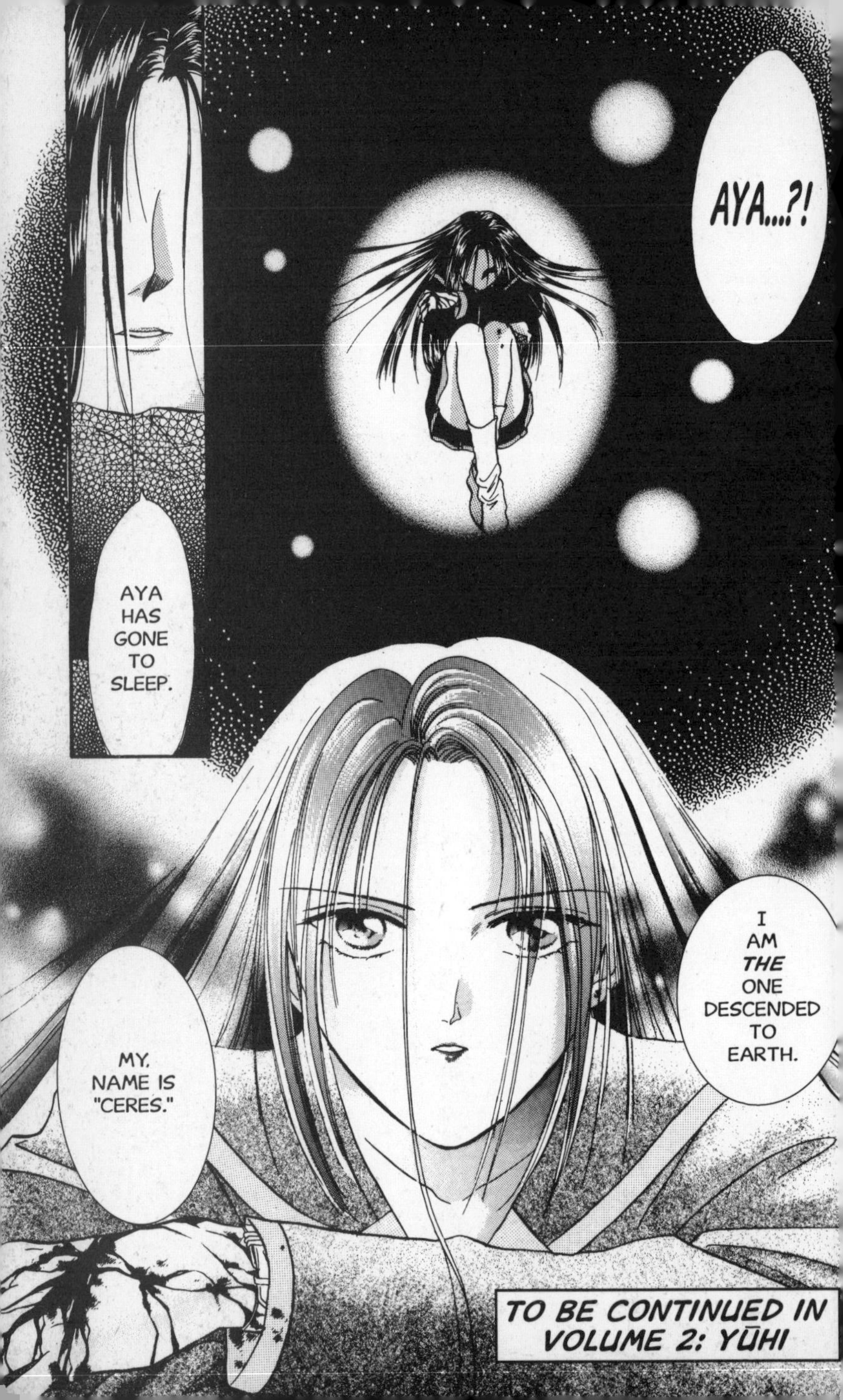
AYA...?!
AYA HAS GONE TO SLEEP.
I AM *THE* ONE DESCENDED TO EARTH.
MY. NAME IS "CERES."
TO BE CONTINUED IN VOLUME 2: YŪHI

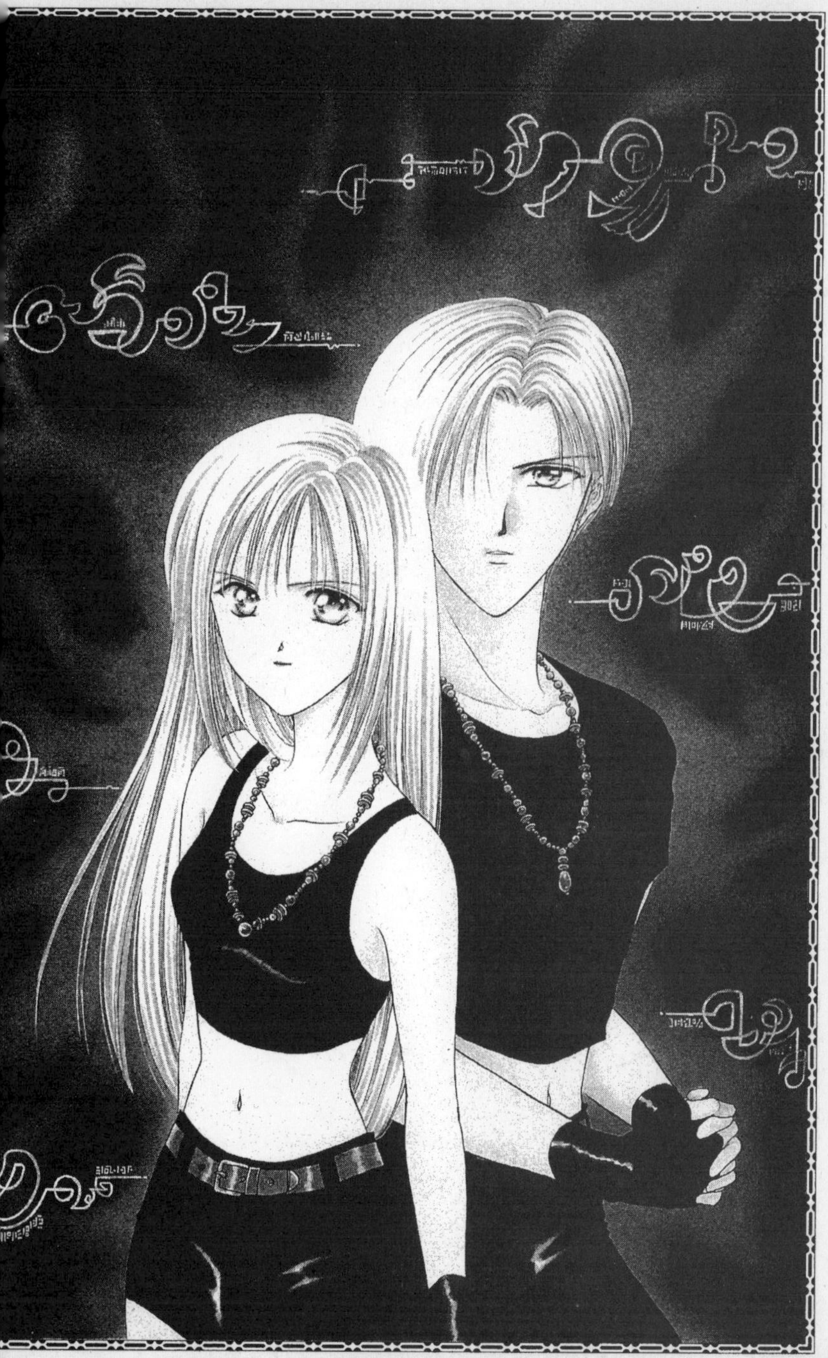

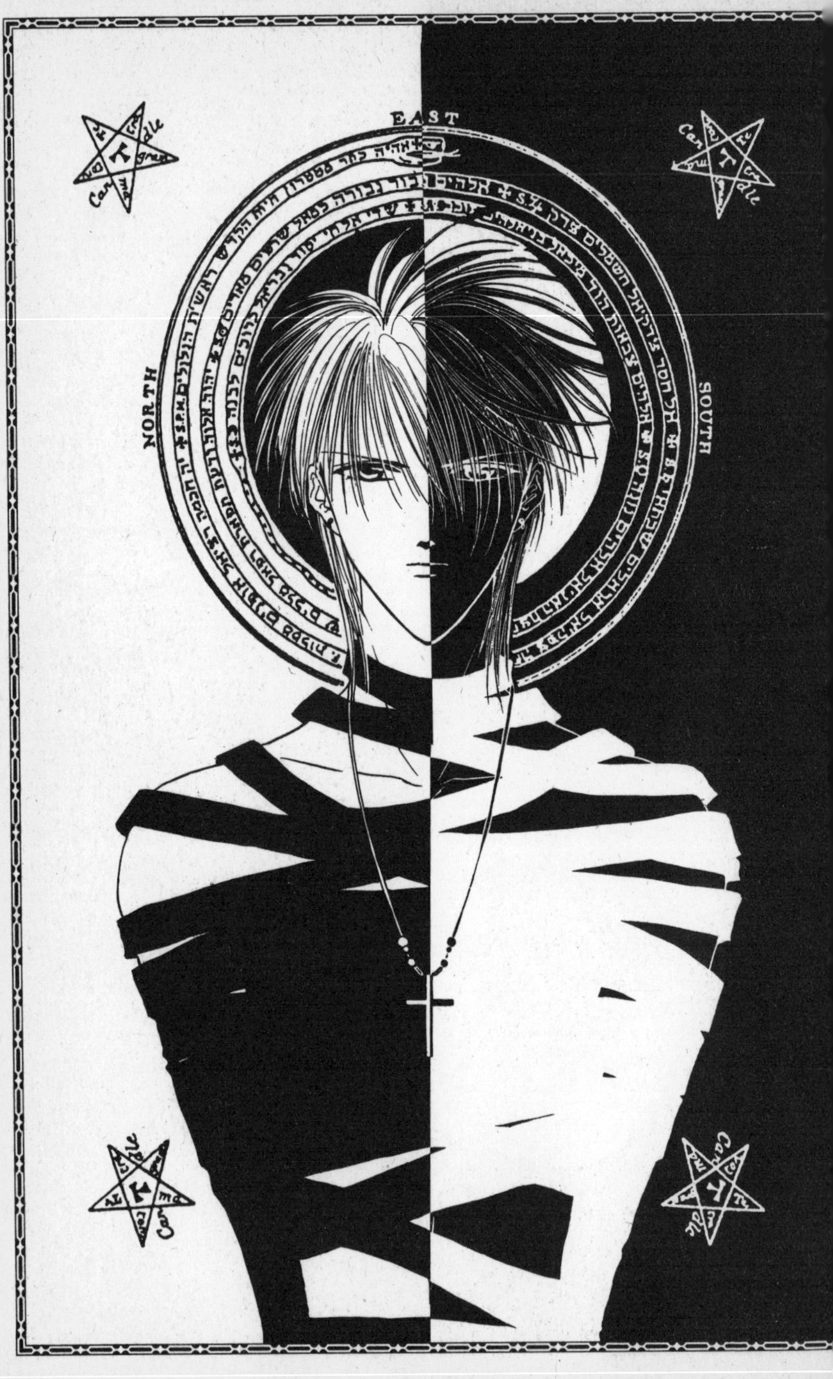
EAST
NORTH
SOUTH

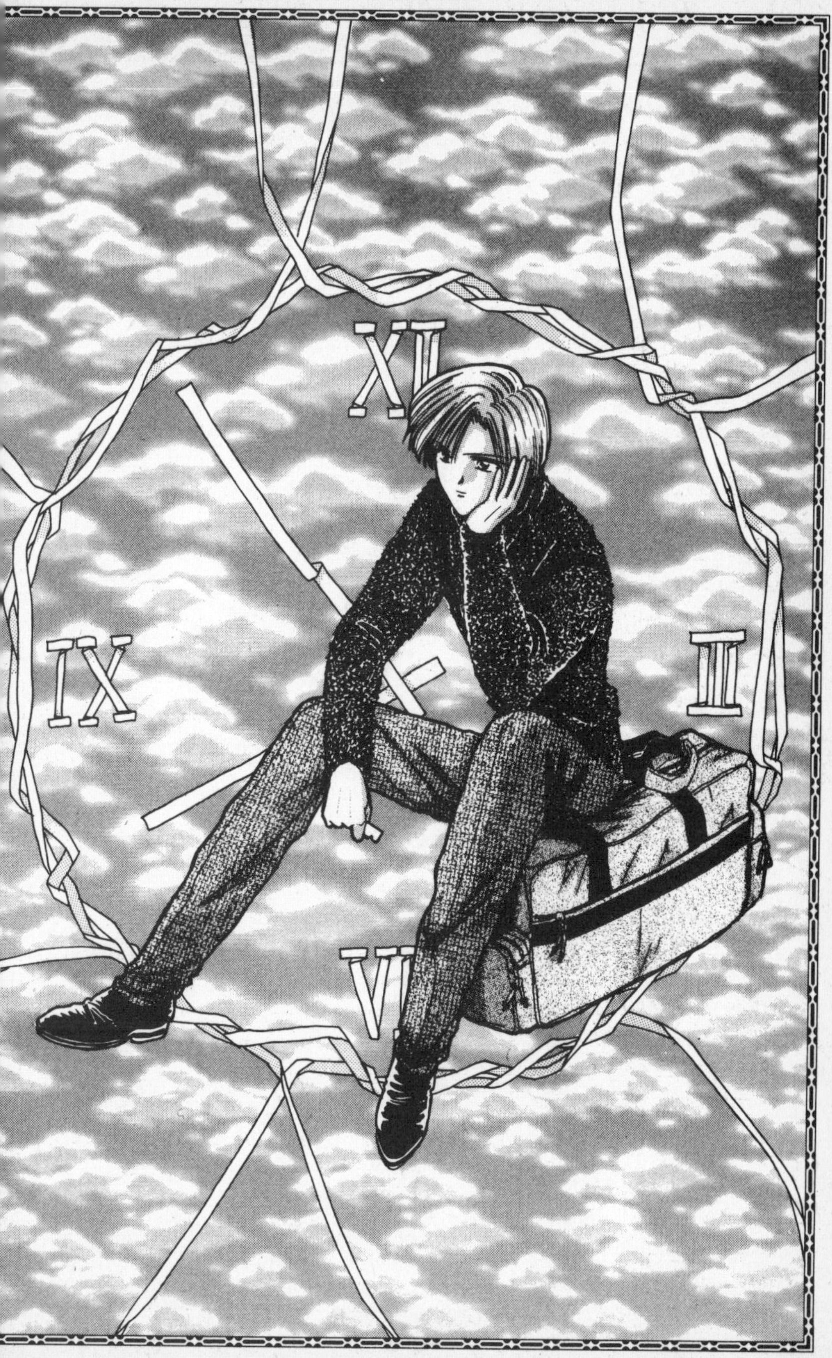
XII
III
VI
IX

The Ceres Guide to Sound Effects

We've left most of the sound effects in Ceres as Yû Watase originally created them — in Japanese. VIZ has created this glossary to help you decipher, page-by-page and panel-by-panel, what all those foreign words and background noises mean. Use this guide to impress your friends with your new Japanese vocabulary. The glossary lists the page number then panel. For example, 2.1 is page 2, panel 1.

32.6 — FX: PAN [clap]

34.1 — FX: KA [flash]

34.2 — FX: GORO GORO [rumble rumble]

34.3 — FX: BATAN [slam]

— FX: JIWA JIWA JIWAJI [nostalgic sound of cicadas]

35.4 — FX: GACHA [click of door]

38.1 — FX: BATAN [click of door]

38.3 — FX: SU [entering]

38.4 — FX: GATAN [clunk from getting up]

39.1 — FX: SURURI [fabric slipping off]

39.2 — FX: DOKUN DOKUN [ba-dump ba-dump]

39.3 — FX: DOKUN DOKUN [ba-dump ba-dump]

39.4 — FX: DOKUN DOKUN DOKUN [ba-dump ba-dump ba-dump]

39.5 — FX: DOKUN DOKUN DOKUN [ba-dump ba-dump ba-dump]

39.6 — FX: KAPO [creak of wood box opening]

40.1 — FX: DOKUN [ba-dump]

40.3 — FX: KIII [high-pitched sound]

41.1 — FX: KIII [high-pitched sound]

— FX: DOKUN DOKUN DOKUN DOKUN DOKUN [ba-dump ba-dump ba-dump ba-dump ba-dump]

41.2 — FX: BURU BURU [tremble tremble]

41.4 — FX: ZAWA [gasp, murmur]

42.1 — FX: BA [fash]

42.2 — FX: BURU BURU BURU [tremble tremble tremble]

42.4 — FX: GATA GATA [clatter clatter]

43.1 — FX: BAN [shatter]

43.2 — FX: FU [fft]

43.3-4 — FX: HA HA HA HA [huff huff huff]

44.1 — FX: BURU BURU BURU [tremble tremble tremble]

44.2 — FX: JIWA [seep]

44.3 — FX: BA [slash]

44.4 — FX: BABA [spurt]

45.2 — FX: BABA [gouge]

7.3 — FX: BIKU [twitch]

11.3 — FX: BAN [slam]

12.4 — FX: KI [glare]

13.2 — FX: PACHI PACHI [clap clap]

13.3 — FX: HA [uh]

14.2 — FX: ZUN ZUN [bass sound]

14.3 — FX: PIKU [getting angry]

14.4 — FX: GASHAAN [crash]

— FX: DOTA BATA [clamber]

14.5 — FX: CHA [readying camera]

15.1 — FX: KASHA [click]

16.1 — FX: KYAA [a scream]

17.5 — FX: PASHI [snag]

18.5 — FX: GAKU [trip]

20.4 — FX: HA [GASP]

21.1 — FX: FU [momentary float]

22.1 — FX: PAA [beep]

22.3 — FX: KIKIKI [screech]

23.2 — FX: DOKUN DOKUN [ba-dump ba-dump]

23.3 — FX: DOKUN DOKUN [ba-dump ba-dump]

24.1 — FX: DOKUN [ba-dump]

24.2 — FX: SARA [fine hair]

25.1 — FX: ZAWA ZAWA [murmur murmur]

25.2 — FX: ZAWA ZAWA [murmur murmur]

25.4 — FX: UHYOO [whoo]

26.1 — FX: SU [retreating]

26.4 — FX: NIKO [smile]

28.4 — FX: BASHII [whap]

29.2 — FX: DOSU [thump]

30.4 — FX: KUN [yank]

31.2 — FX: GAN [klonk]

31.3 — FX: DOKU DOKU [gush gush]

31.6 — FX: PITA [stopping]

32.5 — FX: GORO GORO [rumble rumble]

45.3—FX: FU [fft]

46.5—FX: KATAN [getting up]

47.2—FX: GATA GATAN [several people getting up]

49.1—FX: PO PO [plip plop]

49.2—FX: SAA [rain]

49.3—FX: KA KA [tap tap, walking with cane]

49.4—FX: KA [tap]

50.1—FX: AHAHAHA [laughter]

50.5—FX: BIKUN [gasp]

51.1—FX: KOTSU KOTSU [walking]

51.5—FX: KII [creak]

51.6—FX: PATAN [closing quietly]

52.3—FX: BAN [slam]

52.4—FX: GU [clutch]

53.2—FX: GIRI GIRI [hands squeezing]

53.4—FX: BIBIBI [shiver]

—FX: GATA GATA GATA [rattle rattle rattle]

54.1—FX: KA [glare]

54.2—FX: BAN [crash]

54.3—FX: SAA [rain]

56.1—FX: SUPAPAPA [chop chop chop]

56.2—FX: BOCHA BOCHA [plip plop]

56.4—FX: KAAN [klong]

56.5—FX: GARA DOSSHA [clatter smash]

—FX: GASHAAN [crash]

57.1—FX: GAA [grr]

58.4—FX: SAA [fsshh]

59.1—FX: KASHAN [clink]

59.2—FX: KASHAN [clink]

59.4—FX: MIIN MINMIN [cicadas]

59.6—FX: MIIN MINMIN [cicadas]

60.2—FX: BIKU [urk]

60.4—FX: DOSA [thud]

61.1—FX: MIIN MIIN [cicadas]

61.2—FX: HA [gasp]

61.4—FX: SAAA [fsshh]

62.1—FX: BIKUN [yipes]

—FX: GOSHI GOSHI [rub rub]

63.5—FX: GYU [squeeze]

64.2—FX: FUWA [flap]

65.3—FX: PATA PATA [running]

—FX: PIKU [twitch]

66.3—FX: GUI [tug]

66.4—FX: KASHAN [clatter]

68.2—FX: SAA [rain]

68.4—FX: BASHA BASHA [splash splash]

68.6—FX: KASHAN [clatter]

69.1—FX: BASHA BASHA [splash splash]

70.1—FX: GYAAAA [a scream]

70.2—FX: DOKI DOKI [ba-dump ba-dump]

71.1—FX: CHA [ka-chak of gun]

71.3—FX: DOKUN DOKUN DOKUN DOKUN DOKUN [ba-dump ba-dump ba-dump ba-dump ba-dump]

71.4—FX: SHU [fwoosh]

71.5—FX: TON [tap]

72.1—FX: GURA [stagger]

72.2—FX: PASHI [snap]

72.3—FX: DOSU [wham]

73.1—FX: BASHAN [splash]

74.3—FX: TON [shove]

75.1—FX: FUWA [float]

76.1—FX: BASHA [splish]

76.2—FX: SA [fsshh]

76.4—FX: BASHA BASHA [splash splash]

77.2—FX: PASHA [splash]

78.1—FX: ZAA [rain]

—FX: BASHA BASHA [splash splash]

79.1—FX: DOSA [fwump]

79.2—FX: BATAN [slam]

80.1—FX: MUSU [hmph]

80.2—FX: PATAN [closing door]

80.6—FX: BURU BURU [shiver shiver]

80.7—FX: CHAPUN [splish]

81.1—FX: GU [squeeze]

81.3—FX: DOKI [ba-dump]

82.2—FX: TOKUN TOKUN [heartbeats]

82.3—FX: ZAPA [splash]

82.4—FX: PISHAN [splish]

83.1—FX: GUWARA [zhoop]

83.4—FX: DOKA BASHI GESHI GOKI BASU [pummel whack bash crack]

84.1—FX: PISHAN [slam]

84.2—FX: ZAA [fshh]

85.1—FX: BAN [slam]

85.2—FX: PITARI [stopping]

87.1—FX: ZAA [rain]

88.3—FX: KASA [rustle]

88.6—FX: GAAN [shock]

89.1—FX: FUWA [float]

89.2—FX: BA [fwap]

89.3—FX: PATA PATA [whiff whiff]

89.5—FX: PATA PATA [flutter flutter]

—FX: SOYO SOYO [light breeze]

90.2—FX: KARA KARA [rattle rattle]

90.3—FX: PISHAN PISHAN [slam slam]

91.1—FX: SAAA [fshh]

91.2—FX: BASHA BASHA [splash splash]

91.4—FX: BAN [slam]

—FX: MUKU [pop]

92.2—FX: PON [toss]

93.2—FX: SAA [fshh]

94.1—FX: BURORO [car engine noise]

94.6—FX: KII [creak]

95.1—FX: KASHAN [clatter]

95.2—FX: BIKU [urk]

97.2—FX: PATAN [door closing]

100.6—FX: ZUGAAN ZUGAAN [blam blam]

101.3—FX: PATA [slump]

102.1—FX: ZURU [slip]

102.3—FX: DOKUN [ba-dump]

102.4—FX: BURU BURU [tremble tremble]

102.5—FX: ZAA [emanating power]

103.1—FX: FU [light fading]

105.1—FX: CHAKI [chak]

106.1—FX: SARA SARA [light rain]

108.1—FX: GYU [squeeze]

108.2—FX: YORO [stagger]

108.3—FX: GACHA [door clicking]

108.4—FX: GACHA GACHA [clack]

108.5—FX: BAN [bam]

112.1—FX: PATA [slump]

112.2—FX: DOKUN [ba-dump]

113.1-6—FX: DOKUN DOKUN DOKUN DOKUN DOKUN DOKUN DOKUN DOKUN [ba-dump ba-dump ba-dump ba-dump ba-dump ba-dump ba-dump ba-dump]

114.1—FX: DON [boom]

115.4—FX: PIKU [twitch]

116.1—FX: HA [gasp]

117.1—FX: FUN [unf]

117.1—FX: GYA GYA GYA [tires squealing]

117.2—FX: GON [bonk]

117.5—FX: BAA [vroom]

118.2—FX: GYA GYA [squeal squeal]

118.3—FX: GASHAN [crash]

118.4—FX: KIKII [screech]

118.5—FX: HA HA HA [huff huff huff]

—FX: GACHA [click]

—FX: YORO [stagger]

119.1—FX: PISHI PISHI [crack crumble]

—FX: ZUZUZU [rumble]

121.3—FX: JIIN [glowing]

122.5—FX: BA [leap]

123.1—FX: BARI BARI [zak]

123.2—FX: BIKUN [gasp]

123.3—FX: FU [fft]

124.2—FX: SUPAAN [whack]

125.1—FX: SU [raising gun]

126.1—FX: KACHI [click]

126.4—FX: BATAN BATAN [slam slam]

126.5—FX: GYURURURU [vroom]

128.5—FX: URO URO [pace pace]

128.6—FX: BATA BATA [running]

—FX: GARA [rattle]

131.3—FX: CHI CHI CHI [chirp chirp chirp]

135.1—FX: KYU [tying ribbon]

—FX: KYU [pulling socks]

136.6—FX: TOTA TOTA [tump tump]

137.1—FX: GUWARA [zhoop]

137.4—FX: DOKA BASHI GESHI GOKI BASU [pummel whack bash crack]

138.1—FX: PISHAN [slam]

139.1-3—FX: BISHI BISHI BISHI [wisp wisp wisp]

175.2 —— FX: BUROROO [vroom]

176.1 —— FX: ZA [slash]

177.3 —— FX: ZA [slash]

177.5 —— FX: DON [slam]

178.1 —— FX: FU [lights going out]

178.5 —— FX: DO [thud]

179.2 —— FX: PATA PATA [tump tump]

179.3 —— FX: PATA PATA [tump tump]

179.4 —— FX: PASA [hair coming undone]

179.5 —— FX: GACHA [click]

180.1 —— FX: GAKU GAKU [tremble tremble]

180.2 —— FX: PETA [slump]

180.3 —— FX: DOKUN DOKUN [ba-dump ba-dump]

180.4 —— FX: DOKUN DOKUN [ba-dump ba-dump]

183.3 —— FX: DON [wham]

183.4 —— FX: DON DON DON [bam bam bam]

184.1 —— FX: DON DON [knock knock]

185.3 —— FX: SHU [slice]

185.5 —— FX: ZUZUN [thud]

—— FX: SU [smash]

—— FX: GASHAN [crash]

186.2 —— FX: KUN [sniff]

186.3 —— FX: SHUU [gas swooshing from burner]

—— FX: KACHI [click]

186.4 —— FX: GACHA GACHA [jiggling door handle]

187.1 —— FX: GA GA [stab stab]

187.2 —— FX: GA GA [stab stab]

187.3 —— FX: DOKUN [ba-dump]

187.4 —— FX: DOKUN [ba-dump]

187.5 —— FX: DOKUN DOKUN DOKUN DOKUN DOKUN DOKUN [ba-dump ba-dump ba-dump ba-dump ba-dump]

188.1 —— FX: DOKUN DOKUN DOKUN DOKUN DOKUN DOKUN [ba-dump ba-dump ba-dump ba-dump ba-dump ba-dump]

189.2 —— FX: GA GA [stab stab]

189.3 —— FX: GA GA [whack whack]

190.2 —— FX: GUGU [grab]

190.3 —— FX: BAN [wham]

190.4 —— FX: DOKA [thunk]

140.1 —— FX: GUI [tug]

140.2 —— FX: BARI BARI [zak]

141.4 —— FX: KII [screech]

141.5 —— FX: BUTSU BUTSU [mumble grumble]

143.6 —— FX: PITA [stopping]

144.5 —— FX: PATAN [door closing]

145.1 —— FX: KOPOPOP [pouring]

146.4 —— FX: BAN [wham]

147.4 —— FX: ZAA [fshh – faucet running]

148.1 —— FX: BASHA BASHA [splash splash]

148.3 —— FX: ZAA [fshh – faucet running]

149.2 —— FX: BIKUN [unh]

149.3 —— FX: BASHA BASHA [splash splash]

149.4 —— FX: YORO [stagger]

150.3 —— FX: BAN [slam]

151.2 —— Sign: SHIKISHI [autograph board]

151.3 —— FX: DAA [dash]

—— FX: HA [GASP]

151.4 —— FX: ZA [rustle]

151.5 —— FX: ZAWA ZAWA [rustle rustle]

152.3 —— FX: GYU [clench]

152.5 —— FX: KAA [blush]

153.1 —— FX: SU [stepping away]

155.3 —— FX: SU [raising arm]

155.5 —— FX: JARI [gravel cracking]

158.1 —— FX: ZA [rustle]

159.2 —— FX: DOKI [ba-dump]

159.3 —— FX: GYU [squeeze]

161.2 —— FX: KAAN KOON [ding dong]

—— FX: ZAWA ZAWA [chatter murmur]

161.5 —— FX: MUSU [hmph]

162.5 —— FX: BATAN [slam]

163.2 —— FX: GACHA [click]

163.4 —— FX: BATAN [door closing]

166.2 —— FX: HA [oh]

167.2 —— FX: KACHA [click]

167.6 —— FX: ZAKU ZAKU [chop chop]

168.2 —— FX: DOBABA [ploof]

170.3 —— FX: GU GU GU [bubble bubble bubble]

171.3 —— FX: KIIN KOON KAAN KOON [ding dong]

171.5 —— FX: PISHAN [zhoop]

172.6 —— FX: IRA IRA [grr grr]

173.2 —— FX: BURURU [phone vibrating]

Yû Watase was born on March 5 in a town near Osaka, Japan, and she was raised there before moving to Tokyo to follow her dream of creating manga. In the decade since her debut short story, Pajama De Ojama ("An Intrusion in Pajamas"), she has produced more than 50 compiled volumes of short stories and continuing series. Her latest series, Zettai Kareshi ("He'll Be My Boyfriend"), is currently running in the anthology magazine Shôjo Comic. Watase's long-running horror/romance story Ceres: Celestial Legend and her most recent completed series, Alice 19th, are now available in North America published by VIZ. She loves science fiction, fantasy and comedy.

IF YOU ENJOYED *CERES*
HERE ARE SOME OTHER MANGA
VIZ RECOMMENDS YOU READ:

©1992 Yuu Watase/Shogakukan

FUSHIGI YŪGI

is Yû Watase's popular fantasy shôjo series about a junior high school girl who suddenly travels to a fictional version of ancient China, where she finds love, betrayal and adventure.

© 1996 SAITO CHIHO/IKUHARA
KUNIHIKO & BE PAPAS/Shogakukan

REVOLUTIONARY GIRL UTENA

is the captivating tale of a teen princess who wants to become a prince, just like the man who saved her when she was a little girl. Years later, as her search continues to find the prince, Utena discovers her world is not what it seems and is forced to fight duels for the power to revolutionize the world.

© 1995 Kazuya Kudo/Ryoichi
Ikegami/Shogakukan.

MAI THE PSYCHIC GIRL

is Ryoichi Ikegami's acclaimed story about an outgoing, 14-year-old girl who seems just like her friends, but there's one thing that makes her different. She has incredible psychic powers, which the evil Wisdom Alliance wants to use for world domination.

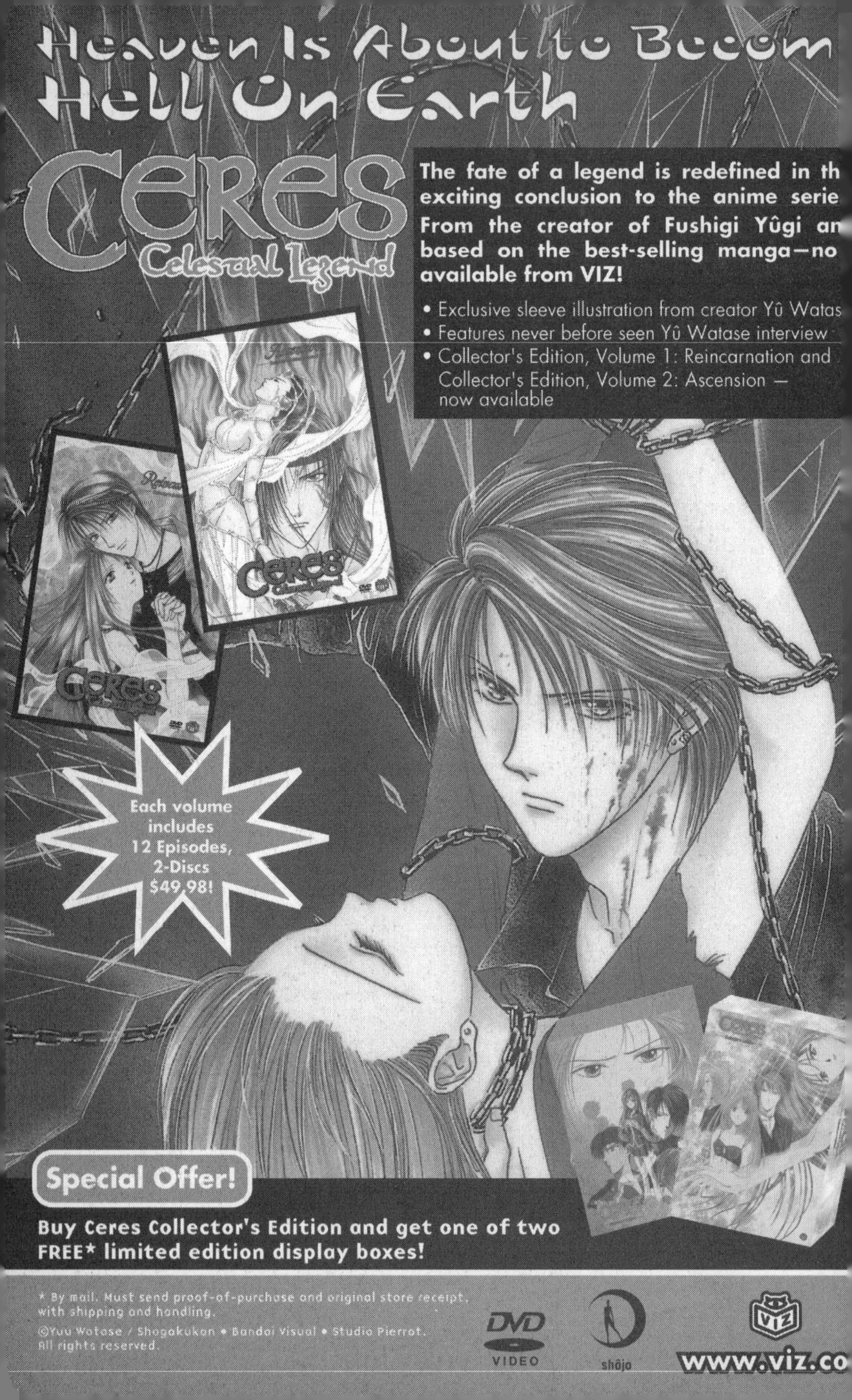
Heaven Is About to Becom
Hell On Earth
Ceres
Celestial Legend
The fate of a legend is redefined in th exciting conclusion to the anime serie From the creator of Fushigi Yûgi an based on the best-selling manga—no available from VIZ!
• Exclusive sleeve illustration from creator Yû Watas
• Features never before seen Yû Watase interview
• Collector's Edition, Volume 1: Reincarnation and Collector's Edition, Volume 2: Ascension — now available
Each volume includes 12 Episodes, 2-Discs $49.98!
Special Offer!
Buy Ceres Collector's Edition and get one of two FREE* limited edition display boxes!
* By mail. Must send proof-of-purchase and original store receipt, with shipping and handling.
©Yuu Watase / Shogakukan • Bandai Visual • Studio Pierrot. All rights reserved.
DVD VIDEO
shôjo
VIZ
www.viz.co

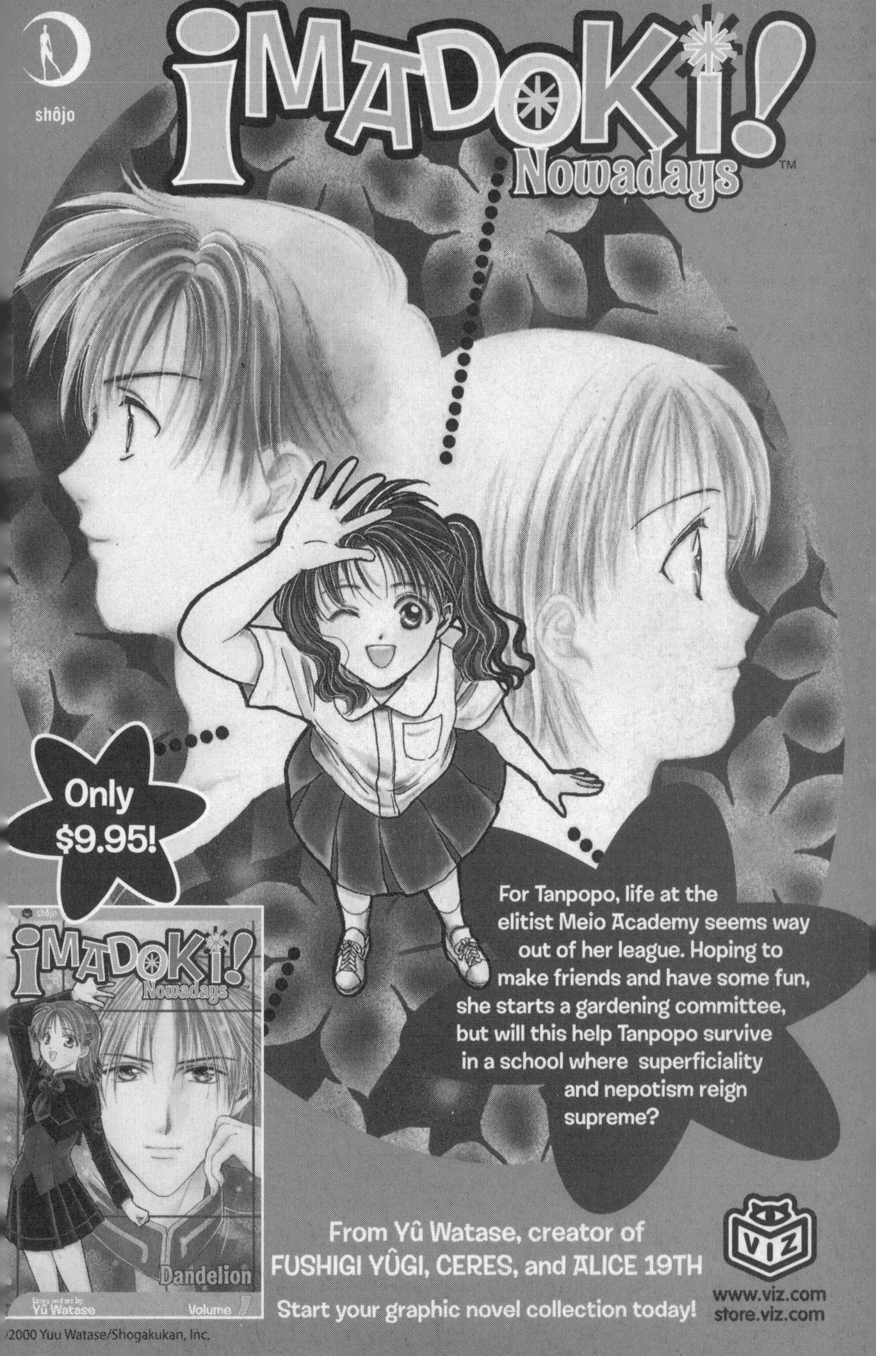
shôjo
iMADOKi!
Nowadays™
Only $9.95!
iMADOKi! Nowadays
Dandelion
Story and art by Yû Watase
Volume 1
For Tanpopo, life at the elitist Meio Academy seems way out of her league. Hoping to make friends and have some fun, she starts a gardening committee, but will this help Tanpopo survive in a school where superficiality and nepotism reign supreme?
From Yû Watase, creator of FUSHIGI YÛGI, CERES, and ALICE 19TH
Start your graphic novel collection today!
VIZ
www.viz.com
store.viz.com

COMPLETE OUR SURVEY AND LET
US KNOW WHAT YOU THINK!

☐ Please do NOT send me information about VIZ products, news and events, special offers, or other information.

☐ Please do NOT send me information from VIZ's trusted business partners.

Name: _____

Address: _____

City: _____ **State:** _____ **Zip:** _____

E-mail: _____

☐ **Male** ☐ **Female**   **Date of Birth** (mm/dd/yyyy): ___ / ___ / ___   (Under 13? Parental consent required)

What race/ethnicity do you consider yourself? (please check one)

☐ Asian/Pacific Islander   ☐ Black/African American   ☐ Hispanic/Latino

☐ Native American/Alaskan Native   ☐ White/Caucasian   ☐ Other: _____

What VIZ product did you purchase? (check all that apply and indicate title purchased)

☐ DVD/VHS _____

☐ Graphic Novel _____

☐ Magazines _____

☐ Merchandise _____

Reason for purchase: (check all that apply)

☐ Special offer   ☐ Favorite title   ☐ Gift

☐ Recommendation   ☐ Other _____

Where did you make your purchase? (please check one)

☐ Comic store   ☐ Bookstore   ☐ Mass/Grocery Store

☐ Newsstand   ☐ Video/Video Game Store   ☐ Other: _____

☐ Online (site: _____)

What other VIZ properties have you purchased/own? _____

_____

How many anime and/or manga titles have you purchased in the last year? How many were VIZ titles? **(please check one from each column)**

ANIME	MANGA	VIZ
☐ None	☐ None	☐ None
☐ 1-4	☐ 1-4	☐ 1-4
☐ 5-10	☐ 5-10	☐ 5-10
☐ 11+	☐ 11+	☐ 11+

I find the pricing of VIZ products to be: **(please check one)**

☐ Cheap ☐ Reasonable ☐ Expensive

What genre of manga and anime would you like to see from VIZ? **(please check two)**

☐ Adventure ☐ Comic Strip ☐ Science Fiction ☐ Fighting

☐ Horror ☐ Romance ☐ Fantasy ☐ Sports

What do you think of VIZ's new look?

☐ Love It ☐ It's OK ☐ Hate It ☐ Didn't Notice ☐ No Opinion

Which do you prefer? **(please check one)**

☐ Reading right-to-left

☐ Reading left-to-right

Which do you prefer? **(please check one)**

☐ Sound effects in English

☐ Sound effects in Japanese with English captions

☐ Sound effects in Japanese only with a glossary at

THANK YOU! Please send the completed form to:

NJW Research
42 Catharine St.
Poughkeepsie, NY 12601

All information provided will be used for internal purposes only. We promise not to sell or otherwise divulge your information.